"Finally . . . a work by Gary Black about Dallas Willard! Are you kidding me? This is great. Dallas Willard has impacted countless numbers of us looking for a fresh perspective on the dynamic, surprising, compelling life Jesus invites us into. And Gary has been on the leading edge of helping explain this new movement that's brewing and how it's helping so many people find the vibrant Christian stream that's been flowing for a while now. People from a broad range of perspectives will find Gary's clear, informed, nuanced and hopeful voice a welcome guide as we navigate the shifting landscape we're living in."

—ROB BELL
Best Selling Author, Speaker and Pastor Emeritus of Mars Hills Church in Grand Rapids, MI.

"We might want to consider disqualifying any leader of the church, based on whether or not they have read this book. Quite possibly some of the theologically richest, deepest and most well formed thoughts for God's church are in these pages. Excavating below leadership tactics and spiritual formation approaches lies this breathtaking vision of God. Read slowly, savor and ponder. Let it simultaneously affect your heart and your mind. It is a distant light, leading us home."

—NANCY ORTBERG
Author of *Non-Linear Leadership*

"There is simply no one whose understanding of Jesus and his good news has the power and depth of Dallas Willard. Gary Black offers us all a tremendous gift—a journey of thought that will illuminate your faith and change your life."

—JOHN ORTBERG
Author of *Who Is This Man?*

"No one has had a greater impact on my understanding of spiritual formation and life in God's kingdom than Dallas Willard, and I know of no one who has a more thorough grasp of Willard's teachings than Gary Black. . . . The hopeful vision of life in God's realm expertly summarized in this book has the potential to revolutionize the church and our world—if only we summon the courage to make it our way of practice."

—MARK SCANDRETTE
Author of *Practicing the Way of Jesus*

"Gary Black writes a comprehensive and penetrating survey of the thought and context of one of American evangelicalism's most influential reformers. The resulting analysis—*The Theology of Dallas Willard*—is worth studying and then studying some more, because Dallas Willard is that important to the future of the church in North America."

—DAVID FITCH
Author of *Prodigal Christianity*

"Black has given us a window into Willard's thoughts, showing his deep and systematic approach to living life as a disciple of Jesus. This is an excellent read for understanding the depth and beauty of a contemporary theological giant. I highly recommend it!"

—KEITH J. MATTHEWS
Coeditor of *Dictionary of Everyday Theology and Culture*

"The present volume is a masterful and accessible presentation of Willardian theology, which is, at its heart, an invitation to step into a real, present, holistic, experiential, and incarnational form of Christian faith. This is an important book."

—GARY W. MOON
Author of *Apprenticeship with Jesus*

The Theology of
Dallas Willard

The Theology of Dallas Willard

Discovering Protoevangelical Faith

Gary Black, Jr.

PICKWICK *Publications* • Eugene, Oregon

THE THEOLOGY OF DALLAS WILLARD

Discovering Protoevangelical Faith

Pickwick Publications
An Imprint of Wipf and Stock Publishers
199 W. 8th Ave., Suite 3
Eugene, OR 97401

www.wipfandstock.com

ISBN 13: 978-71-62032-963-4

Cataloguing-in-Publication data:

Black, Jr., Gary.

The theology of Dallas Willard : discovering protoevangelical faith / Gary Black, Jr., with a foreword by Scot McKnight.

xxiv + 244 pp. ; 23 cm. Includes bibliographical references.

ISBN 13: 978-71-62032-963-4

1. Willard, Dallas, 1935–2013. 2. Evangelicalism. 3. I. McKnight, Scot. II. Title.

BV4511 B412 2013

Manufactured in the U.S.A.

To my family—all of them—natural and extended. Thank you for your love, support, and grace to engage this life changing pursuit of the gospel. It has been worth it all.

Contents

Foreword

When someone looks back in 2050 at the previous century's evangelical church influencers in North America, only a few names will rise to the top. I venture to suggest N. T. Wright will be the Bible expert, John Piper will be the Calvinist resurgence leader, Bill Hybels will be the seeker-friendly church innovator, and Dallas Willard will be spiritual formation leader. Dallas Willard, whose theology is examined in this exceptional book by Gary Black, Jr., has changed the landscape and the shrubbery in the North American posture toward spiritual disciplines and spiritual transformation.

Most evangelical Christians were suspicious, to use a milder category, of anything smacking of rummaging around in the Catholic and Orthodox traditions for help with spiritual growth, very few were willing to use the typically Catholic expression "spiritual formation," and even those who did nourish themselves in these traditions did not say so in public or from the pulpit. To have quoted St. Theresa of Avila or St. John of the Cross was to court furrowed frowns that would likely lead to a meeting with the Deacon or Elders.

Dallas Willard provided the intellectual and historical basis for a spirituality grounded in the great traditions of the church, but he did so in the context of emerging trends in the American evangelical scene. Gary Black, Jr.'s sketch of that emerging evangelicalism is masterful and deserves careful reading. In fact, this opening chapter is one all pastors and seminary students need to read. It sets the context for comprehending, in a thick description, the vision of Dallas Willard.

Black expertly takes the reader through Willard's theology of Scripture and tests his views on conversion, activism, and the cross. But Willard has famously refused to sit comfortably in traditional evangelical recliners. Willard presses the famous quadrilateral ideas back to the Bible, through the grids of the great church traditions as well as classical philosophical ideas, to fashion a protoevangelicalism that continues to nurture, and will continue to do so, for all those who want to live out the gospel in our world. Black coins the term protoevangelicalism to describe Willard's deeper probing of pneumatology, anthropology, theo-ontology, Christology, and ecclesiology—all lines of thinking that expand the borders of evangelicalism by getting behind it to rediscover its roots. Where protoevangelicalism lands is the *essentia Dei*, the nature and essence of God. What one finds there is a God of love. This journey of seeking and finding is essential to the transformative process, one designed to make us lovers of God and others.

In contrast to almost all theoretical discussions of philosophy, theology, and hermeneutics, Dallas Willard's recapturing of the whole always leads to the transformative process. God speaks to us, we listen, and as we turn toward God we are overcome by the goodness of God so that we become transformed unto Christlikeness. Any theology that does not lead to transformation is not Christian theology and neither is it what Dallas Willard has left to us. Black guides us through the depth and breadth of this authentic Christian theology that should stand the test of time.

Scot McKnight
Professor of New Testament
Northern Seminary

Acknowledgments

No one writes in a vacuum. Although I believe this to be true, it perhaps has never been more true than in this work. So many wonderful people have participated in the production of this work that even the idea of a vacuum vaporizes in light of the concert of minds and voices that have motivated, directed, guided, supported, and enlightened my heart and mind. There are so many players in this orchestra of co-conspirators pursuing the gospel of Jesus, that pages could be filled simply ascribing to each of them ample credit for their skills and contributions. Yet, like those perennial movie stars who "run out of time" during their gilded moment at awards shows, I too fear omitting someone whom I deeply love, and admire—up close and from afar—whose contribution was integral to this project. For those whom I may not recognize in the confines of these pages, please know I sincerely appreciate your inestimable worth in the completion of this book.

Even still, there are those whose influence was not only beneficial but also essential. These are individuals who impacted me and the direction of my life to a point where even the possibility of pursuing the subjects of this work could become a reality. These are individuals who did more than affect my words and ideas; they also contributed to the transformation of my character. It is the heavy lifting of these precious individuals whom I wish to specifically acknowledge here.

Let's start geographically. The paint first hit canvas on this project in Novato, CA, during a long, long, long conversation over coffee with Dieter Zander. Thank you, Dieter, for your courage, childlike faith, and patience with me while I listened to your story and began to reform my own. Also, thanks to Larry Boeck for making that introduction and for being the most consistent voice of encouragement since I walked into his Sunday School class as a sixteen year-old teen who didn't know what he didn't know. Arm in arm with the Boeck family are Craig and Susie Dillon who never ceased fanning into flame what was invisible to everyone else. This is also true for the Davis family who graciously opened their home to me while I completed this research. More importantly, Sandy and Morgan are expert models of genuine hospitality, the limitless benefits to gut-level mentoring and the character-building humility available in innumerable defeats at boardgames! Thanks also to Ray Johnston for being the first pastor in my life to encourage me to become a leader. Thanks to Sam Williams who was ahead of his time and implemented much of what is in these pages long before anyone knew what he was doing. A special thanks to Keith Matthews. Keith introduced me to Dallas Willard, both the man and his works. I've never known someone as devoted to helping people discover and achieve their highest potential. He is a great coach, mentor, and friend. Thanks for always passing me the ball. I look forward to the next chapter together.

To those I met during our time in Southern Oregon: My sincere gratitude to my colleagues and partners at Edward Jones for your support and encouragement. This could not have happened without you. To the Sniders and Andersons for their fearless creativity during those Monday nights in our living room and for the small brave community that came out of those gatherings. These were precious moments and became my first inspirations to pursue what authenticity might look like inside the Kingdom of God. Thanks to Rob Bell for helping me see what story we are in, displaying the courage to ask tough questions and being more committed to *agape* than to tradition or fear of change. Thanks to Scot McKnight for his scholarly devotion to the evolutions of contemporary evangelical faith in America and that wonderful little book about a parakeet that I simply could not put down. Thanks to Donald Miller for the first biography of a Christian that seemed to even remotely resemble my real life. Thanks to Steve Spotts for walking me out of a dark place with laughter, intelligence, wisdom, pure grit, and raw faith.

To those I met while in Springfield, Missouri: Thanks to Melody Palm, Johan Mostert and Doug Oss who spent many wonderful hours with me during the turbulent seminary years, breaking bread together on warm summer evenings, listening, encouraging, and demonstrating genuine collegiality. Thanks to the Carla and Chris Weber family for their friendship, their wonderful cabin, and enduring late night conversations with feigned interest but loving smiles. Thanks to Andrew Goodall who first allowed me to see the power of these ideas reflected in someone else's eyes.

To those I met in England: Thanks to Keith Langdon and those at Sarum College for sharing their hospitality and grace while I was a long way from home. Thanks to Michael Delashmutt who read every word and listened to every idea with generosity, biting wit, gentleness, and an honesty that only exudes from those who truly know what they are talking about.

Thanks to Esther Reed who helped me navigate British academia with skill, humor, and grace.

Thank yous to all the leaders and participants of Oak Hills Church, Re: Imagine, Holy Trinity Anglican Church and ACCD. Of specific note thank you to Mike Lueken, Kent Carlson, Mark Scandrette, Todd Hunter and Dan Tochini. Beyond my wildest imaginations, these individuals, and the organizations they lead, demonstrated over and over how the ideas on these pages are applied where the rubber hits the road.

A special note of appreciation to Barbara Hayes for her insight, encouragement and mastery of the English language. Thanks to Christian Amondson at Wipf and Stock for giving this work a chance to be seen.

Thanks to my family. To my sister Donna for her gentle, strong spirit and mastery of the English language. To my brother Patrick for never changing his opinion of me, in success or failure, victory or defeat—you are neither impressed nor disappointed, always loyal, always true. You have given me the gift of a deep reservoir of unconditional brotherly love. Thanks to Peyton, Jack, and AJ—the admiration and honor reflected in your young eyes calls me to become ever worthy of your respect. Thanks to my mother and father for not only giving me life, but also raising me well and showing me what both endless grace and unbending courage can accomplish together. This work is part of your legacy. I hope it serves you well. Thank you to my beautiful and brilliant daughters, Taylor and Jacy—this work is for you most of all. In some measure your faith is my duty. I pray these words and ideas help you and your generation form an imagination of what is possible, to walk your own unique path into the kingdom of God, to speak truth in your own voice, and to see God's grand universe with new eyes and fresh hearts. Thank you for your sacrifice in my absence and your patience with this task. You, better than any, know where these ideas and their truths have yet to re-form my heart and soul. Yet, both of you are my inspiration to never stop being transformed into the reality these pages describe. To Susie—my wife, companion, partner, most excellent helper and loyal friend—thank you for your devotion, strength, encouragement, and smile. I could not and would not have completed this without you. I came late to this party. Thanks for waiting for me. Journeying with you is the greatest treasure and pleasure of my life. It is a great gift being married to a better person. You are my beloved.

Finally, in the process of publishing this work, Dallas succumbed to pancreatic cancer. I have felt and experienced his loss in profound and poignant ways. Yet, I am grateful he was able to read this manuscript in its entirety shortly before his death. I will forever cherish his words of encouragement and affirmation. In part, it was this work that sparked conversations about co-authoring a sequel to *The Divine Conspiracy,* which is now in the final stages of completion.

Words fail to express my great appreciation, and how deeply I benefited from Dallas' devotion to me over the years. His approval, participation, and support as a scholar, theologian, and disciple of Jesus have been wonderfully illuminating, empowering, and validating. I will be eternally grateful. The immense talents Dallas combined with an authentic humility are testament to and a product of exactly the kind of life and reality he described. He knew exactly to whom and what he bore witness.

May this be only one of many more investigations, explorations, and analyses into the implications of Dallas' perspectives on the kingdom of God and the gospel of Jesus. I have done my best to describe and articulate the nature and effect of his perspective. I pray these pages only advance what Dallas long endeavored to establish and achieve for God's glory in and through his church. Amen.

Introduction

A RADICAL SHIFT APPEARS to be progressing through contemporary forms of Christian faith in the United States. Amidst this transition a few strains of theology have emerged and are gaining increased attention. Several theologians, writers, and practitioners are linked to this theological evolution. This work specifically explores the single tread of theology in this evolving theological tapestry connected to the writing and teaching of philosopher and theologian Dr. Dallas Willard.

Grounded in earlier traditions of American evangelicalism, Willardian theology seeks to capture the visceral qualities emblematic of Christian movements of the past.[1] At its core Willardian theology pursues, articulates, and forcefully defends the proposition that the impact and essence of the original (proto) gospel (*euangelion* or evangel) Jesus preached, manifested, and taught remains a vital ontological reality, which is understandable, incarnational, relational, and as readily available today as it was two millennia prior. Henceforth, the term "protoevangelical" will be applied throughout this work to describe Willard's overarching desire to recapture the essence of the visioning message Jesus originally delivered in the New Testament Gospel accounts.[2]

Willardian theology is first and foremost a pursuit of the quality and nature of this "good news." Willard works to uncover, explain, and

1. There are several similarities to renewal, reform movements of the past, that carry several of Willard's theological values. One of the most notable was John Wesley and his renewalist theology of Anglicanism. Willard suggests Wesley's method was perhaps the most complete modern disciple making approach in American evangelical history. Dallas Willard, "Day 6, Session 3, Topic-Wesleyanism, Recorded Lecture."

2. I am indebted to Dr. Randy Walls for his insights into the history of this concept. The original use of the term comes from the discussion regarding the concept of the "Q" source for the New Testament gospels. See Udo Schnelle, *Theology of the New Testament*. There is also a common theological reference to the proto-evangel referring to the "first" occurrence in Scripture where the salvific intent of God is described. Often cited is Genesis 3:15–21. See Cronk, *The Message of the Bible*, 45–46.

illustrate how and why Jesus has revealed, and continues to reveal, the fundamental nature of God and his kingdom. Further, Willard demonstrates how entering into an apprenticing relationship with Jesus and learning his "way" of life and truth is the primary means through which God's kingdom reality is accessed.

Consequently, Willardian theology holds any proper "evangelical" form of faith must equally pursue the depth and breadth of life Jesus describes in this kingdom realm. The expectation of life and living from this reality necessitates demonstrating the resources, exposing the purposes, representing the ethos, and manifesting the effects intrinsic to a God-permeated world. The possibility of, and invitation into, such a life is what Willard contends was the focus and intent of the original gospel (proto-evangel) Jesus articulated in the first century. In this way, Willardian theology is quintessentially a practical theology since it is devoted to the development and experience of a holistic vision for the type and quality of life offered through Christ under the direction of God's good and perfect will. Appropriately, Willard focuses on describing the reasons, ways, and means by which one can come to terms with the spiritual, metaphysical, existential, and ontological reality of the kingdom of God applied to one's entire life.

In forming this protoevangelical vision, Willardian theology tends to advocate a move away from mainstream forms of American evangelical faith that have become progressively mired in denominational separatism and doctrinal wranglings over issues ranging from the authority of the Bible, esoteric atonement theories, eschatology, etc., and their concomitant effects on soteriology and ecclesiology. Willard became a prominent figure of reference within groups of evangelicals who began searching for a more holistic, authentic, and incarnational form of Christian faith. The first groups demonstrating their dissatisfaction with mainstream evangelical religion were those involved in what has come to be termed the Spiritual Formation Movement (SFM). The SFM saw Willard's theological vision as more intellectually robust and existentially vigorous than that commonly offered in many evangelical church settings. In more recent years, Willard's protoevangelical vision has also drawn increasing attention in both non-evangelical and postmodern/postevangelical Christian circles as well.

Despite maintaining an enduring following within the SFM, and developing new interest with "emerging" generation Christians, overall, Willard's works have not received widespread consideration from the theological academy. It is impossible to discern exactly why this is the case, but several issues may be at work here. First, Willard does not consider himself a modern or systematic theologian. Willard's resistance to applying a straightforward systematic theological method—still the preferred means of evangelical theological inquiry—may be the primary reason his work continues to elude wider scholarly engagement. Such a decision is not haphazard but rather an intentional, purposeful characteristic of the values inherent to Willard's overall theological objective. He is working from an inherent critique of modern epistemological hubris that he perceives to be active within the doctrinal-centric values and interests in modern systematic theologies.

Simply stated, Willard remains critical of systematic theological methodology. He suggests evangelicalism has been undergirded by a systematic theological approach that has overseen a significant increase of sectarian division over the past two hundred years. This is evidenced in the thousands of different Christian denominations worldwide that now apply some degree of systematic theology to prove innumerable competing and conflicting doctrinal claims.[3] The exacerbation of competing systematic theologies inside modern evangelicalism also perpetuates guilds and special interest groups that too often splinter what otherwise could become areas of common agreement and fellowship.[4] His resistance to the systematic theological apparatus is also a likely candidate for explaining why Willard does not engage the established, on-going theological discussions nearly as prodigiously as is the established habit of professional theologians. Thus, Willard resists the systematic methodology; sensing theological systemization carries inherent historical and epistemological limitations that intensify inappropriate assumptions that lead to overly modern, rationalistic, and anthropomorphic conclusions and practices.

Nonetheless, the scope of Willard's *Renovation of the Heart* provides an encompassing overview of the breadth of Willard's knowledge regarding the integrative necessity of Christian theology and spirituality. Furthermore, many of the components of what would normally be required of a classic systematic theological exposition are available, although not intentionally so, across the sum of Willard's published work. When considering the whole of Willard's corpus, including his numerous journal and magazine articles, in combination with other book publications and philosophical work, Willard's theological horizon easily covers the length and breadth of western evangelical theological horizon, and much of modern Christendom as well. Yet, Willard's theological overview or platform is couched not inside the limits of rigid systematic categories but rather appears in a more organic form. This platform includes and encompasses several biblical/anthropological/philosophical frameworks that deal with the holistic nature of every

3. Willard, *Renovation of the Heart*, 22. Hereafter referred to as ROH.

4. An excellent defense on this topic is provided by conservatives Dockery, Neste, Tidwell, and Mohler, *Southern Baptists, Evangelicals, and the Future of Denominationalism*, and more progressive voices, Viola, *Reimagining Church*.

aspect of human life and existence. Willard draws this structure first from biblical forms, widely reproduced across many academic disciplines, which pursue the dynamics of human life and being.

The potential impact of Willard's work could be significant if more broadly engaged by academic theologians. To this point only a few scholars studying the transition of evangelical theology into postmodern contexts have found reason to compare Willard, in terms of similar levels of influence, to theologians N. T. Wright, George Ladd, Lesslie Newbigin, Stanley Grenz, and Eugene Peterson.[5] High praise indeed. Still, the broader theological academy has, as of yet, largely bypassed his work.

Even more inexplicable, proponents of Willard's work tend to restrict their perspectives of his impact to the areas of discipleship and spiritual formation.[6] This leads to the second potential cause of Willard's lack of wider recognition by the academy. By his own admission, Willard's works tend to have a "pastoral" impetus. By this he does not mean to suggest an interest or proclivity to provide simplistic theological reductions or personal anecdotes often indicative of literature attributed to the category of "Christian Spirituality." Instead, Willard's pastoral emphasis means each of his theological publications was initially motivated from first considering how to best help those he knew within his social and relational sphere deal with struggles or questions that tended to elude them. Hence, Willard's subjectival spectrum was initially motivated to provide aid and guidance to issues and problems as they arose within his unique "congregational" setting. The result is the production of several detailed and rigorous theological and philosophical engagements of key topics of Christian thought and life.

Inadvertently, his pastoral emphasis may have created the impression his approach to theological concepts and ideologies originates from a more pragmatic perspective that seeks a reductionistic or utilitarian end. Such an assumption is evidence only of guilt by association. Yet, this puts Willard's work into something of a double bind. If one analyzes Willard expecting to find a systematic theological perspective, there is an inherent risk of overlooking his more substantive practical theological motive and intent. Yet, if one comes to Willard's work expecting the fluff of a "how to" or "fill in the blank" sermon series recitation, then one will be sorely disappointed and quickly overwhelmed.

5. See Gibbs and Bolger, *Emerging Churches*, 15. Keck, *Pneumanaut*, 14, 45. Flory and Miller, *Finding Faith*, 32. For the sake of space, this work provides no distinguishing comparative analysis of the above-mentioned theologians.

6. An example of this is seen in an entire issue dedicated to Willard's work found in *Journal of Spiritual Formation and Soul Care* 3.2 (2010).

Until now, no attempt has been made by others to organize or provide an explanation that articulates Willard's theological perspective and motive. Therefore, this work provides an in-depth practical theological organization and investigation of Willardian theology. At its end, I conclude any limiting of Willard's theology to topical opinions on the subject of spiritual formation represents a significant oversight and naïve reduction. Certainly, Willard engages these subjects. However, the topic of spiritual formation is not the primary motive or drive behind Willard's theological examination. Furthermore, it will be shown here that Willard's corpus provides a fairly universal theological perspective. His body of work covers nearly all the significant points of doctrine pertinent to nineteenth-, twentieth-, and twenty-first-century evangelical theological inquiry. Yet, his intent in the endeavor is to always provide a more rooted understanding of the nature and intent of the gospel of Jesus Christ as a fulfillment of the *Missio Dei* revealed throughout the entirety of Scripture and history.

As such, Willard stands as a potential corrective or renewalist voice to American evangelical theological reflection in general and not simply one interested in the nuances or esoteric benefits within the delimiters of systematic theology, spiritual formation, and/or discipleship. Certainly, an original, totalizing theological volume would be helpful and potentially aid in the wider acceptance, engagement, and clarity of Willard's work. However, I propose a comprehensive treatise currently exists in the entirety of Willard's corpus—one that is holistic, discernable, and increasingly attractive to those currently reconsidering evangelical theology and praxis. This work aims at assisting that movement.

To accomplish that task this work provides a means of organizing and prioritizing the sum of Willardian theology and represents the culmination of a complete examination of the entirety of Willard's theological corpus and pertinent aspects of his philosophical work as well. This analysis was compiled from both public and private resources that were referenced and cross-referenced in order to best clarify the subjects Willard engages.[7] To organize and describe Willard's theological insights a considerable contribution of Dr. Willard's personal time and effort was spent in private discussions and written correspondences. His openness to discuss anything and everything "on-the-record" was of upmost importance to this project. His generosity, graciousness, patience, candor, and cooperation allowed this

7. These resources included over 150 hours of conference lectures and DVD recordings, fifty-eight hours of original classroom lectures, and twenty-seven hours of recorded personal interviews and private conversations. These means are used to supplement the written literature to compile the best, most detailed, and holistic perspective possible of Willardian thought.

author to present Willardian theology as accurately, clearly, and completely as possible. These interviews probed the philosophical, epistemological, ontological, psychological, and theological frameworks Willard formed to support the conclusions presented in his publications. However, any and all misunderstandings or mistakes in articulating Willard's views belong exclusively to me and me alone.

Since Willardian theology is a practical theology, it is appropriate to analyze his work in the same vein. Although a relatively recent field of theological inquiry, several perspectives delimit the practical theological arena. Specifically, Willard applies a practical theological motive likened to that of practical theologians Edward Farley, J. W. Fowler, David Tracy, and others. Farley, Fowler, et al. have positioned their view of practical theology as a means of engaging the doctrines, beliefs, perspectives, and ideas of Christian theology for the betterment of both the individual and the ecclesial community. In their collective perspective, practical theology should also maintain and foster an intellectual rigor that resists reducing theology to pragmatic concerns related only to ministerial skills required for managing ecclesiastical organizations. In contrast, the practical theological school of thought employed here values and pursues understanding regarding how groups conceptualize their tradition and are wrestling, adapting or forming new responses to their religious heritage. Such a priority is a significant pursuit of Willardian theology as well.

A second methodological means required to best understand Willardian theology is found in the social scientific method of intellectual historiography. Since many of the theological concepts in Willardian theology either speak directly to or oppose some deeply held traditional evangelical beliefs, an intellectual historiography enables the tracing of where these key beliefs generated within American evangelical history and to what lingering effect. The historical research required to best understand Willardian theology traces the intellectual progression through parts of two centuries. During these periods several key evangelical concepts, their transitions, adaptations, and conflagrations with other socio-cultural realities within American life worked to form and influence Willard's theological response. This historical perspective frames both how and where Willardian theology represents either a corrective or reforming influence to traditional evangelicalism. This multidisciplinary approach will also allow us to investigate the historical, intellectual, theological, social, and philosophical contributions to the development of contemporary evangelicalism, which includes its contemporary derivatives and protestations found in Willardian theology.

Since it is inappropriate to systematically analyze Willardian theology, instead, an overarching schema is presented here. To elucidate this schema the proceeding chapters have been structured by two priorities. First, precedence was given to those specific works that directly respond to or critique contemporary evangelical theology. Secondly, those topics most related to the development and explication of Willard's protoevangelical vision were prioritized.

To better illuminate and understand Willard's protoevangelical vision the first chapter describes and utilizes David Bebbington's four evangelical distinctives as a platform from which to compare and contrast Willard against the mainstream evangelical perspective. Bebbington's quadrilateral provides a framework from which Willardian theology can be more clearly juxtaposed.[8] Complementing Bebbington's analysis is Randall Balmer's recent work on American evangelicalism.[9] As will be shown, Balmer improves upon Bebbington's analysis by presenting four historically integral transitioning events which both define evangelical progress in American society but also describe the basis from which the postevangelical impetus or protest has formed.[10] The first chapter will also serve as a means of situating Willardian theology within its historical and contemporary contexts.

The second chapter provides a coalescing of the adaptations Willardian theology makes to Bebbington and Balmer's key evangelical distinctives. The third chapter describes the core of Willardian theology and the construction of his protoevangelical vision. Chapter four expressly states where Willardian theology offers more specific corrections and critique to mainstream evangelical theology and praxis. The fifth chapter presents an important discussion on how Willard's application of philosophical realism informs his critique of modern and postmodern epistemology and their corresponding effects on evangelical theology. The final chapter discusses the potential Willardian theology has to affect existing forms of evangelical and postevangelical theology and praxis.

Two final points of clarification as to the overarching objective of this work are in order. First, it is important to note—and Dr. Willard certainly concurred—that many, many other crucial voices, working in concert, have combined to effect what this work seeks to describe. That this book focuses most exclusively on Dr. Willard should in no way be construed as an attempt to ignore or diminish the contribution of the broader community of which he was but one essential member. In many substantial ways, Willard's influence stands on the shoulders of innumerable others. Secondly, the subjects

8. Bebbington, *Evangelicalism in Modern Britain*.

9. Balmer, *The Making of Evangelicalism*.

10. In addition to Bebbington and Balmer, this work is significantly informed by and appropriately references the works of other noted historians such as Martin Marty, George Marsden, Richard Kyle, Roger Olson, Donald Dayton, and others.

this book pursues are of paramount importance to contemporary forms of Christianity in the United States. The impact and influence of evangelicalism is widespread and has been well established. The vital socio-politico-religious connection to American history and culture will be more deeply pursued in subsequent chapters. Hence, a vibrant and authentic Christian faith that exemplifies and manifests the good news of God's availability, love, and grace carries potential benefits that are simply too monumental to ignore.

The fact that increasing numbers of Americans and Christians alike no longer sense the inherent goodness in the evangelical news is therefore a dilemma worthy of pursuit. Growing but influential minorities of evangelicals are beginning to suggest change is not only needed but essential to recapture any resemblance of an authentic Christian expression within evangelical forms of faith. This conflict, its nature, implications, and its characters represent the broader arena wherein Willardian theology is posited. It is to the depth and breadth of this specific strand of theology working its way through the changing tapestry of American evangelicalism that we now turn.

List of Abbreviations

DC	*Divine Conspiracy*
SD	*Spirit of the Disciplines*
HG	*Hearing God*
ISOG	*In Search of Guidance*
GO	*The Great Omission*
KCT	*Knowing Christ Today*
ROH	*Renovation of the Heart*

Chapter One

Willardian Theology in Context

To best grasp the scope of Willardian theology, its protoevangelical vision, and its corresponding effect on contemporary forms of evangelicalism in America, we must begin by delineating from where Willardian theology has evolved. Interest in Willard's protoevangelical theology arises out of, and responds to, significant shifts occurring within existing forms of American evangelicalism. The variables of these shifts are important to understand in order to track why Willardian theology has become increasingly attractive. It is therefore helpful to highlight at least some of these shifts as described by relevant empirical social scientific research.[1] What appears to be emerging from the data is a growing number of disaffected and disillusioned evangelicals or what have been termed "post" evangelicals.[2] It is the nature and purpose of the postevangelical protest where Willardian theology appears to be making its most significant impact.

First, we must define what the term "evangelical" means in our contemporary setting, after which we will be better positioned to appreciate the qualifying prefixes "post" and "proto." Secondly, the intellectual historiography of American evangelicalism presented in this chapter defines, contextualizes, and traces the development and evolution of distinct themes within the evangelical movement. Tracking this intellectual lineage better contextualizes the pertinent issues currently active in contemporary settings wherein Willardian theology is understood and applied. To accomplish these two goals a selective and summative review of American evangelicalism frames the historicity of these key themes. Future chapters are then

1 See pages 47-50.

2. This term was perhaps first coined by Dave Tomlinson in his book *The Post Evangelical.*

better positioned to more clearly discuss these same doctrinal themes in light of Willard's unique perspective and critique. Together, chapters two through four form a foundational understanding from which current manifestations of evangelical, postevangelical and protoevangelical theology and praxis can be properly compared and contrasted.

Defining Evangelicalism

Throughout the past two centuries the terms "evangelical" and "evangelicalism" have carried various meanings and connotations. Even today definitions of these terms can span a wide horizon of theological, ecclesiastical, and practical variance. In some contexts the words can be used as synonyms for "conservative," "revivalist," "fundamentalist" "born-again" or even "reformed."[3] For others, especially those in Western European contexts, the words can connote "liberal," "ecumenical," or "progressive."[4] Ironically, depending on the situation and context, "evangelical" can carry in one environment the exact opposite meaning one might expect or intend in another.[5] In the United States the ideas and images associated with the terms evangelical and evangelicalism are loaded with a plethora of intended, unintended, and hidden meanings or agendas.[6]

Theologically, "evangelicalism" also covers a broad range of dissonant or divergent definitions.[7] This is exacerbated by denominational affiliations across a wide spectrum of inconsistent beliefs and practices. Evangelical denominations with theologies as varied as the Assemblies of

3. Hankins, *American Evangelicals*, 13, 98, 185.

4. Catherwood, *The Evangelicals*, 98. In recent years media outlets ascribing contentious and even malevolent attributes to the terms "evangelical" and "evangelicalism" have exacerbated this confusion.

5. An example of this can be discerned by comparing and contrasting these definitions of evangelicalism discussed in the works of Lloyd-Jones, *What is an Evangelical?*, Shepherd, *Our Evangelical Faith*, Randall, *Evangelicals Etcetera*, and Stott, *Evangelical Truth*.

6. This is seen most pervasively when considering the political and sexual controversies regarding evangelicals. There is something of a cottage industry devoted to investigating and revealing the worst of evangelical hypocrisy. See *Religulous*, directed by Larry Charles, Lions Gate Entertainment, 2008; *The Trials of Ted Haggard*, directed by Alexandra Pelosi, HBO Entertainment, 2008; and *Lord Save Us from Your Followers*, directed by Dan Merchant, Big Finish Media, 2008. For a broader analysis of the terms evangelical and evangelicalism see Balmer, *Encyclopedia of Evangelicalism*, Blumhofer and Carpenter, *Twentieth-Century Evangelicalism*, Brint and Schroedel, *Evangelicals and Democracy in America*; Hunter, *American Evangelicalism*.

7. Seller, *America's Definition*.

God, Missouri Synod Lutherans, Southern Baptists, Wesleyan and United Methodists, Church of the Nazarenes, Church of Christ, the Presbyterian Church in America, and thousands in between, all consider themselves in some measure or form "evangelical."[8] Yet, evangelical Christians can also be found in Roman Catholicism, Eastern Orthodox faiths, and various other sub-groups within mainline Protestant denominations.[9] Timothy L. Smith likens evangelicalism to a mosaic; while individual "stones" remain unique and distinctly separate, when joined together, each evangelical group becomes part of the same overarching evangelical objective.[10]

However, a significant question in this work arises when attempting to determine exactly what the "evangelical objectives" are. Some theologians suggest the high levels of diversity within evangelicalism, the plurality of its distinctives and the divergence of its groups, have convoluted the term to the point of irrelevance for providing clarity or consensus on evangelical claims, purposes or objectives. Donald Dayton writes,

> I try to avoid the use of the word "evangelical" as much as possible. It is, in the words of British analytic philosophy, an "essentially contested concept" in which the basic meaning of the word is so at dispute that it is impossible to use it with precision or without participating in an ideological warfare that empowers one group over another.[11]

Dayton suggests a moratorium on the word could allow theologians and scholars to better reengage the phenomenon of American Christianity more coherently and precisely. To that end Dayton argues for three very different but irreducible ways of using "evangelical" in contemporary contexts. He recognizes these definitions conflict, which well represents the theological struggle inherent across American evangelical religions.

The first meaning Dayton offers harkens back to a specific Lutheran theological advocacy. Evangelicals in this sense of the word tend to advocate for a Jesus-centered, New Testament/gospel-centric theology and ecclesiology focused on the Reformational *solas*.[12] Hence "evangelicals" in this view tend to position traditional Lutheran Protestantism over and against traditional Catholic or Greek Orthodox theology and ecclesiology.[13]

8. Seller, *Defining Evangelical in Polling and Research*. This study suggests even evangelicals have trouble self-defining their own faith.

9. Balmer, *The Making of Evangelicalism*, 35–44.

10. Smith, "The Evangelical Kaleidoscope," 125–40.

11 Dayton, "Are Charismatic-Inclined Pietists," 40–49.

12. Ibid.

13. Martin Luther's advent of the five "*solas*" became theological touchstones for

Secondly, Dayton suggests the definition of evangelicalism can also include the Wesleyan theological view.[14] This position is founded on eighteenth- and nineteenth-century revivalism. As a corrective movement Wesleyans reacted against the forms of nominal or civil forms of Christianity in Europe and sought to establish a more personal "religion of the heart."[15] The results came in The Great Awakenings and a more robust focus on discipleship or sanctification that was deemed inseparable from salvific faith.[16] Third, Dayton describes the evangelical faction of "neo-evangelicalism" rising from the mid-twentieth-century reaction to the extremist views of fundamentalism.[17] Led by evangelist Billy Graham, theologian Carl Henry, and others, neo-evangelicalism rejected the separatism advocated by fundamentalists and instead sought a more culturally engaged, socially active role in American society. Although now significantly diverse and segmented in its own right, neo-evangelicalism is perhaps the most widely recognized and comprehensive display of evangelicalism in America today.

Dayton recognizes these differing sects of evangelicalism often conflict radically in terms of theological preferences and priorities. At times these conflicts have risen to the point of creating stark opposition, division, and warring factions. The significant point to be made of Dayton's insights here is that American evangelicalism has carried forward over two centuries of adaptation and mutation. Therefore, contemporary evangelical religion in America currently represents the collective result of multiple streams of theological, cultural, and sociological thought and experience which now coexist simultaneously. Dayton recognizes that each of the definitions he proposes, although carrying severe distinctions and differentiations, also contains dominant similarities that tie each sub-group to a common and distinctive "evangelical" thread. In the end, Dayton draws the picture of a proverbial evangelical family tree with thousands of various branches. Each branch claims some degree of autonomy yet remains dependent on a common root system.

Scholars George Marsden, David Bebbington, and Randall Balmer each help more clearly define and describe these theological roots.

---

the Protestant Reformation. In Latin they are understood as sola: *fide, gracia, scriptura, Christus,* and *gloria.* That there is more than one "sola" is an infamous theological oxymoron. Contemporary theologian Alistair McGrath is an example who advocates for such an understanding. See McGrath, *Christianity's Dangerous Idea.*

14. Dayton, "Are Charismatic-Inclined Pietists," 40–49.

15. Ibid.

16. Ibid.

17. Ibid.

As a historian specifically interested in American evangelical religion, Marsden modifies and deepens Dayton's proposal.[18] Marsden supports the position that evangelicals are groups of Protestant Christians who share a common theological prioritization of the "gospel of Jesus."[19] The focus on the New Testament revelations of the person, mission and purpose of Jesus, above all other religious or Scriptural priorities, is what Marsden suggests has historically remained the preeminent focus for American evangelicals. Secondly, Marsden argues evangelicalism can be understood to describe a distinctly Protestant ecclesiological movement as well, one that has maintained significant cultural and theological disparity. Nevertheless, Marsden notes evangelicals have retained many mutual traditions, influences, and experiences with other forms of non-Protestant Christianity that allow for evangelicals to participate in a shared and unifying Christian worldview. Third, Marsden senses a more recent generalizing trend that has created what he calls a "trans-denominational" effect within evangelicalism.[20] These trans-denominational groups demonstrate more fluid infrastructures than traditional evangelical denominations while remaining formidable enough to create coalitions and common fellowship.[21] Marsden uses evangelist Billy Graham, and his parachurch organization, as an example of trans-denominationalism. Although Graham is a lifelong member of the Southern Baptist denomination, in his career as an evangelist, Graham's ecumenism has demonstrated a significant commitment to the broader arena of evangelical theology and practice than the more limited perspectives or advocacies indicative of a single denomination.[22]

Bebbington's Evangelical Distinctives

Marsden's reflections and typology of evangelicalism become a lens through which to better perceive Bebbington and Balmer's classifications of evangelicalism. First, Bebbington's analysis of evangelical theological distinctives has perhaps remained one of the most commonly cited works on the subject.[23]

18. Marsden, *Reforming Fundamentalism*, 2–5.

19. Ibid.

20. Ibid.

21. Ibid. Marsden suggests members or participants of trans-denominational groups often remain active in non-evangelical churches while remaining committed to an overarching evangelical ethos.

22. Along with Marsden, see Wacker, "Billy Graham's America," 489–511. Butler Jr., "Billy Graham."

23. Bebbington, *Evangelicalism in Modern Britain*.

Bebbington identifies four key evangelical distinctives and theological prioritizations. These priorities are defined in the terms conversionism, activism, crucicentrism and biblicism.[24] Bebbington's quadrilateral, first published in 1989, has maintained wide acceptance in both scholarly and popular evangelical circles.[25] Likewise, the Bebbington evangelical quadrilateral will serve this work as a standard against which contemporary forms of evangelical and postevangelical theology and practice are gauged.[26] Finally, Bebbington's characterizations of evangelical theological values carry meaningful significance for clarifying Willardian theology, how it is perceived within contemporary evangelical circles, and where it corrects or adapts evangelical ideals and distinctives. Therefore, chapter two will compare and contrast Willard's theological critique and reform against the same four distinctives.

Conversionism

Bebbington suggests the classical or traditional evangelical understanding of Christian conversion refers to the life-changing event whereby a person receives or achieves a confidence (faith) in the deity, sanctity, and salvific capacity of Jesus Christ. Other evangelical theologians describe conversionism as a "new birth" experience that often radically alters a convert's life.[27] Frequently, evangelicals conjoin conversion with a moment of existential crisis whereby an individual comes to the awareness of their "lost" condition. This awareness motivates the pursuit of a remedy for their sin through the atoning work of Christ.[28] Hence, for the evangelical, families of origin, nationality or ethnicity have nothing to do with Christian identification. One must become a Christian either by a predetermined act of

24. Ibid., 3.

25. See Hankins, *American Evangelicals*, 1. Haykin et al., *The Advent of Evangelicalism*; Dockery et al., *Southern Baptists, Evangelicals*; Wells, *No Place for Truth*.

26. While Bebbington's analysis has been added to and challenged over the past several decades, the quadrilateral has remained a worthy standard from which to measure compliance or deviation from traditional, historical evangelical distinctives. For agreement with Bebbington see McGrath, *A Passion for Truth*, 22. For additions to Bebbington see Harris, "Beyond Bebbington," 201–18. For a limited critique see Sweetnam, "Defining Dispensationalism," 191–212; Larsen, "Defining and Locating Evangelicalism"; Stewart, *Continuities in Evangelical History*. An excellent summary of Bebbington's distinctives is made by Fahlbusch and Bromiley, *The Encyclopedia of Christianity*, 216–19.

27. McGrath, *Passion for Truth*, 22. Dayton agrees with Bebbington's prioritization of conversionism and suggests evangelicalism is primarily concerned with "convertive piety." See Dayton, "The Limits of Evangelicalism," 48. Hankins, *American Evangelicals*, 45.

28. Shibley, *Resurgent Evangelicalism*, 21.

God's grace, a personal choice, or perhaps both acting in concert. One is not born an evangelical Christian. One becomes an evangelical Christian through conversion.

Evangelical conversion also carries eternal and supernatural properties affecting one's destiny in the afterlife. Yet, evangelical Christian conversion also includes the assumption of temporal changes that shift the teleological and ontological paradigm of a convert towards that of a Christian worldview. Evangelical theologians tend to describe conversion in totalizing terms since conversion affects a volitional shift resulting in "actual turning of the sinner in repentance and faith in Christ. Passive conversion is also termed 'regeneration' because it involves the renewal of the sinner's will. Active conversion, or the actual turning of the sinner to Christ, is often termed simply 'conversion.'"[29]

As noted in the quote above, conversion and salvation are related in evangelical theology since the converted are considered saved and the saved are believed to have converted.[30] Whether by means of predestination or the result of an act of the human will, conversion remains strongly emphasized in the evangelical enterprise.[31] Gathering conversions became the primary focus of the revivalism of the second Great Awakening and continue to the present as a primary focus of much evangelical missiology around the globe.

Activism

Evangelicalism has also remained historically tied to the proselytizing act of "evangelism." Both terms come from the root *euangelion*.[32] Evangelical theologians interpret this Greek word used in the New Testament as, "that which is proper to an *euangelos*, or messenger of good news.[33] *Euangelion* is often translated in the New Testament "gospel."[34] In a wider sense the term "evangelical" has been applied since the Protestant Reformation to those churches or individuals placing preeminence on the activities involved in

29. Greenough et al., *Dogmatic Theology*, 953.

30. There is debate in evangelical circles as to the durability of conversion. This debate traces its roots to the theological conflicts between John Calvin and Jacob Arminius. This discussion remains an issue in evangelicalism into the First and Second Great Awakenings, the significance of which will be discussed later in this chapter regarding the effect it has produced in evangelical theology and practice. Also see Olson, *A–Z of Evangelical Theology*, 430; Thuesen, *Predestination*; Feinberg et al., *Predestination & Free Will*.

31. Balmer, *The Making of Evangelicalism*, chapter 1.

32. Balz and Schneider, *Exegetical Dictionary*, 70.

33. Fahlbusch and Bromiley, *The Encyclopedia of Christianity*, 446.

34. Ibid.

preaching and teaching the properties of the "gospel" specific to salvation.[35] The active, purposeful proliferation of this "news" as an inherently "good" opportunity has traditionally remained a primary evangelistic and missionary activity. Evangelicals place the mandate of this activism on the Great Commission, a declaration of Jesus described in Matthew 28:16–20 for his followers to go into the entire world, spreading his teachings and making Christ-following disciples.[36]

Bebbington suggests evangelical activism represents a key distinctive which separates evangelicalism from other forms of Protestant Christianity.[37] Further, the desire to fulfill the Great Commission has remained a significant pillar in evangelical priorities and is a predominate value in the Southern Baptist denominational Faith and Mission Statement as well as the Assemblies of God's "16 Fundamental Truths."[38] The former represents the largest evangelical denomination in the United States. The latter is the fastest growing evangelical denomination in the world.[39]

Biblicism

Bebbington describes evangelical biblicism as the priority placed on the efficacy and reliability of the Bible as the solitary, authoritative source for all theological and ecclesiological formation.[40] What is key for evangelical

35. Yet, as we shall see later, the history of evangelicalism reveals a continuously evolving debate regarding a) exactly what the gospel is, b) which qualities of the gospel (good news) are in fact "good," and c) to what degree such qualities should or must be emphasized within the essence and content of evangelical theology and doctrine. Hence, the evangelical understanding of the gospel as a representation of the Christian metanarrative remains an evolving and changing subject of varied opinion and emphasis over the centuries, this despite more contemporary claims of the gospel's inviolate, singular and eternally constant nature. This has been a continuing claim from conservative evangelicals regarding the passage in Jude 1:3. Conservatives interpret this to mean the gospel has only one valid or orthodox meaning and interpretation. See Bauckham, *2 Peter and Jude*, 34. Also see Piper, *Jesus: The Only Way to God*.

36. See Klauber and Manetsch, *The Great Commission*.

37. Using a generalization, Bebbington suggests mainline Protestant faiths tend to prioritize the satisfaction of more eminent, physical needs such as hunger, shelter and social justice issues. In contrast, Bebbington notes evangelicals tend to focus on the transcendent, spiritual needs of eternal salvation of the soul. This emphasis dictates an activism of proselytizing the unsaved. Bebbington, *Evangelicalism in Modern Britain*, 74.

38. See the Southern Baptist Faith and Message doctrinal statement at http://www.sbc.net/BFM/bfm2000.asp. The Assemblies of God 16 Fundamental truths can be accessed at http://www.ag.org/top/beliefs/statement_of_fundamental_truths/sft_full.cfm.

39. Lindner, *Yearbook of American & Canadian Churches*.

40. Bebbington, *Evangelicalism in Modern Britain*, 12.

biblicism is the holiness of Scripture and its unique representation as the divine revelation of God. Therefore, Scripture plays a supreme, totalizing and absolutist role in evangelical theology and practice. Held as inspired by God's Holy Spirit, evangelicals consider the Bible as containing the normative instructions for all of human endeavors while also establishing divine doctrines for the organization and purposes of the church catholic. Evangelicals often differ significantly regarding particular views of biblical inspiration or among esoteric understanding of inerrancy or infallibility.[41] However, there exists overarching agreement between evangelicals that Scripture, in cooperation with the interpretive guidance provided by the Holy Spirit, carries an authoritative function to direct human life and living. Typically, evangelical debates regarding Scripture surround how and what measurement or degree of authority, inerrancy, infallibility, or accuracy should be applied, not if such a standard is necessary or appropriate.[42]

Crucicentrism

The final of the four Bebbington distinctives is crucicentrism. Evangelicals contend the first century crucifixion of Jesus of Nazareth represents both a historical event and a manifestation of the penultimate act of divine grace, love, and atonement leading to eternal salvation.[43] Generally, evangelical theology holds God's overarching mission (*missio Dei*) in human history, and perhaps Jesus' single objective in his earthly ministry, was the triumph of good over evil accomplished through an atoning blood sacrifice and subsequent resurrection.[44] Additionally, many evangelicals contend the overarching narrative of the Scriptures is a long foreshadowing or prophetic illustration of the atonement Christ ultimately accomplishes through the crucifixion.[45] Thus, for evangelicals, the power and credibility of Christian-

41. This is seen during the period called the "Bible Wars" where fundamentalist and liberal factions debated the viability of Scriptural accuracy and authority. See Wright, *The Last Word*; Lindsell, *The Battle for the Bible.*

42. Malley, *How the Bible Works.*

43. Bartlett, *Cross Purposes*; Driscoll and Breshears, *Death By Love*; Green and Baker, *Recovering the Scandal of the Cross*; MacArthur, *Ashamed of the Gospel*; Piper, *The Future of Justification.*

44. A history of the development of the theology behind the confluence of *missio Dei* with salvation itself is found in Fahlbusch and Bromiley, *The Encyclopedia of Christianity*, 563. As H. H. Rosin has shown, not only did *missio Dei* serve to identify God as the genuine subject of Christian mission, but the phrase became a means to enlarge substantially the horizon of salvation itself. See Rosin, *Missio Dei.*

45. Lewis and Demarest, *Integrative Theology*, 432–45.

ity as a whole hinges upon the metaphysical events leading up to, surrounding and proceeding from Christ's death on the cross.

Additionally, evangelicalism positions personal piety metaphorically in terms of accepting the death of one's carnal, disobedient willfulness through the idea of "picking up of ones cross daily" or becoming "crucified with Christ."[46] Here the symbol of the cross represents an existential reality of a life dedicated to obedience and submission to Christ's example. Furthermore, the suffering, sacrifice, and ultimate victory of "good" implicit in the resurrection are considered emblematic of the same or similar types of demonstrations of God's sovereignty and love in the personal life of the believer.[47] Hence, evangelicals place a significant level of representative meaning on the cross that includes, but also transcends, the physical act of Jesus' execution.

Again, Bebbington argues that the way crucicentrism is prioritized in evangelicalism is unique when compared to other forms of Protestant Christianity. Doctrinally, some mainline Protestants, depending upon how literal their interpretation of Scripture, may tend to accentuate the moral or ethical witness of Jesus' teachings or focus on a symbolic meaning to the death and resurrection of Christ.[48] Therefore, the crucifixion becomes not a literal but a representative, transcendent symbol of a divine type of love humans should attempt to emulate as an ultimate model. Conversely, evangelical doctrine holds to literal, historical, physical, bodily resurrection described in the gospel accounts. They contend this event legitimizes Jesus of Nazareth's teachings and therefore by implication Christian doctrine which proceeds from the same.

Further, the good news evangelicals are tasked to actively spread is objectively centered on the atoning sacrifice Jesus provided. The crucifixion made available God's merciful forgiveness of all sin, effectively rescuing humanity from the consequences and penalty of their transgressions.[49] For evangelicals, the crucifixion and resurrection are tangible evidences, not symbolic representations, which prove God's existence, the divinity and authority

46. Stott and McGrath, *The Cross of Christ*, 271.

47. Blackaby, *Experiencing the Cross*.

48. Here Bebbington makes fleeting reference to the Bultmann debates. See Bebbington, 253. Also see Borg and Wright, *The Meaning of Jesus*, Davis et al., *The Resurrection*.

49. Again, the nature of the penalty of sin and hell is a matter of some debate in evangelical circles. Recently wading into this quagmire was popular evangelical pastor and writer Rob Bell in his book *Love Wins*. Bell introduced many evangelicals for the first time to long standing theological debates regarding the nature of hell and the afterlife. Bell drew significant condemnation from many conservatives for simply engaging these issues.

of Jesus, the necessity of defending biblical authority and the efficacy of Jesus' overarching salvific mission the Scriptures describe.[50] The four theological distinctives are mutually dependent, each reinforcing of the other.[51] Crucicentrist priority funds conversionism, the activist impetus, and vice versa.

However, Bebbington perhaps fails to recognize or elucidate the impact biblicism tends to make on the entire evangelical enterprise. Traditionally, evangelical theology has positioned the Scriptures as the premier authority over all subsequent doctrinal interpretations and evaluations.[52] Consequently, the existence of the four evangelical tenets Bebbington describes each stems from an *a priori* assumption regarding the supremacy of Scripture. Consequently, despite whatever diverging interpretations may come from Scripture, evangelicalism has tended to elevate biblicism above the other three distinctives. Sometimes this prioritization has led to claims of a myopic over-prioritization of Scripture and even assertions of "bibliolatry."[53] Placing the Bible on such a lofty perch has required evangelicals at times to vehemently defend the Bible against any real or perceived attacks on its authority, since the Bible tends to become the linch pin that stabilizes the entire evangelical vision of Christianity as a whole.[54]

Modern Evangelical Theology

Randall Balmer's more contemporary history of American evangelicalism adds further texture to Bebbington's quadrilateral.[55] Balmer discusses four imperative, transitional events in American evangelicalism he believes altered or added key doctrinal positions within Bebbington's overarching distinctives. The first transition centers on the soteriological shift between the first and second Great Awakenings. The second key modification is tied to the influence of premillenial/postmillennial eschatology resulting from John Darby's dispensational theology. Third, Balmer connects the devel-

50. See Wright, *The Resurrection* and Stott and McGrath, *The Cross of Christ*.

51. Bebbington, *Evangelicalism in Modern Britain*, 17–19.

52. This is what Clark and Feinberg track as the reformational edict of *sola scriptura* within contemporary evangelical theology. See Clark and Feinberg, *To Know and Love God*, 221–23; Wells, *No Place for Truth*, 128.

53. George, *Pilgrims on the Sawdust Trail*, 176. Also see Robbins, *Between Faith and Thought*, 135; Balmer, *Mine Eyes Have Seen the Glory*, 195.

54. This will become of increasing importance when discussing the effect of postmodern hermeneutics in more contemporary representations of evangelical faith, specifically the Emerging Church Movement, as well as its effect on Willardian theology as a whole. See Hankins, *American Evangelicals*, 109–32.

55. Balmer, *The Making of Evangelicalism*.

opment of sectarian separatism and a fundamentalist subculture with the nineteenth-century rise of theological liberalism and scientific empiricism. Finally, Balmer highlights the attempt to re-acculturate evangelicalism into American socio/political arenas through the affiliations and agendas of the Religious Right. D. M. Oldfield connects the growth of the Religious Right with the popularity and acceptance of the seeker-driven, Church Growth Movement ecclesiology.[56]

Each of these evolutionary events plays a key role in the development of the contexts wherein Willardian theology has emerged and gained increasing attention. Therefore, a brief investigation into each of these adaptations will better illuminate the unique issues, clarifications, or critiques found in both Willardian theology and the protoevangelicalism it advocates.

Soteriology

Balmer begins his analysis with a discussion of the evolving nature of evangelical soteriology. Historically, Balmer points to soteriology as representing perhaps the most essential, divisive, and yet consistently evolving aspect of American evangelicalism. For centuries evangelical theology has attempted to identify more clearly both what one is saved "from," what one is saved "to," and the existential or ontological nature of the "saved" condition itself. Balmer argues that each of the evangelical transitional events he investigates revolves around a prioritization of one soteriological ideal or belief over another. Balmer appears to believe that soteriology lies at the heart of what evangelicals deem the entirety of the Christian gospel represents. Further, both Balmer and Bebbington agree that soteriology is a core thread that conjoins evangelical biblicism, conversionism, activism, and crucicentrism inside the evangelical theological tapestry. Therefore, the debate on the nature and essence of salvation involves theological constructs that lie at the quintessential heart of the evangelical gospel message. Perhaps one of the most consistent and penultimate goals of evangelical theology, which is also true of Willardian theology, is to clearly articulate a biblically valid soteriology. Therefore, understanding the historical progression of the evangelical soteriological debates starting in the Great Awakenings will clarify where the postevangelical protest generates and why Willardian protoevangelicalism is seen to offer an attractive correction and alternative.

Balmer agrees with Bebbington, Marsden, and Martin Marty's assertions that evangelicalism in the United States traces its origin primarily to the forms of Protestantism evident in the first (1730–50) and

56. Oldfield, *Right and the Righteous*, 195.

second (1800–1835)[57] Great Awakenings.[58] Centered largely on the revivalist preaching of Jonathan Edwards, Charles Finney, John Wesley and George Whitefield, evangelicalism spread quickly throughout the American colonies.[59] The "Awakenings" left a permanent soteriological impact on American religion. Edwards and Wesley's evangelical understandings of both the process and effect of Christian salvation significantly altered previous articulations of Protestant theology. These itinerant missionaries presented vast audiences with a Christian gospel emphasizing an increased sense of personal responsibility for individual holiness and the desperate need for a rescuing forgiveness from the consequences of sin.[60] The crucicentrist focus on the need for forgiveness, provided through the atoning work of Christ, allowed an escape from an eternal destiny in hell.[61]

The evangelical emphasis on personal conversion and individual forgiveness increasingly pulled evangelical converts away from prior Christian reliance on sacred rituals, priestly rites and church liturgies significant in more traditional, "higher church" forms of Protestant ecclesiology.[62] These evangelistic messages were frequently delivered in a flowing rhetorical style

57. The dates of the second Great Awakening are disputed among historians. The arguments tend to rest on whether one considers the second Awakening as simply the results of the Yale College and Cane Ridge revivals which began in 1801 and ended a few years later. See Olson, *Arminian Theology*, 27ff. There is also debate as to whether evangelicalism predates the Great Awakenings. Prominent evangelicals John Stott and J. I. Packer argue that evangelicalism is in essence nothing but first century Christianity, recovered by the Reformation reinstated by the Puritans and popularized by the Awakenings. See Hughes and Armstrong, *The Coming Evangelical Crisis*, 45; McGrath, *Christianity's Dangerous Idea*, 37–61; Stewart, "Did Evangelicalism Predate the Eighteenth Century," 152.

58. So pervasive was its growth, Marty calls the period from 1776 through 1877 the century of the "Evangelical Empire." Marty, Marsden, Olson and Balmer all suggest the early American evangelicals were a mix of what Balmer describes as the three Ps—New England Puritanism, Continental Pietism, and Scottish-Irish Presbyterianism. Some might add a fourth P for Scottish Pragmatism. Marsden, *Understanding Fundamentalism*, 86, and Olson, *The Story of Christian Theology*, 491.

59. Marty, *Righteous Empire*. It is well understood that other key figures contributed to both the First and Second Great Awakenings other than Edwards, Wesley and Finney. However, for the theologically illustrative purposes of this work, a limited perspective on these three figures is sufficient.

60. Kidd, *The Great Awakening*, Marsden, *Jonathan Edwards*, and Harper, *The Way to Heaven*.

61. This salvific message remains largely unchanged in mainstream evangelical theology today. See Piper, *Jesus: The Only Way to God*, Mohler, *The Disappearance of God*; MacArthur, *Experiencing the Passion of Christ*; Driscoll and Breshears, *Doctrine*; Erickson, *Christian Theology*.

62. Marsden, *Jonathan Edwards*, 353; Olson, *The Story of Christian Theology*, 432.

to large revival meetings and often evoked impassioned "awakenings" or conversions within their hearers. Revival homiletics fostered intensely personal feelings of spiritual guilt, emotional anxiety and the need for salvific relief. As a result, the "revived" Christian was expected to lead a more introspective, contemplative, morally upstanding life, devoted to developing a Christlike character.

By the start of the second Awakening the progressive advancement of Enlightenment humanism was gaining increased traction in both Western Europe and the American colonies.[63] One effect of this transition was a recognition, acceptance and application of what philosopher Charles Taylor describes as an evolving epistemology.[64] Taylor describes this paradigmatic change as the introduction and development of the "buffered self."[65] Enlightenment humanism, Taylor argues, allowed seventeenth- and eighteenth-century Western civilizations to increasingly apply a newfound volitional capacity to act as independent agents, on their own behalf, and from their own resources. This allowed human beings to become progressively aware of their "buffered" personhood, one no longer permeable and controllable by outside "spiritual" forces of good or evil.[66]

Connecting to Taylor's sense of the "buffered self" Balmer argues that several important soteriological changes occurring during the Awakenings produced long-lasting effects in American evangelical theology. Jonathan Edwards' soteriology consisted of a fairly straightforward Calvinistic or Reformed view of divine election and predestination.[67] Balmer suggests Edward's Calvinism worked well with a more "permeable" or un-buffered and therefore passive, pre-Enlightenment audiences of the First Great Awakening. Calvinists expected a spiritual force (the Holy Spirit in this case) to actively pursue and work to convert the soul.[68] This left the recipient rather passive in the conversion process.[69] Consequently, Edward's preaching did not attempt to persuade non-believers toward a conversional, salvific

63. Lovelace, *Dynamics of Spiritual Life*, 44–49; Wright, *No Place for Sovereignty*, 17–43.

64. Taylor, *A Secular Age*, 38.

65. Ibid.

66. This is a very abbreviated synopsis of the humanistic progression. Gay, *Age of Enlightenment*; Gergen, *The Saturated Self*; Heelas et al., *Religion, Modernity, and Postmodernity*; Israel, *Radical Enlightenment*; and Taylor, *Sources of the Self*.

67. Balmer, 20. Also see Thuesen, *Predestination*.

68. Cherry, *The Theology of Jonathan Edwards*, 55–61.

69. Balmer, 21.

decision. Rather Edward's sermons tended to focus on calling pre-existing believers to a more devoted and pious Christian life.[70]

The changing philosophical and epistemological environment of the mid-19th century facilitated the more individualistic and empowering Wesleyan/Arminian theology, which advocated and encouraged the engagement of the personal will in the salvific process.[71] Hence, Wesleyan soteriology aligned with the more democratic humanism already working its way through American socio-political consciousness. As Wesleyan Arminianism gained ground in the American colonies, and the new sense of empowerment found its way into the soteriology of the Second Awakening, evangelicalism also shifted toward incorporating the "manifest destiny" ideology inside the still pliable American political consciousness.[72]

It is important to understand this transition. Edwards' Calvinist soteriology was in stark contrast to that of Wesley. Wesley endeavored to spur non-believing listeners to voluntarily *choose* God's gift of repentance.[73] He preached that sanctification was the completing, or second act of conversion, evidenced by the display of a disciplined, pious life.[74] Edwards tended to argue conversion was exclusively an act of predetermined grace on which human will had no effect. Wesley and later Charles Finney also positioned salvation as an act of divine grace, but conjoined the attainment of grace with a specific act or move of human volition. This recognition and proliferation of individual free will carried with it the accompanying potential, and obligation, to persuade or evangelize. Combined with the development of the industrial revolution which sought to attain higher degrees of efficiency and effectiveness, Finney and other evangelists soon comingled their evangelistic call of persuasion with a pragmatism to achieve the greatest numbers of conversions as expeditiously as possible.[75] To wit, both Finney and Wesley wrote extensive methodological treatises on how to most effectively convince revivalists to make choices they felt were eternally beneficial in light of the evangelical gospel they advocated.[76]

70. Helm, "Calvin, A. M. Toplady and the Bebbington Work," 199–220. Marsden, *Jonathan Edwards*, ch. 17.

71. Balmer, *The Making of Evangelicalism*, 22. Also see Bryant, "Original Sin, " 536–38.

72. Anheier and Hammack, *American Foundations*; Brint and Schroedel, *Evangelicals and Democracy*; Corbett and Hemeyer, *Politics and Religion*; Lippy, *Being Religious*; Noll and Harlow, *Religion and American Politics*; Hunter, *American Evangelicalism*.

73. Hart, *The Lost Soul of American Protestantism*, 12.

74. Finney, *Sanctification*.

75. Wauzzinski, *Between God and Gold*, 120–24.

76. Working off Wesley and Finney's revivalist agendas B. W. Gorham's 1854

This passive vs. active soteriological conflict produced many substantial consequences. Three are key for our purposes here. First, the Edwards/Wesley debate within evangelicalism became a genesis for two very different characterizations of the personhood or doctrine of God and his relationship to humanity.[77] Secondly, humanity's ability, or lack thereof, to respond to God created two different teleological interpretations and responses to Christian life. The combinations of these two points build the third result. Evangelicalism now had two widely endorsed, biblically supported, yet conflicting "gospel" messages. The introduction of pluralism, and the lack of a single cohesive message, would cause bitter and enduring splits, sectarian denominationalism and centuries of competition for authority and orthodoxy between warring factions inside the evangelical ranks.

However, despite this division, Edwardian Calvinists and Wesleyan Arminians widely concurred on one key evangelical tenet. Both agreed any revival deemed a success should produce the conversion of both lost souls and the transformation of human lives into more obedient disciples pursuing Christlike virtues.[78] Regardless of the bitter free will/determinist conflict, the first century of American evangelical theology maintained a soteriological position that conjoined the two priorities of soul conversion with an increasingly transformed lifestyle. Justification and sanctification remained of equal value in both the Edwardian/Wesleyan evangelical theologies that proceeded from the Great Awakenings.[79] Collectively, Edwards and Wesley's work reveals a prioritization for the converted to progressively demonstrate a noticeable effect resulting from their salvific condition. Both soteriologies conjoined the redemptive state with a life of disciplined obedience to the commands and teachings of Christ.[80] This pursuit was often termed "holiness." As we shall later discover, at least soteriologically, the Great Awakenings prioritized the objectives of evangelical theology and praxis in very similar terms to those espoused in the Willardian protoevangelical vision of life in the kingdom of God.

publication of the *Camp Meeting Manual* provided detailed blueprints on how to most effectively and efficiently conduct a successful revival meeting. See Finke and Stark, *The Churching of America*, 98.

77. This will be developed in Willard's *essentia dei* theological perspective in chapter three.

78. Tracy, *The Great Awakening*, 422–31.

79. See Calvin, *Golden Booklet*; Edwards and Moore, *Pursuing Holiness*; Finney and Parkhurst, *Principles of Holiness*; Wesley and Weakley, *The Nature of Holiness*.

80. Armstrong, "How John Wesley Changed America."

Eschatology

The second transitional event in American evangelicalism to consider is the rise of eschatology and the influence of John Darby's esoteric, yet influential, dispensation theology.[81] Gaining popularity in evangelical circles roughly in the mid-nineteenth century, millennial eschatology became a key theological and sociological phenomenon.[82] The conflicts between post-millennial, a-millennial, or pre-millennial dispensationalism still maintain wide influence in contemporary theological discussions.[83] Yet, the power of a- or post-millennial eschatology in the nineteenth century stems widely from its confluence with the pious, "perfectionist" theology that developed inside Wesleyan Methodism after the second Great Awakening.[84] During this era, Methodism hinted at the potentiality of such widespread personal piety that larger systemic societal ills would progressively be overcome.[85] The development of "perfectionist" theology, combined with millennial eschatology, fueled a zealous desire for widespread social reform.[86] Built largely on the Old Testament apocalyptic imagery, prophecy and visions within the writings of Isaiah, Daniel, and Ezekiel, combined with the New Testament writings in Revelation, a new form of socio-religious activism came to the forefront. Following a desire to usher in or assist God's kingdom influence into broader society, postmillennial and amillenial evangelicals sought to implement a Christian ethic they believed could and should lead to an increasingly Christlike civilization.[87]

Furthermore, many nineteenth-century evangelicals believed the American nation state, and even the world at large, would become evermore positively affected by the acceptance and application of Christian piety.[88] This societal-focused gospel included all the soteriological, biblicist, con-

81. Balmer, *The Making of Evangelicalism*, 34.

82. Gribben, *Writing the Rapture*, 19–22.

83. The widely popular "Left Behind" series or theo-novels are evidence of Darby's long legacy. See Isaac, *Left Behind Or Left Befuddled*, and Frykholm, *Rapture Culture*.

84. Kostlevy, *Holiness Manuscripts*, 9–20.

85. Bucke, *The History of American Methodism*, 337–401.

86. White and Hopkins, *The Social Gospel*, 5–15.

87. Most evangelicals advocating for such a social transformation held to an a-millennial or post-millennial eschatology. These theologies held that during, (a-millennialism) of after, (post-millennialism) one thousand years of Christian advocacy, Christ would return and complete what was still yet to be perfected. See Feinberg, *Millennialism, the Two Major Views*; Baumgartner, *Longing for the End*; Marsden, *Fundamentalism and American Culture*, 92.

88. The connection between nationalism and millennialism is discussed by Smith, *Nationalism in the Twentieth Century*, 16–21.

versional, and crucicentrist features previously asserted. Yet, it also added this new, post-conversion, divine edict to participate and contribute to an ever expanding, improving period of socio-religious activism resulting in the eventual unveiling of God's kingdom ethos until the return of Christ.[89] Marsden writes this postmillennial vision dominated nineteenth-century evangelicalism and created the view that "America has a special place in God's plans and will be the center for a great spiritual and moral reform that will lead to the golden age or "millennium" of Christian civilization."[90] Thus moral reformation—personally, socially, and politically—was considered a hastening of God's overarching will and plan.[91]

This optimism was eventually crushed by the tragic longevity and severity of the Civil War (1861–65). The progressive socio-religious vision was replaced by a deep consternation over the inhumanity of warfare and racism. The close proximity and prolonged debauchery of battle no longer supported the belief in an ascendency of civil righteousness and the triumph of a millennial kingdom ruled by virtue and righteousness. Human decency appeared to be in a free-fall decline within both Christian and non-Christian groups alike. Growing pessimism opened the door for a new theological understanding of divine providence. Once again evangelical theology demonstrated evidence of a continuing plasticity to changing contexts.

In the post-Civil War gloom, John Nelson Darby (1800–1882) offered renewed hope for evangelicals looking to make sense of their disappointing, yet grand social project. Darby's hermeneutical configuration was well suited to the biblicist, conversionist, and activist propensities of nineteenth-century evangelicalism. In short, his dispensationalism argued the Bible should be divided by eras (dispensations).[92] These eras carried separate and distinct attributes that governed God's action with humanity.[93] Each dispensation was understood in terms of divine covenants God made with key patriarchs of Scripture such as Adam, Moses, King David, etc.[94] And like all contractual agreements, Darby's theology taught each covenant had its unique terms and conditions through which God's personal action was

89. Reichley, *Religion in American Public Life*, 207.

90. Marsden, *Understanding Fundamentalism*, 92–112.

91. Many examples of the benefits of the so-called social gospel are still available. The abolition of slavery, the six day work-week, child-labor laws, the public school system, women's suffrage, and the beginnings of equal rights are all traced to the social activism of evangelical theology in the nineteenth century. See Marty, *Religion and Republic*, 116, and Dorrien, *Social Ethics in the Making*.

92. Prosser, *Dispensationalist Eschatology*.

93. Couch, *Dictionary of Premillennial Theology*.

94. Olson, *The Westminster Handbook*, 112.

mediated. Hence, the era or "dispensation" for those struggling to make sense of the tragic events of the Civil War was significantly different from previous eras described in Scripture.

Darby's exegesis/eisegesis of Scripture posited the dispensation of the nineteenth century was one of trials and tribulations, in which worldwide evil would grow and spread.[95] Consequently, Darby prophesied the immediate future would be marked by an increasingly tumultuous climate. Faithful Christians should therefore expect and prepare for the imminent return of Jesus to rescue (rapture) true believers from the trials and destruction of a tribulation period. Darby described this hellish purgation of evil from the world as the pouring out of God's wrath as a judgment on those "left-behind" during the rapture.[96] As a result, pre-millennial dogmas formed around the tenet Jesus would return before (pre) the millennial rule to rescue (rapture) the faithful from his divine punishment. After the tribulation, Jesus would return with the faithful and establish his millennial reign in a purged and purified world.[97]

Pre-millennial dispensational eschatology grew and spread largely through the preaching of Dwight L. Moody, (1837–99) and Charles Spurgeon (1834–92).[98] Now undergirded with the eminence of premillenial rapture eschatology, evangelicals following Moody's vision of the gospel saw a divine imperative to reach as many unsaved souls as quickly as possible.[99] As a result, the Moody-esque nineteenth-century revival preaching departed from the more holistic Edwardian/Wesleyan message that articulated a growing spiritual maturity as a result of salvific faith. Instead, evangelists proliferated a confrontational call directed specifically to the non-churched and unsaved.[100] Premillennialism evoked a fear response to the impending delivery of God's

95. Newport and Gribben, *Expecting the End.*

96. This is where the title of the best selling "Left Behind" series by La Haye and Jenkins gained its inspiration.

97. There are several descriptions of this theological proposition. Much of it remains key to mainstream contemporary evangelical theology. See Erickson, *Christian Theology*, 1212–16. Also Meissner, *Thy Kingdom Come*; Blomberg and Chung, *A Case for Historic Premillennialism*.

98. Influenced by the theology and works of William Carey (1761–1834) and Andrew Fuller (1754–1815), Moody combined his pre-millennial dispensationalism with renewed focus on a fulfilling the Great Commission. Carey and Fuller departed from the traditional English view of evangelism and missions of their day believing instead that, in view of the Great Commission, pastors and churches were given a divine responsibility to call the lost to conversion, not existing believers to a holier life. Terry, "The Great Commission and International Missions: A Historical Look," 70.

99. Bebbington, *The Dominance of Evangelicalism.*

100. Ibid.

wrath.[101] Thus, Moody's focus was primarily on justification of the unsaved, not sanctification of the believer. His revivals focused almost exclusively on conversion.[102] Combined with Darby's pre-millennial eschatology, Moody's soteriology highlighted the urgency of removing sin guilt through a profession of faith in the viability of Christ's penal substitutionary atonement. Such a profession saved one from both the trials of the tribulation, the world-ending battle of Armageddon, and the fires of eternal damnation.[103]

In light of the demise of humanity and the end of time, matters such as piety and spiritual maturation became increasingly marginalized. By the time of the publishing of the Scofield reference Bible in 1909, premillennial dispensational theology had taken deep root, replacing Methodism's socially transforming gospel as the embodiment of American evangelical Christianity.[104] Again, this soteriology fit well with the growing American sense of democracy and populism. The result was another broadening of evangelical prominence in America. The priorities of personal piety, character transformation, development of the intellect, concern for liturgy and the pursuit of sound theology carried forward in the writings and ministries of stalwart evangelicals such as Luther, Calvin, Edwards, Wesley, Whitefield, Edwards, and Finney gradually diminished.[105] Moody and Spurgeon's form of revivalism, which eventually led to the popularity of bombastic evangelists such as Billy Sunday and Aimee Simple McPherson, dramatically changed evangelical theological priorities and values.[106]

Consequently, American evangelicalism migrated toward becoming an anti-intellectual, historically un-rooted, populist movement set on evoking emotional religious conversion experiences in large crowds led by famous personalities. This populist version of evangelicalism became increasingly well known through Billy Graham's Crusades and remains prevalent in the plethora of tele-evangelist organizations today.[107] Entering the twentieth century, premillenialism had built an evangelical missional superstructure around a myopic obligation to save as many souls as possible from both a hellish tribulation and hell itself.[108]

101. Weber, *Living in the Shadow of the Second Coming*, and Rice, *We Can Have Revival Now*, 199.

102. Long, *The Revival of 1857–58*, 128.

103. Ibid. Moore, *The Kingdom of Christ*, 90–93.

104. Marty and Appleby, *Fundamentalisms Observed*, 170; LaHaye, *Revelation Unveiled*, ch. 34; Rice, *We Can Have Revival Now*, 199.

105. Ibid. Moore, *The Kingdom of Christ*.

106. Fox and Kloppenberg, *A Companion to American Thought*, 219–23.

107. Sweet, *Revivalism in America*, 24–25; McClymond, *Embodying the Spirit*, 132.

108. This is an incredibly interesting confluence of factors that come together at a

As will become increasingly clear, Willard's holistic theology of the kingdom of God starkly opposes the effect, if not all the doctrinal eccentricities, of Darby's premillenial dispensationalism. Further, Willard's emphasis of discipleship evangelism contradicts the conversion-focused, soul-saving impetus of Moody/Graham's populist revivalism. However, other contributing factors were also building during the late nineteenth century. The rise of fundamentalism would radically affect evangelical theology and practice over the next century. The long-ranging influence of fundamentalism is the topic to which we now turn.

Fundamentalism and Liberalism

In conjunction with the proliferation of premillennial dispensationalism and revivalism, the third key influence on American evangelical religion is the rise and effect of fundamentalism.[109] Inspired by Moody's teachings, two wealthy Chicago businessmen compiled and published a collection of twelve books, containing some ninety essays, titled *The Fundamentals: A Testimony to the Truth* in 1910.[110] Written by conservative evangelical scholars and pastors, these essays reveal a deep concern over the increasing influence of modern empiricism, specifically evidenced in the new application of German higher criticism of Scriptural texts.[111] One-third of the essays in the *Fundamentals* dealt specifically with the issues of biblical inspiration. Together they attempted to forge a bulwark defense to protect and preserve Christianity from the perceived encroachment of modernism and its accompanying liberal theology.[112]

Chief among the defenses pursued in the *Fundamentals* were a strict belief in the supernatural acts of God and a clear doctrine of verbal, plenary inspiration of the Bible that produced an absolutely inerrant Scriptural text. This inerrancy extended to all genres of Scripture and created a literalist hermeneutical methodology to all the historical, theological, as well as supernatural events described in the Bible.[113] *The Fundamentals* also conveyed

fortuitous period in evangelical history. For an excellent discussion on this see Yong, *In the Days of Caesar*, 316–23.

109. Marsden, *Fundamentalism and American Culture*, ch. 3. In fact, the premillenial rapture theology became one of the fundamentalist evangelical beliefs. Torrey et al., *The Fundamentals*, 400.

110. Ibid.

111. Marsden, *Fundamentalism and American Culture*, xiii.

112. Torrey et al. *The Fundamentals*, 22. And Couch, *The Fundamentals for the Twenty-first Century*, 22.

113. Christian historical theologian Roger Olson notes that most reformed

strong opposition to any and all deviations from their stated orthodoxy. Infamously stated, "the literal exposition of all the affirmation and attitudes of the Bible and the militant exposure of all non-biblical affirmations and attitudes" were essential in the fundamentalist ethos in order to properly discern orthodoxy in evangelical Christian faith.[114] The *Fundamentals* soon became the reliable litmus test for judging acceptable practice of evangelical faith. They also became useful as a defensive playbook in the fight against the encroachment of liberalism. Darby's interpretation of the New Testament book of Revelation argued for a widening refutation of the gospel as a whole in the run-up to the rapture and tribulation.[115] Conjoined with premillennial dispensational theology, fundamentalists saw higher literary criticism as a providential sign of the predictable and systemic rise of evil that Darby prophesied would occur during the end times.

By the beginning of the second decade of the twentieth-century, evangelical fundamentalism had achieved wide-spread popularity in America. Marsden notes that during this period, American evangelicalism and fundamentalism were nearly synonymous. He writes, "There was not a practical distinction between fundamentalist and evangelical: the words were interchangeable."[116] Princeton University served as headquarters for fundamentalist theological training where J. Gresham Machen, A. A. Hodge, and B. B. Warfield led sway from 1812–1921.[117] Presiding over *The Princeton Review*, Warfield editorialized the benefits and virtues of exclusivist, separatist fundamentalism.[118] According to Warfield, anyone who did not accept the specific doctrines depicted in the *Fundamentals* "forfeits the right to be called a Christian. There could be no legitimate position in between."[119]

---

protestant fundamentalists disregarded the fact that their early reformed forefathers did not teach anything like meticulous, perfect Scriptural inerrancy. Inerrancy rose in interest only after liberal theology put the Bible in question. Previously verbal, plenary inspiration and meticulous inerrancy were an unnecessary proposition for Christian orthodoxy. Thus, inerrancy is a fundamentalist reaction, not a traditional doctrine. Olson, *The Story of Christian Theology*, 548–608. Also see Rogers and McKim, *The Authority and Interpretation of the Bible.*

114. Dollar, *A History of Fundamentalism.*

115. Ironically, in an apparent acquiescence to modern rationalism, the complexity and chronological classifications within dispensationalism provided a rationalistic means of developing a systematic intellectual foundation that fundamentalists hoped would conserve evangelical theology. Darby, *Notes on the Book of the Revelation.* See also Krapohl and Lippy, *The Evangelicals,* 119–29.

116. Marsden, *Reforming Fundamentalism*, 48.

117. Livingston et al., *Modern Christian Thought,* 315.

118. Ibid.

119. Hutchison, *Religious Pluralism in America*, 146.

His exuberant theological claims became a lasting trademark of the narrow, rigid legalism inherent to fundamentalist Christianity.[120]

When the Scopes Trial opened in 1925, fundamentalist Christianity in America had positioned itself in direct competition to the rise of modern thought.[121] The Scopes Trial is formally known as The State of Tennessee vs. Scopes. It is also informally known as the Scopes "Monkey" Trial. The case represents a landmark American legal battle between the State of Tennessee and high school biology teacher, John Scopes. Scopes was accused of violating Tennessee's Butler Act which made it unlawful to teach evolution in public schools. In addition to the Scopes issue, fundamentalists found themselves fighting liberalism on many fronts. What the Scopes trial represented was the coalescing threats from Enlightenment humanism versus the inerrant authority of the Bible. In addition, the troubling propositions in Charles Darwin's theories of evolution raised significant concerns with the fundamentalist beliefs regarding the origins of humanity.[122]

Although the prosecution, led by fundamentalist William Jennings Bryan, officially won the Scopes trial due to the popularity of fundamentalism in the south, in the larger court of public opinion, Bryan's brand of anti-science, anti-reason, anti-modern, biblical literalism was broadly lampooned by the newly formed media culture. Newspaper journalists and radio broadcasters painted caricatures of fundamentalists as the stereotypically intolerant, rural, backward, ignorant, over-zealous, and bigoted underbelly of American Christianity. With these broad stroking depictions, increasing numbers of evangelicals became disassociated, alienated, and marginalized from the wider American culture.

Balmer classifies this as the creation of the "evangelical subculture" and the beginnings of a separatism that defined evangelicals for more than forty years.[123] Fundamentalism's reaction to the scientific revolution remains a lingering issue in evangelicalism's attempt to conjoin their theology and political policy. Public discourse about the separation between faith and reason, or science and faith, has at times created a widening dualistic gap regarding the appropriate means of attaining knowledge and what kind of education should be provided in public institutions.

120. Boice and Ryken, *The Doctrines of Grace*, 58–61.

121. See Hankins, *American Evangelicals*, 81.

122. These are extremely complicated issues that are very interesting and intricate. They are mentioned in summary here due to their complexity and the space it would require to give full credence to their heft. For a review of these issues see Bowler, *Monkey Trials and Gorilla Sermons*; Cornwell and McGhee, *Philosophers and God*; Harris, *Fundamentalism and Evangelicals*, 327–29.

123. Balmer, *The Making of Evangelicalism*, 43.

In the aftermath of the Scopes trial, large groups of evangelicals faced dwindling public acceptance, a dispensational eschatology that perceived the events of WWI and WWII as poignant signs of the eminent progression of the apocalyptic tribulation and its accompanying persecution, secularization, and ultimate rejection of Christianity.[124] In response, evangelicals retreated from the public square to begin a four-decade building spree. The result was the development of an autonomous religious infrastructure that fundamentalists hoped would maintain the purity of their doctrinal beliefs.[125] During the period from roughly 1930 through 1976, evangelicalism developed into a broad-scaled subculture of local churches, national denominations, private schools, Bible colleges, publishing houses, and parachurch groups.[126] The majority of these organizations remained cloistered from the influences of both secular and mainline religious institutions of the day.[127] "Evangelicals burrowed into their own subculture. They socialized almost entirely within that world . . ." and were able to function virtually independently from the larger American culture.[128] Ironically, forty years later this separatist subculture—first created as a response to the perceived threat of religious liberalism and civil secularism—would produce one of the largest and most powerful conservative political activist organizations in the history of American society.[129] It is to this highly political brand of evangelicalism where we now turn.

The Religious Right

Theologian Robert Webber reminds us that fundamentalism never left the evangelical tent. Webber, a long time evangelical scholar at Wheaton University from 1968–2000, chronicles his first-hand experience of both neo-evangelicalism and the "younger evangelical" movements of the 1970s-90s.[130] He argues fundamentalism began to reshape itself during the 1960s when Americans widely reacted to the proliferation of the "peace, love, and dope" sentiments of the counter-culture movement. In concert with the tragedies and protests of the Vietnam war, Supreme Court rulings on prayer in pub-

124. Kirsch, *A History of the End of the World.*

125. Carpenter, *Revive Us Again*, 7.

126. Peshkin, *God's Choice*; Nezar and Massoumi, *The Fundamentalist City?* 82.

127. Marsden, *Reforming Fundamentalism*, 5.

128. Balmer, *The Making of Evangelicalism*, 50.

129. Utter and True, *Conservative Christians and Political Participation*; Press, *How the Republicans Stole Christmas*; Wald, *Religion and Politics in the United States.*

130. Webber, *The Younger Evangelicals,* and Webber and Bloesch, *The Orthodox Evangelicals.*

lic school, legalization of abortion, and the Watergate scandals, a growing number of Americans rekindled a desire for a more conservative lifestyle. In the wake of these complex social upheavals, Balmer suggests Americans were eager for "a message that cloaked itself in a very simple morality, one that appropriated the language of Christian values."[131]

With the election of evangelical president Jimmy Carter, *Newsweek Magazine* declared 1976 the "Year of the Evangelical."[132] Historian Roger Olson suggests fundamentalist leaning political groups represented by Southern Baptist pastor Jerry Falwell, Pentecostal/Charismatic televangelist Pat Robertson, and Focus on the Family psychologist James Dobson fostered a growing audience for their conservative blend of patriotism and Christian virtue.[133] Falwell's Moral Majority and Robertson's Christian Coalition began to exert tremendous influence in American culture and politics.[134] En masse evangelicals came out of their self-imposed hiatus and exerted their considerable influence on national and local political machines. Backed by the infrastructure and financial clout of radio and television media outlets, universities, publications houses, and para-church organizations built during the preceding four decades of seclusion, Falwell, Robertson, and Dobson blanketed the country with conservative evangelical values, sponsored legislation and endorsed evangelical candidates for public office.[135]

Political parties once avoiding evangelical connections began to court evangelical endorsements. As a result, from the 1980s through the present, conservative evangelicals have played substantial roles in each national election cycle.[136] A considerable amount of research and commentary has given either credit or blame to the "new Christian right"[137] for their role in the two-term presidency of Ronald Reagan,[138] the impeachment of Bill

131. Balmer, *The Making of Evangelicalism*, 55.

132. Meacham, "From the Editors Desk," 6.

133. Olson, *Story of Christian Theology*, 568.

134. Snowball, *Continuity and Change*, and Patterson, *Restless Giant*, 139.

135. Campolo, *Speaking My Mind*, ch. 3.

136. Bromley and Shupe, *New Christian Politics*, 92–97.

137. The term "Religious Right" and "New Christian Right" are interchangeable. Butler, *Born Again*, 4–12.

138. Corbett and Hemeyer, *Politics and Religion*, 369; Djupe and Olson, *Encyclopedia of American Religion and Politics*, 366–71; Haynes, *Routledge Handbook of Religion and Politics*, 389; Queen et al., *Encyclopedia of American Religious History*, 82–86; Martin, *With God on Our Side*.

Clinton,[139] and the two-term election of George W. Bush.[140] Although the issues of abortion, prayer in schools, and moral/family values remain key concerns, conservative right-wing evangelicals have also taken on other contemporary issues such as same-sex marriage, the appointments of federal judgeships, Islamic terrorism, and Jewish-Muslim-American relations regarding the state of Israel.[141] Additionally, the theo-political connection with Republican fiscal conservatism, trickle-down economic policy and the rising popularity of the "prosperity gospel" created a mutually reinforcing ideological symbiosis between conservative nation-state political ideology and conservative evangelical theology.[142]

However, over the past three decades, the political arena is only one demonstration of the increased willingness and ability of evangelicals to exert tremendous influence on American culture. Beginning in the 1960s and running through the present, a more pragmatic and culturally sensitive brand of evangelical ecclesiology began to evolve within younger generations of neo-evangelicals. It is to the creation and effect of the more contemporary evangelical movement that we now direct our focus.

Contemporary Evangelical Movements

The past four sections have set the stage to best understand the contemporary context of American evangelicalism. The biblicist, conversionist, activist, and crucicentrist focus of Bebbington's analysis, combined with the historical transitions in Edwardian vs. Wesleyan soteriology, millennial vs. dispensational eschatology, fundamentalism's reaction against liberalism, and the politically powerful and polarizing "Religious Right" movement, are all essential elements still swirling within contemporaneous forms of American evangelical religion. These issues are integral to Willard's theological proposal as well. This section will consider how each of these previous incarnations and adaptations of evangelical faith have combined to create three expressions or movements within evangelicalism today. First, a review of the rise of the neo-evangelicals will describe what has come to be accepted as the most

139. Berlet and Lyons, *Right-Wing Populism in America*, 305–22; Utter and Storey, *The Religious Right*.

140. Benson and Heltzel, *Evangelicals and Empire*; Erdmann, *So Help Me God*; Williams, *God's Own Party*, 282.

141. Green et al., *The Christian Right in American Politics*; Campolo, *Red Letter Christians*; Oldfield, *The Right and the Righteous*.

142. Balmer, *The Making of Evangelicalism*, 61; Wolfe and Katznelson, *Religion and Democracy in the United States*, 34; Gerber, "Behind the Prosperity Gospel," Editorial.

prevalent mainstream form of evangelical doctrine and practice. Secondly, the Church Growth Movement (CGM) reveals yet another pragmatic move in the ongoing contextualization of the evangelical gospel and the goal of fulfilling the Great Commission. Finally, a short discussion will investigate the rise of postevangelicalism evidenced in the Spiritual Formation movement (SFM) and Emerging Church Movement (ECM). Each of these groups carries significant implications on the motive and intent of Willardian theology.

Neo-Evangelicals

Evangelical fundamentalism has maintained a long and illustrious influence on American life.[143] However, after WWII a new brand of evangelicalism would attempt to break from fundamentalist hegemony. By the mid-point of the twentieth century the first signs of a more moderate evangelical perspective began to emerge.[144] The separatism advocated by fundamentalists created a split with moderates over the issues of cultural integration in an increasingly secular society. Moderates resisted fundamentalism's overvaluing of the eminence of doctrinal primacy and the desire to remain pure through reclusively resisting the broader culture.[145] Instead, this new breed of moderates, or "neo" evangelicals, attempted to maintain devotion to the core tenets of evangelical orthodoxy while also appropriately engaging the wider culture.[146] Instead of separatism, neo-evangelicals sought increasing degrees of acculturation in an effort to both evangelize their communities and constructively affect the moral and spiritual direction of society at large.

Significant numbers of key evangelicals began to dispute the separatist tendency of the fundamentalist majority. Larry Pettigrew points to a Southern Baptist source from 1956 entitled "*Is Evangelical Theology Changing*?" which lists the key indicators of a "new" or neo-evangelicalism.[147] The article described moderate neo-evangelicals as representing

143. The National Association of Evangelicals (NAE) created in 1942 listed key fundamentalist leaders Bob Jones, Sr., John R. Rice, and Harry Ironside as founding members. Rice, *The Charismatic Movement*, 15–17. As such, much of American evangelicalism has German Protestant roots which eventually transitioned into Lutheran Pietism.

144. Webber presents an excellent study of this history. Webber, *The Younger Evangelicals*. Also see Sweet, *The Evangelical Tradition in America* and *Post-Modern Pilgrims*.

145. Marsden, *Understanding Fundamentalism and Evangelicalism*, 108.

146. Kyle, *Evangelicalism*, 135.

147. Pettegrew, "Evangelicalism, Paradigms, and the Emerging Church," 159–75; Christian Life Magazine Editorial, "Is Evangelical Theology Changing?" 16–19; Olson, *A-Z of Evangelical Theology*, 43; Marsden, *Reforming Fundamentalism*, 163; Marty, *Modern American Religion, 1941–1960*, 524.

- Friendly attitudes toward science
- Willingness to re-examine beliefs concerning the work of the Holy Spirit
- More tolerant attitudes toward varying views of eschatology and a shift away from so called "extreme dispensational" theology
- Increased emphasis on scholarship and intellectual pursuits
- A more definite recognition of social responsibility
- Desire to re-open the subjects of biblical hermeneutics and inspiration
- A growing willingness to dialog with liberal theologians

Pettegrew notes fundamentalists were quick to offer a chastening response to the article.[148] The fundamentalists' critique also leveled concerns of an increased reliance on the experiential or transcendent aspect of Christian spirituality instead of maintaining a dependence on the veracity of imminent, concrete biblical doctrines that define salvific faith.[149] Ironically, these critiques suggest perhaps an unconscious acquiescence to modernity and a scientistic, empirical rationalism motivating a doctrinal-centric focus.

Some neo-evangelical theologians such as Jesse Bader argued the neo-evangelical movement was simply a new manifestation of old evangelical pietism and not a foundational shift in evangelicalism at all.[150] Carl Henry, a

148. Alva J. McLain responded to the article by stating the worst part of new evangelicalism was a focus on "new birth" as opposed to contending for accuracy and orthodoxy in doctrines of faith. He clearly stated a deep fear that new evangelicalism focused significant attention on the "subjective experience" of new birth and not the "objective matters" of faith. He concluded, as a result "real" conversions would soon become impossible. See McLain, "Is Theology Changing in the Conservative Camp?" Additionally, Richard Clearwater, then the first President of the self-described fundamentalist seminary Central Baptist Theological Seminary, directly confronted the flaws of new evangelicalism by suggesting it "depreciated doctrinal differences, neglected outward churchly arrangements, and highlighted human experience." See Clearwater, "The Bible: The Unchanging Evangelical Volume." Many other sources of similar responses are available in the literature. Perhaps the best examples may be Bader, *Evangelism in a Changing America.*

149. There is a significant connection to the increasing influence of Pentecostalism within evangelicalism in America that appears to coincide with this concern of the experiential noted by fundamentalist theologians above. However, the revivalism of the nineteenth and early twentieth century, led by fundamentalist preachers, was clearly not a Pentecostal expression of evangelical faith. It did create many schisms within evangelicalism. Pentecostalism will again rise to the forefront later in the research as the post-evangelical movement spawns the Vineyard Churches through John Wimber. Wimber had a significant influence on the ministry training of Todd Hunter. See McGee, *Miracles, Missions, and American Pentecostalism* and "William J. Seymor and the Azusa Street Revival." Especially helpful was Goff and Wacker, *Portraits of a Generation.*

150. Bader, *Evangelism in a Changing America.*

theologian at Trinity Evangelical Divinity School was a key figure who argued for a studied engagement with broader culture.[151] As a result of Henry's exegetical prowess and substantial evangelical credentials, neo-evangelicals found a biblical basis to distance themselves from fundamentalism separatist dogma. Joining Henry were influential pastors and evangelists Harold Ockenga, Charles Fuller, and Billy Graham.[152] Each came to recognize the liability in the public's conjoined fundamentalist/evangelical perception. Such a view greatly limited their ability to evangelize non-believers.[153] Neo-evangelicals moved to re-shape an evangelical future defined as more positive, non-legalistic, inclusive, evangelizing, and more culturally relevant.

However, as the neo-evangelical splinter evolved, most if not all of the fundamentalist theological positions remained, including premillennialism, literal biblicism, free-will Wesleyanism, and Moody's revivalist activism and soul-winning conversionism. The key difference was the manner by which neo-evangelicals pursued their faith. As Pettigrew's taxonomy described, neo-evangelicals engaged in more open dialogue and intellectual engagement in non-condemning, non-judgmental ways in hopes of portraying a more attractive faith.[154] Additionally, neo-evangelicals increased their participation in popular culture, putting more attention and effort into public relations.

Eventually, Ockenga, Fuller, and Henry joined to form Fuller Theological Seminary in Pasadena, CA. Ockenga led Fuller Seminary as President from 1947 to 1954, and again from 1960 to 1963.[155] His leadership pushed Fuller Seminary to assume, like Princeton half a century prior, a seminal role in developing the newer, non-fundamentalist, neo-evangelical movement.[156] In 1956, Ockenga and Graham also established the widely successful evangelical periodical *Christianity Today*, which remains the most influential voice of mainstream evangelicalism today.[157]

Neo-evangelical participation in secular American culture created disequilibrium in evangelical circles.[158] Fundamentalist groups continued to express discomfort, warning against increasing levels of worldly integration. This apparent dichotomy of being "in the world but not of the world"

151. Henry, *The Uneasy Conscience of Modern Fundamentalism.*

152. Marsden, *Understanding Fundamentalism and Evangelicalism,* 180–86.

153. The very term neo-evangelical was an attempt by Ockenga to create distance between evangelicalism from fundamentalism. Smith and Emerson, *American Evangelicalism,* 11.

154. Also see Kyle, *Evangelicalism,* 134–37.

155. Marsden, *Reforming Fundamentalism* 146n.

156. Marty, *Modern American Religion, 1941–1960,* 445–46.

157. Smith and Emerson, *American Evangelicalism,* 12.

158. Dalhouse, *An Island in the Lake of Fire,* 2.

represents a long-standing debate in evangelical circles.[159] In his PhD dissertation, Farley Butler suggests this separation between evangelicals and fundamentalists is further evidenced in the increasingly tense relationship between the young upstart Graham and his fundamentalist mentors.[160] Butler describes how Graham's sermons began to propose a version of evangelicalism focused on "matters of the heart" and not the pursuit, profession, and maintenance of fundamentalist doctrinal orthodoxy.[161]

Even Graham's popularity did not prevent him from coming under severe scrutiny, and even repudiation, by fundamentalists who condemned his ecumenical work with non-evangelical denominations as heretical.[162] The result of Graham's decision to remain open to non-evangelical Christians created a clear departure from fundamentalist exclusivism and highlighted differences in neo-evangelical objectives. Marty notes neo-evangelicalism was "devastating to the flank that wanted to keep ties to separatist fundamentalism and liberating to those who promoted Ockenga's 'new evangelicalism.'"[163]

159. This phrase, although often quoted as if from the Bible, is not actually written as such. It seems to come from a culmination of phrases Jesus makes in a prayer recorded in John 17 or a statement in John 15:19–20. It may also have some connection with the apostle Paul's letter to the Romans in chapter 8, verse 12.

160. Billy Graham notes in his autobiography that Jones, Rice, and McIntire provided a significant degree of influence on the then young evangelist. Both Bob Jones Sr. and Bob Jones Jr. were a part of Graham's first evangelistic crusade through the south, staring in the Carolinas. As a one-time student at Bob Jones University, Graham had significant ties to Jones and the fundamentalism Jones advocated. Graham, *Just as I am*, 34–42, 303–4.

161. Butler, Jr., "*Billy Graham and the End of Evangelical Unity.*"

162. This is one of the most compelling and seemingly untold stories in American evangelical history. Mark Noll, an evangelical scholar and historian, recalled this tension in an article for the fifty-year anniversary edition of *Christianity Today.* Noll noted Graham's crusade in New York city was a key turning point for highlighting key differentiating features and marked a decisive break from the fundamentalist past. Graham's overwhelming popularity allowed him to cooperate with whomever would assist his evangelistic endeavors. This included mainline Protestants and Catholics, many of whom conservative evangelicals considered dangerously liberal. When fundamentalist critics challenged this strategy, Graham stood firm. Graham notes that the divide between him, Jones, McIntire, and Rice was difficult. Graham writes the battle started over "their objections to my growing ecumenism, of course, but the New York Crusade marked their final break with our work. I studied and prayed over their criticism, wanting to accept their indictments if they were right. But I came to the firm conclusion that they were not and that God was leading us in a different direction. Ruth, likewise studied the whole matter; we discussed the issue and prayed over it frequently. Her conclusion was the same as mine. In addition, my study of the major evangelists in history also showed me that the issue was not new; every one of them—from Whitefield and Wesley to Moody and Sunday—had to contend with the similar criticism, both from the right and from the left." See Wacker, "Billy Graham's America," 494. And Graham, *Just as I Am*, 302–3.

163. Marty, *Modern American Religion*, 447.

Historian Mark Noll suggests neo-evangelicalism was crucial in the progression, development, and popularity of current evangelical expressions.[164] He draws a straight line from Graham/Ockenga/Henry's neo-evangelical vision to the popularity of modern, contemporary evangelical pastors Bill Hybels, Rick Warren, and Timothy Keller.[165] These contemporary neo-evangelicals, led by Graham's example, promoted neo-evangelicalism by entering the world and attempting to convert the lost out of secular society and into a more accepting and savvy evangelical subculture.[166]

Once called liberals by conservative fundamentalists, neo-evangelical theology now represents the mainstream, theological, ecclesiological, and doctrinal norm from which evangelical orthodoxy is measured.[167] No longer a minority, neo-evangelicals now claim the most prestigious positions in each of the most significant evangelical institutions once held by their fundamentalist forbearers.[168] The exclusive, separatist approach of early twentieth-century fundamentalism is now no longer normative even within conservative evangelical circles. The preponderance of mainstream evangelical institutions, universities, and denominations now employ some semblance of Graham, Henry, Ockenga, and Fuller's theological, ecclesiological, and missiological perspectives.[169]

The Baby-Boomer/Church Growth Movement

Quick on the heels of the neo-evangelical transition from fundamentalism came the ever-dynamic "Baby Boomer" phenomenon.[170] Richard Quebedeaux notes the genesis of this Baby-Boomer theological transition in his

164. Noll, "Where We Are and How We Got Here."

165. Ibid.

166. Ibid.

167. This is not to suggest there are not both liberals and conservatives now within the neo-evangelicalism. There are such distinctions and they are regularly in conversation. This phenomenon is called the "evangelical tent." See Clark and Feinberg, *To Know and Love God*, 221–23. Sweet, *The Evangelical Tradition in America*, 84. Basden and Dockery, *Southern Baptists & Evangelicals*, 40, 231.

168. Neo-evangelicals are now leading many of the publishing houses, seminaries, magazines, universities, and para-church organizations once held by their fundamentalist forbearers. See Lindsay, *Faith in the Halls of Power*.

169. Marsden, *Reforming Fundamentalism*. Also, the media appears to understand evangelicalism from this perspective as well. See two studies from Seller, *Defining Evangelical in Polling and Research* and *America's Definition*.

170. Baby-Boomers are classically considered the generation born to WWII veterans between 1945 and 1965. See Easum and Miller, *How to Reach Baby Boomers*; Wuthnow, *After the Baby Boomers*.

1974 work *The Young Evangelicals*. He records the continuing evolution of neo-evangelicalism and reveals the fermentation and coalescing of theology and practice currently representative of mainstream evangelical thought.[171] Quebedeaux suggests the "younger" evangelicals of the mid-1960s began to move away from the remnants of fundamental theology that remained inside Graham, Ockenga, and Henry's neo-evangelicalism.[172] While neo-evangelicalism had become increasingly popular and taken firm hold in American culture during this period, younger neo-evangelicals became more interested in political and social policy. Due to the conflicts surrounding the injustices within the Vietnam War, younger evangelicals demonstrated a capacity for prophetic criticism of the state and a greater openness to engaging both non-evangelicals and non-Christians.[173] Further, the charismatic forms of evangelicalism gained increasing popularity in both their ecclesiological and theological frameworks. These are the first signs of what would eventually propel the CGM.[174]

Organizations such as Calvary Chapel and the Association of Vineyard Churches became significant evangelical movements during this period.[175] John Wimber, the founder of the charismatic Vineyard movement, was also a professor of Church Growth at Fuller Theological Seminary.[176] This period also marked the beginnings of Bill Hybel's and Rick Warren's careers and their introduction to the CGM ideology through Robert Schuler, the first protégé of Fuller Theological Seminary professor and CGM founder Donald McGavran.[177] The two influences of the charismatic and pragmatic would eventually transform neo-evangelicalism into the current manifestation widely recognized in contemporary American society at present.[178]

Centered mostly on college campuses and beach communities on the west coast, the "Jesus People" Vineyard/Calvary Church movement of young adults, later called the "Baby-Boomer" generation, became a focal point of a growing number of "adumbrated evangelical hippies of the late 1960s."[179]

171. Quebedeaux, *The Young Evangelicals.*

172. Ibid.

173. Ibid.

174. Wacker, *Heaven Below*, and "Uneasy in Zion: Evangelicals in Postmodern Society," 17–28.

175. Miller, "Routinizing Charisma, 216–39.

176. Sweeney, *The American Evangelical Story*, 151.

177. Hybels and Hybels, *Rediscovering Church*, 69; Einstein, *Brands of Faith*, 61–65.

178. The history and evolution of the CGM is best presented in a paper presented to the American Society of Church Growth on the past and future of the movement. See Stetzer, "The Evolution of Church Growth, Church Health, and the Missional Church."

179. Hunter, "The New Class and the Young Evangelicals," 155–69.

Comprised largely of students, recent seminary graduates, street people, intellectuals, activists, pastors, evangelists, politicians, and concerned laity, younger evangelicals attempted to form evangelical churches significantly different from, and more aesthetically appealing to, their counter-cultural generation.[180] Quebedeaux discusses a number of intellectual and theological catalysts for the younger evangelicals. Among these influences, he cites the works of C. S. Lewis, Dietrich Bonheoffer, and Francis Schaefer.[181] The influential works of George Ladd and the broader contribution of other scholars at Fuller Theological Seminary are also noted as significant contributing factors.[182]

Quebedeaux also notes younger evangelicals placed greater weight on discipleship as the necessary effect of a genuine Christian conversion. The transformational effect of a gospel that spoke to the "whole person" and not simply the conversion of a "soul" rose in importance as well. This inclusive, whole-life conversion traces back to the early ministries of Wesley and Edwards but was also a focus of evangelical Leighton Ford, Billy Graham's brother-in-law, and the development of organizations such as Inter-Varsity Christian Fellowship and the Urbana 70 conferences.[183] Both Quebedeaux and Webber also describe an increased desire for making a substantive impact on societal condition and a deeper, more valid, systemic change in their individual lives.

However, as with their neo-evangelical parents, younger evangelicals resisted doctrinal innovation and maintained Bebbington's basic evangelical tenets. The Bible retained its core authoritative position as divine revelation.[184] Premillenial dispensationalism also remained. A focus on crucicentrist conversionism was the premier focus of Ladd, Bonheoffer, and Schaefer's

180. They also desired an honest dialog on what appeared to some as an inappropriate level of complicity in the syncretism of conservatism in both evangelical theology with American political policy. Many works catalogue these events and people in addition to Quebedeaux. Gish, *The New Left and Christian Radicalism*; Yoder, *The Politics of Jesus*; Marty, *A Nation of Behavors*; Brown, *The Christian Revolutionary*; Hunter, "The New Class and the Young Evangelicals," 261–67; Webber, *The Younger Evangelicals*; Webber and Bloesch, *The Orthodox Evangelicals*.

181. Quebedeaux, *The Worldly Evangelicals*, 107–9.

182. An excellent review of the significant influence of Fuller Theological Seminary is compiled by Marsden, *Reforming Fundamentalism*. Fuller is at the forefront of the new evangelical movement discussed here. Several EC leaders who teach adjunct classes or seminars at Fuller have welcomed the evolution of evangelical theology wherever it leads.

183. Gibbs and Bolger, *Emerging Churches*, 49.

184. The eventual split between Chuck Smith and John Wimber was largely over how literally one chose to interpret the Bible on the issue of spiritual gifts. See Poloma, *Main Street Mystics*, 148.

missiological soteriology and ecclesiology. Once again, the theological difference between neo-evangelicals and their evangelical offspring was one of emphasis and application, not content.

As the new aesthetically and culturally "hip" younger evangelical/Jesus People movement grew, McGavran's publishing of *Understanding Church Growth* provided an ecclesiological platform for the enterprising Baby-Boomer generation to follow.[185] McGavran and C. Peter Wagner's unique conceptual mix of corporate organization, brand marketing, and missiology encouraged accommodation to local culture as an essential element to successful evangelistic efforts.[186] To capitalize on the key evangelical pursuit of the Great Commission, McGavran and Wagner buoyed pastors and leaders to focus efforts on evangelizing non-believers through first advocating the benefits of church affiliation, then conversion, and eventually church membership. To best accomplish this evangelization McGavran encouraged churches to create religious programs and structures that meet "felt needs" of relatively homogenous culture groups.[187] To track the quality of church membership, McGavran suggested modern quantitative accounting methods to evaluate and measure specific determiners of church "success."

Therefore, the CGM methodology gradually emphasized the accumulation, public reporting, and management of key metrics and measurements of congregational accomplishment.[188] These measurements focused on the number of new converts, membership growth, church service attendance, and financial giving.[189] McGavran's overt focus on quantitative—not qualitative—measurements created an ideological and theological rationalization for developing entertaining, attractional religious programming to compete in what Barry Kosmin calls a religious "free-market" ideology.[190]

185. McGavran, *How Churches Grow*; McGavran, *Church Growth and Christian Mission*; and McGavran and Wagner, *Understanding Church Growth*.

186. McGavran eventually created the Institute of Church Growth at Fuller Theological Seminary. Towns and McIntosh, *Evaluating the Church Growth Movement*, ch. 1.

187. This proved to be one of McGavran's most controversial suggestions. Yet still, many Church Growth advocates still sense McGavran's pragmatic wisdom in maintaining cultural and even racial segregation in growing churches. See Malphurs, *Planting Growing Churches for the 21st Century*, 320, and McGavran and Wagner, *Understanding Church Growth*, 223.

188. Each subsequent reissuing of McGavran's *Understanding Church Growth* shows a progression of more pragmatic language and the use of increasing "thermometers" of church growth. There are currently three editions, one published in each decade from 1970 to 1990. Also see Towns and McIntosh, *Evaluating the Church Growth Movement*.

189. McGavran called these measurements "facts." See chapter 6 of each edition *of Understanding Church Growth*.

190. Kosmin and Keysar, *Religion in a Free Market*, 11.

To both participate and win in this competitive environment, churches applied business model marketing strategies, hoping to attract as many potential purveyors as possible to their evangelical "storefront."[191] The now popular "seeker-sensitive" or "seeker-driven" methodology that spawned the megachurch phenomenon was the culmination of upstart, enterprising Baby-Boomer pastors applying the CGM theology and missiology.[192]

There are four essential principles that define the CGM as applied in the "seeker" church model.[193] As mentioned earlier, quantitative measurements of determining success play a significant role. Metrics such as worship attendance, increases in cash receipts, and number of new converts are considered significant determiners for discerning if proper contextualization is occurring and to what degree. If "crowds, cash, and converts" are growing, then successful contextualization of the gospel into the culture is believed to have occurred. This represents the second goal of the CGM/Seeker methodology and the overarching objective of the movement. Third, applying the latest, modern consumer marketing techniques and technologies is essential for displaying cultural acumen, creating an entertaining atmosphere, and maintaining brand loyalty in a competitive religious marketplace. The technology and marketing efforts focus directly on the Sunday morning "worship service." This typically becomes the calling card or primary focal point of the entire church organization. Each segment of the service, from the sermon, music, drama, video, etc., is carefully choreographed to convey a pleasurable, relevant, user-friendly, and palatable Christian message.[194] Thus, the seeker-driven worship service became significantly centered on the creation of a performance event or spectacle that would equally entertain as it would inform and enlighten.[195] The outcome is an acculturated church experience using popular communication styles, entertainment trends, and beneficial programs to satisfy "felt needs" in an attempt to accomplish an evangelistic priority.[196] Finally, the value of networking with

191. Ibid.; also Kyle, *Evangelicalism*, 2.

192. Wuthnow, *After Heaven*, and Roof's two works, *A Generation of Seekers*, and *Spiritual Marketplace*.

193. Roof, *A Generation of Seekers*; Roof *Spiritual Marketplace*.

194. To draw and not offend the seeker, CGM organizations strive to implant or mimic the larger cultural milieu into their religious services, reducing the contextual conflicts between the non-religious and religious environments. A wonderful description of this is provided by Carlson and Lueken, *Renovation of the Church*. Also Hoover, "The Cross at Willow Creek," 145–60; also Malphurs, *Strategy 2000*, 93.

195. DeWaay, *Redefining Christianity*, 6; Warren, *The Purpose Driven Church*.

196. Warren, *The Purpose Driven Church*, 75–80, 251–308; Hybels and Hybels, *Rediscovering Church*.

like-minded churches and church leaders allows younger leaders to learn from veterans of the movement and pass on "what is working" in terms of growth strategies for competitive advantage.[197]

The seeker-oriented churches were vastly successful at corporately applying McGavran's ecclesiology and missiology.[198] The goal was to contextualize and implement popular forms of secular culture to first attract, then to convert, attendees to evangelicalism and finally membership to a particular church.[199] In the process megachurch pastors often became minor celebrities in their own right. Following the example set by Robert Schuller at his Crystal Cathedral and its weekly service televised as the *Hour of Power*, megachurch organizations worked with noted business consultants such as Peter Drucker and John Maxwell, professional athletes, famous entertainers, and celebrities to spread and endorse their populist evangelical ethos.[200] As such, this era of American evangelicalism tended to present a fashionable, persuasive, and attractive group of cultural icons and leaders across a broad spectrum of American society who gave convincing testimonials and endorsements for the benefits of evangelical brands of faith in their lives and professional careers.[201]

Leith Anderson, a CGM advocate, puts perhaps the best spin on the contrast between the more traditional neo-evangelical and CGM ecclesiology. He writes, "We cannot view the church as an island isolated from the rest of society. It cannot be isolated. As the culture changes, the church changes."[202] Critics such as scholar Os Guinness commenting on the CGM suggest, "Fundamentalism prided itself on being world denying by definition. Today [evangelicalism] has become world affirming in a worldlier and more compromising way than liberalism."[203] In less strident terms, Mark Noll says mainstream CGM evangelicalism is exceedingly "flexible and adaptable" and that evangelicals have become "pervasively shaped by their particular cultures."[204] Other scholars and writers label this move not simply enculturation but rather a secularization of evangelicalism itself.[205]

197. For additional insight into the "Seeker" movement other than Wuthnow and Roof see Stetzer, *Planting New Churches in a Postmodern Age*.

198. Einstein, *Brands of Faith*, 61–65; Warren, *The Purpose Driven Church*, 29; Gortner, *Transforming Evangelism*, 25.

199. Sargeant, *Seeker Churches*.

200. Pritchard, *Willow Creek Seeker Services*, and Douglass, *Truth Matters*, 14.

201. Dorrien, *The Remaking of Evangelical Theology*, 171; Kyle, *Evangelicalism*, 272.

202. Anderson, *Dying for Change*, 43.

203. Guinness, "Sounding Out the Ideals of the Church," 92, 154.

204. Noll, *American Evangelical Christianity*, 14

205. Lee and Sinitiere, *Holy Mavericks*; Guinness, *Dining with the Devil*; White and

Despite its critics, the seeker oriented/CGM brand of evangelicalism has become the prevalent stream of evangelicalism in American culture. The mega and "super-mega" church phenomenon continues to spread across the nation often at the expense of smaller, less fiscally robust congregations.[206] Timothy Weber interprets the seeker-driven megachurch trend as evidence of the height of evangelicalism's enculturation into the broader American society.[207] Driven largely by the works and publications of Hybels and his Willow Creek Association, and Warren's publication of the *Purpose Driven* series of books and study guides, the CGM's seeker model continues to attract the largely suburban, Baby-Boomer audience.[208] Expansive building programs have been commonplace during this era. Outside business consultants often assist with professional fundraising strategies, management direction, and leadership development.[209] Church campuses tend to resemble modern shopping malls.[210] Theatrical lighting, smoke machines, laser lights, and large projection video and sound equipment continue to entertain larger and larger crowds. Some congregations have even taken over stadium venues to accommodate larger audiences, convinced increased attendance represents affirmation and often a degree of divine blessing.[211]

For those without the financial wherewithal or desire to build increasingly larger church campuses, many megchurch leaders have chosen to create a satelite or franchise structure. In this model satellite churches are planted using the same branding logos, similar names, marketing materials, even the same Sunday morning sermon. The preacher of the "franchisor" becomes what Bob Smietana calls a "High-Tech Circuit Rider"

Yeats, *Franchising McChurch*; Davis, *More than a Purpose*; Ostwalt, *Secular Steeples*; Einstein, *Brands of faith*, 61–65.

206. Loveland and Wheeler, *From Meetinghouse to Megachurch*, 127–80. Definitions of the term "mega" church vary. However, most commonly, a mega church is categorized as regularly drawing more than 2000 in weekly attendance. "Super" megachurches are those with over 10,000 weekly attendees. Approximately fifty churches in America are in the "Super" category. Thumma and Travis, *Beyond Megachurch Myths*, 186. And Thumma and Bird, "Not Who You Think They Are."

207. Weber, "Fundamentalism Twice Removed," 428–30.

208. Warren makes it clear how significant the teaching of McGavran was on his early development. See Warren, *The Purpose Driven Church*, 29. Hybels and Warren recognize the influence of megachurch television pastor Robert Schuller as the first "seeker driven" church model. Hybels and Warren studied with Schuller prior to the planting of their churches. Einstein, *Brands of faith*, 62.

209. Elisha, *Moral Ambition*, 50–55; Ammerman, *Pillars of Faith*, 104–8.

210. An interesting investigation into the connections between shopping malls and religion is done by *Malls R Us*, directed by Helene Klodawsky. Also see Gruber and Hungerman, "The Church Versus the Mall," 831–62.

211. Witham, *Marketplace of the Gods*, 91.

often delivering live sermons via internet connection or tape-delayed, prerecorded sermons cast over a large-screen video system. A non-preaching "franchisee," or multi-site minister, is available to direct all other aspects of the service, leading worship, prayer, etc. According to Smietana, "The idea behind multisite or franchise churches is the same one that's made chain stores successful – take a system that works, and duplicate it over and over."[212]

Thus, at the dawn of the twenty-first century, American evangelicalism had more than recovered from their early twentieth-century malaise. Evangelicalism became a popular, articulate, attractive, well-managed organizational structure that pursues business-like methods and excellence in many of its endeavors. Evangelicals learned well from the American corporate culture how to market, brand, lead, strategize, and mobilize evangelicalism through popular media outlets into both mainstream American society and its political institutions.[213]

Post-Evangelicalism

However, exactly what determiners are used for defining "success" or "a system that works" were key factors up for debate with many postevangelical groups. In response to the expanding influence of the seeker oriented/CGM methodology, theology and paradigm for defining a "successful" ecclesiology, several groups of evangelicals began to expresses concerns. Sociologists J. B. Watson and Walter Scalen describe "counter movements" that rose to correct perceived excesses and oversights in the CGM's ecclesiological syncretism with American individualism and consumer culture.[214] They suggest these groups are contemporary versions of counter or protest movements of the past and offer five common yet integral critiques. The first critique centers on the prioritization of individualism and the acquiescence of consumerism in the evangelistic strategies of the CGM. These critiques argue consumerism and competition drive church activities toward the single goal of attracting more and more attendees. One result is to pay less attention on the development and maturation of existing member's faith. This absence of focus on the development of Christian character became a more obvious concern as

212. Smietana, "High Tech Circuit Riders," and Jethani, *Discovering a Faith Beyond Consumer Christianity.*

213. White and Yeats, *Franchising McChurch*; Ostwalt, *Secular Steeples*; Smith and Emerson, *American Evangelicalism;* Taylor, *American Evangelicals and Religious Diversity.*

214. Watson and Scalen, "Dining with the Devil," 171–80.

prominent evangelical leaders were discovered engaging in various sexual, financial, and political improprieties.[215]

Second, as a corollary to the first critique, the soteriology communicated in the CGM ecclesiology often carried a Moody-esque focus. CGM-styled evangelicalism tended to climax at the moment of conversion. Lacking in the seeker/CGM theology was a holistic vision of life after conversion. The concepts of discipleship and "holiness" discussed earlier were not a primary concern beyond the civility required for church membership. This absence left increasing numbers of evangelical church attendees desiring a more holistic, satisfying, and robust Christian experience.[216] Thirdly, the sheer size of many megachurch organizations is not conducive to the development and maintenance of intimacy in personal relationships.[217] Communal engagement can be difficult. Increasingly, some megachurch attendees began to sense the loss of a church "family" and desired more meaningful relational interactions. The result was the beginning of the "cell" or "small group" movement.[218]

Fourth, premillenial eschatology provided a strong motive for CGM organizations to evangelize the world. However, the premillennial rapture theory carried significant repercussions. One repercussion was an overarching disinterest in responsible environmental care.[219] Since premillennial rapture theory holds Christian will be removed from the earth before the Tribulation period while the planet is destroyed and recreated, Christian environmental groups became increasing concerned about the cavalier approach to pollution, destruction, and over-consumption of natural resources these eschatological views elicited.[220] A second repercussion of premillenialism was the creation of an insider/outsider mentality within many evangelical groups. The overwhelming popularity of the *Left Behind*

215. The lists of writers and references on this subject are plentiful. Yet, very few are objective. For a sampling, see Wallis, *The Great Awakening*; Genda, *Republican Conservative Hypocrisy*; McElvaine, *Grand Theft Jesus; and* Greenwald, *Great American Hypocrites*. For a conservative view, see Cupp and Joshpe, *Why You're Wrong about the Right*, and Cupp, *Losing Our Religion*.

216. This is perhaps best described in the *Reveal* study conducted by seeker church advocate and mega church Willow Creek led by Bill Hybels. See Hawkins et al., *Reveal: Where Are You?*.

217. This is best described by home church advocate Viola, *Finding Organic Church*, and *So You Want to Start a House Church?*

218. Mahaney, *Why Small Groups*, 3–16. Donahue, *The Willow Creek Guide to Leading Life-Changing Small Groups*; Donahue and Robinson, *Building a Church of Small Groups*.

219. Habel and Balabanski, *The Earth Story in the New Testament*, 171. Beisner, *Where Garden Meets Wilderness*, 33.

220. Bradley, *God is Green*; Merritt, *Green Like God*.

novels, an eighteen-book series of biblio-fiction describing the premillennial apocalypse, capitalized on the literalist biblicism advocated by fundamentalists in the early twentieth century.[221] The book series drew a number of significant critiques.[222] Perhaps the most troubling aspect of the series was the extremely violent and wrathful portrait of God that was widely accepted and praised by millions of mainstream evangelical readers.

One or more of these four central issues motivated particular counter movements and created what Watson and Scalen describe as "emerging schools of thought much larger than simply a response to the CGM, [which] in some cases have a long history."[223] Barna's research group has also tracked specific reactions within younger generations of evangelicals against the neo-evangelical theological distinctives and the CGM ecclesiology.[224] Watson, Scalen, and Barna's research suggests these counter-reactionary movements are primarily comprised of disaffected evangelicals and not influenced by outside or non-evangelical agendas. As such, each counter-movement shares a similar evangelical, historical, and theological context. In particular, two of these counter-movements are most pertinent to Willardian theology.[225]

Spiritual Formation

The "Spiritual Formation" movement (SFM) is one of the more pronounced counter-CGM/seeker movements.[226] The subject of Christian spiritual formation is a vast, multi-layered, and historically diverse phenomenon within both evangelical and global forms of Christianity. Thus, there is no attempt here to define or localize the movement in general. However, the Renovaré ministry became increasingly popular in evangelical circles through its reemphasizing of the concepts of character formation and "holiness," once so prevalent

221. There are eighteen books in the Left Behind series. LaHaye and Jenkins, *Left Behind.*

222. A good survey of the critiques of the Left Behind theology is found in Tischler, *Encyclopedia of Contemporary Christian Fiction*, 190–96. And Isaac, *Left Behind Or Left Befuddled*, and Efird, *Left Behind?*

223. Watson and Scalen, "Dining with the Devil."

224. Barna, *Baby Busters*, 158; and *Generation Next*, 107. Barna and Hatch, *Boiling Point*, 233–35. Dale et al., *The Rabbit & the Elephant*.

225. The two other counter movements described by Watson and Scalen are the "cell" or "house church" movement and the "small group" faction. See Barna and Viola, *Pagan Christianity*, and Viola, *Who is Your Covering*. Also, *So You want to Start a House Church?*

226. Watson and Scalen, "Dining with the Devil," 171–80; Barna, *Growing True Disciples*.

in early years of evangelical faith.[227] Led by philosophers, theologians, and psychologists such as Richard Foster, Larry Crabb, Gary Moon, John Ortberg, and Willard, the SFM centered on the development of Christian character and discipleship.[228] Significant in the SFM message was the professed attempt to focus more exclusively on the gospel Jesus preached—one centered on transformation of the human heart—that enables Christ followers to manifest Godly character in everyday interactions and events. Such a virtuous life was described as one inhabiting the kingdom of God.[229]

In time, Renovaré and other spiritual formation/discipleship ministries such as Navigators, joined with the relatively new sub-discipline of Christian Psychology to reintroduce the traditions and practices of Christian formation in the distinctly therapeutic format of mental health.[230] The growing arena of Christian counseling increased interest and attention in the forming and re-forming of human personality and character.[231] The use of personal retreats and the spiritual disciplines such as contemplation, silence, solitude, and service were also reintroduced and re-emphasized.[232] To this end, the SFM initiated many evangelicals into the classic devotional and contemplative readings from ancient church fathers such as St. John of the Cross, Brother Lawrence, Augustine, and Thomas Merton.[233]

The ideals and values of the SFM offered a sometimes stark alternative to the individualistic, corporate, and consumerist values of the CGM ethos. Willard, Hull, Foster, Crabb, and others, conveyed warnings against the overt pragmatism inherent to the CGM and its focus on proliferating larger church organizations simply for the sake of attaining numerical

227. Matthews, "How Is It with Your Soul?" 42–45.

228. Willard describes this shift well in his book *The Great Omission*, hereafter referred to as GO. For a description of the SFM impetus, see Foster's books, *Prayer*, and *Celebration of Discipline.* Willard's *Hearing God*, Moon's, *Apprenticeship with Jesus*, Roller and Graybeal, *Connecting with God.*

229. Several Renovaré authors describe this kingdom life principle. For an inclusive explanation, see James Bryan Smith's foursome, *The Good and Beautiful Life*, *The Good and Beautiful God*, *The Good and Beautiful Community*, and *The Kingdom and the Cross.*

230. Crabb and Scazzero, *Emotionally Healthy Spirituality*; also Scazzero and Bird, *The Emotionally Healthy Church.*

231. John Ortberg and Gary Moon were early advocates of the connection between SFM and psychology. See Ortberg and Willard, "What Makes Spirituality Christian?" 16–17; Ortberg, "Rethinking the Kingdom of God," 306–17; Moon and Benner, *Spiritual Direction and the Care of Souls.*

232. Foster, *Celebration of Discipline*, and Willard, *The Spirit of the Disciplines.*

233. See Renovaré website for reading list http://www.Renovaré.us/SPIRITUALRENEWAL/FollowingJesussFollowers/ClassicDevotionalWritings/tabid/2504/Default.aspx.

growth.[234] They warned congregational size, large budgets, and expansive buildings could become antithetical to what SFM leaders understood as the intent of the biblical message of Jesus, the mission of the kingdom of God, and the historically orthodox purposes of the church. Some of these critiques rose to the level that suggested the SFM's vision of the kingdom of God posed direct opposition to the CGM's propensity to build a "kingdom of the church."[235]

Over time, the SFM's theology of the kingdom of God also became a prominent focus of the Emerging Church Movement (ECM), which Watson and Scalen suggest is the second influential evangelical counter-movement. Early leaders in the ECM wrote of being widely attracted to the ideas of the kingdom of God offered by writers such as Willard, N. T. Wright, George Eldon Ladd, and Eugene Peterson.[236] Thus, we now shift our focus to this genesis and impact of the ECM and its effect on contemporary evangelicalism.

Emerging/Emergent Church Movement

The roots of the ECM are varied but the history is rather clear.[237] Like previous evangelical generations described in this chapter, the ECM arose as Gen X evangelicals attempted to adapt and correct the theology and praxis they inherited.[238] As a protest/counter-movement, Watson and Scalen claim the ECM embodies the most direct and complete critique to the perceived inadequacies of the CGM, the influence of modern philosophical empiricism and its quest for certainty, and the lingering fundamentalism in neo-evangelical theology.[239]

234. This is seen clearly in Willard's, *The Great Omission,* Hull's, *Choose the Life*, and Crabb's two works, *Connecting* and *Becoming a True Spiritual Community.*

235. Dooley, *Praying Faith,* 181. Towns and McIntosh, *Evaluating the Church Growth Movement*, ch. 2. Also an early theologian discussing the difference between the kingdom of God and traditional evangelical theology was Fuller Theological seminary professor George Eldon Ladd, *The Gospel of the Kingdom.*

236. Gibbs and Bolger, *Emerging Churches*, 63.

237. Excellent descriptions are provided by several key ECM leaders. See Gibbs and Bolger's *Emerging Churches*; Pagitt, *A Christianity Worth Believing*; Pagitt and Jones, *An Emergent Manifesto of Hope*; and Jones, *The New Christians.*

238. The term "Gen X" generally refers to those born after the Baby-Boomer generation. Also called the "baby-buster" generations they are commonly considered individuals born between 1965 and 1976. Brabazon, *From Revolution to Revelation*, Mitchell, *Generation X.*

239. Watson and Scalen, "Dining with the Devil," 171–80.

Furthermore, when considering the whole of ECM literature, it becomes evident several ECM leaders have not only questioned but also opposed seminal interpretations of each of the previously listed characteristics of Bebbington and Balmer's evangelical distinctives. In total, the ECM has critiqued, and often resisted, the hegemony of the religious right, the consumerism of the CGM, the fundamentalist anti-intellectualism of premillennial dispensationalist theology, and the effects of modern Enlightenment epistemology in systematic theology prevalent within neo-evangelical institutions, denominations, and universities. The ECM's protest of these aspects of evangelicalism demonstrates an essential desire to recapture an authentic recontextualization of Christian faith within their postmodern cultural setting.[240] These same sentiments are present in Willard's theological pursuit, albeit with a different outcome. Thus, the overall sentimentality, ethos, and objective of the ECM's pursuit found a sympathetic conversational companion in Willard's corpus and therefore become indispensable topics for consideration in this work.

The first seeds of discontentment are articulated in the early works of ECM writers and leaders such as Brian McLaren, Tony Jones, Doug Pagitt, Dieter Zander, Mark Scandrette, Karen Ward, and Todd Hunter. While positing different views and offering varying solutions, each recognized a significant degree of American nationalism, corporate-styled leadership structures, consumer driven ecclesiology, and fundamentalist theology that became synergistically conjoined inside mainstream evangelical theology and practice.[241] By 1995, a "conversation" between groups of younger (under forty) youth and young adult pastors, formalized into what was first labeled The Young Leader Network. These pastors, coming from mostly mainstream evangelical churches and megachurches, were seeking to find a means of recontextualizing the neo-evangelical gospel to a changing generational dynamic.[242]

Early in its evolution, few ECM proponents suggested outright dismissal of evangelicalism. Initially, the ECM focused primarily, but not exclusively, on more stylistic differences or preferences in worship styles, evangelistic

240. Each of these issues is seen in Brian McLaren's works. See McLaren, *A Generous Orthodoxy*.

241. Each of these issues is chronicled by Gibbs and Bolger in interviews with those noted above. See Gibbs and Bolger, *Emerging Churches*, 49. Also, Frank Viola later describes a similar but more pointed critique in *Pagan Christianity?*

242. Pagitt was the leader of this first group. In an interview with Pagitt, he describes being funded and tasked by Bob Buford, an evangelical author and speaker, to find "the next Bill Hybels" for the Gen X crowd. Doug Pagitt, "Skype Interview" interviewed by author, 10/29/2009.

endeavors, and leadership structures. Since many early ECM leaders started ministry careers in evangelical churches with CGM type structures, their first instinct was to discover or create new and more effective ways of communicating the fundamental principles of traditional evangelical theology. Therefore, like previous CGM advocates, many ECM leaders believed the Gen X crowd required only another re-contextualizing adjustment in order to re-appropriate the gospel into more culturally relevant terms. However, others in the ECM soon sensed the CGM's pragmatically focused, corporate-styled structure that advocated consumerism, conservatism, and theological fundamentalism had re-created an insider/outsider culture of separatism and a tendency to celebrate the "profane elements within established evangelical religion."[243] As such, the differences between the Gen X/emerging culture and the CGM's Baby-Boomer culture quickly came into more striking relief.

Trying to make sense of this difference, ECM leaders began discussing postmodern philosophy and epistemology. Some argued the postmodern proclivities of Gen X groups caused a rejection of more than the seeker-sensitive, purpose-driven ecclesiology. To many in the ECM, a recontextualization of neo-evangelicalism in total was required in light of the tenets of postmodern epistemology.[244] Hence, ECM leaders began to write and discuss the philosophical concepts and potential effects of philosophical postmodernism and how the cultural phenomenon of postmodernity might impact the receptivity of evangelicalism to Gen X groups.[245]

During the early development of the ECM, leaders like Brian McLaren, Dieter Zander, Mark Scandrette, Todd Hunter, and others were all experiencing similar epiphanies about the difficult conflicts inherent to modern vs. postmodern perspectives on a variety of sociological, ecclesiological,

243. Kosmin and Keysar, *Religion in a Free Market*, 39–59.

244. In an interview with Dieter and Val Zander, they describe trying to work a "church-within-a-church" model at Willow Creek. The concept was to have both a Gen X and a Baby-Boomer church meeting on the same campus but in different venues. Others mentioned trying this approach as well. In the end, the church-within-a-church model failed. Dan Kimball, Doug Pagitt, and Dieter Zander all state the concept failed because senior pastors of the established churches could not handle the church having two contextualized theologies. As long as the only differentiating feature between the two in-house churches was a worship style, but the content of the sermons was the same or similar, the church-within a church model was acceptable to them. This proved to be an impossible task for most CGM leadership structures. Dieter Zander and Valerie Zander, "Research Interview" interviewed by Author, Novato, CA., June, 2009.

245. These conversations would eventually become essential to a group called Re:Imagine. Re:Imagine was originally a small group of five or six evangelicals in the San Francisco Bay Area who were struggling to find out how to contextualize their faith into the postmodern cultural context of California. See Scandrette, *Soul Graffiti*.

and theological problems mentioned above.[246] Scott Bader-Saye describes this period as one when the implications of postmodern philosophy and hermeneutics began to cause some ECM leaders to investigate alternative, essentially non-evangelical theological values and goals.[247] Bader-Saye describes the significant amounts of literature, blogs, and websites attributed to the ECM beginning in the mid-1990s, much of which deconstructs and exposes significant flaws in the CGM/neo-evangelical theology and practice.[248] One seminal work published during this period came from author and pastor Dave Tomlinson. Tomlinson was the first to discuss the concept of a postevangelical vision for evangelical reform.[249] However, Tomlinson was not alone in his conclusions. The works noted below represent a marked interest and angst within a growing, critical segment of younger evangelicals.[250] Also, Barna continued to publish research detailing the changing attitudes of the Gen X and Gen Y evangelicals. Sensing that evangelicalism was not prepared for the cultural changes these groups would require, Barna increasingly raised warnings forecasting evangelicalism's inability to attract future generations of believers.[251]

Several writers in the ECM have suggested the key issue, and perhaps one of the most significant hurdles, in both the ECM's adaptation or contextualization of mainstream evangelicalism and the postevangelical reconstruction of an authentic Christian praxis is the conundrum within the rise of postmodernism and its effect on epistemology. Tony Jones has consistently declared the proverbial "it" that funded the overall impetus of the ECM was the philosophical implications of postmodernism.[252] Doug Pagitt also recalls, early on in the evolution of the Young Leader Network, discussions and discoveries of postmodernism began to develop an agenda surrounding the subject of epistemology.[253] These discussions soon began to trump all other

246. Percy, "Review of Reinventing American Protestantism," 406.

247. Bader-Saye, "The Emergent Matrix," 20–25.

248. Ibid.

249. Tomlinson, *The Postevangelical*, 1995.

250. An example of this early literature is seen in Middleton and Walsh, *Truth is Stranger Than It Used to Be*, 70–75; McLaren, *Reinventing Your Church*; Miller, *Blue Like Jazz*; Bell, *Velvet Elvis*; Burke and Pepper, *Making Sense of Church;* Kimball, *The Emerging Church*; Long, *Emerging Hope*; Sweet et al., *Church in Emerging Culture*; Van Gelder, "Mission in the Emerging Postmodern Condition," 113–39.

251. Barna's work on the subject includes, *The Invisible Generation, Generation Next,* 107, *Evangelism that Works,* 176, and *Baby Busters,* 158.

252. He claims Brad Cecil, another young leader in the movement, was the first to articulate the postmodern ethos at a meeting Pagitt organized for what was then called the Young Leader Network (YLN) in Colorado Springs in 1997. Jones, *The New Christians.*

253. Pagitt, "Skype Interview" interviewed by Author, 10/29/2009.

topics. According to Jones, philosopher John Caputo, one-time student of Jacques Derrida and a professor at Syracuse University, was the first voice within the ECM regarding the issue of postmodern epistemology.[254] Gibbs and Bolger also suggest postmodernism came into increasing focus and interest as the ECM deconstruction of evangelicalism progressed.[255] McLaren's seminal book, *A New Kind of Christian*, refers continually to the concepts of postmodernism.[256] Key scholars and researchers of the ECM often refer back to McLaren's references to postmodernism.[257] Certainly, McLaren is not the first to introduce the potential effects of postmodern epistemology on American evangelicalism. Theologians Lesslie Newbigin, D. R. Griffin, Stanley Grenz, and others had previously bracketed the subject.[258]

By the turn of the millennium the ECM's protest against neo-evangelical theology and praxis was becoming more visceral. Some ECM writers suggested, at points, the institutionalization of neo-evangelicalism threatened to escape the limits of biblical Christian faith and the traditional purposes of the Church.[259] Eventually, some postevangelical writers and leaders began to inch toward advocating a separate and distinct post-evangelical theology and praxis. Still other postevangelicals remained sympathetic to a preponderance of evangelical theological distinctives. Biblical authority, activism, and conversionism remained key measures of Christian orthodoxy. However, with the growing interest in postmodern hermeneutics, gone was the literalist interpretations of Scripture, and a more communal hermeneutic became preferred.

Additionally, postevangelicals no longer expressed the overt desire to evangelize their world with a wrath-filled, pre-millennial, crucicentrist gospel wedded to a penal substitutionary atonement theory. Postevangelicals considered this an anemic soteriology, one perceived as offering only membership in a megachurch and an ambiguous description of life after death. Overall, the CGM gospel was uninspiring, theologically reductionistic, and increasingly anthropomorphic to postevangelicals.[260] Such a message was received as impotent in its ability to positively shape the broader culture,

254. Jones, *The New Christians*, 41.

255. Gibbs and Bolger, *Emerging Churches*, 26.

256. McLaren, *A New Kind of Christian.*

257. Ibid.; also Labanow, *Evangelicalism and the Emerging Church.*

258. Griffin, *God and Religion in the Postmodern World*; Olson, "Postconservative Evangelicals Greet the Postmodern Age," 480–83; Brown, "Theology in a Postmodern Culture"; Erickson, *Postmodernizing the Faith*, 163.

259. See Garrison, *Jesus Died for This?* Smith, *A Lover's Quarrel with the Evangelical Church*; Bakker, *Fall to Grace.*

260. Viola, *Pagan Christianity?*

while also appearing ineffective in transforming the lives of those within the evangelical congregations applying its practices and beliefs.

As a result, an increasing sense began to grow among many ECM leaders that something foundationally altering would need to occur within modern evangelical forms of faith to accomplish their objective of recontextualizing the gospel into postmodern culture. At this point, a shift occurred in the new ECM leadership. One time ECM leader Mark Driscoll describes a moment when he felt the ECM conversation moved from reformation, recontextualization, and deconstruction of orthodox Christianity into heretical propositions against not only evangelicalism but also Christianity at large.[261] Driscoll ceremoniously distanced himself from the movement and became a prolific opponent of his former colleagues, going as far as labeling some as heretics and non-Christians.[262] In a much less demonstrable way, Todd Hunter describes sensing that the ECM conversations appeared to him to be suggesting the reconstitution of some liberal theological pursuits reminiscent of the early twentieth century.[263] Thus, for those inside the movement, as well as its outside critics, rumors of "warmed over" liberalism began to hover over the ECM ethos.

The ECM literature, and its extensive "blog-trail," appears to suggest that some, but not all, of the theological "conversations" within the ECM have broadly evolved. One of these early conversational shifts marked a transition from questioning how to progressively recontextualize existing neo-evangelical theology toward more deconstructive efforts to eradicate the influence of modern, rationalist epistemology in contemporary evangelicalism. Some ECM leaders even reconsidered the efficacy and/or value of such a "modernized" Christian faith.[264] In the pursuit of these questions, the ECM tended to employ their more egalitarian, diverse, inclusive and communal hermeneutical methods. Whether these factors actually prove claims of theological "liberalism" in the ECM as a whole depends specifically on how the "liberal" label is defined, by whom, and for what purpose.

Certainly, the postmodern/modern clash created as divisive–and as slippery—a theological slope as that which existed during the turn of the

261. Driscoll, "The Emerging Church"

262. Driscoll's infamous description of Rob Bell as a heretic is well known in ECM lore. See Driscoll, "The Emerging Church Highway," and his podcast: Driscoll, "The Emerging Church," found on the web at http://theresurgence.com/2008/02/27/convergent-conference-session-3-the-emerging-church (accessed 2/9/2010).

263. Hunter, "Research Interview" interviewed by author, 7/13/2010.

264. This is best described by Tony Jones' description of the development of the ECM ethos in Jones, *The New Christians*, 41–52. Jones picks up and fills in where Gibbs and Bolger stopped their research in 2004. See Bell, *Velvet Elvis* and Pagitt, *A Christianity Worth Believing*.

20th century.[265] Yet, there are undeniable differences as well. Unlike previous liberal/fundamentalist clashes, the Bible, the cross, Christian activism, and conversion/transformation remain key components and priorities within both the mainstream evangelical and Emerging/Emergent Church movements. The question is not ***if*** these two movements share traditional evangelical distinctives and priorities. The question to pursue is ***how*** these two groups manifest their shared theological priorities, and as a consequence, have developed different expectations and results. It is the contemporary representations of these long-standing questions we now must investigate.

Contemporary Context

So far this chapter has reviewed specific instances in American evangelical history that continue to shape and affect contemporary forms of evangelical theology and praxis. Within the past five years, findings from several independent socio-religious research endeavors point to momentous change within the religious environment of the U.S.[266] Tracing trends over several decades, the *General Social Survey* (GSS) and *American Religious Identification Survey* (ARIS) conducted in 2008 and published in 2009, both revealed a decrease in American's identification with Christianity in general and evangelical denominations in particular.[267] GSS provides comparative data over four decades, and the 2008 data revealed a rather sudden and dramatic increase in the percentage of respondents with no religion affiliation; from under 7 percent in the 1970s to over 16.5 percent in the 2008. The category of "non-Christians" also moved from under 11 percent of respondents in the 1970s to over 21 percent of respondents during the same period. Further, the GSS shows "Baptists," which includes the largest evangelical denomination in the United States, have seen the most rapid decline over the past decade.[268] The 2008 ARIS study also revealed a 10.2 percent drop in Christian identification in the US from 86.2 percent to 76 percent. This was the first

265. Jones routinely engages these issues on his blog. http://www.patheos.com/blogs/tonyjones/. See especially his debate with David Fitch on the topic of labeling and liberalism on Fitch's blog http://www.reclaimingthemission.com/?p=3600 (accessed 6-10-13).

266. Dickerson, *The Great Evangelical Recession*.

267. See Smith, *General Social Survey*, and Kosmin and Keysar, *American Religious Identification Survey*. These studies also revealed, when comparing other Christian religions, a higher percentage of evangelicals left their faith than those of other Christian religions. Also Olson, *The American Church in Crisis*.

268. Specifically Southern Baptists comprise the largest Baptist denomination in the world and the largest Protestant evangelical denomination in the US. Lindner, *Yearbook of American & Canadian Churches*, 11.

major slide recorded since the study began in the mid 1950s. Additionally, identification with Protestantism dropped 9.1 percent from 60.0 percent to 50.9 percent during the same period.[269] In total, the GSS and ARIS research revealed significant weakening among American Protestantism in general since their peak in 1990s, with evangelicals as a subgroup representing the steepest decline of all.[270]

George Barna, an evangelical pollster, also reported a dramatic increase in what he calls the "unchurched" over the past decade. Although performed on a smaller scale to the ARIS and GSS reports, The Barna Group studied a thirteen-year period from 1991–2004 and found a 93 percent increase in American adults who no longer attended a Christian church.[271] More recently, Barna has discovered that the growing population of young adults and teenagers (ages eighteen to twenty-nine) represents one of the fastest growing unchurched or "de-churched" demographics.[272] Also, the

269. Both the GSS and the ARIS studies are well-funded studies that review large sample sizes and compare data over several decades. Both are well received in the academic community and are widely used in a plethora of other scholarly articles across many academic disciplines. The GSS is the largest sociology project funded by National Science Foundation and has been described as a national resource. It is second only to the U.S. Census in funding and allocation of resources. Over 16,000 research uses in articles, textbooks, monographs, dissertations, etc., have been documented. See National Opinion Research Center, University of Chicago, http://www.norc.uchicago.edu/gss/. The 2008 ARIS is the third in a landmark time series of large, nationally representative surveys that track changes in the religious loyalties of the U.S. adult population within the forty-eight contiguous states from 1990 to 2008. The 2001 and 2008 surveys are replicas of the 1990 survey and are led by the same academic research team using an identical methodology. The ARIS 2008 survey was carried out from February through November 2008 and collected answers from 54,461 respondents. See http://www.americanreligionsurvey-aris.org/reports/methods.html. In an analysis of the ARIS and GSS studies, one report discussed the methodological difficulty with figures and degree of growth or decline due to the range of definitions available for evangelicalism. Hacket and Lindsey validate the credibility of the GSS and ARIS studies and discuss the means of best dealing with issues regarding how to accurately count evangelicals. See Hacket and Lindsey, "*Measuring Evangelicalism*,"11–20.

270. The GSS also revealed one in five Americans rejects religious identification, 20 percent of Americans believe that the Bible is a book of fables (up from under 14 percent in 1984,) and that 18 percent do not believe in a "god" (up from 13 percent in 1988.) Thus the GSS data suggests rejection of religion is growing in America and Christian hegemony is breaking down in American culture.

271. See Barna, at http://www.barna.org/barna-update/article/5-barna-update/140-number-of-unchurched-adults-has-nearly-doubled-since-199 (accessed 10/14/2010).

272. Barna's research is published in Kinnaman and Hawkins, *You Lost Me*. Kinneman and Barna collaborated on a study of teens and young adults based on research conducted for the Faith That Lasts Project, which took place between 2007 and 2011. The research included a series of national public opinion surveys conducted by Barna Group. In addition to extensive quantitative interviewing with adults and faith leaders nationwide, the

Southern Baptist Convention (SBC), the largest evangelical denomination in the US, published an internal 2011 report that reinforces the ARIS, GSS, and Barna Group results. The SBC recorded four straight years of declining membership, baptisms, and church attendance.[273] In 2011 the Pew Forum on Religion and Public Life presented the results of a survey of church leaders from around the world. Eighty-two percent of evangelical ministers from the United States indicated their movement was losing influence in their communities. This represented a higher percentage loss of ministerial influence than in any other country studied.[274] Commenting on these overarching trends, the *USA Today* stated, "The percentage of people who call themselves in some way Christian has dropped more than 11 percent in a generation. The faithful have scattered out of their traditional bases: The 'Bible Belt' is less Baptist. The 'Rust Belt' is less Catholic. And everywhere more people are exploring spiritual frontiers—or falling off the faith map completely."[275]

Prior to the publication of these key studies, little quantifiable evidence existed to suggest anything but the continuation of evangelical Christianity as a growing and sometimes dominating force in American culture.[276] However, the summation of these studies suggests that American Christianity in general, and evangelicalism in particular, has entered a state of flux and shows signs of a significant decrease in the hegemony it once held in American culture. The data also suggests increasing numbers of self-identified evangelicals have

main research examination for the study was conducted with eighteen to twenty-nine-year-olds who had been active in a Christian church at some point in their teen years.

273. In conjunction with their four-year decline in memberships, 2010 had the lowest number of baptisms Southern Baptists recorded since the 1950s. Smietana, "Southern Baptists Consider New Name to Broaden Appeal." Lawless and Gibbs appear to attempt a calming influence on the SBC in light of the apparently unforeseen statistics of their rapid decline. See Ed Stetzer, "A Year is Not a Trend," at http://www.edstetzer.com/2008/04/a_year_is_not_a_trend_decline_1.html (accessed 10/12/2010). Also Lawless, *The Great Commission Resurgence*, 2–23. Also see Stetzer's most recent description of the four-year downward trend in the Southern Baptist denomination at Allen, "SBC Reports Statistical Decline," http://www.abpnews.com/content/view/6478/53/ (accessed 6/15/2011).

274 Dickerson, *The Decline of Evangelical America.*

275. Grossman, "Most Religious Groups in USA Have Lost Ground Survey Finds." The Christian Science Monitor also covered the release of this data in March, 2009.

276. These studies marked the first indication of a significant reversal of past trends revealed in both ARIS and GSS data. Previous ARIS and GSS studies conducted from the mid-1970s through the 1990s predicted a different outlook. Those results indicated significant measures of evangelical growth was expected to continue nationwide with exponential increases in middle American and southern states. A good example of this confidence is seen in a *Time Magazine* article on evangelicalism. See Staff reporter, "100 Most Influential Evangelicals."

begun reevaluating and altering previously held opinions regarding the role Christian religion plays in their lives. It is in this theological transition where Willardian theology has grown and offers increasing numbers of evangelicals a new platform from which to engage their desire to reimagine and/or recontextualize their Christian theology and praxis.

Specifically within evangelical circles, these research reports, and the flux they describe, have been met with a wide variety of responses from social commentators, evangelical practitioners, and scholars alike.[277] Popular as well as scholarly publications investigated, chronicled, and editorialized the various issues and challenges American evangelicalism faced theologically, ecclesiologically, politically, and philosophically.[278] Evangelical theologians have attempted to suggest cause and effect relationships in order to describe, understand, and perhaps reverse the transitional tide. Such proposals cover a range of explanations and justifications.

However, those with theologically conservative perspectives tended to offer a rather univocal account of the decline of evangelicalism as stemming from the popular rising, widening influence and effects of secularism and postmodern epistemology. The combined effect of these ideological forces is often pointed to as posing a broad-scaled threat to Christian faith in general and, therefore, represents the greatest areas of concern for evangelicals.[279] The literature represents a significant collection of conservative authors and scholars offering multiple tangential opinions on this main proposal. Perhaps the most prolific conservatives representing these views are Dr. Albert Mohler, president of Southern Baptist Seminary,[280] systematic theologian

277. Kushiner, "Decline of Christianity Stunning Survey Notes," and Flannely et al., "Religion in America-1972–2006," 875–90; Goetzman, "So Many Gods, So Little Time," 79; Spencer, "The Coming Evangelical Collapse," Editorial.

278. Example of these works are Smith and Emerson, *American Evangelicalism*; Emerson and Smith, *Divided by Faith*, 18; Woodhead and Heelas, *Religion in Modern Times*; and Wuthnow, *The Crisis in the Churches: Spiritual Malaise, Fiscal Woe*. Olson, *The American Church in Crisis*; Wicker, *The Fall of the Evangelical Nation*; and Smith, *A Lover's Quarrel with the Evangelical Church*.

279. Colson, "The Postmodern Crackup"; Dockery, editor, *The Challenge of Postmodernism*; Köstenberger et al., *Whatever Happened to Truth?* Henry, "Postmodernism: The New Specter," 34–52; Middleton and Walsh, *Truth is Stranger Than It Used To Be*.

280. Mohler, *Culture Shift* and *The Disappearance of God*. Also Mohler and Hart, *Theological Education in the Evangelical Tradition*, 320. Finally, Mohler, "Confronting Postmodernism."

Millard Erickson,[281] New Testament theologian D. A. Carson,[282] and author/pastor John Piper.[283]

Furthermore, each of these authors also suggests the surfacing, development, and influence of the ECM represents the most poignant example of the theological, philosophical, and cultural maelstrom threatening the mainstream evangelical theology and praxis. Some evangelical leaders began to consider the ECM phenomenon as either evidence of the reemergence of theological liberalism or the outcome of the unholy union between postmodern constructivism, relativism, and pluralism and the modern rationalism in systematic evangelical theology.[284] More outspoken conservative evangelicals went so far as to decry ECM leaders as heretical opponents to the Christian gospel itself.

ECM leaders have attempted to defend themselves against such claims but with mixed results.[285] Perhaps their difficulty is largely due to the fact the movement never anticipated nor intended to engage in vitriolic epistemological or theological battles with conservative institutions and their leaders. Theologically, critics and supporters alike have suggested the ECM's well-intended attempts at fostering an open, conversational environment for theological, pastoral, and ecclesial reflection was more difficult and problematic than initially expected. At times the ECM's inclusiveness and considerations of so many varied opinions and perspectives led to levels of ambiguity that triumphed over the substantive ability to discern a coherent proclamation of Christian theology or praxis. Further compounding this problem, ECM advocates have yet to agree philosophically on an epistemological position that addresses the logocentrism of historic Christianity and

281. Erickson, *Postmodernizing the Faith*; Erickson, *The Postmodern World;* Erickson et al., *Reclaiming the Center,*

282. Carson, *Becoming Conversant with the Emerging Church*; Carson, *Telling the Truth*; Carson, *The Gagging of God;* and Carson, *Christ and Culture Revisited.*

283. Piper, *Tulip*; Piper, *Jesus: The Only Way to God*; Piper, *The Future of Justification*; Piper and Taylor, *The Supremacy of Christ in a Postmodern World.*

284. Carson, *Becoming Conversant with the Emerging Church*; Erickson, *Reclaiming the Center*; Hunter, *Christianity beyond Belief*; Bohannon, "Preaching and the Emerging Church"; Mohler, "Confronting Postmodernism"; Smith, *Truth and the New Kind of Christian.*

285. The entrance of several ECM's leaders into the political arena and their advocation of liberal Democratic political issues heightened these concerns. Some emerging generations of Christians appeared just as reticent to engage the politically polarizing issues on the Liberal Left as they were the issues of the Religious Right. See Henard and Geenway, *Evangelicals Engaging Emergent*; Jones, "Is Emergent the New Christian Left?"; Carson, *Becoming Conversant with the Emerging Church*; and, Johnson, *Reforming Or Conforming?* 76.

the potential conflicts such a position maintains with postmodern hermeneutics, nominalism, and philosophical constructivism.[286]

Whether it is a fair assessment of the ECM to describe it as either a threat to evangelical orthodoxy or as a manifestation of the effects of postmodern epistemology and secularism is a matter with as much diversity as the ECM leaders themselves.[287] However, the data suggests, over the past two decades, increasing numbers of disaffected evangelicals have left mainstream evangelical churches.[288] Additionally, many emerging generations of Christians have been drawn to the increasingly popular, nondenominational, postevangelical type churches that specifically avoid the political positions, doctrinal-centric theology, leadership hierarchies, and consumeristic ecclesiology indicative of contemporary evangelical institutionalization. Often termed "Gen X," "postmodern," "recovering," or "postevangelical" Christians, this relatively young constituency (aged eighteen to forty-five) appreciate the more inclusive, ecumenical leanings of the ECM, with its emphasis on equality, social justice, environmentalism, doctrinal

286. Dockery and Thornbury, *Shaping a Christian Worldview*, 85. Each of these issues, separately and in combination, has resulted in the exodus of some early ECM leaders from Emergent Village affiliation and "Emergent/Emerging" church terminology as a whole. In recent years the separation in terms between "emerging" and "emergent" may be a separation between postevangelicalism and liberal theology. Emerging churches are questioning praxis. Emergent churches are questioning key aspects of modern theology and epistemology. This is seen in the public distancing of Dan Kimball, Scot McKnight, Erwin McManus, Leonard Sweet, Rob Bell, and Shane Claiborne from direct affiliation with Emergent Village or the ECM. The most vocal ex-ECM leader is Mark Driscoll. There is also a move inside the ECM ethos to create what has been termed the Missional Church movement, which takes much of the ECM ecclesiology but retains a much more conservative theology. By 2008, the Emergent Village was significantly restructured and has since diminished in its national organizing role. However, many of the original Emergent Village leaders continue to pursue and advocate for Emergent/Emerging Christian ideals and still host or sponsor periodic conference events. The evolution of the ECM has been well chronicled. See Driscoll, "The Emerging Church Highway"; Armstrong, *Reforming Pastoral Ministry*, 212; Bohannon, *Preaching and the Emerging Church*, 109–27; Kwon, "Interview: Brian McLaren on Sin, Hell, New Kind of Christianity"; Claiborne, "Red Letter Christians"; Shields, "Ten Years Out"; Croft, *Mission Shaped Questions*, 91; Bergquist and Karr, *Church Turned Inside Out*; Hirsch, *The Forgotten Ways*, 17; Jones, "Theoblogy: Which Missional Church"; Obrien, "Emergent's Divergence"; and Keffe, "Tony Jones Out as Emergent Village Head."

287. Important to note, the Emerging Church movement is a global phenomenon with a significant degree of its original impetus coming from Western European Christians of the late twentieth century. However, this work is concerned specifically with the branch of the ECM centered in the United States. For a description of the European roots of the ECM, see Gibbs and Bolger, *Emerging Churches*. The ECM is described in depth in chapter 2.

288. Duin, *Quitting Church*; Dyck, *Generation Ex-Christian*; Lyons, *The Next Christians*; Kinnaman and Lyons, *Unchristian*.

humility, mystery, and a priority placed on relational living.[289] Dave Tomlinson, perhaps the first to coin the phrase postevangelical, defines postevangelicals as those evangelicals who progressively have found it difficult to reconcile their experience of evangelicalism with their "personal values, instinctive reactions, and theological reflections."[290] This tension often creates a considerable level of relational conflict and interpersonal angst that spawns a search for relief.

Tomlinson makes clear that "post" evangelical is not to be confused with "ex" or "anti" evangelical. Instead, the "post" prefix should be considered a type of evangelical that "takes as given many of the assumptions of evangelical faith, while at the same time moves beyond its perceived limitations."[291] Additionally, Tomlinson suggests postevangelicals tend to relate to their world both culturally and epistemologically from a postmodern perspective. Thus, postmodernism and/or postmodernity is the "cultural environment that influences the way they think about the experience of their faith, and this is the context in which the integrity and credibility of their faith must be tested."[292] The deeply felt connections, heritage, and experiences of the evangelical culture and theology make this transition difficult.

The issue of soteriology has been demonstrated as a historically evolving and contested theological doctrine. Starting with the Calvinist/Arminian debate that progressed into Moody revivalism, Methodist social activism, and finally arriving in the contemporary distinctions and juxtapositions between fundamentalist separatism, the Religious Right, the CGM/seeker movement, and the ECM's protest of the same, a commonly agreed upon definition of salvation remains an elusive and divisive pillar in the postevangelical enterprise. The presence of a dichotomous soteriological message continues to fragment the movement.

The result is a multitude of competing, oppositional, and polarizing factions struggling to claim the "biblical" authority for what an evangelical convert can and should become as a result of applying an evangelical brand of faith. Past and present examples of evangelical priorities directed toward cross-purposes are plentiful. Pre-millennial fundamentalists choose to abstain from social and political interaction, while the Religious Right strives to overwhelm the American political process. The seeker/CGM ecclesiology attempts to attract the highest quantity of non-believers as possible to church

289. Kimball, *They Like Jesus But Not the Church*; Kimball, *The Emerging Church: Vintage Christianity for New Generations*; Scandrette, *Soul Graffiti*; Celek and Zander, *Inside the Soul of a New Generation*; Gibbs and Bolger, *Emerging Churches*.

290. Tomlinson, *Postevangelical*, 2.

291. Ibid., 7.

292. Ibid., 9.

complexes the size of sports arenas, while the SFM attempts to focus on developing the highest quality of individual character through small communities gathered in living rooms. Evangelicals committed to modernity advocate the benefits of doctrine and find the concepts of certainty, mastery, and predictability inherent to systematic theology to be warmly securing.

Conversely, postmodern evangelicals champion humility in the face of a mysterious, ambiguous, dangerously unpredictable, yet awe-inspiring God. Each of these opposing perspectives finally stems from different expectations, interpretations, and assumptions about the core message Jesus presents in the New Testament gospels. Yet, this lack of consensus on the end product of evangelical faith creates a dearth of confidence that is devastating to young evangelical generations looking for guidance and direction on the same, bedrock evangelical priorities of Scripture, the cross, Christian activism and spiritual transformation while engaging these questions in a post-Christian, post-foundationalist, secular, global, multi-cultural, and cross-cultural society.

The ECM protests have offered significant critiques against secular acculturation by neo-evangelicals in the seeker/CGM ecclesiology, fundamentalist theology, and the Religious Right. Even some neo-evangelicals leaders agree with the insights and constructive criticisms of the excesses of mainstream evangelicalism exposed by the ECM. James Davidson Hunter makes a poignant insight in describing how significant the dichotomy exists between younger and more traditional evangelical visions of Christianity. In describing the stark difference between the two, Hunter questions whether young evangelicals are actually intending to be missional to non-believers or if, in fact, their goal is to re-evangelize traditional evangelicalism itself.[293] The impact of that statement is profound. Postevangelicals have perhaps unwittingly sought the means to evangelize their neo-evangelical progenitors into a gospel void of the traditional trappings of modern epistemology, fundamental theology, literalist bibliology, secular enculturation, sectarian factions, and grandiose political or social aspirations. In short, postevangelicalism seeks a Christianity deemed worthy of its namesake and funded solely by the same.

It is a significant and troubling irony that postevangelicals sense evangelicalism has evolved into a form of Christendom devoted to esoteric doctrines that no longer well represent the "*euangelion*" Jesus articulated in the New Testament. Joining historians Kyle, Marty, Olson and Marsden, and theologians Grenz, Gibbs, Bolger, Guinness, and Webber, the ECM sensed a troubling paradox of theological and epistemological compromise inside

293. Hunter, "The New Class and the Young Evangelicals," 155–69.

mainstream contemporary evangelicalism.[294] Each of these scholars in his or her own way articulates evangelicalism's steady approach toward a line that separates relevance to, versus absorption into, the surrounding culture. Therefore, this intellectual historical review reveals the lingering volatility, plurality, and plasticity in the American evangelical tradition that now appears to be on a trend of steady decline in the United States.

What is important to grasp from the ECM phenomenon is the level of divisiveness and attention the emergence of the postevangelical ethos created within the largest and most powerful of evangelical institutions in America. This conflict serves to illuminate both the instability, insecurity and tension currently present within evangelical Christianity in America. At the same time the nature and scope of this conflict reveals, in part, why many welcome Willard's protoevangelical vision as a potential remedy.

It is the nature of this remedy that establishes both the subject and context for the following chapters. Within this volatile and sometimes tumultuous evangelical milieu, Willard's rather unassuming, practical protoevangelical perspective has emerged and gained increasing influence in postevangelical circles. A closer examination of the pillars that support Willardian theology will consume the rest of our focus.

294. Marty and Hunter write of this paradox in Kyle's *Evangelicalism*, 3, 2ff.

Chapter Two

The Willardian Adaptation

This chapter is organized in specific reference to the forms and expressions of evangelicalism described in the preceding chapter. Both Bebbington and Balmer's descriptions of the evangelical distinctives and key transitional events will serve to structure and clarify the Willardian theological response. Consequently, this section will review Willard's perspectives on biblicism, activism, conversionism, and crucicentrism. It will also review Willard's perspective on the significant soteriological implications Balmer describes. This will include an investigation into the specific critiques Willard makes of evangelicalism in America. At its conclusion, these descriptions, comparisons, and analyses of Willardian theology, contrasted against both the history and polity of mainstream evangelicalism, build a platform for understanding Willard's protoevangelical quest.

At the onset, before engaging Bebbington's key theological distinctives, it is important to mention that when discussing Bebbington's work with this author, Willard admitted to not agreeing with an equal evaluation of Bebbington's four evangelical theological distinctives.[1] Willard did agree that evangelicalism has traditionally focused intensely on the areas of biblicism, activism, crucicentrism, and conversionism. Therefore, as a descriptive analysis, Willard was in agreement with Bebbington's work. To the degree Bebbington attempts to offer a prescriptive or evaluative analysis of evangelical theological priorities, Willard contended only biblicism and conversionism are quintessential to orthodox Christian expression. Even still, Willard's perspectives on biblicism and conversionism were far more encompassing than Bebbington allowed. Yet, Willard suggested the

1. Written notes of this discussion were made during one of Willard's doctoral cohorts for Fuller Seminary held at Mater Dolorosa, CA., June 14, 2011.

full complement of Bebbington's evangelical priorities should naturally emerge from an appropriate consideration and application of Christian biblicism and conversionism. Willard argued, when an intimate engagement of Scripture is undertaken, and when one desires to convert one's life to the realities and opportunities of the kingdom of God, the results will include a progression of maturity which develops a worldview inclusive of activism, crucicentrism, along with much more.[2]

Biblicism in Willardian Theology

Willard contends the creation of Scripture required two aspects, the human and divine, working in concert. With regards to the human aspect, Willard suggests there is nothing in the authorial creation of Scripture to suggest that the Bible was preserved and produced by anything less than highly competent individuals who were at least as intelligent and devout as any contemporary peoples within modern society. Willard expects the biblical authors would have been fully capable of both accurately interpreting their own experience and then presenting what they heard, witnessed, and understood within the language of their historical community.[3] As such, Willard suggests that the Bible can and should be considered a reliable and authoritative representation of the story and truth God willed to be revealed to humanity.

However, Willard does not dogmatically propose the Bible to be strictly inerrant, nor does he make overt claims of plenary inspiration in conjunction with normative fundamentalists/literalist positions. He offers some nuance to the biblicist argument in his statement,

> The Bible is inerrant in its *original form* and infallible in *all its forms for the purposes of guiding us into a life-saving relationship with God in his kingdom.* It is infallible in this way precisely because God never leaves it alone. . . . [T]he Bible reliably fixes the boundaries of everything God will ever say to humankind. (italics added)[4]

2. Ibid. Willard states, "It's not biblicism as much as it is the 'life' describes in the Scriptures that is important. The devotional life to Scripture, meditating, and applying its truths . . . this is what is most important. And when this happens, one is changed or converted. And thus we receive what John chapter 3 is revealing a new life from above. So yes, . . . the Bible and conversion go hand in hand. And everything else proceeds from those."

3. Willard, *Divine Conspiracy*, xvi. Hereafter referred to as DC.

4. Willard, *In Search of Guidance*, 141–42. This was rereleased as *Hearing God: Developing a Conversational Relationship with God.* References in *In Search of Guidance* will be referred to hereafter as HG.

Here, Willard may be attempting to dance a bit through the proverbial biblicist minefield while also desiring to uphold some historic orthodox issues at hand. While using similar wording, the quote above does not necessarily communicate what many inerrantists might assume of it. Willard's statement does not appear to unequivocally condone the concept of a strict fundamentalist view of biblical inerrancy. Nor does this statement expressly support the inerrancy of the many proceeding translations of Scripture. As a result, Willard's statement bypasses the fundamentalist tendency toward the application of a literalist hermeneutic.[5]

Interestingly, Willard does not mindlessly assume the total, unmitigated objectivity of every description, elucidation, or interpretation in the biblical record. As witnesses, commentators, participants, and/or hearsayers of these events, Willard assigns to the writers of Scripture a veracity and integrity both assumed in their task and conveyed in their work. As such, the events of the Bible are accurate (inerrant) descriptions of the testimony provided or event witnessed in direct relation to the author's own beliefs, perceptions, and experiences. Hence, the Bible presents no outright fallacious attempt to deceive or mislead its reader. However, Willard seems to give credence and allowance for the nature of witness testimony and the limitations of individual perspectives when compared to the omniscient circumference of the "God's eye view." Thus, the human aspect in the creation of Scripture adds a necessary degree of subjectivity to the text. The result appears to be a position in which the Bible represents a mixture of both the objective, accurate, perfect, and unadulterated revelations from God, along with subjective, imperfect, or incomplete perceptions, reactions, and interpretations of that revelation. Ultimately, Willard contends God can and should be trusted to compile and preserve the totality of the biblical message in such a way as to guard against any human limitation, misinterpretation or misperception that would be fatal to either the contributions of its ancient writers or contemporary readers pursuing its truths.

Willard separates the divine "purposes" of the Scriptures and an "error-proof" biblical manuscript. What the statement quoted above affirms is the inerrant and infallible *ability* of the Bible to fulfill the "purposes"

5. Willard recognizes that none of the original autographs are available. Therefore, the proposition the original manuscripts are "inerrant" is a faith claim, one Willard suggests is "most likely true." Yet, the proposition all the subsequent copies or translations accurately match the original autographs is also impossible to empirically verify. What Willard understands as the motive behind the evangelical "inerrant" dogma is the desire to maintain the veracity and authority of Scripture through applying some form of rational or empirical methodology. In his view, this can perhaps unintentionally take modern evangelical theologians far afield from what he perceives are the key issues regarding the role of Scripture in the Christian life and the nature of divine revelation.

of God.[6] These are treated as altogether separate issues. Consequently, Willard bypasses the more banal disputes in what has been traditionally labeled the "battles over the Bible."[7] Willard does argue the divine contribution to the creation of Scripture necessitates that God is both willing and competent to arrange and steward the biblical record, including the record of Jesus, to emerge and be preserved in reliable ways that will secure his sovereign, benevolent intentions for humanity at large. Willard mentions that for those who maintain a faith in the God the Scriptures describe, such a proposition will be untroubling.

Willard's position cautions against conservative or fundamentalist assertions regarding their claims to the infallible participation of human beings in the inspired transcription of the Bible. Such claims may be valiant attempts to protect the priority of Scriptural authority against early twentieth-century attacks from liberal theologians employing higher criticism. However, Willard suggests such overreaching declarations often end in the transparent application of unreasonable rationalism and/or legalistic dogmatism. Equally critical of liberal theologians, Willard does not believe the message of the Bible can be left in the hands of twentieth-century scholars engaged in the esoteric applications of modern literary critique. Willard recognizes higher critics are unable to agree even among themselves on which of their theories best determines exactly what the Bible consists of, or even its general purposes.

The Divine Logos

In place of either liberal higher criticism or fundamentalist literalism, Willard's biblicism takes the Scriptures outside of traditional evangelical arguments of the past century. Instead, Willard describes the Scriptures as a physical, written manifestation of God's revealed presence among humanity. The Scriptures are a means, but not the only means, used to represent the Greek, and later Christian, concept of the divine *Logos*. Willard understands the *Logos* as both a metaphysical and spiritual presence that represents and encapsulates the ultimate and final order of reality.[8] Hence, the *Logos* is present in the Scriptures, in history, in nature, and also discovered in the lives of individuals.[9]

6. Willard suggests the infallible role of Scripture to communicate God's "Word" is inherent to all the "forms" or translations the Bible takes.

7. For an explanation of these issues see Lindsell, *The Battle for the Bible*.

8. Willard, *Fuller Seminary Doctoral Class* (6/16/2010).

9. *Logos* translated in English is "Word." Furthermore, the Trinitarian presence of

In discerning the difference between the Christ discussed in John 3:16 (God's Son), the person of the "Word" described as present in John 1:1, and the historic person of Jesus of Nazareth, the *Logos* represents the member of the Trinity of which Jesus of Nazareth claimed of himself "Before Abraham was, I am."[10] Willard suggests this claim is a reference by Jesus to his identity as the member of the Trinity, understood as the "cosmic Christ."[11] This is the same individual described as the divine *Logos*, of whom Jesus of Nazareth was the physical manifestation on earth during the first century. Willard argues revealing the divine personhood of Jesus is a major point of John's Gospel. John seeks to distinguish between the historical Jesus as a human being, which is different and unique from the embodying spirit of the *Logos*, which empowers the life of Jesus of Nazareth. This differentiation seeks to highlight the spiritual nature of the kingdom of God, created through the *Logos*, made accessible through Christ, and utilized by humanity in the empowerment of the Holy Spirit. Each of these features of the Trinity is therefore essential to the existential reality of life in the kingdom of God.[12]

What makes this subject pertinent to Willard's bibliology is the proposition the Bible does not only communicate the exclusivity of Jesus the Nazarene but the exclusivity of the Trinitarian cosmic Christ, revealed in the *Logos* and made manifest in Jesus of Nazareth. Therefore, the Scriptural exclusivity of Christ does not necessitate knowledge of the historical individual of Jesus of Nazareth referred to in the New Testament.[13] This is due to the *Logos* being both a physical and non-physical reality. The *Logos* became incarnated (in Jesus) and yet still remained the same Spirit that was

---

God is also equally present in each of these divine manifestations as well. Willard does not develop a specific doctrine of the Trinity. However, it is a consistent theme in his works. See specifically DC, 318, 386–289. ROH, 184–85, KCT, 228ff. Willard et al., *The with God Bible*, 87 and 477.

10. John 8:58

11. Willard discusses the *Logos* at length in chapter 7 of *Knowing Christ Today* where he reviews the concept of Christian pluralism, hereafter referred to as KCT in the notes. Willard, *Knowing Christ Today*, 169.

12. This divine-human-cosmic-Trinitarian characterization of Jesus is simply a mystery, largely indiscernible and far beyond the scope of this thesis. Willard suggests, however, that since the subject lies largely beyond human purview and thus, a matter from which only the divine is fully equipped to engage, understanding necessitates an approach at the level of the heart (internal motives and desire) and not only at the level of the mind or intellect. Hence, Willard argues spiritual matters are best approached and understood at the level of spirit. This is one of Willard's insights and critiques regarding the anemia of purely academic theology.

13. The Scriptural references that surround the question of exclusivity that is in question here are found in Acts 4:7–12 and John 3:16.

with God at the beginning of creation.[14] This understanding maintains and allows the *Logos* freedom to be an omnipresent creative and communicative force throughout the cosmos. It also allows for the manifestation of the *Logos* in various other forms. Likewise, Willard argues the Bible contains the words of God, but the Bible does not exclusively represent or encapsulate the existential reality of the *Logos* (Word). The *words* printed in the Bible are significantly different from the *Word* it describes and bears witness to.[15]

Unlike theologian Karl Barth, who asserted that the Bible is the Word of God only when God uses it to speak, Willard states God has certainly and unequivocally communicated to the world through the Scriptures.[16] Thus, the message of the Word (*Logos*) is always available in the Scriptures, whether effectively interpreted or not. Willard also contends the Bible reveals the *Logos* when God uses it to convey his will. However, in contrast to Barth, Willard contends the Scriptures consistently represent God's revelation at all times. Willard believes God speaks continually through the Bible, not simply periodically or circumstantially. Willard also recognizes God's readiness to use the Scriptures as a medium to communicate to humanity. Yet, there must also be a commensurate willingness or desire on the part of humanity to actively listen.[17] Willard is keen to say God is not the only one who can use the Scriptures as a communicative means. Satan and human beings also maintain the ability to use and misuse the Scriptures and have done so toward ignominious and tragic ends.[18]

Furthermore, the written manifestation of the *Word*, or Scripture, is bound by language. Thus, the Scriptures are an objective presence of the *Logos* in the world. Yet, the Bible is never to be considered an all-inclusive representation of the *Logos*. The Bible remains a very important, necessary, and powerful presence in human history. However, it cannot and should not be confused with God himself. The living *Word* (*Logos*) transcends language.[19] Willard suggests that Romans chapters 1 through 11 reveal that the *Logos* speaks in nature and through the lives of the Old Testament patriarchs, the New Testament saints, and in Jesus himself.[20] When Jesus states "man shall

14. John 1:1–3.

15. This position encompasses what Willard describes as "Christian pluralism" and has significant impact on the evangelical idea of crucicentrism. This will be discussed in greater detail in this chapter.

16. Barth, *Church Dogmatics*, 525.

17. Willard, *Fuller Seminary Doctoral Class* (6/16/2010).

18. Ibid.

19. An excellent overarching discussion of this subject is covered in Smith, *Thinking in Tongues*.

20. Specifically Rom 1:18–21; 2:17–28; 3:21–31; 4; 5:12–20; 6–11.

not live by bread alone but by every word that proceeds from the mouth of God," he is not suggesting humanity should live from every word written in the Hebrew Torah or the Greek Septuagint.[21] Rather, Willard suggests Jesus is revealing the reality of the sustaining metaphysical substance of the *Logos*. This is God's substantive communication for sustaining life and cannot be bound or limited to the words written in the Bible.[22] Willard argues this is why the apostle Paul commands Timothy to preach the *Logos*—which is larger than simply the written language limited to the manuscripts of the Scripture.[23] Hence, the kingdom of God is found in all the various complementary manifestations of the *Logos* of God.

As a whole, Willard believes the Bible is God's gift to the world through his church, not through scholars or theologians of either the conservative or liberal persuasion. Its purposes are primarily practical, not academic or dogmatic. Therefore, an intelligent, careful, and intensive but straightforward reading, one not governed by obscure and faddish theories or by a mindless orthodoxy, is required to receive appropriate direction for life in God's kingdom. Any other approach threatens to derail the vision God desires to reveal in and through the *Logos*.[24]

Willard also admonishes against a mindless, routinized reading of the Bible. Methodological consistency alone will not overwhelm or transform the will. One's expectations imputed onto the Scriptural texts, whether liberal or conservative, are rarely overcome or significantly altered through ritually reading the Bible.[25] More commonly, one's perusal of Scripture becomes an act seeking to justify a pre-existing expectation of the text or condone a preferred behavior. Such an approach routinely re-entrenches the self-appropriated hermeneutical lens with every subsequent engagement of the text. Ironically, the ability of the Scriptures to then break through these biases decreases the more "devout" one becomes. Willard recognizes this conundrum and recalls how such biblicism has been used over the centuries to catastrophic effects.

Willard advocates the application of an epistemic humility to Scripture in order to interrupt this dynamic. His advice in overcoming this tendency is to allow the Scripture to set its own intents and purposes. One must come to

21. Matt 4:4.

22. This is a very Jewish understanding of God's creative act in Genesis, which stems from the act of originating speech. Genesis 1:1–26 and referenced in John 1:1–3. Wenham, *Genesis 1–15*, 8.

23. The Greek translation of Paul's advice: See Aland et al., *The Greek New Testament*, 554–55. 2 Tim 4:2.

24. Whether such an argument uses circular reasoning is left to consider.

25. Willard, "Willardian Theology," interviewed by author, 2/10/2011.

the Scriptures and let its values and agenda set the tone, not vice versa. This assumes some degree of intentional and renewable naïveté when approaching the Scriptures. Anything less threatens to devolve into a method of justifying anthropocentric aims and overwhelming divine communion altogether. Humbly approaching the Bible creates a disposition capable of apprehending its prophetic and corrective intents to "teach, correct, rebuke and train in righteousness (*dikaiosune*)."[26] Willard reminds, the Bible, as a tool of the *Logos* in tune with the character of God, does not set out to overcome the human will. Consequently, the message of the Scriptures must be willingly accepted. The Scriptures do not aggressively wrangle the human personality into submission simply through the course of reading its words. Willard laments this fact is often misunderstood and misapplied within the evangelical propensity to saturate its members in Bible studies, Sunday schools, exegetical sermon series, commentaries, and read-thru-the-Bible-in-a-year devotionals.

In summary, Willard agrees with the primacy and centrality of biblicism as a key tenet in any vibrant Christian faith.[27] The Bible is a coalesced representation of all the essential aspects and arenas of human inquiry compiled in a coherent manner. As such, the Bible is a treasure because it reveals God's perspectives on all essential aspects of life and reality. It also creates a platform of ideas and thoughts that makes relational depth with God and his world accessible.[28] Willard's bibliology also brings into greater relief his theo-ontological perspective. He argues the Scriptures present a reliable description of the substantive metaphysical reality of God's kingdom. The Scriptures illuminate a tremendous body of research, giving insight into the spiritual realm within which this reality rests.

For Willard, Jesus' statement, "the words that I speak to you they are spirit and they are life" characterizes the totalizing metaphysical quality and benefit of both the Scripture in specific and divine revelation in general.[29] As both a phenomenologist and epistemologist, Willard recognizes the power of words and the ideas they represent. Therefore, his perspective of Scripture is one that appreciates the potential of words to illustrate and reveal

26. 2 Tim 3:16. *Dikaiosune* is a key concept in DC, 144. The term is often translated as "righteousness" in the New Testament. Willard suggests the term connotes the idea of the ability to both know and do the right thing. In ancient Greek text the term was often translated virtue. See page 125.

27. Willard, *Fuller Seminary Doctoral Class* (6/16/2010).

28. However, Willard recognizes it would be difficult to comprehend how these factors are presented in the Bible by reading the Bible alone. Good teaching and preaching must accompany individual Bible study for well-rounded comprehension of the Bible to be attained. The lack of this in modern evangelicalism is something Willard commonly laments.

29 John 6:63

the substance of life and reality, all of which falls under the direction of the cosmic *Logos*. Such a perspective exponentially affects the potentiality one places on the power of Scripture to affect human life and perception.

Finally, key to Willard's biblicism is the advocation of putting the guidance provided in the Bible into practice. This brings the knowledge of the reality the Bible describes into proper fruition and perspective. The knowledge and wisdom the Bible imparts, in Willard's view, creates the opportunity for freedom because one is given the resources for manifesting, incarnating, and inhabiting the God-permeated reality the Bible describes. Willard suggests one's "view" of Scripture intellectually or theoretically, although important, is not of greatest consequence. Of greatest importance is actually doing or applying the concepts and truths described in the Bible, "getting the words to come off the page," as it were.[30] For Willard, this represents the "highest" view of Scripture, regardless of one's academic or intellectual reasoning about what the book may or may not represent. If one maintains an inaccurate view of Scriptural authority, such a position could easily make applying or placing value in the Scriptures increasingly difficult. Additionally, certain perspectives of Scripture, even those historically identified with particular views of "orthodoxy" can also make realizing the overarching message of Scriptures increasingly difficult as well.[31]

Conversational Revelation

Based on the unlimited creative and communicative ability of the divine *Logos*, it follows that Willard's understanding of how a follower of Christ receives divine revelation would exceed the singularity of the written Scriptures. In his first theological work, *In Search of Guidance*, Willard tackles this historically controversial topic.[32] He proposes individuals have the potential, and should expect to experience, the reality of hearing God communicate or "speak" personally and directly. Willard's specific intent is to provide the reader with a clearer understanding and greater confidence in the practical means God uses to guide individuals within a communicative relationship. *Guidance* strives to reveal this deep, spiritual, and relational

30. Willard, *Fuller Seminary Doctoral Class* (6/16/2010).

31. As an example, Willard cites double-predestination as a traditionally orthodox view in many conservative Calvinist theological arenas. However, to ascribe fully, such a doctrine may create a situation where belief in God's overarching goodness, justice, and loving character becomes increasingly difficult. Such an example illustrates losing the "biblical forest in the doctrinal trees."

32. *In Search of Guidance* was re-released by Intervarsity Press as *Hearing God* in 1999.

interaction with God that builds and develops through the result of the maturation process of discipleship. Part of this maturation and development is realizing the availability of God's directive communication.

However, Willard states hearing God is neither the end nor the goal of discipleship. Rather . . .

> The great height of our development as disciples of Christ is not that we shall always have guidance, but that we shall be trained under the hand of God in such a way that we are able to stand even without guidance, at our appointed time and place, in faith, hope, and love.[33]

Discipleship, like all theological or ecclesiological endeavors in Willardian theology, is not an end in itself. Instead, discipleship represents only a means into the existential reality of life as God's "children of light" in his kingdom, which begins now and stretches for all eternity.[34] Part of that kingdom ethos involves direct communion with God, both through the *Logos* of God revealed in the Scriptures but also through direct, unmediated interaction. As a manifest reality of a citizen in such a kingdom, ruled by a benevolent King, Willard proposes God is not only both willing and able to communicate individually but in fact does communicate with "ordinary" human beings.[35] Therefore, when one is taught to expect and listen for divine communication, such training can allow for entering into the established kingdom reality of relational life "with God."[36]

Although Willard contends there should be no inconsistencies in divine revelation, whatever form it takes, his position puts him at odds with evangelicals advocating cessationist dispensationalism.[37] In response, using a multitude of Scriptural accounts, Willard identifies the ways God has communicated to individuals throughout the ages and argues against the

33. HG, 225.

34. Willard, *Renovation of the Heart*, chapter 12. Hereafter referred to as ROH.

35. HG, chapter 5.

36. This is also a common phrase in the Renovaré Bible in which Willard was a co-editor. See Willard et al., *The With God Bible*.

37. Cessationism is still a very active dogma in conservative evangelical circles. It stems from the belief the miraculous and the miraculous "sign gifts" described in the New Testament such as prophesy, speaking in tongues, healing, etc. are no longer part of the current dispensation experienced by the church. Cessationism is strongly connected to dispensational theology and became a key issue in B. B. Warfield's fundamentalist evangelical theology. In this case, many cessationists contend hearing God's voice would be included as a miraculous event and, therefore, outside the limits of the current dispensation. For an excellent discussion on this issue referencing several points of view, see Gaffin et al., *Are Miraculous Gifts for Today?* And Warfield, *Counterfeit Miracles*, 4–5.

cessationist view that neither the establishment of the church, nor the establishment of a closed canon of Scripture, excludes God's communicative ability or desire.[38] Furthermore, Willard asserts God has always communicated through means other than the Scriptures. In addition to general revelation (creation) God continues to uses specific events or circumstances, angelic messengers, visions and dreams, miraculous events such as signs, prophetic messages, and the widely accepted concept of "a still, small voice," as viable and reliable platforms upon which to communicate with persons in contemporary contexts.[39]

Ironically, Willard suggests that of these communicative choices, God has traditionally chosen to use more dramatic communicative methods with those in a less spiritually mature condition.[40] The most common means God uses, Willard suggests, is the "still, small voice."[41] This juxtaposition presents an insight into Willard's concern with the spiritual condition of the more flamboyant spiritual leaders and television evangelists who regularly offer incredible claims of divine communication.[42] However, Willard also suggests that the outright absence of any revelations from God may not be a sign of maturity but, instead, an indication of resistance or even spiritual deadness. Both these extremes—either no communication or continual spectacular, and incredulous revelations—suggest dangers and distractions to the original purposes of God to develop an intimate communal relationship. Instead, God seeks a rapport to aid and guide human beings toward an attentive and responsive knowledge of his character, regardless of the means of communication. Open dialog is maintained through what Willard describes as the intentional act of constantly "keeping God present to the mind."[43] This constant interaction with the voice of God slowly builds the nature and character of Christ into ever-fuller maturity in the life of a believer.

38. HG, 106.

39. HG, 108–10.

40. Many examples are evident in the biblical account. The apostle Paul's conversion conversation is one poignant example. Additionally, the "burning bush" example with Moses is a case in point, after which it appears Moses needed less dramatic communicative encounters with God.

41. HG, 91.

42. As a means of manipulating or cajoling their followers, several televangelists claim God routinely and dramatically "speaks" to them. Such is the immaturity Willard discusses. See Fishwick and Browne, *The God Pumpers*, and Johns, *The Popes of Pentecostal Television*.

43. HG, 214

Willard's view of divine revelation is very practical and reasonable. He advocates a proper theological understanding of God should recognize divine relationship with humanity not in abstract, literary, propositional, doctrinal, or theoretical terms as may become the expectation of an overtly biblicistic faith. Rather, as a person engaging persons, God desires a level of open, interactive, and dynamic engagement simply unimaginable with a book. Hence, as a "father" or parent, Willard suggests God desires good and moral choices to be made by his children within the context of the freedom essential for the development of fully capable, loving human beings. God's will, Willard suggests, is for individuals to embody the character which empowers them to freely "be" who they were created to be.

Therefore, the Bible should not be used as a mind-dumbing index of legalisms or obligations. Rather, God desires humanity to learn properly "to grow in the grace and knowledge of Christ," developing a godly character that is capable of discerning God's "law of love."[44] Willard recognizes this as a very close representation to the Augustinian precept, "love God and do as you please."[45] Consequently, the purpose of all divine communication, including the Bible, works toward the internalization of the ethos of God becoming so thoroughly integrated as to become essentially "written on the heart."[46]

In summary, Willard's biblicism argues the Bible itself illustrates that the written Scriptures should not be considered the exclusive means for divine communication and revelation. Therefore, Willard's bibliology does not limit God to the predetermined theological assumptions and interpretations of the written Scriptures. One does not have a relationship with a text. This position does not so much contradict, but rather expands the mainstream evangelical view to include a broader understanding of the divine *Logos*. Willard also resurrects the pre-cessationist spirituality reminiscent of the earlier Christian theology prior to Darby's dispensational theology.[47] This presents an opportunity to reinvigorate and put substance to the overly used but sparsely understood evangelical phrase "relationship with God." As such, on a subject that many evangelicals remain concerned about, and which some see as a threat to the nature of what it means to be in rela-

44. 2 Pet 3:18 and Jas 2:8.

45. Burnaby, *Augustine: Later Works*, 316.

46. Rom 2:13–15. This statement is an apparent reference the apostle Paul makes to Jer 31:33.

47. This pre-dispensational theology is seen in the early Christian mystics. Examples of this spirituality are seen in Willard's references to the ancient works of Teresa Avila, St. Jerome, Brother Lawrence, Bonaventure, Athanasius, Ignatius Loyola, and others in his class syllabus for the Fuller Seminary Doctoral seminar.

tion with God, Willard unveils a biblically validated vision regarding divine revelation that includes, but also transcends, the issues described in Bebbington's evangelical biblicist apologetics.

Yet, the much larger goal in relationship to God is to grow into the kind of person who not only desires to hear God's voice but also equally endeavors to obey, or heed, what the divine voice requires. Hearing God, attaining knowledge of the Scriptures or placing high doctrinal authority on the validity and veracity of the Scripture all maintain value in and of themselves. Regardless of these esoteric points of doctrine and theology and despite whatever one might or might not claim about the traditional liberal vs. conservative arguments over the Bible, Willard contends obedience demonstrates the highest view of Scripture. Ultimately, the goal of relationship with God is to grow into the kind of person who desires to not only hear God through any and every means available, but is also willing and able to follow that call.

Conversionism in Willardian Theology

Conversionism too plays a significant and enduring role in Willardian theology. However, Willard rarely uses the exact term. The most accurate and useful synonym in Willardian theology for conversionism is transformation. The idea of converting and transforming in Willardian theology are nearly identical. In both words the focus is placed on the action of change from a preexisting status or condition. As mentioned in the preceding chapter, evangelical theology has historically considered Christian conversion a moment or a choice wherein an individual either receives or chooses the forgiveness and grace offered through Christ's atoning sacrifice on the cross. This event alters the spiritual and existential nature of the human being. In what is commonly termed justification, the convert's sins are atoned or "redeemed." As a result, one is rescued or delivered from the eternal consequences or penalty of the previously unjustified or unsaved condition. The concept of sanctification, following justification, becomes quite another matter, an issue encountered subsequent to the atoning, salvific choice (Armenian), or act of God's grace (Calvinist).

In short, Willardian theology reconnects the justification/sanctification event that evangelical versions of conversionism previously separated. He positions justification (atonement) as something accomplished solely by the Trinity and therefore altogether beyond human intervention or effect.[48]

48. An entire article is devoted to Willard's view of the atonement in Moon, "Getting the Elephant Out of the Sanctuary."

Willard argues conversion/transformation is not the same as atonement. Instead, conversion is the initial step or action of placing one's confidence in the reality and consequence of divine love and grace. This new outlook begins the process of "converting" the entire life and worldview. Conversion is therefore identical to transformation, alteration, and renovation of the entire person. Willard suggests the convert's ontological position becomes progressively adapted through discipleship to Jesus into the metaphysics of the kingdom of God. Willard reconnects the historically divided and bifurcated terms of justification and sanctification, unifying their qualities and objectives as elements of the same convertive process in the transformational journey. In short, Willard views conversion as a simultaneous conjoining of justification and sanctification to the point a convert can be considered equally both "saved" and "being saved."

Willard's most popular work, *The Divine Conspiracy,* focuses on describing the existential condition and process of living in this convertive state. Willard also spends the majority of *Renovation of the Heart* discussing the reasons and hurdles that prevent persons from entering into the "easy yoke" of transformation with Jesus as a guide. *Renovation* pursues the roles anthropology, psychology, sociology, and epistemology play in the theological understandings of individuals and groups attempting to convert/transform their previous worldviews and enter into a relational interaction with the kingdom of God.[49] This process is what Willard describes as the biblical understanding of *metanoia* or repentance, an important theme carried throughout his description of the apostle Paul's encouragement to become "transformed by the renewal of the mind."[50] Willard defines repentance as "rethinking one's thinking" or "reconsidering one's considerations."[51]

Willard suggests that Christianity, rightly understood, represents not a belief system as much as a unifying philosophy, as it were, that when appropriately applied in a consistent manner eventuates conversion and transformation of every aspect of the human condition. The general outline

49. ROH represents a significant aspect in Willard's engagement with larger fields of inquiry (anthropology, psychology, sociology, philosophy, etc.) and consequently evokes a wider vision of a more robust practical theology. To classify *Renovation* as a work specifically limited to the subject of spiritual formation, as some of Willard's peers are apt to do, is an oversight. Again, as mentioned earlier, Willard sees theology as nothing if not practical. Yet, *Renovation* also is perhaps Willard's most philosophical treatment of the subjects surrounding conversion or transformation and the effect of the protoevangelical gospel Jesus articulated on these issues.

50. Rom 12:2.

51. DC, 227–29. Trevor Hudson and Jan Johnson use Willard's definition of *metanoia* in their works. See Hudson, *Discovering Our Spiritual Identity*, 94; and Johnson, "Guilt Odyssey."

provided in *Renovation* presents an ample vista that captures the depth and breadth of Willardian theology as a whole and what potential alterations a convert faces (*metanoia*) once introduced to the theo-ontology of the kingdom of God. Combined, *Renovation* and *Divine Conspiracy* provide bookends of Willard's theology and praxis, demonstrating both personal application and theological insight on individual and corporate conversion/transformation into the kingdom of God.[52]

More specifically, *Renovation* focuses primarily on unfolding Willard's understanding of the multi-layered, interdependent, symbiosis involved in the individual parts of the human self. Here, each aspect of the person (the heart, mind, body, social relations, and all-encompassing soul) carries specialized needs and aspects that require progressive transformation into Christlikeness. Willard starts this dissection of the self by reviewing Jesus' gospel announcement of the reality and availability of God's theo-ontology in every arena of human existence.[53] Willard intimates, such a Christlike life is not only possible, but has been attained by many dedicated disciples over the ages.

Secondly, *Renovation* points to how and why Jesus must be considered Christianity's primary teacher and guide for Christian living. Thus, converting one's life, mind, heart, body, and soul to Jesus is an act of confidence in Jesus' ability and wisdom to competently guide his followers into this worldview. This theme is also referenced as the soteriological opportunity Jesus articulates in the New Testament and is the central theme of *Divine Conspiracy*.[54] Finally, Willard moves into his description of not only what holistic conversion would look like in the life of a disciple, he also describes how churches and their leaders can facilitate such a transformation and what curriculum would be required to facilitate such a change. In some respects, *Renovation* picks up on Willard's eschatological vision and continues providing details where *Divine Conspiracy* ends.

Perhaps *Renovation's* most pertinent chapter deals with the issue of how spiritual conversion occurs and why it often does not occur. Willard deals briefly with the issue of "intentionality" in *Divine Conspiracy*, while *Renovation* devotes an entire chapter to the concepts involved in creating a "general

52. Moreover, reviewers seemed to miss that ROH represents Willard's comprehensive treatment of kingdom theology through his detailed descriptions of each segment of the self. Chapters 4, 12, and 13 specifically can be considered a clarified restatement of the overarching object of Willard's theological goals in general.

53. This is a major focus of the section on anthropology, pp. 97-113.

54. The first two sections of *Renovation* are deeply theological and, as such, repeat some of Willard's earlier writings. Yet, *Renovation* also evidences a refinement and clarity of theological explanation and insight that may have been missing in previous works. See DC, 273, 316.

pattern of personal transformation."[55] As an answer to what components are required for any sustainable change, Willard presents the acronym "VIM" that represents the terms, Vision, Intention, and Means. Willard makes the all-encompassing claim that "If this VIM pattern is not put in place properly and held there, Christ simply will not be formed in us."[56]

Willard points to each aspect of the VIM pattern as containing necessary components required to progress to the next stage of Christlike development. Thus, change starts with a vision of what is possible in the potentially changed life. Vision provides the necessary establishment of hope that the change advocated or promised is not only possible but is significantly better than that currently experienced. A proper vision of who Jesus is, what message he is delivering, and what kind of life he is understood to advocate for and provide must be properly understood and communicated.

Building on the topic of vision, Willard offers a theological critique of the differing soteriological ends within competing professions of the evangelical gospel.[57] What vision of life one is asked to convert to, or accept as normative, is paramount in the conversion process. This is why Willard believes pastors, preachers, and teachers hold such significant roles in the process of conversion and transformation. He sees ecclesiastical leaders as either keepers and tenders of the gospel of Jesus, or proliferators of its competition. When the message preached or taught is altered significantly from the vision Jesus professed, the experience is changed as well. In short, this is precisely the view Willard takes with regard to most neo-evangelical theology and preaching today. The evangelical gospel preached from many contemporary pulpits has been adapted to the point where a different story, with a different vision for life and purpose, is communicated, one essentially different from the original message of Jesus, present in the *protoeuangelion* and revealed in the biblical accounts.

The next step, intention, is specifically a responsibility of the individual and not a duty laid on Christian leaders, teachers and pastors to persuade, manipulate or cajole. However, intentional decision-making is not completely separate from the vision cast. The two are somewhat dependent since the essence of the vision compels the intention to follow Christ's lead.

> The vision of life in the Kingdom of God through reliance on Jesus makes it possible for us to intend to live in the Kingdom as he did. We can actually decide to do it. . . . If we do not count on

55. ROH, chapter 5.

56. ROH, 85.

57. More will be discussed on this topic in the section titled "Willard's Critique of Evangelicalism" beginning in chapter four.

> him as "the one," we will have no adequate vision of the Kingdom or of life therein and no way to enter it. He is "the door;" he is "the way." Find another whoever can.[58]

Willard goes on to make a significant critique of other ideologies and theologies regarding the nature of conversion. He bases this critique on his understanding that intention is the pivotal link between the declaration of good intentions and the reality of actual change. Most pointedly, two of the more extreme ideological/theological camps within evangelicalism garner Willard's disparagement.

First, Willard offers correction to the more fundamentalist/conservative strands of evangelicalism that traditionally position the profession of belief in correct doctrine as occasioning conversion and achieving a salvific end. As a result, these groups have viewed obedience in discipleship and its transformative properties as an unnecessary or optional aspect of Christian life and experience, to which Willard suggests,

> Indeed no one can actually believe the truth about [Jesus] without trusting him by intending to obey him. It is a mental impossibility. To think otherwise is to indulge a widespread illusion that now smothers spiritual formation in Christlikeness among professing Christians and prevents it from naturally spreading worldwide.[59]

Willard argues any "saving" faith must exemplify itself in a will directed toward obedience. Something less, by definition, should be considered suspect as to its effectiveness or intent. Such a claim, if broadly applied to the statistics regarding the lack of discipleship evident in contemporary evangelicalism, is staggering to consider and a reality Willard comes back to again and again in his work.

Secondly, Willard advises against the promotion of any form of "super" natural transformation. Pentecostal/charismatic forms of evangelical conversionism tend to advocate wholesale transformation of the personality "in a moment." This advocates or accentuates an undisciplined, unprepared, and decidedly passive role in transformation. These theologies tend to encourage specific reliance on a miraculous production of Christlike behavior, character, or knowledge, while in the moment of need, or what Willard calls "on the spot." This is a significantly mistaken understanding

58. ROH, 87.

59. Ibid.

and appreciation for the power of the human will in combination with a lack of awareness and recognition of the unobtrusive nature of God's character.[60]

> One of the greatest temptations that we face as evangelicals—for the moment I include in that what is sometimes called the charismatic stream of the church—is the idea that the personality and the heart are going to be transformed by some sort of lightning strike of the Spirit. You can call it revival or whatever you want. There is going to be the great boom and then suddenly you will be transformed in every aspect of your being. There will be no need for a process—it will all be accomplished passively and immediately.[61]

As a result, charismatic/Pentecostal perceptions of "on the spot" empowerment requires an expectation, imploration, and infusion of divine intervention to either overcome or transcend the weaknesses of the "flesh." Such a view of the "Spirit-filled life" can become essentially a "Spirit-contravening" life that happens despite the individual will, not because of it. "God is not going to pick us up by the seat of our pants, as it were, and throw us into transformed kingdom living, into holiness."[62] It is important to note that Willard fully places spiritual formation and conversion as a work of the Spirit, an activity he terms a "Spirit-driven process."[63] It is the passivity inherent in many forms of popular charismatic/Pentecostalism that Willard warns against. "Well informed human effort is certainly indispensible, for spiritual formation is no passive process."[64]

Converse to many supernatural transformational proposals, Willard recognizes the power of deeply established habits and tendencies of the mind, emotions, and body in their ingrained status, which routinely present themselves stronger than even the most valiant desire of the heart "in the moment." While not dismissing God's omnipotent ability to act as he sees fit, in whomever he chooses, and at any stage of a person's maturation, Willard articulates the normative means God has established for spiritual transformation is routinely different from the abstract and inconsistent reality of the "super" natural means that remains at his disposal. Instead, Willard suggests the biblical record demonstrates "off the spot" training through meditation, prayer, study, solitude, and other spiritual disciplines. These activities allow one to become the individual who routinely and ordinarily—not

60. ROH, 90

61. GO, 56.

62. ROH, 91.

63. ROH, 22.

64. ROH, 23.

extraordinarily or spontaneously—engages and extends the power of God's grace and love.

> Sanctification is not an experience, though experiences of various kinds may be involved in it. It is not a status, though a status is maintained by means of it. It is not an outward form and has no essential connection with outward forms. It does, on the other hand, become a "track record" and a system of habits.[65]

Therefore, Willard proposes such a "track record" is validated by the righteous character one is capable of displaying "on the spot," which is a result of the training engaged through the spiritual disciplines "off the spot." These represent the consistent and reliable means toward attaining a regularly sustained conversion experience true to the teachings of Christ and exemplified in his life.[66]

Activism in Willardian Theology

As the previous section has already described, Willard's discussion of the subject of Christian activism is spread throughout his corpus. However, his most condensed statement on the topic is found in *The Spirit of the Disciplines: Understanding How God Changes Lives.*[67] Published in 1988, this work presents an intellectual, philosophical, psychological, and theological justification and explication of the essence and nature of the activist Chris-

65. ROH, 226.

66. *Renovation* has been widely repackaged and re-publicized, with Willard's permission, by accompanying authors. Perhaps the best received of these re-publications came from John Ortberg, a long-time Willard advocate, who accumulated increasing popularity as a mega-church pastor at Bill Hybels' Willow Creek Church. Ortberg is a prolific author in his own right and as such has brought increasing attention to Willard's work. Ortberg's *The Life You've Always Wanted* is self classified as a "Dallas for dummies." Apparently a reference that suggests the book represents a rendition of Willard's work for the popular reader. See Ortberg, *The Life You've Always Wanted*, 10. Ortberg is not the first to re-package Willard's words in a more "user friendly" manner. Randy Frazee published a youth edition of *Renovation of the Heart;* see Willard and Frazee, *Renovation of the Heart: Student Edition*. Similarly, Don Simpson released a less theologically sophisticated and simplistic version of *Renovation of the Heart* entitled, *Revolution of Character.* See Willard and Simpson, *Revolution of Character.*

67. Willard, *The Spirit of the Disciplines*. Hereafter referred to as SD in the notes. *Disciplines* can be viewed as perhaps a more academically rigorous handling of Foster's *Celebration of Discipline*. Combined with Willard's *Spirit of the Disciplines,* Foster and Willard are co-dependent volumes on the same subject. Foster's work focuses his interest in orthopraxis, and Willard bolsters Foster by providing a history of the subject. See article with Foster and Willard interviewed together. Tennant, "The Making of the Christian" 42–44.

tian life. It also investigates and discusses what Christian conversion is and how it is affected in the life of the Christ follower.

This points to Willard's primary departure from evangelical traditions regarding the subject of activism. Bebbington argues evangelicals have focused primarily on a revivalist, proselytizing view of activism made popular by Moody, Graham, and later the CGM. In a summative statement, Willard argues:

> Christian evangelism today is rooted in a misunderstanding of salvation. People have been told they are Christians because they have confessed they believe that Jesus died for their sins, but the total package is presented in such a way that it leaves the general life untouched. Biblically, salvation means deliverance; the question is, "Deliverance from what?" The common message is "deliverance from guilt." But the full concept of salvation in the New Testament is deliverance from our present sins. This deliverance from sins comes from the new life of God's Kingdom when we place our confidence in Jesus the person. The problem is that we have been obsessed with this idea that the real issue is "making the cut" to get to heaven. We have taken the discipleship out of conversion.[68]

Instead of focusing on evangelizing the world with a salvific message constrained to deliverance from sin guilt and a heavenly dwelling place after death, Willard proposes an activism based on "discipleship evangelism."[69] To this end, his discussion of the spiritual disciplines starts with unveiling the proper motivations required to fund the disciplined life and what corresponding effects discipleship activities should produce.

Disciplines suggests discipleship/activism is quintessential for Christian life. Willard asserts, "My central claim is that we can become like Christ by doing one thing—by following him in the overall style of life he chose for himself. If we have faith in Christ, we must believe that he knew how to live."[70] To substantiate this claim, Willard employs what might be similar to a general education survey of previously applied Christian perspectives on what the ends of Christian faith can and should produce in the life of a follower of Jesus. The result is a consideration of the various Christian means (practices and doctrines) currently employed in contemporary Christianity, many of which Willard suggests have most often not resulted in a transformed life or a Christlike community.

68. Willard, "Rethinking Evangelism."

69. DC, 304–5.

70. SD, ix.

Disciplines makes other definitive statements regarding the role of practical theology as a means of theological inquiry that conjoins activism and praxis in order to make clear

> . . . how we can be like [Christ] not as a pose or by a constant and grinding effort but with the ease and power he had—flowing from the inner depths, acting with quiet force from the innermost mind and soul of the Christ who has become a real part of us.[71]

This is the most poignant and clear description of Willard's view of an appropriate Christian activism. He suggests activism is essentially identical to the understanding of praxis defined here as "ideology of action." As such, an appropriate theology should reveal "the manner in which our actions interact with God to accomplish his ends in human life."[72] Accordingly, Willard suggests everyone has both an active, practical theology, even that of the atheist. Further, every theology vitally directs the course of individual life. To wit, the presence of a thoughtful activism is as powerful as a thoughtless activism, since, at its end, each praxis fuels the answers to questions about how one goes about perceiving and living life. In this way, Christian theology should equally have as its goal the development of practical, implementable methods by which "women and men interact with God to fulfill the divine intent for human existence."[73] This is the heart of the activist objective Willard encourages.

In connection with such a vision, Willard indicates the goal of ecclesiology should be focused solely on

> the effective proclamation of the Christian gospel to all humanity, making disciples from every nation of ethnic group, and the development of the disciples' character into the character of Christ himself. . . . If these are done well, all else desirable will follow.[74]

Christian leaders, pastors, and teachers are therefore those tasked with preparing and developing Christian (Christlike) character within the lives of those inside the ecclesial organizations they lead and serve. Here, Willard quotes the apostle Paul who suggested that the task of leadership is to "equip the saints for the work of ministry."[75] Willard recognizes this has

71. SD, 14.
72. SD, 14.
73. Ibid.
74. SD, 15.
75. Eph 4:12.

been a less than consistent practice throughout the history of the church. "Our leaders have not always been sufficiently wise and powerful in their work."[76] Willard laments the historical emphasis and zeal in accomplishing the Great Commission through global expansion and missional endeavors, which articulate only a sin-guilt/heaven bound gospel that has "deflected us from an adequate emphasis upon the understanding and practice of growth in Christlikeness *after* conversion."[77]

Specifically, the misinterpretation of Jesus' message and mission as a whole is where Willard finds the primary flaw within modern evangelical activism. He comes back to this theme again and again. Willard disagrees with the overt advocation that Jesus' primary, if not solitary mission on earth, was to provide "forgiveness of sin." As a consequence, evangelical activism has interpreted the life, death, and resurrection of Jesus through the monolithic lens of the atonement. By extension, most other facets of evangelical theology have been adapted to align with the crucicentric bias. Willard argues modern evangelical activist theology has in fact "robbed" the restorative, redemptive meaning from the traditional Christian understanding of salvific faith by perpetuating the hegemony of "special theological interests."[78]

This represents one of Willard's most significant critiques of American evangelicalism. Such a critique strikes at the heart of the biblical, soteriological, conversionist, activist, and crucicentrist assumptions of evangelical faith. Willard recognizes there are moments within both historical and contemporary manifestations of evangelical faith that have become singularly focused on attaining either professions of faith or forgiveness of sins to the exclusion of all other priorities. Willard warns any missionary endeavor, Christian organization or denomination perpetuating a Moody-esque activism that focuses singularly on issues of forgiveness and eternal rewards risks missing the entire point of the *protoeuangelion* Jesus preached. Such a condition presents what Willard understands as the "great omission from the Great Commission."[79]

Willard devotes the whole of chapter 3 of *Spirit of the Disciplines* to asking and answering the central questions related to what evangelical soteriology comprises and to what degree that understanding is contrary to and in opposition of what he understands biblical activism should represent.[80] Here is where Willard reveals his clearest, most summative thinking,

76. SD, 15.

77. Ibid.

78. SD, 33.

79. See Willard, *The Great Omission*. Hereafter referred to as GO.

80. SD, 28–43.

command of Scripture, and logical consistency. Although his conclusions threaten established evangelical orthodoxy, the force of his arguments reveal a mix of a philosopher's temerity with an evangelist's zeal. In the end, it seems clear Willard endeavors to use all of his considerable resources to plead his case to his own evangelical family in hopes of encouraging a reconsideration of misapplied values, blind faith, and deadening legalisms tied to an almost fanatical proselytizing zeal. Willard takes great pains to entreat his readers to reposition their misplaced evangelical activism onto a more accurate and contextually honest application of Jesus' original message.

Although he does not venture into all the "specific theological interests" he considers culprits of this shift toward a proselytizing agenda, he does mention one specific interest. It is the uniquely evangelical view of grace that Willard suggests is improperly understood and therefore misapplied across the spectrum of evangelical theology. He asserts evangelicalism has developed a theological position which reduces, limits, and situates grace as only a divine means employed to provide eternal life. Such a partial and narrow designation of grace has driven a dividing wedge into evangelicalism's ability to inculcate an incarnational and activating Christian life. Willard contends such a marginalization reduces the concept of grace to only that required for the forgiveness of sin. As a result, this limited vision of God and his grace loses its restorative power to reconstitute a vital spirituality demonstrating effectiveness in the kingdom of God and positively affecting the present needs and circumstances of daily life.

Instead, Willard argues for the need for "radical rethinking of the Christian concept of salvation."[81] His articulation of discipleship and the employment of the spiritual disciplines are both fully funded by and accomplished through regular and sustaining infusions of God's ongoing participatory grace. Furthermore, with such a limited definition of grace, neither discipleship nor the engagement of spiritual disciplines can be engaged with any degree of confidence or expectation. To prove this point, Willard exemplifies that current teaching and preaching largely omit the work of grace in discipleship. Willard asks the rhetorical question, "What is your group's plan for teaching your people to do everything Christ commanded?"[82] Due to his long tenure of engagement with evangelical churches, Willard is all too aware of the answer.

> The fact is that our existing churches and denominations do not have active, well designed, intentionally pursued plans to accomplish this in their members. Just as you will not find any national

81. SD, 32.

82. SD, 16.

> leader today who has a plan for paying off the national debt, so you will not find any widely influential element of our church leadership that has a plan—not a vague wish or dream, but a plan—for implementing all phases of the Great Commission.[83]

For modern evangelicalism, which has historically forged its identity on the singularity of the Great Commission's command to "make disciples," such an omission in its applied values is not only striking but also equally catastrophic to the integrity of the gospel it professes.[84] Therefore, Willard spends the rest of *Disciplines* highlighting exactly how Jesus and his followers through the ages learned to embody Godly character in their daily lives. This act of embodiment, the shaping of character, and the freedom it provides, is what Willard understands as Jesus' "way" of entering into the "easy yoke" of the kingdom of God.[85] Further, Willard suggests the Christian understanding of the righteous life (*dikaiosune*) is the indirect outcome of the directed efforts of spiritual disciplines, with God's grace.[86] God's grace is manifested when human beings are able to accomplish what they could never accomplish by their own efforts.[87] Transformation of the human life is therefore evidence of the conjoining of both God's grace with human effort to effect a previously unattainable result. Such a life, one both willing and able to follow the commands of Christ and achieve supernatural results is unfortunately roundly missing in both evangelical doctrine and experience.

According to Willard, much of evangelical dogma actually discourages the "easy yoke" of Christ. He argues the more Reformed understandings of evangelical doctrine misinterpret the Wesleyan theologies of perfection. The Calvinist suggestion that effort placed on holiness is antithetical to the doctrine of grace is but one example of where "heavy burdens" become inhibitors to meaningful Christian discipleship and the practice of spiritual disciplines.[88] Conversely, Willard argues from experience and history for the spiritual disciplines as a self-validating means by which a person becomes able to do what needs to be done when it is required of them. Such is the nature of freedom, but so, too, is the nature of a disciplined life.

83. Ibid.

84. Matt 28:16–20. Ironically, the Great commission's task is to make disciples, not converts or activists.

85. SD, 3.

86. The Greek concept *dikaiosune* will be dealt with in greater detail on page 125. See DC, 144.

87. GO, 60–68 and ROH, chapter 1.

88. SD, x.

> The general human failing is to want what is right and important, but at the same time not to commit to the kind of life that will produce the action we know to be right and the condition we want to enjoy. This is the feature of human character that explains why the road to Hell is paved with good intentions. We intend what is right, but we avoid the life that would make it reality.[89]

Thus, there is not an oppositional relationship between human efforts and God's grace, as positioned in the Edwardian/Wesleyan debate. Instead of hoping for an infusion of grace "in the moment" when moral courage is necessitated in a crisis of life's challenging circumstances, Willard posits that God has provided the means, in the spiritual disciplines, through which a person can actively choose to develop the poise required to do the good simply because he or she has become "a good person."

Lastly, Willard's view of Christian activism is much broader and deeper than the single activity of evangelization posited by contemporary evangelicalism. Rather, his holistic vision of activism represents the result of a whole-life pursuit of God's kingdom through discipleship to Christ, employing the time-tested disciplines that train one's own will to gain "ever increasing sway over our embodied selves."[90] Through applying the disciplines, with God's grace, one gains freedom from addictions or compulsions to social convention, self-consciousness, hate, fear, greed, emotionalism, and the many other obstacles present within the human condition and experience of life. Willard believes Jesus, and the protoevangelicalism he advocated, presents an unmitigated understanding of how the human life can be lived to the fullest capacity. Fortunately, Jesus also demonstrated what means need be employed to accomplish that end. Thus, *Disciplines* articulates Willard's view of the vision Jesus presents of the kingdom life and the appropriate activities "activist" Christians can employ to engage the reality of God's reign.

Crucicentrism in Willardian Theology

Finally, building on the reforms Willard advocates to the traditional evangelical views on biblicism, activism, and conversionism, crucicentrism is another arena of significant adaptation as well. Willard's view of the all-encompassing reality present in the absolute beneficence of God as King of

89. SD, 6.
90. SD, 86.

his kingdom substantially reformulates his view of the cross and its effects. Willard agrees with evangelicals that

> Embracing the cross with Jesus is to be our salvation. It is to release ourselves into the realm of God, into God's care, and to stop trying to work the human system of power and desire to get what we want.[91]

However, Willardian theology posits the contemporary evangelical understandings of atonement, justification/sanctification, and salvation, which have often been segmented in crucicentrist investigations, are best dissolved into parts of the same objective whole. "They are distinct but inseparable"[92] Thus, a consideration of how Willard understands the three crucicentrist arenas of atonement, justification, and sanctification is appropriate.

First, justification, for Willard, simply describes the act of restoring relationship to God. Willard does not prescribe to the evangelical theologies of justification that delimit the cross to a transactional propitiation attained through Jesus' sacrificial payment paid on the cross. Such a view of justification, for evangelicals, has often created a situation in which humanity is believed cleansed of all sin, to the point where a person returns to a perfected condition as if sin had never occurred, to which Willard states,

> I think it's very unfortunate the way we use [justification] and say, "It's just as if I'd never sinned." It will never be that way. I will always be a redeemed sinner, and that's going to be part of the mental and spiritual furniture that helps me live before God for eternity. It will never be "just as if I had never sinned."[93]

Instead, Willard sees justification as initiating the resumption of relationship, also described as attaining "peace with God," "being reconciled to God," or perhaps "God being reconciled to man." All of these descriptions Willard will accept as adequate descriptions of what justification accomplishes. However, the atonement is a much more ambiguous concept in Willard's view.

> Atonement is God's act that makes this [justification] possible, and that act is the giving of His Son. The giving of His Son is much bigger than His Son's death on the cross. When we read John 3:16, [we] have to understand that the whole passage is not

91. Willard, "The Craftiness of Christ."

92. Moon, "Getting the Elephant Out of the Sanctuary."

93. Ibid.

> about forgiveness. It is about life that comes in our relationship to the Son—and that is atonement; that is a gift.[94]

Willard recognizes the atonement is inseparable from placing confidence in Christ's ability to reestablish relationship with God. This interconnectivity becomes increasingly difficult for traditional evangelical theology to accept or perhaps agree with, purposively due to Willard's delineation that justification is not only a forensic act. "And that's what John 3:16 is about. It's about life from above, and that is atonement."[95] When considered from a phenomenological perspective, exactly how Jesus saved humanity on the cross, Willard humbly suggests, is a mystery no one will probably ever be able to answer.[96] It is a mystery as deep as the incarnation, the creation, and the Trinity itself and, therefore, too deep for words and/or the human intellect to describe and understand fully.

Consequently, Willard's definitions of both atonement and justification necessitate a reconsideration of the evangelical understanding of salvation as well. Willard recognizes how contemporary evangelicalism conveys the concept of deliverance has broad ranging implications. Some evangelicals, depending upon their theory of atonement, can completely miss the relational focus of justification mentioned earlier and instead focus solely on the penal substitutionary concept of a transaction of credit. Such a view allows for an inappropriate confidence that, "now your sins are paid off and you have a kind of contract with God that you will not be punished for your sins."[97]

Salvation, for Willard, is centered on the act of deliverance. Exegetically, salvation is described in Scripture as the escape or rescue from harm.[98] *Soteria* (deliverance) is the same word used in the Septuagint to describe God's miraculous efforts in the exodus or escape of the Israelites from Egyptian slavery by traveling through the Red Sea (Exod 14:13).[99] Willard argues the biblical proposal referenced in the New Testament presents salvation as not the imputation of a meritorious condition, but a different form of life, one not focused and dependent on the self but rather fully cognizant of God. Thus, the hermeneutical contexts of the usage of the term salvation need be properly discerned in order to determine if the usages refers to living with God in an eternal kind of life mentioned in John 14:6, or

94. Ibid.

95. Ibid.

96. Ibid.

97. Ibid.

98. Vine et al., *Vine's Complete Expository Dictionary*, and Brown and Townsley, *The New International Dictionary of New Testament Theology*, 339–401.

99. KCT, 186.

whether the term is used to describe deliverance from some degree of physical affliction (as in Peter healing the lame man in Acts 3). Willard states it is the former definition which Jesus is most cognizant about describing. "And that, I think, is what John and Paul and the New Testament generally understand [salvation] to be . . . that people now have a life from above, and their salvation, their deliverance, is a matter of having that life and living that life with God."[100]

Therefore, salvation is not a matter of forgiveness of sin and deliverance from a consequential destiny in an eternal state of heaven or hell. Willard states, "Associated with this agreement that the issue in salvation is only heaven or hell is a further agreement that being saved is a forensic or legal condition rather than a vital reality or character."[101] To summarize these positions Willard states,

> I would say that justification is a new beginning for a relationship that has been broken, and it is made right by forgiveness, but that's just the doorway into the resumption of relationship. The relationship [itself] is atonement, and that involves Christ becoming one with us. [Atonement] means that we now [can] walk with Him and that He is in us, and we are in Him. We have eternal life, and that is what atonement is. The result of atonement is deliverance or salvation. We are not under the power of sin and death anymore. Justification, atonement, and salvation are three aspects of one thing.[102]

Thus, the most poignant crucicentric issue for Willard is not where a person goes after death. This is not what he believes is the focal point of Jesus' emphasis on the cross or eternal life and salvation. Instead, Willard suggests the Scriptures articulate a concept of salvation that is attained not after life, but while living as a disciple of Jesus. The discipled life is an ongoing salvific experience consisting of an ongoing existential engagement with *agape* that inexorably involves forgiveness, faith, and hope. But this life also includes a new kind of existence that has no limits of these eternal qualities. Faith, hope, love, and life become unlimited by time, quantity, or quality. This describes the nature of the life Jesus offers and depicts in his use of the terms "from above," "abundant," "eternal," "overflowing," and "heavenly." What one is saved to is this life from above. What one is saved from is their own self-centered attempts at achieving an ever elusive illusion of human flourishing.

100. Ibid.

101. DC, 47.

102. Moon, "Elephant Out of the Sanctuary."

In Willard's view, conservative evangelical crucicentrism and penal substitutionary atonement theory can completely miss the object of Jesus' gospel message. Salvation is neither about "demerit and merit." Nor is salvation attained from mental ascent to a certain salvific "belief," a doctrine one must profess, or a forensic agreement. Rather, for Willard, salvation is a state of being, one inescapably tied to a certain type of life, a vital reality, and a personal character. Willard suggests the Scriptures demonstrate the concept of faith and righteousness as an active, participatory, interactive relationship with God. Such vibrant and relational communion with God brings with it forgiveness as a natural product of relational interaction based on love.

What is not evident in Scripture is a doctrinal astuteness test on atonement theories. This is Willard's response to the idea there is a significant difference in placing one's confidence (faith) "in the real person of Jesus, with all that that naturally involves, versus trusting some arrangement for sin-remission set up through him—trusting only his role as guilt remover. To trust the real person Jesus is to have confidence in him in every dimension of our real life."[103] This entire subject is summed up well in Willard's perception that

> The sensed irrelevance of what God is doing to what makes up our lives is the foundational flaw in the existence of multitudes of professing Christians today. They have been led to believe that God, for some unfathomable reason, just thinks it appropriate to transfer credit from Christ's merit account to ours, and to wipe out our sin debt, upon inspecting our mind and finding that we believe a particular theory of atonement to be true—even if we trust everything but God in all other matters that concern us.[104]

The emphasis on heaven, for Willard, is commensurate with the emphasis Jesus places on it. He cites Jesus' definition. "This is eternal life, that they (disciples) may know you, the only real God, and Jesus the anointed, whom you have sent" (John 17:3). This knowing—again an epistemological mainstay with Willard—refers to "an intimate, personal, interactive relationship" and not a mental ascent to a set of theological propositions.[105]

The conservative evangelical views of the atonement that focus only on blood sacrifice and death resulting from the cross do not place the believer in a position to understand Paul's argument that God is working reconciliation and deliverance "by his (Christ's) life" (Rom 5:10). Willard suggests that the concept of Jesus' saving death, and not his life that triumphs over

103. DC, 49.

104. DC, 49.

105. Ibid.

both physical death and a death-like existence, confuses the entire point of such atonement theories discussed above. As a result, this "death-centric" as opposed to "life-centric" soteriology places the believer in a position where,

> . . .the body and therefore the concrete life we find ourselves in are lost to the redemption process. And when that happens, how else could we see the disciplines and the spiritual life but as historical oddities, the quaint but misguided practices of troubled people in a far-off and benighted time. [106]

Therefore, Willard's theology places significant and appropriate value on the cross of Christ. Yet, Willard's crucicentrism is tempered by a more theologically encompassing soteriology that he believes is biblically rooted in a more holistic understanding of the type and quality of life, made available after the cross and resurrection of Christ, in the kingdom of God. Willard argues the New Testament gospels demonstrate and advocate for a crucicentrism that rests not on *profession of belief* in the cross but rather on the believer picking up one's own "cross," and dying to the "old self," by assuming a discipleship relationship with Jesus. This is the level of active confidence (faith) Jesus knew must be present in the individual will in order to allow full participation with the grace and power of God to deliver or rescue his or her entire person from the bondage of sin and death. Such a view, if applied across the evangelical spectrum, would necessitate a radical shift away from the theological interests and practices of revivalist conversionism that earmarked the Moody/Graham/CGM era. Even still, Willard is very aware any potential for change in evangelical crucicentrism must eventually pass through the current dedications and commitments conservative evangelicals have made to penal substitutionary atonement theories,[107] to which Willard is fond of replying, "it is not about getting people into heaven but getting heaven into people."[108]

After discussing Willard's perspective, analysis, and adaptation of Bebbington's four evangelical distinctives, the next chapter will present a constructive description of Willard's overarching theological motif and serve to coalesce each of the various parts into a unified whole. Two central themes that run throughout Willard's work will be revealed and discussed. These themes are defined under the terms *essentia Dei* and the theo-ontological understanding of the kingdom of God. This will serve to construct a more positive overarching perspective on Willardian theology as a whole.

106. SD, 34.

107. Willard, "Discipleship."

108. ROH, 238.

Chapter Three

Essentia Dei and The Protoevangelical

After describing the specific aspects of Willardian theology as compared against Bebbington's evangelical distinctives, this chapter will articulate a positive vision of Willard's entire theological perspective. In order to frame Willardian theology and the protoevangelical vision he offers, an overarching schema will also be presented. This schema—termed *essentia Dei*—ties all of Willard's work together through a coalescing of his perception, understanding, and personal experience of the theo-ontological range and reality of the kingdom of God.[1] This chapter will also articulate the implications of Willard's schema as understood within the classic categories of systematic theology (pneumatology, anthropology, Christology, etc.).

The *Essentia Dei* is defined as a mental pattern in Willardian theology that prioritizes the consistent pursuit of discovering the nature or essence (*essentia*) of God. *Essentia Dei* colors Willard's view of anthropology, pneumatology, soteriology, the atonement, sanctification, ecclesiology, eschatology, and thus all the objectives of Christian life and faith. However, more than just applying to these broader categories of theological inquiry, Willard's application of the *essentia Dei* schema can also be seen in the more minute aspects of his theology. These more specific topics might be aspects of individual motive, personal thoughts, internal dialogue, or interpersonal relationship issues. Thus, Willard's perspective on the *essentia Dei* applies to every aspect and application of his theology.

Willard continually calls his readers and students toward a deeper, more specific understanding and awareness of the personality, temperament,

1. After lengthy conversations with Willard on the topic, this author proposes the term *schema* is appropriate to convey a mental pattern of organizing a certain perspective.

and disposition of God that is described by the *Logos* of Scripture, made manifest in Jesus, and currently present and experienced through the Holy Spirit and the church. Further, Willard's writing and teaching consistently extract and highlights this knowledge of God's essence or disposition from the situations and people described in Scripture. Similarly, the New Testament gospels demonstrate Jesus teaching and explaining to his disciples, not only the nature of the kingdom of God, but also the nature and essence of God himself. Willard argues the *protoeuangelion* Jesus conveyed was focused first and foremost on introducing or re-introducing humanity to his benevolent Father.

This schema sets the stage for all Willard's theological insights. His understanding of the *essentia Dei* wills, pulls, and empowers his Christian experience and theology toward its goal of appropriate knowledge of God, God's creation, and his purposes for humanity. Similar to Farley's description of *theologia habitus,* Willard assumes such an intimate encounter and awareness of God's magnificence will provide all the motivation needed for theological inquiry and Christian living.[2] So central is *essentia Dei* to Willardian theology, in order to properly understand the more concrete details of his vision of the kingdom of God, or the means of personal character formation and discipleship Willard proffers, one must first come to grasp the quality, disposition, and temperament of the King who governs this order. Such awareness correspondingly affects exactly whom human spiritual formation, and Christianity at large, seeks to find as its sustaining model.

As a description of the *essentia Dei*, Willard often uses Adam Clark's portrayal of God. Clark states God can be conceived as,

> The eternal, independent and self-existent Being; the Being whose purposes and actions spring from himself, without foreign motive or influence; he who is absolute in dominion; the most pure, the most simple, the most spiritual of all essences; infinitely perfect; and eternally self-sufficient, needing nothing that he has made; illimitable in his immensity, inconceivable in his mode of existence, and indescribable in his essence; known fully only to himself, because an infinite mind can only be fully comprehended by itself. In a word, a being who from his infinite wisdom, cannot err or be deceived and who from his infinite goodness can do nothing but what is eternally just and right and kind.[3]

From Clark's description, Willard suggests the key characteristic—perhaps the only vital characteristic—of God's character is the eternally manifesting

2. Farley, *Theologia: The Fragmentation and Unity of Theological Educaiton.*
3. Clark, "Definition of God," 903–4.

presence and effluence of *agape*. This love-focused understanding of God is expressed and experienced through several means. Yet, all of the expressions of God's love come to humanity in a relational manner. This, Willard recognizes, is identically representative of an enduring tenant within evangelical Christianity—the personal experience of relationship to God.[4] In Willard's view, such a God as Clark describes, expresses his loving character through relational communication and endless displays of grace. Again, Willard defines grace as "God's action in the lives of human beings that allows them to do what they could not do by their own efforts."[5] Thus, many aspects of the Christian life can be considered actions or evidences (communications) of grace, including the provision of Scripture, the body of Christ (church), nature, salvation, etc. Additionally, Willard proposes that God is not limited or self-confined to such implicit displays of grace. As mentioned earlier, God's loving desire compels him, when appropriate, to overtly or explicitly reveal himself to humanity conversationally, through direct communication.

Furthermore, Willard's vision of the *essentia Dei* contains a parental aspect as well. God is considered a protective, supportive, and nurturing Father, giving guidance about what to avoid in life, what to pursue, and how to flourish. God is also seen as a provider of every "good and perfect thing" needed for life in his kingdom.[6] Furthermore, God is as equally concerned about the individualistic needs of the one as he is the corporate needs of the group. Therefore, Willard presents a parental characteristic of God that remains intensely aware of the detailed events and concerns of human life as well as maintaining his universal, dynamic control over the entire cosmos.

Together, God's *agape* nature, his communicative and caring character, and his parental concern combine to create a vision of a Christian existence Willard describes as a "with God life." Such an existence creates a paradigm, or worldview, and a theology, that Willard suggests is exemplified in many of the characters depicted in the Scriptures. These characters and their stories (Abraham, Isaac, Jacob, Joseph, Moses, David, Solomon, Sampson, Daniel, John the Baptist, John, Peter, Paul, etc.) all reveal that God's goodness and grace is trustworthy and unconditional. Further, these biographies reveal a God that continues to faithfully "walk with them" despite their temporality and frailness. God is seen to continually provide communication, protection, encouragement, and guidance—all displays of love—despite malfeasant behavior, undeveloped character, or simple lack of understanding.

4. Willard, *Fuller Seminary Doctoral Class* (6/16/2010).

5. GO, 67.

6. Jas 1:17.

These biblical characters and their stories reveal various degrees of improper choices, often motivated by a lack of confidence in God's character, and the consequential results of those choices. Yet, in each instance, God's faithful character, and his integrity to covenant loyalty, remains unfettered. This, Willard suggests, is the goal and intent of the Scriptural account and the *euangelion* of Jesus: to reveal the nature and character of God among his people, in both their success and failures, and to proclaim the possibility of what life with such a benevolent God can make manifest if chosen and applied. As such, all theology and ecclesiology, in Willard's view, should be acid tested for how it articulates, reveals, and exalts a vision of God's loving character.[7] After establishing the roots of the *essentia Dei* schema, we can now track how Willard applies this concept through each aspect of his larger theology.

Pneumatology

Closely related to Willard's concept of *essentia Dei* is his pneumatology. In fact, pneumatology is a central and catalytic feature of the entire Willardian project. One gets the impression Willardian theology reacts against modernity's resistance to the metaphysical or the supernatural, which has deeply robbed Christian spirituality of its essential nature. As a result, Willard, like some more recent Renewal theologians such as John Rodham Williams, Ray Anderson, or more recently Amos Yong, suggests the significance of the role of the Holy Spirit, along with the spiritual nature of life and faith, needs significant reemphasizing in Christian theology. Where Willard may depart from these aforementioned scholars is in the degree to which the Holy Spirit should be given more attention and acclaim. Nevertheless, Willard agrees and supports the notion that much of evangelicalism in the modern era has neglected both the nature of spirituality and role of the Holy Spirit in Christian life. As a result, the pneumatological nature of both the Christian religion, in general, and its essential role in conveying an accurate anthropological definition of humanity have significantly hampered the application of Christian theology in a practical manner. Simply stated, Willard posits that to ignore or remain ignorant of the spiritual nature of humanity and the spiritual nature of the kingdom of God is to risk missing the bulk of the nature of God in total.

A more complete discussion of anthropology is still to come, but briefly mentioned here, Willard believes the human being is essentially a living, embodied spirit, created in God's likeness, which is inexorably spiritual

7. DC, 328.

in nature and essence.[8] The ontological nature of God is spirit. God is not simply spiritual but his existential disposition is spirit. In creating human beings, the Genesis narrative describes God's imparting an aspect of his nature (image) into human beings by "blowing" spirit, or breath, into the body of Adam. This bestowing act delivers the spark of animation to Adam's body. This description provides a basic understanding of human ontology and its intrinsic connections and relations to the properties and functions of the spirit or pneumatology. Hence, to understand humanity, one must equally engage spirituality. This gives reason to why Willard sees a contemporary renewed interest in spirituality. This interest is a natural curiosity into the fundamental reality of the human condition. This curiosity is not a passing fancy but a significant human need, as Willard views it. It reveals the metaphysical and ontological drives to understand the nature of what is real, how things exist in the world, and from whence they came to "be."

Willard suggests that the nature of life itself should be understood always and everywhere in terms of an inner "power" to relate to other things in certain and specific ways.[9] All living things, human and non-human alike, have an inherent power that connects with that which is beyond itself, drawing from this "beyond" to enhance and extend its own being, effect, and influence.[10] Additionally, life has the ability to contact and selectively take in from a surrounding environment whatever supports its own survival, extension, and enhancement.[11] Here, one can see the building blocks of Willard's use of phenomenology. His phenomenology does not simply consider how a thing (in this specific instance, the subject under consideration is "life") is produced. Rather, Willard seeks to describe what distinct and essential qualities and properties uniquely make life that which it is. Hence, Willard strives to describe and understand the nature or essence of "life" and how it separates or distinguishes itself from other objects or subjects, in order to differentiate uniqueness and facilitate clarity and identification. This is the work of phenomenology and Willard employs these skills and motives throughout his theological and philosophical pursuits to elucidate his perspectives.

This makes clearer the connection Willard makes between anthropology, pneumatology, and ontology, since the biblical view presents both God and humanity as spiritual beings. The creation narrative describes humans as spiritual beings but not exclusively spiritual. Unlike God, humans are

8. See also page 97.

9. SD, 57.

10. Ibid.

11. Ibid.

embodied spirits. As such, Genesis unveils the concept there is an invisible (spiritual) nature to the world that has the power to effectuate all visible reality. Willard defines spirit as "unembodied personal power."[12] As such, a spirit is capable of interacting with, influencing, and in some manner inhabiting a body. Thus, spirituality is the common heritage of the human race. Ultimately, Willard argues, God is unbodily, personal power. There also exists unembodied, non-personal powers such as electricity, gravity, magnetic forces, etc. In short, human spirituality is defined as "embodied personal power." For Willard, the unseen spiritual realm of both embodied and unembodied personal and non-personal powers fills the teleological void of the material world. Purpose is found not in matter or power itself but rather in that which lies "beyond" the matter and the power. It is the originating Spirit of God that undergirds reality and forms the means from which the physical universe literally attains its substance. Willard argues this platform underneath physical reality is the spiritual realm. It is the non-material, spiritual reality that actualizes, controls, creates, and forms the physical realm.

At its end, when considering the universe of life forms, Willard perceives human life as distinct and unique in its purposive individuality and internality.[13] He argues the far-reaching ability humans have to use that which is beyond themselves for their own purposes gives some indication and insight into the potential human beings posses. The degree and expanse of power that humans have increasingly learned to generate, accumulate, harness, and manage is staggering to consider. Just the nuclear arena alone reveals the presence of enough accumulated and directed power to cause complete destruction of all life on earth. This is a sober realization of Willard's point. Yet, there is a troubling moral absence or emptiness in the raw physical accumulation of power without a positive purpose, since power is by definition the ability to effect change or to do work. The same absence of purpose is equally troubling and damaging when applied to an individual life as well.

Willard's definition of spirit helps clarify why spirituality has become so problematic and counterintuitive to more modern empirical understandings and investigations of the physical world. Here, Willard describes the problems Da Vinci faced when attempting to explore and explain the role of the invisible forces of nature in a socio-religious context controlled by a medieval Catholic church. Willard also references Isaac Newton's critics who held his non-visible, non-physical concept of gravity was necessarily

12. SD, 64.

13. SD, 60.

occultist because gravity, too, is an unembodied "force."[14] Similarly, in what Willard terms the theology of E=MC2, he suggests Einstein's theory not only presents an equation that explains the amount of mass that is in energy, it also equates the amount of energy required in order to create the amount of mass one finds in the universe.[15] Energy is power, the capacity to make change. Thus, thinking about God as disembodied power (energy), one can see how Willard understands the nature of the physical world as one inextricably full of or energized by a non-physical, spiritual power. In fact, one senses he believes them to be inexorably linked. Thus, Willard argues it is a simple matter of logic to require a non-physical cause for the creation of the physical world. In Willard's view, the physical universe, and human life, requires an alternative explanation and justification from those currently provided by the physical sciences. Yet, the most pressing issue for his theology lies in the existence, presence, and experiences of non-material reality.

Similarly, in our contemporary context, the primacy physicalism and scientism now hold in our culture are well demonstrated in a very interesting hypothetical Willard that presents to his students. He suggests students consider the hypothetical of a brain transplant. If it were possible to transfer the brain of one person into the cranium of another, who—or whose personality—would awake from the anesthesia? This hypothetical is meant to reveal a bias. If the answer given is that the original donor of the brain should wake, now housed in a new body, Willard argues the student maintains a bias which assumes the personality or soul is somehow housed in the physical structure and tissues of the brain. Conversely, if the student suggests the recipient of the brain transplant were to awake from the surgery, then the assumption is that the personality is maintained in the entire body, not specifically or exclusively in the brain. In the second response, the brain is considered simply an organ like any other organ (heart, liver, kidney) essential to human life.

This hypothetical question searches to understand where one assumes the locus of human existence lies. Willard refers back to earlier periods of medical advancement, specifically when the first heart transplant procedure was considered. Many ethical discussions during that time suggested there were personal characteristics of the donor that were resident in the organ tissue. Willard argues against such physicalism to suggest human beings "are not our brains." Rather, the human being is best understood as working spirit that energizes both the mind and the body. Therefore, the brain is certainly unique and essential to life, yet no more or less so than

14. Ibid.

15. Ibid, 53.

any other organ and therefore as spiritually "inert" as a kidney or liver. That such a proposition is widely disputed in many scientific and medical circles suggests to Willard the lack of depth in understanding and appreciation for the nature of the pneumatological significance of human existence, the consequence of which is displayed in the increasing absence of ontological imperatives and an increasing moral, ethical, political, philosophical, and theological drift experienced across western society as a whole.

In summary then, if and when a human being, or any life form, is separated from its source of nourishment—that which empowers its life and living, it literally and figuratively shrivels or wastes away from "the inside out." Identically, human beings, as embodied spirits, receive their life and sustenance from God and the spiritually sustaining nature of his Word (*Logos*). Therefore, when separated from the source of life, there is a need to replicate or replace that which is lacking. While searching for a means of sustenance in the material world may be intuitive, for human beings this search can become increasingly counter-productive. The spiritual nature of human life, and the description Jesus uses to articulate the eternal type and quality of life, must be generated in the realm of God, which exists "above" and "beyond" the limits of the physical world. Therefore, Willard argues Jesus' teachings about the Spirit and spirituality are describing both the essence and nature of a spiritual kingdom of God, God himself, and the humanity he created.

Hence, to live in the good news and from the resources of God, one must develop an understanding and appreciation for the pneumatological realties and conditions of not only human life but of all life and reality, material and non-material, physical and spiritual, under God's control. All religious life, Christian and non-Christian alike, can be defined as a significant belief in, or awareness of, an invisible, non-physical reality that controls, or is influential in, the visible, physical world. For Willardian theology, that spiritual, invisible reality is in, through, and by God and becomes experiential inside the governance of his kingdom. Willardian theology and pneumatology contends that to enter this kingdom, as Jesus told Jewish leader Nicodemus, one must be "born again." The first birth is physical. The second birth is no less real, but beyond the physical. Such is the quintessential nature of the spiritual life.[16]

Competing Pneumatologies

There are other competing spiritualities, of course, and Willard recognizes them. He defines a human spirituality, in contrast to a Christian spirituality,

16. John 3:5–8

as one marked by a significant reliance on natural ability. This is what Willard sees the scriptures referring to as the "flesh." In his article, *What Makes Spirituality Distinctly Christian,* he separates and distinguishes Christian spirituality from, for instance, the "Power of positive thinking" or an "Oprah" spirituality. Such spiritualities tend to be guided by an active or aggressive imposition of the will toward that which one senses is the most right thing to do. There is a tendency to advocate something of a "willing" or "visualization" of situations and circumstances into reality. This may connect to versions of spirituality that suggest one can join with the "Star Wars" version of the "force." These are distinctly non-Christian in origin or substance, in Willard's view. Nor does Willard subscribe to the version of naturalism or its differing varieties of panentheism or pantheism. Different from the belief God's being exists and can be found in all creation, or that God, in fact, exists in all things, Willard subscribes to the position that God's spirit sustains all things and created all things. However, God remains uniquely separate from his creation. Bearing the image of God is not the same as containing God or his existential or ontological presence.

All of these different spiritualities, including the more recent interest in angels and demons, suggest to Willard there is a deep hunger in the human heart that yearns to learn, reach out to, and connect with the underlying sustaining reality of God and the power of his character. Willard states that each person, in some measure and in different ways, at one time or another senses or struggles to understand the nature of the crucial non-physical factors from which much, if not all, their existence and experience proceed. Love, joy, longing, awe, community are all spiritual, non-physical expressions and emotions that transcend the biological mechanisms associated with them. This is where religion has always stemmed from and, in Willard's view, where Jesus' teachings meet the human longing and search for purpose.

Unfortunately, Willard recognizes this renewed desire for understanding the nature and depth of spirituality presents a problem for many contemporary churches. The theology and experience of a large segment of Christian congregations espouses ecclesiology centered on acts, beliefs, or organizational objectives that are not transcendent enough to meet even the common level of curiosity in these subjects. Willard senses the renewal movements (charismatic/Pentecostal) and also the early revival movements were both signs of a similar basic yearning; the established church and its theologies and ecclesiologies of the time were not as spiritually sensitive, interested, and focused on the pursuit of spiritual truth as the people seeking such enlightenment. Furthermore, Willard sees the rise and success of secularized spiritualities, like those present in Alcoholics Anonymous, as a verifiable sign pointing to the dearth of spirituality that still exists in the many churches and denominations today.

Yet, at one time in history, Willard suggests the works of Brother Lawrence, Thomas à Kempis, and other similar catholic spiritualists, were heavily focused on the spiritual aspects of Christian faith. He recognizes and laments how modern evangelicalism often starts its story of the Christian faith not at the creation of humanity in Genesis 1 but at "the fall" of humanity and the need of an atonement discussed in Romans 1. For Pentecostal Christians, Willard suggests the story of Christianity starts not in the creation account of Genesis, nor with the progression of the fall and atonement in Romans, but rather proceeds from the Day of Pentecost described in Acts 2. As a result, these reductions largely ignore human spirituality, the ministry of Jesus, the *essentia Dei,* and by implication, the kingdom of God as a whole.

Contrarily, Willard proposes the functional aspect of the Gospels, and the entire run-up of the Old Testament, conveys the proposition that both the world (cosmos) and the human being are deeply ingrained in the spiritual realm by their very essence and purpose. Thus, God and his kingdom, as evidenced in the curriculum of discipleship covered in Jesus' ministry, is interested and devoted to the entire person—heart, soul, body, mind, and relationships. Quoting Teilhard de Chardin, Willard suggests, "We are not human beings having a spiritual experience but spiritual beings having a human experience."[17]

The last point where Willard's pneumatology affects his view of theology is witnessed in his sense of the effect secularism and modernism have had on the Christian perspective of human ontology. Secularism presents the theory of reality, which has become increasingly authorized by the historical progression of western rationalism over the past several centuries. In so doing, it has attempted to provide mastery over every aspect of the human project. Modernism, humanism, and secularism each contends for a level of human domination of life, living, and environment—ecologically and economically—to be both plausible and beneficial. Such a position in Willard's view is nothing short of "self-idolization, the Faustian drive of humanity [that] is rooted in original sin."[18]

It follows that Willard senses Christian theology and its understanding of spiritual realities and their properties need never back away from physics or science, something he fears has become all too common in recent years. When it comes to the definition of ultimate reality, Willard senses that

17. De Chardin, *The Phenomenon of Man,* 211.

18. Willard, *Fuller Seminary Doctoral Seminar Reader,* 10.

theology, and its emphasis on the spiritual, has as much to offer in terms of "knowledge" as that of the strictly physical or "hard" sciences. That theology is engaged in a spiritual inquiry does not in any way diminish its value to the pursuit of truth in the real world. To allow such diminishment is to entreat the committal of disobedience to the first commandment of Mosaic Law—the worship of an alternative god or idol. He writes, "Our accepted intellectual systems today, often called 'scientific' or 'naturalistic,' are in reality idolatry, though usually not intended as such. Education fails us by not teaching us to be intellectually thorough but to conform."[19]

Likewise, Christian inquiry should be liberally open to all truth. There should be no fear of the pursuit of truth nor of what is found and proven as a result of such an inquiry. Again, Willard ascribes to an understanding of God (*essentia Dei)* that suggests if there is truth outside of Christian knowledge, God is the sort of person who would desire one to have it, regardless of the implications that might come about in orthodox Christian faith.

The direct, critical, or classical realist pneumatological perspective uniquely casts Willard in a complicated light. His phenomenological approach to realism and his pneumatological understandings about the nature of spirit do not necessarily contradict. In fact, they complement each other when considering Willard's view that phenomenological realities can be discerned in and of themselves to determine their efficacy. Therefore, it would appear Willard is applying, or brings to bear, his extensive philosophical disciplines to the arena of spirituality and theology in order to investigate the claims of Christ regarding the essence of life. The fact his investigation uncovers no inherent contradiction makes for a strong case as to the reliability of Christianity's knowledge claims regarding the nature of human existence and the spiritual properties undergirding the physical universe.

Anthropology

After establishing the vital link that the protoevangelical gospel of Jesus centers around and proceeds from a motive of revealing the *essentia Dei* to humanity, Willard begins to describe the nature and essence of what it means to be human. For Willard, human beings are also essentially spiritual in nature. And this reality begins to unveil the extent to which he understands how the gospel is to affect and transform the human condition within the kingdom of God.[20] Willard's first detailed treatment of anthropology is found in *Spirit of the Disciplines.* Yet, since his anthropology is distinctively

19. Ibid.

20. Willard, *Fuller Seminary Doctoral Seminar Reader*, 10.

pneumatological and based on the human-divine relationship, all his works seek to describe, in various degrees and vantage points, his anthropological perspective.[21]

Using a quote from Wesley, Willard suggests that human beings are far more than what they have chosen to define themselves as.

> We consider that the body is not the man; that man is not only a house of clay but an immortal spirit; a spirit made in the image of God; a spirit that is of infinitely more value than the sun, moon, and stars put together; yea than the whole material creation. Consider that the spirit of man is not only of a higher order, of a more excellent nature, than any part of the visible world, but also more durable; not liable either to dissolution or decay.[22]

Additionally, Willard quotes C. S. Lewis' view of the underlying "glory" of the human condition.

> It is a serious thing to live in a society of possible gods and goddesses. To remember that the dullest and most uninteresting person you talk to may one day be a creature which, if you saw it now, would be strongly tempted to worship, or else a horror and a corruption such as you now meet, if at all, only in a nightmare. All day long we are, in some degree, helping each other to one or other of these destinations. It is awe and the circumspection proper to them, that we should conduct all our dealings with one another, all friendships, all loves, all play, all politics. There are no ordinary people. You have never talked to a mere mortal.[23]

Both of the above statements paint a clear picture of the invaluable worth ascribed to all humanity as well as to each human being. Willard upholds these valuations and contrasts them against the existentialist philosopher Jean Paul Sartre's impression that "Man is a useless passion."[24]

In contrast to Sartre's view, as divine image holders of God, Willard understands humans as eternal, never ceasing beings with an eternal destiny in God's great universe.[25] Thus, human beings, understood as embodied spirits, do not die simply when the body dies. For the follower of Jesus, at least, Willard asserts that death is abolished, meaning that the experience

21. SD 45–50.

22. Wesley, "What is Man? Sermon 109," 573.

23. Lewis, *The Weight of Glory*, 15.

24. Sartre, *Existentialism and Human Emotions*, 90.

25. DC, 86.

of that person, passing from earthly existence, will be uninterrupted even through the period of the body's demise.

According to Willard—as a never-ceasing spiritual being of immeasurable worth—humanity is created to "reign" with God over all creation in mutually collaborative and creative governance. Human life on earth is understood as the place where one is trained for progressive empowerment and reasonability. In so doing, Willard believes God's original and final intent for the universe will become a reality. The *missio Dei* consists of the Trinitarian dwelling with humanity and nature, each enjoying a mutually beneficial relationship, as described in the opening of the Genesis account. Such a condition, albeit altered significantly due to the events of the past several millennia, will be redeemed and restored. Thus, the *Missio dei* represents the universal restorative and redemptive plan of God.[26] This is Willard's primary subject and intent as carried through *Renovation of the Heart.*

Yet, there is a problem. And this problem lies primarily in the intrapsychic conflict inside every human heart that stems from an ongoing resistance or desire for independence from the reality and natural consequences of the existence of God's person. This intrapsychic conflict, Willard argues, is what Jesus is describing in his articulation of the fallen condition of the human heart. To better understand how the heart is quintessential to the protoevangelical objective, Willard takes great care in describing and diagramming his understanding of the interlocking and interdependent aspects of the "person" or the self. (See figure 1).

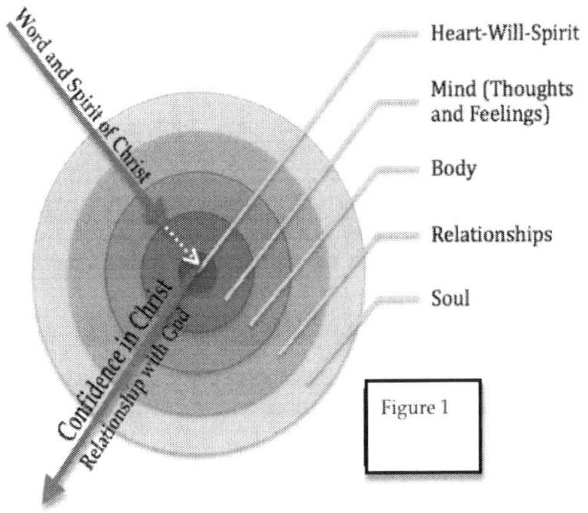

Figure 1

26. Although Willard does not use this term specifically, his vision of the kingdom is similar to the point of identical to what Christopher J. H. Wright has described in this exhaustive work *The Mission of God.*

Interestingly, one of the unique aspects of Willardian theology is his definition of the self. It is also one of the aspects of his theology where one can see his classical or direct realism acting through his phenomenological methodology. Willard states that although all the aspects of the self noted in figure one may not be obvious, it does not follow that they are wholly mysterious.[27] He argues that God is not interested in "hiding" the essential things of life and living. In fact, the opposite is true. God has created all things in ways and through means that can be discerned and intelligently approached as to gather increasing understanding. All aspects, objects, and subjects of human life, in both the material and non-material realm, have "parts." These parts then have properties and relationships between separate parts to the larger whole. Wholes then also have relationships to other wholes, etc.

This structure of increasing relatedness from the individual or particular to the larger collective applies to atoms just as easily as it applies to solar systems and human persons. For Willard, mystery lies in the inherent "otherness" of God who is the undercurrent or cause/creator of all things. Therefore, at one level, there remains a sense of mystery in terms of the inexplicable nature of the divine. Yet, at the same time, Willard's epistemology allows and requires the pursuit and attainment of increasing levels of knowledge about God and our world. Certainty or omniscience is neither a requirement nor a necessary objective to maintain the potentiality of gaining escalating levels of understanding about real states of affairs. Thus, Willard escapes the rationalism of modern empirical objectivity yet retains a level of mystery and respect for ambiguity by recognizing and honoring the otherness of God. This tension is perhaps nowhere as important in Willardian thought and theology than when considering the aspects of human selfhood.

Willard defines the aspects of the self in relation to the things or qualities that are integral, inescapable, and therefore quintessential to human existence. Together, these six basic aspects work together to form a human "nature."[28] Hence, spiritual formation is that activity or process through which the human spirit, will, or heart is formed in relationship and in concert with the six areas that constitute a person.

The Human Heart/Will/Spirit

Willard believes the primary source from which all human life originates and proceeds can be traced to the unique qualities of the human heart/will/spirit. These three terms are somewhat, although not entirely, synonymous

27. ROH, 31.

28. ROH, 30.

in Willardian theology. Together, these terms are significant to Willardian anthropology due in large measure to their all-encompassing, foundational position, which proceeds through and dramatically alters or affects each of the other aspects of the self. In an overarching way, Willard argues that what is contained in the heart/will/spirit will progressively color and shape each of the outer rings depicted in figure 1 (mind, body, relationships, and soul). Therefore, we will more clearly identify and distinguish these three terms and their unique aspects individually.

Willard uses the biblical description of the "heart" as a metaphor to describe or illustrate that which lies at the "core", or what is "central" and essential to the human system of being. "Will" connotes or carries the concept of the capacity that enables the individual to create, originate, instigate, and express their individuality and unique personhood upon their world and with others. The term "spirit" represents both how and in what way this core, central power of life manifests itself in a person. As mentioned earlier, "spirit" describes "power" or the non-physical properties of empowerment. An individual spirit becomes discernible through the nature and effect of the decisions and character it manifests (will). In describing how these three aspects are interrelated, Willard writes:

> I believe it will become clear that the heart, spirit, and will or their equivalents are words that refer to one and the same thing, the same fundamental component of the person. But they do so under different aspects. . . . But it is the same dimension of the human being that has all these features.[29]

More specifically, when considering volition, Willard understands the will as containing the capacity to not only direct the actions and behaviors of the individual but to also affect an environment in a unique, distinct, and matchless manner. Additionally, genuine creativity and expressive individuality demand indeterminate freedom of will. What follows in this freedom is the power (spiritual capacity) to choose both good and evil. Willard does not believe in outside agencies that "make" or force the individual will to act in certain predetermined ways. For Willard, it is this spontaneous, unfettered ability to act and react to our world that constitutes the existential force of individual life. Human will and its effects represent "us" in a way that no other aspect of the self can approximate. In regards to the spiritual aspect of the will, the force and capacity that enables the act of willing—the volitional capacity that is exercised in the individual human person—originates from

29. ROH, 29.

the nonphysical force or power of the individual spirit. Not separate from the will, the spirit activates and empowers—gives life to—the will.

Whether one's spirit is "alive" to Christ or not is a matter directly attributed to and produced by the will's directed pursuits of God and his kingdom. Therefore, Willardian theology holds that the gospel of Jesus places the heart/will/spirit as the non-physical realities that lie at the core of human existence and are the primary objects of engagement for any Christ-centered understanding of spiritual formation. The human spirit empowers the will, which in turn forms the character and represents the heart, nature, or essence of the individual identity. In this way, the heart/will/spirit acts as an "executive center" where decisions and choices are made for the whole person.[30] Since the heart/spirit/will shapes the overall disposition, it must be "reached, cared for, and transformed" by the practices and disciplines of formation into Christlikeness.[31] Willard goes on to comment that when the heart/will/spirit functions as it should, the person will want the good and be able to respond to life's many circumstances and situations in ways that are both good and right as described and defined by Christ. As such the will/heart/spirit is able to direct and conform the other aspects of the self in appropriate ways in order to create an integrated life working toward consistent ends and goals.

When considering the subject of sin, Willard's description of the heart/will/spirit carries crucial implications. The internal acquiescence or resistance of the human will to the will of God is where sin lies. One's thoughts, the presence of temptation, or even the disposition to sin do not in themselves represent a sinful state. Rather, sin exists when the will agrees and submits to the thought or temptation. Following through with the commission of a sinful act is not necessary. When one comes to the point of becoming willing to engage or commit sin, sin has already occurred. The fulfillment is not required, only the willingness.[32] This is Willard's explanation of Jesus' distinction of committing "adultery in the heart" referenced in Matthew 5:28.

Willard recognizes the other aspects of the self (mind, body, relationships, and soul) often do not work in concert with the will. There are other factors and hurdles to overcome in order for the heart's desire to be implemented across all aspects of the self. Willard sees this fragmentation in Paul's description of the "double-mindedness" in Romans 7:15–20.[33] The

30. ROH, 30.

31. ROH, 34.

32. ROH, 33.

33. Rom 7:15–20 ESV—"For I do not understand my own actions. For I do not do

reduction and eventual elimination of this fragmentation, or dis-integration of the self, (i.e., "a house divided against itself cannot stand") is a significant aspect of the spiritual formational/transformational process.[34] This is accomplished when the divided heart/will/spirit begins to draw the various aspects of the entire life into harmonious synergy.[35]

The Mind

The second aspect of the self is the mind. The mind is made up of two core components, the thoughts and feelings/emotions. Willard defines thoughts as those means by which perceptions and imaginings are brought before the mind that enable consideration and contemplation of possible interrelated connections and meanings. "Thought is that which enables our will (spirit) to range far beyond the immediate boundaries of our environment and the perceptions of our senses."[36] As a result, a human being can begin to consider that which is beyond the limitations of the contexts of time, space, and culture. Here, Willard connects thought to consciousness. Thought—whether applied in the arts, sciences, philosophy, or theology—allows the human consciousness, through either reason or imagination, to probe the past, present, and future and effectively escape the situated limitations of place, time, culture, language, physical senses, empirical facts, etc. This is central to the human ability and drive to both explore and create.

The second aspect of the mind is feelings. This is an interesting and perhaps controversial claim in Willardian anthropology. Many psychologists might tend to place the locus of feelings more in the body than in the mind. Willard, however, argues that feelings act to draw or repel one toward or away from things that come before the mind. Feelings, therefore, create something of either an attractant or repellant to certain thoughts. When connected to thoughts, feelings intone an overarching sense as to whether a certain thought or group of thoughts carries a pleasant or painful, beneficial or hurtful, attractive or repulsive potentiality. Therefore, feelings and

---

what I want, but I do the very thing I hate. Now if I do what I do not want, I agree with the law, that it is good. So now it is no longer I who do it, but sin that dwells within me. For I know that nothing good dwells in me, that is, in my flesh. For I have the desire to do what is right, but not the ability to carry it out. For I do not do the good I want, but the evil I do not want is what I keep on doing. Now if I do what I do not want, it is no longer I who do it, but sin that dwells within me."

34. Matt 12:25.

35. Willard also notes how such individuals have an enormous potential in aligning and directing the omni-focused and distracted groups they both belong to and/or lead.

36. ROH, 32.

thoughts are intertwined. The facts or perceptions of a certain set of facts or circumstances evoke a certain set of accompanying feelings which together work in the mind as a means of discerning and navigating our world. So intertwined and interdependent are thought and feeling that Willard treats them as different aspects of a single whole.

Very quickly, one can get a glimpse of how Willardian anthropology coalesces the aspects of the self in an interdependent relationship. The will undergirds the activities of the mind. Choice involves discerning, thinking, and choosing between different thoughts and feelings in relationship to the intentions of the will. Every choice involves thoughts and feelings. Yet, it is also true that what we think and feel is very significantly tied to our choices. Willard laments the fact this is not widely recognized today.

> Unfortunately, the fact that feelings and thoughts are largely a matter of choice is not widely understood—especially as it concerns feelings. We speak of feelings as passions, and that is a word that implies passivity. But we are in fact very active in inviting, allowing, and handling our passions . . .[37]

Human life does not run on human will alone. But the will does in fact organize the life, if the will is acting appropriately. If the feelings are left to drive the will, addiction and obsession are often the result. Hence, Willardian anthropology places not the mind or the feelings as the essential or primal place where illumination to the truths of God must start. Rather, it is the will that can and must control and direct both one's thought life and emotional life.

The Body

The physical instrument of the human self begins with the body. The body is the first kingdom (environ where the will is enacted) human beings are given to control. Its strengths, talents, appearances, sexuality, artistic creative ability are all manifestations of the personal effectiveness and influence of the individual will. The non-physical, spiritual nature of the heart/spirit/will is that which empowers the human body while the thoughts, words, dreams, feelings, visions, and imaginations of the mind, motivated by the will, are eventually and ultimately expressed in and to the physical world through the instrumentalities of the human body. When the spirit/will and mind are unified with the body, a human being comes into existence. The body is the personalized source from which human personhood is expressed to

37. ROH, 34.

both oneself and to others. Therefore, the body in Willardian anthropology is essential for social life and cannot be properly understood outside of its connection to relationship. The body is "the place where we are stimulated by the world beyond ourselves and where we find and are found by others."[38]

Thus, it is important to note here Willard's understanding and navigation of the monist/dualist issues at play between body and spirit. He is clearly a dualist in the sense that he recognizes the effect of both in human interaction and integration. The spirit empowers the mind and the body. They are in an inseparable relationship. The body is the means provided to accomplish the will. Thus monism, which argues for an either/or necessity of body or spirit and often the assumption of the body as inherently evil, is clearly not an option in either Willard's pneumatology or anthropology.

However, Willard does argue that the body tends to have a capacity all to itself. It is not simply an order-taking machine that lies dormant until receiving a directive from the mind or will. In that way, the body tends to have a "mind of its own" in those autonomic abilities that occur unconsciously and go largely unnoticed. These subconscious abilities are exceedingly beneficial (most notably the autonomic drives such as breathing, heartbeat, etc.) but also carry capacity to learn and act inappropriately, as well. This again is what the apostle Paul describes as the existence of sin in the body's "members" (Rom 7:17). Therefore, like the will and the mind, the body must be re-trained or re-formed. The body is not evil in itself but rather "while it is infected by evil it can be delivered."[39] Key to Willardian anthropology is the sense in which the body is integral to the spiritual transformation. Since the will and mind are embodied, carrying out the functions of the individual in the world, if the body is not included in the process of transformation, in a significant sense, the entire transformative enterprise is in jeopardy.

Relationships

The social context appropriately follows in the Willardian understanding of the aspects of the self. Here, embodied persons meet and interact with other embodied persons both individually and corporately. It is the nature and effect of body-to-body or body-to-bodies where the human self finds its rootedness and belonging. Therefore, the intra-personal transformation of the individual naturally follows as a progression of inter-personal development. Willard argues that a large aspect of human ontology is found as a direct result of relationality to others. Much of who we are specifically, and

38. ROH, 35.

39. ROH, 36.

what possibilities exist as a human being generally, are learned and taught through some form of social interaction or relationship. The essential requirement of a child to bond to a maternal figure has been well documented. Simply stated, a child can suffer incalculable damage, even to the point of death, if this key relationship is withheld. Willard believes part of the essence of human life necessitates this bond in order to begin the process of developing a life and a self. Likewise, the need for significant and sustained contributions, connections, affirmations, and interactions with others is a never-ending requirement of human existence.

Yet, the relational aspect of human life is not limited to human-to-human engagement. Much of the socio-relational sector of human life carries over into the human-divine relationship. For Willard the "most fundamental 'other'" is in God himself.[40] He argues human beings cannot separate their individual or collective identities from God himself, since it is in God where all individuals are ultimately rooted. God represents the common factor that connects all people. Therefore, "our ties to one another cannot be isolated from our shared relationship to him, nor our relationship to him from our ties to one another."[41] For Willard, each relationship is best viewed when accounting for and including God's relational contribution. Hence, our perceptions, experiences, and expectations of our personal relationships are only accurate when properly understood in light of and informed through the symbiotic matrix of God's mutual participation and interest.

It is the social dimension of the self where the inner thoughts, feelings, actions, and will are demonstrated through the body to the outside world and where feedback can be attained. What our thoughts, feelings, actions, attitudes, and beliefs mean, what they create, how they affect the world and others around us come primarily through interactive relationships. And it is in our bodies and from our bodies where these relationships occur. We learn how to express ourselves in our bodies through how we appear to others, and we also learn how to touch, communicate, talk, work, and fight with others in and through our physical presence. Therefore, it is in social relationships where human beings begin and never cease to probe the outer and inner limits of their existence. This is why rejection and humiliation at the relational level can be both physically and spiritually debilitating. For Willard, learning how to "be" with others and allowing others to "be" with us is the realm of human existence where the entire self begins to take shape. However, negative learning and forming of relationships can stunt the development of a holistic personhood.

40. ROH, 36.

41. Ibid.

The Soul

Finally, the human soul is that aspect of the self that connects and maintains continuity or integrity among all the aspects of the self in order to form a single identity or personality. The soul enables the assimilation of a single life, one not consumed by thoughts alone or the will, or the body or a relationship. Instead, the soul manages and mitigates all the integral aspects of human life into a holistic and balanced singular existence. Willard writes, "[The soul] is like a meta-dimension or higher level dimension because its direct field of play consists of the other dimensions (thought, body, and so on) and through them it reaches ever deeper into the person's vast environment of God and his creation."[42]

Willard differentiates between the function of the soul and the common assumption that the soul is "the person." The frequent discussion of persons as "souls" in religious venues confuses the matter. Instead, the soul is the deepest part of the self that, like the body, has the ability to function below the level of conscious awareness. Its inclusivity and somewhat independent nature cause the biblical writers to sometimes speak of the soul in the third person.[43] However, the soul is not an outside third party but rather the overarching organizing aspect of the human life that focuses the self in any given moment in time on the things, ideas, and propensities required. The soul has the capacity to muster the self, in all its fragmented and competing distractions, in order to manifest the personality on the issues and concerns that are most paramount and essential.

Therefore, lack of soul care can have drastic implications and manifest totalizing failures. It is not difficult to imagine how fractured and misaligned an individual could become if the soul is unable to assimilate the various responsibilities, thoughts, compulsions, relational dynamics, illusions, beliefs, conversations, responsibilities, roles, pains, moral obligations, activities, temptations, and needs that occur in the course of everyday life, all of which continually mount by the hour, day, weeks, months and years. The soul, working well, allows a person to remain prepared and capable to respond to the situations and circumstances that affect each or all of the dimensions of self as encountered through daily life in an integrated and appropriate fashion.

42. ROH, 37.

43. See Psalm 42 and Luke 12.

The "Fallen" Condition

The range of the effective will of the human being is considered their "kingdom." It follows then that the human kingdom is the sphere that encompasses the employment of whatever system of power is required to accomplish that which a human being desires (wills) to achieve. This is where the problems and potential for human life, both individually and corporately, are found. If the mind, through thoughts and feelings, considers the message of the gospel beneficial or true to the point of allowing the will to place hope and confidence it its realities, then that initial "seed" of faith is planted in the existential core of one's person heart/spirit/will. This is regeneration and the point at which the reality of God begins to progressively work its effect outward to transform the outer lying aspects of the self. This represents the response, the choice of the will, to the offering of the kingdom of God and its grace.

In discussing conversion or transformation, Willard's diagram reveals how the Word of God or the truth regarding the *Logos* of God and his kingdom reality first enters into the person through the outer layers of the self, (soul, relationships, and body) to initially land on the mind. There, the mind thinks through the proposal of the gospel and attempts to measure the beneficence or goodness of the news regarding God and his kingdom. Here Willard argues that the specific tenets and attributes of whatever "gospel" is presented are of paramount importance, since what a hearer thinks and feels about the message itself largely determines if the concepts will remain in the mind, be expelled from the mind, or be blocked by the mind from entering into the heart and affecting the will. This creates a situation where many may believe they have resisted or rejected the "gospel" of Jesus when in fact they may not have actually encountered his message yet at all. Conversely, some may believe they have accepted the gospel while also remaining largely ignorant of its specific intents and purposes.

Willard defines the human condition apart from God in the term "ruined soul."[44] Willard suggests the prophetic witness of Scripture, seen in the wisdom literature, through the biographies of the lives described throughout the Bible, as well as depicted in many of Jesus' teachings, clearly illuminates the effect and consequences of the lost condition. People suffering from a ruined soul are unable to achieve and experience the life they were created to inhabit. The result is a progressive dis-integration of the soul. Such dis-integration is a direct consequence of a soul's inability to assimilate the parts of the self (will, thoughts, feelings, desires, bodily habits, and social relationships) into a uniformed whole and in a united purpose. Such a lack-

44. ROH, 45.

ing is indicative of a heart/will turned inward and away from the reality of God and his express designs and intentions for human life and living.

This concept directly contravenes the humanistic assumption that "We're okay. I'm okay and you're okay." Willard suggests humanity and the human condition apart from God is not at all "ok," a fact that is easily seen and experienced in everyday life, both collectively and individually.[45] Therefore, the move toward Christ is not motivated from a desire for self-esteem as might be the desire of more secular spiritualities. Here, Willard suggests such spiritualities liberally employ the psychological mechanism of denial. Denial produces an inability or unwillingness to admit or recognize the realities of the human condition and its "lostness" apart from God. Therefore, denial is the primary device that humans use to deal with their own dis-integration. Rejection of reality and self-delusion is a faculty inseparable from the human will. The routine and habitual dismissal of facts and realities of everyday existence is a negative expression of the will's greatest power, all while occurring without being recognized as such. This includes not only the rejection of the actual facts of a matter under consideration; denial also often includes an affirmation or acceptance of untruth.[46] Willard states:

> In a world apart from God, the power of denial is absolutely essential if life is to proceed. The will or spirit cannot psychologically sustain itself for any length of time in the face of what is clearly acknowledged to be the case. Therefore, it must deny and evade and delude itself. As a result, when the light of the fundamental truth and reality, God, is put out of the heart and the soul, the intellect becomes dysfunctional, trying to devise a truth that will be compatible with the basic falsehood that man is god, and the affections, feelings, emotions, even sensations, soon follow along on the path of chaos. The mind is uprooted from reality.[47]

Therefore, Willard recognizes that the ruined soul will remain separated from the intents and purposes God has specifically designed for life and living. At the same time, the will can choose to maintain a level of denial in regards to the overt evidences and realities the lost condition eventuates. This becomes an ever-increasing spiral that leads one further and further away from not only the reality of God and his kingdom but also the hope of escaping the elusive lure of the alternative.

45. ROH, 49.
46. ROH, 52.
47. ROH, 53.

Sensuality

At this point, when the mind is derailed from reality through the continued application of denial, Willard argues that a reliance on senses becomes increasingly critical. The result is a life that becomes increasingly dependent on "feelings" that progressively undergird all motives and drives. The human body becomes the locus of control, replacing the spiritually grounded mind and the will. This elevates sensuality into the primary means of seeking and experiencing pleasure. Bodily enjoyment soon becomes an all-encompassing priority. Desire and satiation steadily grow as the chief avenue through which decisions are gauged and evaluated. The drive for self-gratification creates a life without boundaries where fewer and fewer experiences are considered forbidden as long as one can "get away with it."

The result, Willard suggests, is what the apostle Paul describes in Romans 1:29–32. This passage presents Paul's summary of the results of a sensual-centric life and focus. Such a worldview is vacuous of the pursuit of righteous living (*dikaiosune*). When the knowledge of God is denied, sensuality replaces wisdom, and virtue becomes the victim.[48] Paul's letter to the Romans suggests there was an overwhelming absence of experiential involvement and engagement with God in the broader culture of the first century. As such, Greco-Roman Hellenism was a symptomatic representation of an unlimited capacity and desire to fulfill the "lusts of the flesh." This includes not simply the more sexual perversions and deviations. It also connects to the Greco-Roman enjoyment and proliferation of gladiatorial blood sports and even the use of crucifixion as a means of execution. Each of these areas of Greco-Roman life reveals a level of debasement to human life that, for Willard, represents "a vision of human evil that is off the scale of human capacity to deal with."[49] The presence and proliferation of such a life and view of the world become a force of its own that literally grows out of any one person's control. This is the "lost" condition of humanity at large. The overarching result is demonstrated in a collective societal disorientation and blindness to the *essentia Dei*, God's purposes, and the realities of his kingdom.[50]

48. The significance of the Greek term *dikaiosune* will follow later. It plays a significant role in Willard's view of discipleship.

49. Willard, "The Craftiness of Christ."

50. ROH, 56.

Self-Idolatry

Most poignantly, the ongoing progression of denial and the capitulation to sensuality further devolve into a level of lostness that finally becomes a self-imposed state of self-obsession. Thus, a "ruined" soul, for Willard, is created through the mistaken identification of the self—or one's private person—for God. "They falsely identify and cannot recognize what is closest to themselves. They have become delusional. Such a one really does think he is in charge of his life."[51] Willard references Paul's recognition that "their god is their own belly," the belly representing the feeling center of the body in the first century.[52]

The nature of God being God naturally and consistently offends the self-idolizing psyche. Willard states Augustine was accurate in seeing that if it is true "God is running the universe, and has first claim on our lives, guess who isn't running the universe and does not get to have things as they please."[53] Hence, Willard suggests that it is in the nature of choosing to "captain one's own ship" where sin and the problems of all life and human existence exceedingly dwells.[54] As an example of such an offense Augustine describes, Willard refers to Sartre's suggestion that since there is no God, there is no human nature, thus humanity is required to make of itself what it can.[55] Willard points to the logical absurdity of such a proposition, realizing that a thing with no nature can make nothing of itself, since it can do nothing, including self-identification or self-realization. Thus Sartre, at the end of modernity, is seen by Willard to create a view of existentialism and secular humanism that represents what may be the culmination of human denial. Willard suggests Sartre illustrates exactly how self-idolization results from the progression of the lost soul, starting with denial, through sensuality, and ending in self-deification.

After describing the nature of the ruined soul, Willard recognizes how difficult it can be, even in Christian circles, to understand and appreciate the worth God places on the individual who can proceed so far afield from his ways. Willard points to G. K. Chesterton's remarks that one of the hardest things about understanding Christianity is the amount of worth that is placed on the individual soul, especially in light of the ruined soul as it flails for stability under the influence of a denying will. Willard explains the sin condition

51. ROH, 56.

52. Phil 3:19.

53. ROH 52.

54. ROH, 46.

55. Willard, "The Craftiness of Christ."

does not make the person worthless, only lost.[56] "Lost" is defined as the condition created when something is no longer able to accomplish its intended purpose. Such a condition does not devalue. Rather, "lostness" is a misappropriation that creates a condition making the object or person unavailable for that which is most proper and beneficial. This then creates an insurmountable hurdle that prevents one from achieving one's full potential and maximizing opportunity. Thus the "lost" are simply in a position that prevents them from achieving the intended and rightful purpose for which they were created.

The Restored Soul

In contrast to Sartre, Willard quotes Pico Della Mirandola who suggested that humanity was created by God to possess the responsibility for becoming what it wills to become by the sum total of the choices made during one's lifetime.[57] As such, God requires that human beings choose (will) to act on the basis of their inner desires and therefore must freely decide what one "will" live for. What is chosen through the selections among our many desires for fulfillment determines what kinds of persons we become. Therefore, Willard advocates what a person decides to seek in life is the key to the development of a character which further determines the direction of what that individual's character will continue to develop into. This is an existential spiral ascending toward godliness and truth as opposed to a spiral descending into denial and disintegration.

Here, Willard describes how discipleship to Jesus is the process by which humanity can regain entry to the *missio Dei* and thus accomplish their God-given destiny. The definition of a disciple, or as Willard liked to use "apprentice," is simply someone who has decided to be with another person, under appropriate conditions, in order to become capable of doing what that person does or to become what that person is.[58] A student or apprentice must first realize and acknowledge their "learner" status. To not admit so would allow for the continuation of the condition that led a person into a lost condition originally. Key to this process is the recantation of the idealized understanding of the self and the opinions and perspectives that have gained prominence through institution of habit or desire. Willard describes this process as the recantation of the self-directed will that can only be accomplished through a complete denial of the self. Understood in scriptural terms, this concept is described as the "death of the self." Willard

56. ROH, 46.

57. Willard, "The Craftiness of Christ."

58. DC, chapter 8.

states, "Christian spiritual formation rests on the indispensable foundation of death to self and cannot proceed except insofar as that foundation is being firmly laid and sustained."[59]

Jesus illustrates this concept many times, most commonly seen in his use of irony to describe one's need to lose their life in order to find it, or the need to pick up one's cross in order to live in a Christlike manner. The idea of giving up one's life in order to find true life communicates the requirement to denounce the need to govern one's own existence. Such people,

> ...will for the first time be able to do what they want to do. Of course they will be able to steal, lie, and murder all they want-which will be none at all. But they will also be able to be truthful, and transparent and helpful and sacrificially loving with joy, and they will want to be. Their life will be in this way caught up into God's life. They will want the good and be able to do it, the only true human freedom.[60]

This, Willard understands, is what Jesus is communicating at the essence of his protoevangelical message. The underlying motif in Jesus' gospel is that God is good, trustworthy, wise, and faithfully capable of being trusted. Therefore, in Jesus' advocation of "taking up the cross," he is suggesting, in laying aside denial or one's agenda for one's own life's meaning and purpose, there is salvation from one's own desires to be God. Therefore, the purpose of discipleship is to discover the reality of the goodness of God and his character as it represents itself in all life and living. Then, based on that vision and its potential, people can engage the process and means used to become capable of doing and becoming likened to the master and achieving their own potential.

In summary, Willardian anthropology suggests that apart from knowledge and experience of God, human beings—both individually and collectively—will tend to progressively trend toward denial of reality, increasing levels of sensuality leading to self-deification and self-worship. The only hope to break the devolving cycle of ontological and existential "lostness" is to grasp a vision of the *essentia Dei,* which empowers and motivates the progressive construction of a Christocentric view of oneself that is both accurate and beneficial.

59. ROH, 64.

60. ROH, 65.

Theo-Ontology

The term theo-ontology (often referred to as ontotheology in other works) has a rich and diverse lineage. The concept is perhaps first connected to the works of Immanuel Kant and Martin Heidegger, which is then taken up with subsequent contemporary philosophers and writers such as Jacques Derrida, Jean-Lu Marion, Merold Westphal, and John Caputo.[61] In terms of a classical definition, in Kant's system there were two main categories of theology—reasoned theology and revelatory theology. Ontotheology was a sub-sub category within one of two types of transcendental theology, which is set against Kant's definition of natural theology, which also belongs to the larger category of "reasoned" theology. Transcendental theology had two categories as well—ontotheology and cosmotheology. The difference between the two appears to be one of method. Kant writes:

> Transcendental theology aims either at inferring the existence of a Supreme Being from a general experience, without any closer reference to the world to which this experience belongs, and in this case it is called cosmotheology; for it endeavors to cognize the existence of such a being, through mere conceptions, without the aid of experience, and is then termed ontotheology.[62]

Heidegger takes Kant's ontotheological platform in another direction, roundly assigning all metaphysical pursuits in modern philosophy as degenerating into what has become an ontotheological inquiry. Heidegger strongly critiques the connection of philosophy and theology, desiring to break the correlation and allow each pursuit to probe its subject free from the constraints of the other. He endeavored to de-link the philosophical from the theological, and vice versa, in order to maintain the distinctiveness of each. Heidegger argued that the historical conjoining of theology and philosophy clouded and limited both discourses. Once theology is blended with the philosophical pursuit of metaphysics, it became an issue involved with faith and not thought or reason. As a result, the source and aim of theology's irreducible subject (God) also becomes mired in a non-appropriate framework in which all beings (perhaps created beings) are subjected and limited. It seems Heidegger's argument suggests the problem of ontotheology is its propensity to reduce theological inquiry while allowing philosophy to presume too lofty a perch.[63]

61. See Westphal, *Overcoming Onto-Theology*, and Robbins, *Between Faith and Thought*. Also see Caputo and Scanlon, *God, the Gift, and Postmodernism*, 146.

62. Kant, *Critique of Pure Reason*, 362.

63. See Heidegger, *Identity and Difference*, and Heidegger, *Being and Time*.

Although Kant and Heidegger's perspectives are highly esoteric and deeply convoluted, Willard argues a classical understanding of ontotheology does not disallow the position in either philosophy or theology that a God, in fact, exists as a being among other beings, even while perhaps maintaining the condition of the Supreme Being. There may be issues and critiques about the means or methods by which one comes to these questions. Yet, Heidegger nor Kant completes a theological or philosophical argument that eliminates the realist proposition that attaining knowledge of God is possible, nor do they disprove the development of language suitable to describing and expressing such knowledge. That Kant and Heidegger delimit and segregate their inquires of theology and philosophy does not mandate the requirement to do so.

Willard argues philosophical inquiry should not be separate but is instead of the same motive and intent as any right-minded theological process.[64] Hence, for Willard, his philosophical pursuit allows him to engage at the base level of essential questions of life and living, which supports and conjoins with his theological interest. In some ways, Willard seems to understand and propose that a robust theology would and could reclaim its once lofty perch as the "queen of the sciences."

Unlike the classical definition or description of onto-theology used by Kant and Heidegger, this work uses the term "theo-ontology" to communicate Willard's argument that God's existence and nature are central or essential to all "being," including all creation. In taking a position that tends to combine the Kantian notions of revelation and reason, Willardian theology proposes that the world or cosmos, and everything in it, derives its subsistence specifically from the existence and will of God. Therefore, knowledge of God and his kingdom directly enhances and explicates human existence and living. For Willard, this is not a separate theological pursuit but is a pursuit of the nature and condition of existence or being for all "things" in the cosmos. Hence, Willardian theology reasserts a logocentric priority, one that holds all things stem from an external point of reference. This point of reference and origin is God, or the *Logos,* as described earlier.

Using this definition and understanding of theo-ontology, Willard posits that Jesus' articulation of the kingdom of God endeavors to describe the nature and functionality of all reality and existence. This includes the physical and spiritual realms, embodied personal powers (spirits), disembodied personal powers, and embodied non-personal powers. In all, for Willard, there appears to be very little cause for separating the goals and pursuits of

64. Some, like Jeffery Robbins, have attempted to put back together what Heidegger endeavored to rend apart. See Robbins, "The Problem of Ontotheology."

metaphysics, ontology, and theology in conjunction with the pursuit of the kingdom of God. The only significant methodological distinction may be found in his proclivity toward pursuing biblically theological understandings of anthropology and pneumatology described earlier. In this regard, what a human being "is" existentially, and can become ontologically, must be understood and guided first and foremost by the Scripture's depiction of God and his kingdom ethos. Willard argues the realm of God's rule and reign (kingdom) is where humanity discovers and achieves its highest and best potential. Furthermore, the nature and type of such an existential condition inside the kingdom of God is also both an ontological and theological pursuit within the biblical account. Hence, the two disciplines are here conjoined in hyphenation. The inversion of the word from ontotheology to theo-ontology is due to Willard's primacy on all existence emanating from God.[65]

Willard understands the gospel of Jesus as singularly focused on describing and articulating the possibility and nature of a spiritual reality that enables an embodied spiritual existence in relationship to and under the sustaining authority of God. Willard sees Jesus never wavering nor becoming distracted from articulating and manifesting the kingdom of God as an invisible (spiritual) reality, seen working largely through the implementation and application of words and ideas that transform hearts and minds through the illumination of a vision of, and experience with, the present reality of God and his love. When the truth and experience of this reality begin to coalesce to the point where understanding is built and confident action is applied to these truths, lives become progressively transformed and knowledge is accumulated.[66] Thus, the gospel is inseparable and uniquely characteristic of the spiritual, theo-ontological manifestation of life within the realm of God in this present world.

The assumption and hope for citizens in God's kingdom is to progressively become people who understand the purpose of their lives and direct their will toward the objectives and vision of God as co-laborers in his world. This is, of course, not the result depicted in the Genesis story regarding the fall from the theo-ontological state within the Garden of Eden. Therefore, Jesus is seen re-focusing and re-introducing the original theo-ontological hope for humanity that Willard believes anyone should find

65. In *Knowing Christ Today,* Willard makes a first-cause argument, suggesting there must be a non-physical originator of the material universe. Whatever caused the universe to exist must therefore have been "greater" than that which it created. The ability to initiate activity without oneself having been caused is also tied to the "unmoved mover" proposition. This is precisely the quality Willard ascribes to the God of Christianity. See chapter four Willard, *Knowing Christ Today.*

66. DC, 25–33.

> . . . in every respect—wise, beautiful, powerful, and good—that they would constantly see to be in [God's] presence and be guided, instructed, and helped by him in every aspect of their lives. For he is indeed the living head of the community of prayerful love across all time and space.[67]

Discipleship to Jesus, becoming a student pursuing his theo-ontological platform, is then "the very heart of the gospel. The really good news for humanity is that Jesus is now taking students in the master class of life. The eternal life that begins with confidence in Jesus is a life in his present kingdom, now on earth and available to all."[68]

Willard highlights two parts involved in learning the ways and means of the kingdom of God for a disciple of Jesus. First, the kingdom ethos is demonstrated through God's action to reveal his existence and efficacy to humanity both generally through the material, physical world and more specifically, in a person's heart and mind. While the intent is the same, divine revelation, whether general or specific, can happen in several ways and through innumerable means. Secondly, one must learn to place confidence in Jesus, which motivates one to seek understanding on what and how to become the kind of person with the internal character Jesus both carried and demonstrated in his life, words, and deeds.

> Faith is confidence grounded in reality, not a wild, desperate leap. It is as Hebrews 11:1 says, substance, and evidence or proof, not as contemporary translations usually have it, subjective psychological states such as "being sure of" or "having conviction of." Rather faith sees the reality of the unseen or invisible and it includes a readiness to act as if the good anticipated in hope were already in hand because of the reality of God.[69]

This confidence funds the discipleship pursuit of developing a Christlike character in every aspect of the disciple's world. The discipleship process represents what Willard calls spiritual formation into Christlike character. It is accomplished through the combined application of the spiritual disciplines and the infusion of God's sustaining grace.[70] Such a disposition draws or distracts effort and time away from the physical realities common in ev-

67. DC, 273.

68. DC, vxii.

69. ROH, 129.

70. The primary spiritual disciplines are silence and solitude, prayer and study. These are not all of the disciplines but are those initially essential in order to dispose the heart for accepting God's communication and thus begin the process of understanding and experiencing the spiritual reality of his will and way.

eryday life. Thus, the will must decide and intend to enter into God's vision for life and living. This is the call Willard sees Jesus offering to his disciples in the first century, and it is no different a call today.

A Vision of a Perfected Humanity

Willard's protoevangelical theo-ontology situates the gospel as offering humanity a second opportunity to live again in intimate relationship and fellowship with God as "children of light" in his kingdom.[71] The New Testament gospels demonstrate Jesus re-opening the potential for God to act with or tangibly empower persons who desire and are prepared to conform their will toward his ends. Willard defines this as acting "in his name."[72] Jesus' message (gospel) makes possible, and argues for, the beneficence of such a life "with God." The notion of "Children of Light" carries forward this concept and extends the "with God" existence toward an eschatological perspective which suggests,

> According to the biblical picture the function of human history is to bring forth an immense community of people from every nation and tribe and tongue and people (Rev 14:6) who will be a kingdom of priests under God (Rev 1:6, 5:10 Exod 19:6) and who for some period of time in the future, will actually govern the earth under [God]. They will also, beyond that, reign with him in the eternal future of the cosmos, forever and ever (Rev. 22:5).
>
> . . . What the human heart now vaguely senses should be, eventually will be, in the cosmic triumph of Christ and his people.
>
> . . . And those that have taken on the character of Christ—those children of light in Paul's language—will in eternity be empowered by God to do what they want, as free creative agents. And it will always harmonize perfectly with God's own purposes.[73]

While on earth, through spiritual formation and discipleship to Christ, a disciple encounters a

> . . . constant movement toward the eternal appointment God placed upon each of us in our creation—the kingdom prepared for you from the foundation of the world. (Matthew 25:34) This movement forward is now carried on through our

71. ROH, 218.

72. Willard, "Who Is Your Teacher?"

73. ROH, 218.

> apprenticeship to Jesus Christ. It is a process of character transformation toward complete trustworthiness before God.[74]

Disciples are thus people still imperfect in every sense of the term. They do not live in a perfect world and also live in the world imperfectly. Yet, they are uniquely different from those who do not live from the same source and are aware of the spiritual realm of God's kingdom. As such, disciples of Jesus are understood to "be" different, specifically through determining or adjudicating their unique motives, intentions, behavior and abilities. However, it is not simply the pose they strike. Rather, the difference is found always on the "inside of their life. It lies in what they are in their depths."[75] Thus, the heart, the spirit, or the will forms the nature and character of the person which affects everything produced in thought, word, and deed. Disciples of Christ are both becoming and being transformed in their "inner most parts" into individuals who are existentially and progressively emblematic of the same nature and substance of the character of Christ.

Thus, redemption or restoration is a holistic reality. Here, Willard's very detailed description of the dimensions of the human self, each with his or her own unique but symbiotic characteristics, becomes very instructive. Each dimension—the spirit, mind, body, relationships, and soul—are progressively changed or transformed (converted) as they come into increasing transparency and submission to the knowledge and will of God. This results in a restored, transformed, and transforming person who no longer engages denial, sensuality, and self-deification as a *de facto* or *a priori* position. Instead, the heart and mind are becoming, and have become, increasingly confident, ready, and willing to rely on the ethos, provisions, and empowerments of a loving and relational God and his kingdom.

Willard's definition and description of the theo-ontological realm of God's kingdom reveals his philosophical realist perspective. He understands the kingdom of God to be the "effective range of God's will." Thus, the kingdom is where God is currently or actively reigning. Perhaps one could say it is where God is actually in control or wherever what God wants and desires is accomplished. This brings an interesting potential dilemma into the orthodox understanding of the doctrine of God's omnipotent ability. To state that God's kingdom is where he "reigns" is to equally recognize there are places and people where God's rule and reign does not extend, or where God's will is not currently applied. Certainly one can assume from the activities of contemporary life, both now and in the past, there are conditions and circumstances which it would appear what God would want to occur

74. ROH, 218.

75. Ibid.

does not and has not occurred. Thus, the question arises if God is in fact fully in control and omnipotent.

In response, Willard states God is sovereign over, but not necessarily actively in control of, every aspect of reality. Thus, Willard delineates God's omnipotent ability from its actuality.[76] He states, "The kingdom [of God] is to be sharply contrasted with the kingdom of man: the realm of human life, that tiny part of visible reality where the human will, for a time, has some degree of sway, even contrary to God's will." And again,

> God does not like to be present where he is not wanted. And he knows when he is wanted and when he is not. Similarly, where people are really seeking a response from someone else, he does not intrude—generally speaking. So when our aim is [something other than God' will] he lets us do that and stands aside. Of course, he will eventually have his day. There will be a "day of the Lord," his turn at bat, as it were.[77]

Further, Willard defines a "reign" as where a certain will or governance is effectuated. As such, every person has a reign, a range, or environ where their will is put into place and actively engaged or imputed. Thus, Willard understands Jesus' statement "the kingdom of God is within you" to communicate that the individual will is the deciding factor as to whether the kingdom of God will be manifested in a human life. Moreover, the ethos of the kingdom of God is as close or as far away from the individual as their individual choices allow. Therefore, as intimated above, there are competing "kingdoms" and wills that exist today, many of which are seen and experienced in action, and some of which actively oppose God's will and kingdom desire.

In discussing the issue of the human kingdom and its effective range of influence, it is important to remember how Willard's anthropological and pneumatological understandings discussed earlier are built upon and are more fully illustrated when considering how the human person interacts

76. In recent years, the conversation regarding open theism has gained increasing interest, controversy, and coverage in American evangelical theology. Although it is not necessary to label Willard an open theist, there are parts of his theology, specifically his value of human volition and participation in God's kingdom, that are similar to those issues within some theologians articulating an open theist position. Willard does not find it necessary to assume such labels per se. But some similarities exist in overarching views if not in specific dogmas. See articles in Editorial, "God Vs. God," *Christianity Today*, February 2000; Coffman, "Open Debate in the Openness Debate"; Smith, "What God Knows"; Olson, "ETS Leadership Issues Recommendations on Kicking Out Open Theists."

77. DC, 190.

with these realities in God's kingdom and in light of the *essentia Dei* of the gospel of Jesus.

Therefore, Willard suggests that the human kingdom has a choice which kingdom it will serve—either the kingdom of darkness or the kingdom of light. When the human and satanic kingdoms join in cooperation, Willard suggests there is little they cannot accomplish. Perhaps the best description of these two kingdoms working in tandem to accomplish an incredible feat is described in the trial, conviction, and crucifixion of Jesus.[78] Here, Willard suggests Mel Gibson's artistic portrayal of *The Passion* represents well the classical Christian understanding of redemption. This redemption is from the human condition of lostness and evil that is "actually present in human life" and can become vastly oppositional to the theo-ontological presence and reality of God and his reign. Further, the kingdom of light offers redemption or rescue from the effects and consequences of evil in order to provide humanity an escape from the results of their disastrous destiny.

Christology

After what has already been discovered about Willardian thought and theology, one can see how central and essential his Christology must be to sustain his sense of the *Essentia Dei*, his theo-ontological view of the kingdom of God and discipleship into such a living reality. One might suggest that Christology is central to all Christian theology in some measure or form. Yet, this is never more true than in Willardian theology. Therefore, this section will consider Willard's perspectives on the life and ministry of Jesus of Nazareth and the implications these positions have on his theological project. It will also consider the different view Willardian Christology takes when compared to what Willard himself considers as mainstream or populist evangelical Christology.

Jesus as Master

In Willard's view of discipleship, an apprentice (learner, student) is positioned to ascertain both wisdom and/or skills from a master. This was the accepted understanding of the disciple/rabbi relationship described in the gospel records.[79] Students in rabbinic relationships were devoted to gar-

78. Willard, "The Craftiness of Christ."

79. This view is validated by Witherington, *The Christology of Jesus*; Longenecker,

nering knowledge about the world they lived in and how knowledge of God and the Hebrew Scriptures presented wisdom and insight into those subjects and circumstances. However, in addition to learning information, there was a significant directive and understanding that students would and should emulate their rabbi's ways.[80] In Willardian Christology, the historically biblical understanding of the rabbi/disciple relationship has significant implications when approaching the teaching context of Jesus. His teaching and commandments regarding the knowledge and wisdom of God and his kingdom were never considered merely informational or doctrinal by Jesus' disciples. Jesus is seen conveying expertise on subjects both he and his disciples expect will be manifested as realities in their lives.

Willard suggests the single most differentiating factor of Jesus' rabbinic method, which gave him the authority and credibility to teach, especially when teaching concepts that went against conventional wisdom of the day, was garnered through his ability to tap into then demonstrate an overarching spiritual power embedded in the kingdom of God. Willard suggests these demonstrative "miraculous" insights into the kingdom reality came in three ways. The first demonstration Jesus provided was in his physical manifestation of the kingdom through healings and super-natural miracles. The second means Jesus used to reveal the kingdom was through the proclamation or preaching of the kingdom ethos with rhetorical skill. The third means Jesus used was his teaching, or explication, of kingdom ethos. Here he employed reason, logic, history, and psychology in his pedagogical tasks. Each of these means, the miraculous, the rhetorical, and the explicative, in Willard's view, reveals Jesus as a master teacher who is competent to lead and advise others into all potentialities of human life.

> Quite simply, his work and teaching, as well as the main path of historical Christianity that sprang from him, is essentially based upon the substantial reality of the spirit and of the spiritual world. They cannot be separated from it. . . . [O]ur commitment to Jesus can stand on no other foundation than a recognition that he is the one who knows the truth about our lives and our universe. It is not possible to trust Jesus, or anyone else, in matters where we do not believe him to be competent. We cannot pray for his help and rely on his collaborations in dealing with real life matters we suspect might defeat his knowledge or abilities.[81]

Patterns of Discipleship in the New Testament; and Longenecker, *The Christology of Early Jewish Christianity*.

80. Kasemann, *Commentary on Romans*, 180–82.

81. DC, 94.

As a result, faith in Jesus—for a first century disciple—was not produced from Jesus' position as a well-established or influential rabbi. In like measure, today faith should not proceed exclusively from the doctrinal claim regarding Jesus' position as savior of the world, or even the primacy of faith in the event of his resurrection from the dead. Instead, Willard asserts that confidence in Jesus should proceed from trusting him as a competent, verifiable master and guide into the vagaries of all human existence and endeavor. This would include placing confidence in Jesus' own claims regarding his divinity and his resurrection. But belief in only these two propositional doctrines is not, in Willard's view, positioning confidence in Jesus as the holistic Christ offering a total whole life soteriology proclaimed in Scripture.

> Those who are not genuinely convinced that the only real bargain in life is surrendering ourselves to Jesus and his cause, abandoning all that we live to him and for him, cannot learn the other lessons Jesus had to teach us. They cannot proceed to anything like total spiritual transformation. Not that he will not let us, but that we simply cannot succeed.[82]

Willard then goes on to explain how Jesus justifies himself as a master of all life and living. This includes mastery of the physical, moral, and rational realms of life. We will now consider Jesus as a master physicist, moralist, logician, teacher, and guide.

Jesus as Physicist

Much of the previous sections that discuss pneumatology, anthropology, and theo-ontology have adequately covered the issues and aspects that demonstrate Jesus' mastery of both the spiritual and physical realms. There is, therefore, no need to restate those insights here. Suffice to say, Willard suggests that Jesus' teaching and ministry displays mastery over the pneumatological realm and its interface with the physical world. He also demonstrates a full understanding of how the human being is to live and interact with the synergy of the spiritual and physical realms.

Willard argues Jesus primarily demonstrates his expertise in the realm of the physical universe through the manifestations of his super-natural ability to affect or suspend the laws of nature and physics. At the mundane level, Jesus was in possession of the knowledge of how to manipulate water—at the molecular, atomic, or subatomic level—in order to transform it into wine. It is the same type and structure of knowledge that also allowed

82. ROH, 66.

Jesus to multiply a small lunch of bread and fish into a feast capable of feeding thousands. "He could create matter from the energy he knew how to access from the 'heavens' right where he was."[83] Additionally, this ability to access the power of the "unseen" realm allowed him to calm the seas and change weather patterns. He also demonstrated the ability to engage both the physical and spiritual realms simultaneously as demonstrated on the Mount of Transfiguration. The healing miracles manifested his knowledge and capacity to transform human tissues in the body from that of sickness to health, and death into life. The resurrection demonstrated Jesus' control or mastery over death even in his own body.[84]

Jesus as Moralist

In addition to displaying mastery over the physical and spiritual realms, Willard describes Jesus' mastery over moral knowledge, knowledge of good and evil, right and wrong.[85] In the arena of ethics, Willard suggests Jesus displays a form of expertise that elevates him beyond the greatest moralists of human history. He argues Jesus stands alone in the long line of philosophical and religious thinkers and teachers in his ability to provide the most astute and useful moral insights and answers to the most essential questions of well-being and well-doing—questions that have forever troubled and intrigued the greatest minds of every age. "Jesus provides the best answers to the most important questions of human life."[86]

The moral insights of Jesus invite the most careful intellectual and practical evaluation, side by side, with all other potential alternatives. Willard welcomes and encourages the challenging of any and every alternative philosophy or religious paradigm to an honest evaluation of effectiveness in application of Jesus' ethics on human life. After such scrutiny, Willard and others have concluded the teaching and wisdom of Jesus has had a unique and benevolent effect on the world at large. To bolster this view, Willard quotes Jürgen Habermas at length.

> Christianity has functioned for the normative self-understanding of modernity as more than a mere precursor or a catalyst. Egalitarian universalism, from which sprang the ideas of freedom and social solidarity, of an autonomous conduct of life and

83. DC, 95.

84. Willard gives a very interesting and detailed logical description of the veracity of the miraculous claims ascribed to Jesus in KCT, 117–38.

85. Willard, "Beyond Moral Bewilderment."

86. Ibid.

> emancipation, of the individual morality of conscience, human rights, and democracy, is the direct heir to the Judaic ethic of justice and Christian ethic of love. This legacy, substantially unchanged, has been the object of continual critical appropriation and reinterpretation. To this day, there is no alternative to it. And in light of the current challenges of postnational constellation, we continue to draw on the substance of this heritage. Everything else is just idle postmodern talk.[87]

δικαιοσύνη

Specifically, Willard suggests the unique moral knowledge Jesus offers is specifically directed toward human flourishing. Jesus articulates that well-being, or the "abundant life," is discovered and maintained through engaging in an interactive communion with God. All other means of attaining goodness or flourishing—whether that be through material or financial wealth, power, reputation, fame, or sensual gratification—will eventually and inevitably fall short. Therefore, Jesus presents the ideal "good person" as one worthy of love, support, imitation, and companionship in all things. Willard suggests such a person and condition are encompassed in Jesus' description of a life and character permeated with the same substance and essence of agape love which God himself maintains.

> This person is the one who steps forward into leadership and the professional life with the character and strength to translate the highest ideals into reality. And Jesus tell us that the way into all of the intelligent well-being and well-doing is through becoming his apprentice, right where we are, in kingdom living. We learn to lead our lives with him, thereby learning to live our lives as he would if he were we.[88]

Willard recognizes that such a life is not unique to the Judeo-Christian philosophy and theology. The Greeks understood the ethical or virtuous life as *dikaiosune* (δικαιοσύνη) from the word *díkaios,* meaning just or righteous. In the case of the non-Christ follower, such as Plato and Aristotle, the term would suggest a higher form of ethics that a person adopts as his own standard. *Dikaiosúnē* is therefore a manifestation of conformity to the claims of a higher authority.[89]

87. Habermas, *Time of Transitions*, 150–51. In KCT, 220.

88. Ibid.

89. DC, 144–46. It is the essence of *tó díkaion*, that which is just, or *díkaios*, of him

This appears to be what Willard offers as his understanding of the ancient Greek version of *virtue.* In fact, virtue is what Willard suggests is the desire of Plato's *Republic.* "Plato—following Socrates—tries to give a precise and full account of what true inner goodness is."[90] Willard believes Plato, seeking the means to develop human virtue, understood such a disposition of character was necessary for his vision of how human beings could live well and manage to do right. Aristotle, too, translated or reinterpreted *dikaiosune* into *arête,* or virtue. Virtue was thought to communicate the "combination of skill, wisdom, power, and steadfastness for good that makes it very attractive."[91] The difference in the Greek usage and the biblical usage Willard believes is the connection that *dikaiosune* has with the character of God. Whereas the classical Greek understanding of *arête* predominantly stresses human ability and fulfillment alone.

This distinction becomes important when juxtaposing the old and the new morality Jesus offers in the New Testament.[92] In the Sermon on the Mount, Jesus walks through the previous understanding of *dikaiosune* in the OT and the new *dikaiosune* of the kingdom of God.[93] In this redefinition, Willard senses Jesus is describing a new position on morality. The moral issues at hand that Jesus covers through the entirety of the Sermon on the Mount are the essential dilemmas that span the breadth of human life. Nearly all of these issues involve the nature of human interaction. Jesus discusses issues related to troubled relationships (Matt 5:21–26), sexual desire (5:27–30), marriage relationships (5:31–32), inappropriate manipulation of relationships with words (5:33–37), personal injury (5:38–42), and dealing with one's enemies (5:43–48).[94] In each of these instances, Jesus is seen comparing the old paradigm of righteous or moral thought as a means of dealing with these issues and contrasts it to his kingdom vision and the new moral outlook therein.

The old moral code was to simply perform the proper act according to the law. Thus, the outward behavior had become the final determining

---

who is just or righteous. The *súnē* ending makes this an abstraction. Righteousness thus fulfills the claims of *díkē*, which, in the case of the believer, are God's claims to righteousness and his just ways. Zodhiates, *The Complete Word Study Dictionary.*

90. DC, 145.

91. Ibid.

92. DC, 144–46.

93. In the Septuagint, the Hebrew Scriptures use *dikaiosune* to translate the Hebrew word צְדָקָה (*tsĕdāqâ*), usually translated into English as "righteousness." This root basically connotes conformity to an ethical or moral standard. Harris et al., *Theological Wordbook of the Old Testament*, 752.

94. Willard and Foster, "Marriage and Divorce."

factor of appropriate *dikaiosune*. Conversely, the new code Jesus instigates deals specifically with how life can be imagined and exemplified if the overarching ethic of love and benevolence, and not simply the reduction of outward behavior, is the motivating impetus behind the moral imperative. Jesus is seen replacing behavioral compliance with *agape* love as the primal motivating source and determiner for *dikaiosune*. It becomes appropriate for Jesus to then systematically inspect the things that prevent *agape* from overtaking one's heart. This he does in the sermon by discussing anger, sexual desire, etc.[95]

Therefore as a realist, moralist, ethicist, or philosopher, Willard advocates the careful, yet active comparisons of Jesus' moral imperatives and the reality such impositions produce, against any and all alternatives in order to properly gauge their effectiveness. The lack of attention to such comparisons in much of modern evangelical theology and practice today, Willard suggests, is in part due to the disappearance of moral knowledge in society overall. He presented several reasons for this perspective in a forthcoming work on the disappearance of moral knowledge.[96]

To briefly state his position here, Willard suggests that the knowledge institutions of modernity have largely acquiesced the responsibility for carrying forward moral knowledge.[97] However, in Willard's view, if tested against other competing moral systems or claims, Jesus' moral vision can be validated as offering a solution to the greatest moral dilemmas that have previously eluded the greatest of western philosophers. "The centuries-long attempt to devise a morality from within merely human resources has now proven itself a failure."[98] Furthermore, as a long-standing tenured professor in philosophy, Willard observed how the academy and the project of education in general engages the discussion and discovery of what is good, ethical, best, and true. He sensed that modern education tends to leave students with the information about such matters without ever teaching what is required to either *be* good or how to become a person who does what is good, ethical, best, and true. Such a dearth in moral education, in Willard's

95. Willard, "Beyond Pornography."

96. This is to be published posthumously. See also KCT, chapter 3.

97. In addition to the above mentioned chapter in KCT, Willard has written extensively about the loss of moral knowledge and the loss of the concept of objective truth in the modern academy today. His works include, Willard, "Truth: Can We Do Without It?"; Willard, "The University's Responsibility for Moral Guidance"; Willard, "How Reason Can Survive the Modern University: The Moral Foundations of Rationality"; Willard, "Observations on Current Leadership Issues in Higher Education"; Willard, and, "Beyond Moral Bewilderment: Where is Moral Knowledge?"

98. DC, 185.

view, is to suggest and advocate for the non-existence of such realities. Here, Willard saw the moral project of Jesus as offering a great hope and insight to an otherwise amoral or immoral social imaginary.

Jesus as Logician

In addition to the mastery of the physical and moral realms, Willard also suggests Jesus displays a mastery of logic and reason.[99] In connecting both the moral and logical, Willard offers the opinion that to be moral is equally to be logical. One must try to be logical if one is to attempt to be moral as well. Therefore, Jesus presents himself not only as moral, but equally, as a logician—the smartest person who ever lived.[100] To this end, Willard quotes moral historian W. E. H. Lecky as suggesting Jesus presented "an agency which all men must now admit to have been, for good or for evil, the most powerful moral lever that has ever been applied to the affairs of man."[101] Further, Willard notes scholar Michael Grant who states,

> The most potent figure, not only in the history of religion, but in world history as a whole, is Jesus Christ: the maker of one of the few revolutions which have lasted. Millions of men and women for century after century have found his life and teaching overwhelmingly significant and moving. And there is ample reason . . . in this later twentieth century which this should still be so.[102]

Willard admits the proposition that Jesus was the most intelligent individual that ever walked the planet often elucidates an ironic response, something that often appears, to some, as a sort of mis-categorization. To even consider Jesus as such an individual of worth, warrant and consideration of such a title illustrates a contradiction in terms for many modern minds. Willard contends that modern philosophers, even nominally Christian philosophers such as Immanuel Kant and Freidrich Hegel, played a major role in creating doubt as to the intellectual capacity of religion in general and Jesus' teachings in specific. Further, the search for the "historical Jesus" and the assumption of Jesus as nothing more than an uneducated yet wise peasant sage has exacerbated this problem.

99. Willard, "Jesus the Logician," 605–14.

100. DC, 95.

101. Lecky, *History of European morals*, 338.

102. Grant, *Jesus: A Historians Review of the Gospels*, 1.

Contrary to the modern view, Willard argues against the proposition that knowledge, and a proper understanding of reality that is based upon reason and logic, is an endeavor wholly separate from Christian faith and practice. He posits that modernism, humanism, philosophical constructivism, pluralism, relativism, and secularism have proven incapable of forging a foundation for reason, logic, or truth. Therefore,

> To not see Jesus as smart, brilliant, intelligent, as one might consider Bill Gates, Warren Buffet, Einstein, Plato or other notable intellects of this or any previous generation is to put a "death knell" on discipleship, for it locates (Jesus) outside the company of those who have knowledge and therefore deprives us of the practical power of his teachings.[103]

Jesus as Teacher

It follows then, based on the mastery displayed in the previous arenas of life, Jesus assumes the role and authority of a teacher. Throughout Willard's work, the most consistent and common description or vision he provides for Jesus is as a teacher of life and living. As a career teacher himself, Willard sees in Jesus' pedagogy the marks of a master instructor at work. He laments the loss of the overarching perspective of Jesus as a master teacher within more conservative streams of modern evangelicalism today. He asserts this loss can be traced to the liberal/fundamentalist clash in the early twentieth century. Liberal theologians began to discuss the benefits of Jesus' significantly limited role as only a teacher of moral living and not also the divine Son of God. This caused a "knee-jerk" reaction from many conservative evangelicals who began to hear the label "teacher" as a code word for "only human."[104] Willard quotes Thomas Ogden as stating, "it becomes difficult if not impossible to build a plausible Christology out of a naïve, mistaken, hapless, or ignorant Jesus."[105] As a result, Willard senses that whatever teaching is done in modern Christian churches, there is little effort and sometimes opposition to the idea of teaching people what Jesus taught. Nor is there a focus on how to actually put into practice such an education if it were to be presented in the first place. Willard sees this deficiency as a direct result of the lack of respect given to Jesus as a master of anything.

103. DC, 131.

104. DC, 55.

105. Ibid.

Instead of taking the common strategy of lecture and the profession of facts and information the instructor believes are essential for the student to grasp, Jesus applies a teaching approach that maintains a lasting and impactful impression on his students. In using parables, Jesus literally "lays one thing down beside another" and entreats the students and listeners to consider the implications of the two seemingly equal choices. As a result, Jesus is often seen re-directing the vision of the student's imagination or experience indirectly or implicitly. Such an approach often bypasses the more confrontational or combative style Willard recognizes within much of the contemporary models of preaching and teaching today.

Additionally, Willard admires Jesus' use of analogy and imagination to speak to the heart of an issue, even when such an approach leaves some listeners confused or unfulfilled. Jesus teaches in this manner purposefully, requiring the students to choose to pursue and probe deeper into the subject or issue, engaging the will, and not only the mind or intellect. This approach continually requires the student to demonstrate his or her own motivation in order to uncover the deeper truths available only to those who seek fuller understanding. Unlike much of our contemporary education, Jesus is not primarily concerned with the transmission of information. Rather, Jesus teaches in such a way that those who are driven to seek for the truth and benefits of his teachings, and are equally willing to apply these lessons to their daily lives, must demonstrate the strength of will to hear, see, pursue, and apply such knowledge. The pursuit of knowledge becomes as essential as its attainment. This affects the internal character of the student, which is both built and revealed in the quest for knowledge itself.

Jesus as Guide

After teaching and representing himself as a master of all the previously listed subject areas, Willard understands Jesus as presenting himself as a competent guide, directing followers by example, as to what a character formed and a mind enlightened to the kingdom ethic can do in a God permeated world. For Willard, Jesus still seeks to engage with his follower, in the form of his Spirit, through relational learning, to exemplify and model the appropriate interactions and involvements in the concrete occasions of day-to-day activities. This interactive relationship is what Willard understands as the process of acting "in his name," which is synonymous to "in his authority" or "with his power."

Through the act of prayer, Willard believes God's cooperative power and guidance are enacted. The interactive, communicative, joint project of leading one's life, as it were, becomes the main topic and purpose of prayer. Through prayer, decisions are pondered, knowledge is accumulated, wisdom is provided, direction is gathered, and requests are made. Prayer then becomes the central means by which an individual gathers guidance and discernment in order to effectively "rule" over his or her will and participate with God in the sphere of influence he or she maintains. Through the means of prayer, Willard sees God forming a "power-sharing arrangement with humanity."[106]

In prayer, God desires to complement and engage with the actions and motives of citizens in his kingdom while his followers are simultaneously endeavoring to conform their will to the ethos of the kingdom of God. Willard calls this the "why" of prayer and represents it as the empowerment of life in the kingdom of God. Prayer, then, is understood as the "communication between God and human beings about what is being done together. Fundamentally, prayer is asking, but, of course, only as part of an overall walk with God in which our business is his business and his is ours."[107]

Willard also quotes C. S. Lewis' statement that, "Prayer is talking to God about what we are now doing together. Prayer is action."[108] In contrast to those consistently engaged in prayer, Willard suggests that those who do not pray, yet still expect to be living in the kingdom life, are those who have not yet developed or attained confidence in God at all. To not pray is to reveal a substantive lack of confidence (faith) in God as a master for life. Thus, Willard suggests a person in such a condition remains unwilling or unable to enact God's will and way in the confines of everyday life. As such, one simply cannot bring God, nor can God bring them, into the intimate confidences of a kingdom life and its purposes. In such a state, prayer is not considered a powerful and effective means of influence on God and his reality. Therefore, this state of mind is one of unbelief, or at best, belief in an impersonal god different from the *essentia Dei* described by Jesus.

However, one who has developed confidence in God as master and king over life, and seeks to engage in the power-sharing arrangement of being a steward of God's possessions and resources, is one who also progressively engages with the substance of grace. As mentioned earlier, grace is significant in Willardian theology. Prayer's power-sharing arrangement is the realm in which Willard's understanding of grace as the active participation of God in human affairs begins to congeal. God's grace is marked

106. This is one of Willard's positions that can appear similar to positions of some "open theists." Willard, *Fuller Seminary Doctoral Class* (6/16/2010).

107. Willard, *Fuller Seminary Doctoral Seminar Reader*, 90.

108. Lewis and Hooper, *God in the Dock*, 104.

by his participation and effect in human lives and activities that allow for accomplishment of that which human effort or talent alone could never achieve. Willard does accept the traditional definition of grace as God's "unmerited favor."[109] However, Willard does not subscribe to the idea that nothing of one's efforts can play a role in God's ongoing working in his kingdom. Instead, Willard suggests human ingenuity or effort is a necessary and indispensable component in a cooperative relationship with God. The goal of transformation of the will into conformity to Christ and his kingdom vision is the ability to empower human beings to accomplish everything they desire. In such a condition, what is desired is good and right. God's grace is, therefore, that component of divine interaction that spans the gap between the potential of desire and the actuality of achievement. The significance of character transformation plays the crucial role in the impetus of what desires are appropriate and beneficial. The role of the Holy Spirit is to guide and encourage disciples in this progression toward their fulfillment of their own potential in the kingdom ethos.

Ecclesiology

Finally, Willard posits the sociological implications of this anthropological/pneumatological/theo-ontological and Christological protoevangelical vision will result in an overarching renovation of first the church then the culture at large. Willard sees the church as those individuals gathered or called (*ecclesia*) of God into a discipleship relationship with Jesus who routinely congregate in local groups. In Willard's view, these congregations should look and feel much like hospitals—places where people gather to find healing, honest reflection and feedback, restorative therapeutic assistance, wisdom, correction, and guidance toward regaining the functionality of their intended destiny.[110] The church is also the primary avenue wherein discipleship is advocated, learned, and taught. It is a place one can develop their confidence in Jesus' demonstrated life-way, and where the abundant life can be both encountered and encouraged. Thus, the church represents people gathering in all stations of the journey toward Christ-likeness, needing assistance with various struggles, and ministering in various capacities.

The question of how the church is to go about organizing and pursuing this protoevangelical vision is represented in the previously discussed concepts of vision, intention and means, captured in Willard's acronym VIM.[111]

109 Grudem, *Systematic Theology: An Introduction.*

110. ROH, 234.

111. See pages 72–75.

Willard suggests the church can and must pursue the establishment and maintenance of the kingdom of God through applying the VIM rationale. Just as Jesus demonstrated to the first-century disciples, the Holy Spirit of Jesus still encourages and guides the believer through a consistent transformative process that defines and encapsulates the VIM pattern. Through applying this same process, Willard believes any person or group can develop the habits that will lead to the process of consistent transformation, which is guided and encouraged every step of the way by the presence and grace of Christ. We will now consider how Willard perceived each of the three steps in the VIM process should intersect with ecclesial life.

The *Vision* of the Church

As discussed earlier, Willard asserts that Jesus' first step of ministry was the articulation and demonstration of a vision or an overarching description of what life in the kingdom of God would "look like." Jesus is seen both talking about and encouraging people to reconsider their views of God *(metanoia)*, their understanding of the purpose of their faith, their religious beliefs, their relationships, and their expectations of themselves.[112] Willard views much of Jesus' work in the first-century context as focused specifically on deconstructing then reconstructing a vision of God's *missio Dei*, which many first-century Jews appear to have lost sight of entirely or had perhaps never considered in specific detail. In recasting a vision, Jesus allows his would-be followers to imagine, before they place confidence in him, what life could be like when applying his ethos to their circumstances.

A vision of what is possible, seen in Jesus' use of parables and analogies (the kingdom of God is like . . .), puts listeners in a position where they can compare the life they have against the one purposed. The consideration of the alternative is essential to Jesus' ethical foundations, due to the great value placed on the individual will. Therefore, Willard believes vision is the vital first step in the process of enacting lasting change. Equally then, the loss of such a vision can be devastating and destructive to the change desired.

This is a primary and essential aspect to church life. Throughout the ministries, services, worship, sacraments, fellowship, preaching, hymnody, and teaching of the church, an overarching and all encompassing, holistic vision of life in the kingdom of God must be cast. The next chapter will consider in greater detail what effect the diminishment of such a vision has made on contemporary evangelicals. However, Willard believed the church is to be the keeper and first propagator of the gospel vision Jesus

112. See page 70.

proclaimed and manifested. Kingdom life, both personally and collectively, is to be understood and manifested first in the body of Christ and through its many ancillary functions. Willard interpreted Jesus' metaphor comparing disciples as "lights" who collectively form a "city on a hill," as a direct reference to the purpose and effect of an *ecclesia* or church. He argued a first-century understanding of the word *ecclesia* was simply a group of like-minded persons gathering together for a common purpose. For Willard, a Christian *ecclesia's* purpose is to illuminate, for all to see, the benefits of a flourishing life available in God's will and ways. Jesus understood such persons, or witnesses, are crucial to the establishment and proliferation of the common good. Therefore, disciples cannot be hidden and must not hide their knowledge of God and his good ways of life and living (Matt 5:14-16).

The *Intention* of the Church

After a proper vision of what the kingdom of God both constitutes and offers is properly and clearly articulated, a decision must follow. This is Willard's understanding of intention. Jesus describes the necessity of making an intentional decision as inexplicably tied to the process of repentance *(metanoia).* Willard often refers to instances in Scripture where Jesus encounters individuals and situations wherein it is discovered that, despite their impressions or religious activities, in fact, no explicit decision regarding the reality and truth Jesus has occured. Some biblical examples Willard uses are found in the meeting of Jesus and Nicodemus, Peter's denial of Christ, Paul's conversion, James and John's desire to rule at "Jesus' right hand", the rich young ruler, the man who asks to leave Jesus to bury his father, and even Jesus' own family. In these instances, the true motives or intentions of so-called "followers" are revealed. Their intentions of creating the means of achieving their own vision of life while prescribing their motives to the pious religious devotions become exposed for what they are. These examples reveals a dichotomy between intellectual ascent to a set of facts and the intended move of the heart to actually fulfill the demands of submitting the individual will in obedience to God.

Willard recognizes the many obstacles that can prevent the fulfillment of a decision. Circumstances arise that make the decision difficult or seemingly impossible. But equally important, and perhaps more prevalent, are the hidden habits, procrastinations, relational forces, rationalizations, and inappropriate beliefs that become the greatest inhibitors to the achievement of intended goals. However, at its base, it is not these factors alone that finally and ultimately prevent the kind of Christian life available in the kingdom of

God. Ultimately, Willard senses people may wish for life in the kingdom, or even think it best for themselves and others and, therefore, honestly express their wish for such a life to come upon them. However, what remains missing is the power of an intentional decision. "They did not decide to do it, and their intentions—which may well have begun to develop—are aborted and never really formed."[113]

Therefore, the church serves as a place where followers of Christ hold one lovingly accountable in discerning the level and presence of intentionality in following Christ. Without relationship and community, one can escape the vital reality of submitting the will. Too often, one may stop at the level of mere profession of belief in the veracity of Jesus and his kingdom. In contrast, any confidence in Christ, and the committed intention it can and should manifest, must be robustly inseparable to a decision of the will. The fruit of such a decision must necessarily follow in due course. Anything less is, by definition, less than a decision. Hence, the primary means of discerning one's intentional and faithful commitment is found in the symbiotic structure of common transparent living as part of the body of Christ. This lack of intentionality, and the absence of open and honest accountability in communal life is where Willard finds the most pressing void within modern Christian ecclesiology.

Simply stated, modern Christianity is plagued by either a lackluster or misrepresentative vision of the kingdom and/or an absence of an intentional decision to follow and remain committed to the life and teachings of Jesus as a guide and confident master. Again, in a poignantly chilling statement:

> No one can actually believe the truth about [Jesus] without trusting him by intending to obey him. It is a mental impossibility. To think otherwise is to indulge a widespread illusion that now smothers spiritual formation in Christlikeness among professing Christians and prevents it from naturally spreading worldwide.[114]

Thus, Willard asserts that the gospel is much more than believing things about Jesus and God, however orthodox they might be. If profession of the desire to obey is not accompanied with the intention to do so, and no reasonable attempt is made to regularly validate the reality of this decision, there simply can be no convincing claim of any kind of confidence (faith) in Jesus' true identity, presence, or power at all. Therefore, the church must hold unwavering commitment to actually manifesting the realities of love, grace, peace, power, and joy they profess.

113. ROH, 88.

114. ROH, 87.

The *Means* of the Church

The means, in Willardian thought, are those activities or disciplines one employs to eventuate the decision of obedience to follow Jesus and enter his kingdom ethos. Once the vision and intention are solidified, means are a natural progression for how faith is grown and matured. The means' primary objective is to replace the inner character of the self with the character of Christ. As a result, Jesus' vision of the kingdom, his understanding and interaction with the *essentia Dei,* come into increasing relief in the disciple. Willard understands these means as widely available through "rich resources in the example of Jesus himself, in the Scriptures generally and in his people (the church)."[115] As a result of applying these means (spiritual disciplines), disciples will begin to demonstrate the effects of the kingdom ethos with increasing demonstrations of love, joy, peace, power, and grace.[116]

A full description of Willard's rationale for spiritual disciplines is presented in *The Spirit of the Disciplines.* To avoid redundancy, only a brief discussion of the importance Willard places on the disciplines for formation will be engaged here. He advocates for the implementation of spiritual disciplines for two basic reasons. First, the disciplines offer the opportunity for introspection and contemplation for the purposes of evaluation. Here, both individually and in relationship to others in the body of Christ, disciples first begin the process of uncovering the nature of who they are—good and bad, their feelings, thoughts, habits of will, social relations, and bodily dispositions that often stand against their intention of obeying Christ. Psychological, emotional, and spiritual inclinations toward anger or lust—along with inaccurate ideas about God, the nature of justice, one's "rights" or privileges, and expectations of others—are all examples of areas of the inner character that disciplines such as fasting, silence, solitude, prayer, and study will, by God's grace, gradually expose, in order to be acknowledged or confessed. This same grace can then be employed in working with the will to transform the disciple from one captured by anger or lust, for instance, into one increasingly consumed by the loving, forgiving, merciful ethics and ethos of the kingdom way.

Secondly, once the contemplative steps expose areas where growth is needed, these same disciplines can be useful in the retraining of the self, whether that be in the realm of ideas, emotions, relationships, bodily habits, etc. This is what Willard calls "off the spot" training. It is an intentional practice within one's control engaged in order to prepare for a moment that is not in

115. ROH, 89.

116. This is described both in the ROH, 85, and more specifically regarding Jesus as teacher in Willard, "Who is Your Teacher?"

one's control. This he calls "indirect effort," by which Willard means, one cannot plan in the moment how to react when, for instance, someone cuts them off on the highway. Such a response is considered instinctual. Yet, through the study and contemplation of Jesus, his teachings, his life, and meditation on both the proper and improper outcomes of such responses to unpleasant circumstances, Willard asserts Christians can and will begin to restructure the "instinctual" responses that at one time appeared beyond control. Thus, disciplines engaged both individually and corporately through church life are the means by which one consciously and explicitly practices "self-sacrificial" disciplines in less demanding, grace-filled situations that are "off the spot." These "practices," in concert with God's grace, soon transform "a person for whom looking out for number one is not the framework of my life."[117]

However, if there is no "will," Willard recognizes there is no "way." Those who do not intend to follow Jesus' expertise in the kingdom life will not be transformed, "no matter what means they think of themselves as employing, God is not going to pick us up by the seat of our pants, as it were, and throw us into transformed kingdom living, into holiness."[118] To think of grace as God doing everything required for the believer, as opposed to considering grace as the actions of God for that which one cannot accomplish on their own, separates a concept of grace that can paralyze as opposed to one that enables.

The VIM pattern of transformation is the sum total of what Willard understands as the mission of the church—"To equip the saints for the work of the ministry."[119] Willard suggests such activity and focus should be organized and accomplished through the local church, led and directed by pastors and teachers who cast a vision for the kingdom of God and manifest it in their lives. "Discipleship is for the church. Disciples are for the world."[120] This process is to carry on the work of Jesus himself, presenting unique knowledge of the *essentia Dei* and the *missio Dei* as a total and holistic worldview. *Knowing Christ Today* illustrates Willard's opinion that such a Christian worldview presents a gift of knowledge to the world at large. Therefore, the church should be a gift to all humanity.

For Willard, the church has the unique responsibility and privilege to be prepared by their leaders and teachers to share their experiential knowledge of Jesus and his kingdom with the world. In this process, every possible alternative source of knowledge must be appropriately considered,

117. ROH, 90.

118. ROH, 91.

119. ROH, 234.

120. Meyer, *Whole Life Transformation, intro.*

reviewed, and taken seriously. To do less would not only be unwise but distinctly un-Christlike since Jesus naturally desires for humanity to have every good and perfect thing. Christian religion, theology, and philosophy need maintain no special advantage. Each claim to truth should be evaluated based on its own merits.

Willard asks his readers to consider exactly how much of Jesus' edict in the Great Commission, the making of disciples who obey his commands, is currently being engaged by the church. Or, to consider how much of the time and effort of a pastor or minister is directly focused on these tasks. Willard points to the counterintuitive fact that the tasks Jesus listed in Matthew 28 "[take] no special facilities, programs, talents, or techniques. Anyone can do it. It doesn't even require a budget."[121] All that is required is the intention to confidently engage in the vision Jesus is describing. Such an understanding of ministry and the purposes of the church clears the way for simplicity and effectiveness. He suggests:

> The sufficiency of Christ to all is the basis of our efforts in gathering and service . . . the ministers, pastors, and teachers and others should with time and experience expect to receive from Christ with them profundity of insight, sweetness and strength of character, and abundance of power to carry out their role in the local group. The minister does not need tricks and techniques, but need only speak Christ's words from Christ's character standing within the manifest presence of God.[122]

The questions that churches and their leaders should be asking and answering are: What is reality? What is truth? Does God exist, and if so how? How does God interact with human life? What is considered a good life and a good person? What is the spiritual life in Christ, and how does one enter that life? Questions like these represent very deep, philosophical, sociological, and theological questions which pastors and teachers must probe first for themselves and have come to know experientially and thoughtfully. Only then can an authentic manifestation of that experiential knowledge be effectively delivered and the impact of the reality of these answers come to bear on others in their congregations, then to their communities at large. Willard's statement, "it is not about getting people into heaven but getting heaven into people" is a short synopsis of the overarching goal of discipleship to Jesus.[123]

121. ROH, 11.

122. ROH, 247.

123. ROH, 238.

Jesus' beatitudes listed in Matthew chapter five continue the kingdom principle of inversion.[124] The Sermon on the Mount highlights the failures inherent to the types of "righteousness" demonstrated by the scribes and Pharisees. Such religiosity is at odds with the kingdom of God. Willard sees the Pharisaical perspective as one focused on outward expressions of religious acts, things done or not done in the physical activities of religious expression. However, such spirituality is in opposition—actually, backwards or upside-down—to the spiritual reality of the kingdom, which focuses instead on the internal motivations that develop the personal character. Both Paul and Jesus describe this condition as a "circumcision," not a physical change that represented the markings of a dedicated Jew, but rather the internal manifestation of a dedicated heart.

The confusion of this inner focus is not only a difficulty for the religious Jews of Jesus' day. It presents an equally paradoxical problem for many contemporary Christians, pastors and church leaders alike. Willard points to the story of Nicodemus, a religious leader who is described in John chapter 3, as one who does not seem to understand Jesus' spiritual emphasis and was confused by the ironic inversion of the physical and spiritual nature of the kingdom of God. Jesus articulates this in the famous "born again" phrase that ironically has been grasped as a label for so many evangelicals who, in Willard's view, may not have understood Jesus' teaching any better than Nicodemus did two thousand years prior.

It is important to remember Willard's view of salvation. It is a rescuing of one's self from self-idolatry that lies at the root of rebellion against God and his person.[125] With Nicodemus, Jesus accents this feature of becoming like a "child," without pretense and totally dependent on God's goodness and grace. Not only did Nicodemus have problems understanding this reversal of paradigms, Jesus' disciples also took several years to understand the inverted and re-imagined *missio Dei* that had previously been perceived only through the Jewish-Israeli lens. The book of Acts reveals the disciples, even after the resurrection, still thinking about deliverance (salvation) as relief from the abusive power structures of the day and the reestablishment of a Christocentric physical and political kingdom. Willard suggests that during the period of forty days, between the time of the resurrection appearance and the ascension, Jesus is still teaching and training the disciples to accomplish their tasks of ministry "in the name of Jesus."

124. DC, 88-90.

125. ROH, 65.

Performing as a disciple of Jesus in the kingdom of God is to act "in his name" and on his behalf.[126] Yet, Willard admits, like the early disciples, contemporary Christians remain confused on this point. The early disciples received power on the day of Pentecost and beyond, but they did not receive their expected positional authority as political leaders. Their power came from Christ but had no accompanying earthly, political appointments or religious positions of influence they seemed to expect or hope for. Willard suggests contemporary believers stand in the same position. He asserts that biblical Christianity maintains the same power structure Jesus instituted at Pentecost. Most Christians may never be given, and should not expect, overt positions of power within society. Such positions can be beneficial when used appropriately under the guidance and direction of God, but are unnecessary for most faithful followers of Christ to effectively manifest God's will and way in a particular context.

Again, in a representation of the inversion principle, when Christians look to attain positional authority through leadership roles as the sole means of changing society, Willard suggests, churches tend to remove themselves from the very source of power cultural change requires. Thus, salvation (deliverance) is not the overturning of existing power structures through some political means. Instead, the kingdom of God spreads through the proliferation of spirit and truth. God's movement through history has been marked by the subversive inversions of expectations, philosophies, and paradigms tied to the wisdom of the world by demonstrating "signs and wonders" of grace and power, granted from a heavenly source. The result is to overcome evil with good. It is not by might or power, but by the Spirit of the Lord that deliverance is attained.[127] The church must heed that characteristic "upside down" reality of God's ways.

Summary

In summary, Willard views the church as the body of Christ, made up of members who embody the virtue and faith to administer the reign of God's kingdom. This is also what he understands as the dream or intention of God's will—to share his creative goodness without restraint on everyone who can possibly stand it. Such a will is accomplished by those who willingly choose to join God together, individually, and corporately, engaging the world, as Jesus would do the same, in full reliance and expectation of his presence and grace. This joint participation of the faithful with God

126. KCT, 158

127. Zech. 4:6

represents a symbiotic relationship of mutual dependence likened to the Trinity. Willard suggests the model of such a relationship is represented in John 17 where Jesus entreats the Trinitarian relationship as one in which humanity is mysteriously offered entry into the Godhead communion. This relational picture, Willard asserts, is the model for what kinds of relations we can and should pursue in the church.

The kingdom of God is seen by Willard to triumph over every opposing kingdom in the process of redemption. To best understand the depths of this redemption and how necessary it is, a long quotation is in order. Willard posits that God's redemption, through Christ,

> . . . goes precisely contrary to anything that might be imagined from the human point of view, with its regard for power and its acceptance of the evil that is always required to make human power work. It is an act that allows corrupt humanity, ruled by Satan through its most exalted institutions, to have its way to the upmost extent, to do its damnedest without moving a finger to resist it. The felt absence of God from the scene of the crucifixion in [*The Passion of Christ*] is the ultimate point of non-resistance and the prayer of forgiveness of the immediate perpetrators of such an evil and injustice indicates the complete helplessness of those in the grip of evil. Together by contrast the acts and words of Christ affirm the presence of another world—the world of truth, and not power, of the kingdom of God from which redemption and deliverance from overwhelming evil into goodness is possible.[128]

Thus, the choice is presented to humanity to lay aside their independent rule of their individual and collective lives in order to achieve that which God originally intended as most beneficial for humanity now and forever. But, this is most assuredly a choice. Willard posits a very Arminian position here. If people choose to align themselves to God, Willard argues, they are able to receive their own kingdom and God's. The benefit is that in submission, one's own kingdom is in perfect alignment with God's will. If the choice is made to oppose God, then idolatry is the result and that will remain one's chosen fate.

What Willard makes clear, however, is that religious idolatry is an equally abhorrent alternative to the biblical understanding of the kingdom of God. To put one's religious practices and beliefs as the chief aim or guide, even if these be Christian in origin or directive, leaves one in the same lost, unsubmitted, and narcissistic condition. Willard points to the

128. Willard, "The Craftiness of Christ"

often-recognized reality of Christians who become angry and resentful of God for not giving or doing what they want or expect of him. Willard suggests something like this view is perhaps what Job was facing when God gave him a loving rebuke. More problematic is the rising popularity of the "prosperity" form of the gospel that testifies to a God that exists primarily to bless his "faithful" with material wealth. Such positions and behaviors may, Willard suggests, indicate not Christian religious faith but instead an idolization of God used as a means to a self-directed end. Such religions display forms of modern Christian practice and gather under a moniker of Christian theology yet are Christ-dependent in title only.

What never leaves nor diminishes in Willard's theo-ontological perspective is God's respect of the human will and freedom. If one desires for his or her will to be done, over God's will, even while assuming the permissions and titles of Christian faith, God will allow it, even to detrimental effect. However, if one submits his or her will to God, he will accept such devotion and in the process of discipleship to Christ, in his kingdom way, will build a character that wills the will of God and has the power to accomplish God's intent. Therefore, the church, as God's gathered people, is specifically tasked to pursue the vision, intention and means for individuals, families and groups to taste, see, discover, and engage the will and way of God—first for themselves—then as spiritually empowered witnesses of God's goodness to the world. In this mission, Willard understands, the church of Jesus Christ represents the hope of the world.

Chapter Four

The Willardian Correction

Willard's protoevangelical vision and *essentia Dei* schema often conflicts with or stand in contrast to significant tenets of mainstream theology and praxis within American evangelical religion today. Ironically, Willard's most consolidated critique of evangelicalism is found in *The Divine Conspiracy*, which was also his most widely acknowledged and acclaimed work in mainstream evangelical circles.[1] It epitomizes both Willard's soteriology and his exegetical study of the kingdom of God as articulated in Jesus' Sermon on the Mount. Willard's handling of these two key subjects provides a complete investigation of the many soteriological implications of applying the worldview of Jesus to the human condition—a project Willard began in *The Spirit of the Disciplines*. As such, *The Divine Conspiracy* also represents an inclusive exposé of Willard's conceptualization of what Jesus communicates and embodies as the "God-bathed" existence available to all who chose to enter his kingdom.[2] These two tenets, soteriology and theo-ontology, also represent the basis from which Willard stages his critiques of contemporary forms of evangelical theology and praxis. It is to these critiques we now turn our focus.

Willard's critique of modern evangelical theology and practice is commensurate with earlier appraisals delivered by the likes of G. K Chesterton, C. S. Lewis, Dietrich Bonhoeffer, and Os Guinness. Willard often quotes their works to contravene the established norms found in evangelical theology and offer either a more traditional or less modern perspective. Yet, reviewers also note that *The Divine Conspiracy* presented much more than

1. The *Divine Conspiracy* received *Christianity Today*'s award for book of the year in 1998.

2. Ibid.

a critique of evangelical faith and likened Willard's espousal of the Christ-centered spiritual life to the devotional classics of Thomas à Kempis, Luther, Calvin, and John Wesley.[3] High praise, indeed.

As critical as Willard is of mainstream evangelical theology and practice, one wonders why *The Divine Conspiracy* was so widely received and acclaimed. Although perhaps new to evangelicals, Willard's soteriology is not novel in light of the broader history of the church catholic. Yet, since Willard places such a high value on Scripture, a longstanding evangelical theological bulwark, he is seldom if ever perceived or critiqued as offering a "new" gospel or even an extremist shift in evangelical theology. To do so would require a thorough exegetical, hermeneutical battle, to which reviewers sense Willard's exegetical prowess leaves no opening for substantial critique.[4] Conversely, reviewers who recognize and advocate for his interpretation of the gospel and its corresponding theology realize that, if properly understood, Willard presents a significant and radical departure from the status quo within the preponderance of evangelical settings.[5]

Building on the earlier themes, Willard's critique in *The Divine Conspiracy* posits the foundational premise that the essential nature of God and ethos of the kingdom of God are the central driving forces behind the message Jesus presents. As has already been discussed in the previous sections on activism, conversionism, and crucicentrism, Willard steadfastly argues the *euangelion* Jesus presented is uniquely different from that often presented in many evangelical settings. To reiterate, Jesus' gospel is one not dependent on, tailored for, or giving doctrinal primacy to the concept of "forgiveness of sin." Nor does Jesus focus on the development of methods for his followers to "manage" their sin condition after a "conversion" experience.[6] Rather, Willard argues Jesus is seen in the gospel accounts presenting a vision of both a) who God is, b) the kingdom of God, and c) what type of life is available in a God-permeated reality.[7] Furthermore, Jesus is more than a proclaimer or preacher of good news. He also is seen in the biblical texts exemplifying, teaching, guiding, and utilizing the means and principles for both entering and living in the goodness of a "kingdom" type of life as a master of this realm.

3. Van Der Weele, "Book Review," 719–20.

4. Engle, "Book Review," 217–19.

5. Johns, "Book Review," 327–30, and Galli, "Downsizing Sin," 105–6.

6. The concepts of sin management are discussed beginning on page 146.

7. This is handled directly in chapter 2 of *Divine Conspiracy*. But is also a frame of reference in *In Search of Guidance, Renovation of the Heart, Spirit of the Disciplines, The Great Omission,* and *Knowing Jesus Today.*

Willard uses *Divine Conspiracy* to take the reader in a slow, steady, and methodical way through many of the popular misunderstandings of well-used Christian terms, dogmas, and doctrines such as salvation, grace, heaven, eternal life, hell, love, etc. Willard recognizes and articulates the common usage of these terms and concepts then sets about redefining them in view of the *essentia Dei*, the protoevangelical message of Jesus, and the theo-ontological view of God's kingdom ethos. In this process, Willard shows himself to be an expert evangelical insider, revealing contradictions or anomalies in popular evangelical theology and tracking down ill-gotten doctrines to their sources. Willard also offers pointed, stinging commentaries and reflections about American evangelical religion in general.

Belief vs. Faith

First, Willard suggests the most common and revealing characteristic of contemporary evangelicalism is the lack of any overriding compunction that interactive knowledge of—and not only a profession of faith in—Christ's teaching is vital to Christian life and faith. Willard recognizes the now uniform assumption that mandatory conformity to Jesus' teaching is optional and no longer essential to the evangelical articulation of Christian life. Such a "profession of faith" often represents what amounts to an empty allegiance.[8] Thus, Willard makes his position clear, as one reviewer of *Divine Conspiracy* noted, most contemporary Christians simply "don't get it."[9] Modern evangelicalism's focus on first explicating then garnering belief in correct doctrines has, in fact, left contemporary evangelicals devoid of the very knowledge of reality Jesus sought to provide.

Willard understands Jesus first and only as a pragmatist regarding belief and suggests Jesus advocated belief only as an initial basis from which interaction with God begins. Neither belief itself, nor the profession of belief, should be considered the final goal or end of Christian faith.[10] Rather belief is only the first step that must proceed toward the development and eventual establishment of an interactive knowledge of the reality of God and his character. Thus, the current trend in evangelical teaching and preaching that focuses on what doctrines Jesus, Paul, John, and others "believed" and taught as orthodoxy misses the overall vocation of Jesus' ministry. To the degree that such information is taught correctly, Willard senses most "Christians" want to "believe" what Jesus and Paul, etc., "believed." Yet, Wil-

8. DC, xv

9. Galli, "Downsizing Sin," 105–6.

10. This is a theme also arises in *Knowing Christ Today.*

lard contends the hard facts support the conclusion the majority simply "do not really understand [the gospel of Jesus], and their confidence in its reality is shaky. They are like Peter in his truly earth-shaking confession that Jesus was the only one to save humanity. He had it right, of course, but he had no real idea of what it meant."[11] Accordingly, the most one can claim of such a level of understanding is only a confidence that Jesus himself "believed" in the message he professed. Or perhaps one can hope to attain a certain level of "belief" about Jesus that offers some degree of ethical or moral benefit. Yet, remaining at the level of doctrinal acknowledgement (profession) of a belief is not itself a representation of knowledge nor a demonstration of confidence in the gospel Jesus presented for transformed lives.

This is a stark and pointed criticism of popular evangelical piety juxtaposed against the impetus of Jesus' message. The concentration on "belief" that stops at "knowing the right answers" to doctrinal questions has too often become the entire goal in modern forms of evangelical Christianity. Such "professions" of "beliefs" are opposed to what Willard understands as viable confidence in the person and life of Christ. Willard argues that a biblical description of belief necessitates a dedication to the proposition of a conviction to the point of actively placing one's life in the realities those beliefs represent. Hence, biblical belief represents the willingness to act *as if* that which is "believed" is, in fact, the truth of the matter at hand. Thus, the nature of biblical belief demands a much higher level of confidence in the veracity and reliability of the underlying claim or proposal being acted upon. Consequently, the value Jesus' teachings place on belief requires his followers to engage "the task in ourselves and in others to transform right answers into automatic responses to real-life situations."[12]

Unfortunately, Willard sees the status of contemporary evangelical theology and praxis as largely incapable of attaining the type of genuine "belief" defined either in the Scriptures or used in any non-religious arena.[13] This dearth of a robust and biblical concept of belief is decimating evangelicalism and its credibility across the spectrum of cultural and societal institutions in America. Willard admonishes the church to become the primary means through which to "simply bring people to believe, with their whole being, the information they already have as a result of their initial confidence in Jesus—even if that initial confidence was only the confidence of desperation."[14]

11. DC, 317.
12. DC, 317.
13. Ibid.
14. DC, 318.

This confidence is uncomplicated for Willard and does not include the evangelical version of salvation implicit within the formulaic, doctrinally laden, propositional statements inside the "Romans Road to Salvation" or "Four Spiritual Laws."[15] Instead, faith (confidence) in Jesus is simply and powerfully created with the settled understanding that "Jesus is right. He is the greatest and best."[16] From there, one learns continually, as a disciple, more precisely what that profound yet simple statement involves in every area of life.

Closely tied to Willard's differentiation of professions of belief against biblical faith is his second critique which deals with the absence of intentionality placed on the necessity to follow the example of Christ in obedience. As referenced earlier under the VIM concept, such a commitment to whole-life conversion is a non-negotiable requirement of any faith-based conversional decision. This is an ironic twist in the historic role "decision" has played in evangelicalism over the past two centuries. Willard suggests, in large measure, the "elephant in the church" is the widely unacknowledged but well-known fact that the evangelicals simply do not intend to follow the example of Jesus.[17] This is a striking statement when taken at face value. But Willard suggests the evidence is again overwhelmingly obvious and he provides statistics to prove it.[18] The most significant point finds that, overall, Christians are rarely if ever called to make a considered decision to follow Christ in an obedient, discipleship relationship. In fact, churches are not organized to accomplish such a task nor is it a part of their encompassing vision to do so. Thus, Willard surmises, "in the last analysis, we fail to be disciples only because we do not decide to be. We do not intend to be disciples. It is the power of the decision and the intention over our life that is missing."[19]

Willard recognizes much of the historical evangelicalism described in chapter one defined "making a decision for Christ" to connote the "event" where the "soul" is saved from an eternal destiny in hell. This decision was thought to come in many various forms. However, salvific "decisions" in

15. These are commonly used evangelistic tracks developed to assist in the proselytizing of non-Christians. Bill Bright, founder of Campus Crusade for Christ, created the Four Spiritual Laws pamphlet. The Romans Road to Salvation is a common evangelical term used to describe a series of passages in systematic order from the apostle Paul's letter to the Romans in the New Testament. They are coalesced to form a description of the need for salvation and how to receive that salvation. See McQuade, *How Do I Get to Heaven?* and Bright, *Four Spiritual Laws.*

16. DC, 318.

17. DC, 301.

18. DC, 318.

19. DC, 298.

evangelicalism's past most often described one's reception of Christ's atoning sacrifice on the cross. This came to be understood as God's "saving" act of grace. Thus, mental assent to this "fact" and the realization of oneself as a sinner in need of this grace is now broadly understood to encompass the totality of "the decision for Christ." In Willard's view, such a "decision" is in fact nothing more than a realization. Therefore, such realizations need to be followed by an actual decision to commit oneself to a life of discipleship to Christ. Anything less does not constitute a decision for anything that resembles a biblical form of Christian commitment demonstrated in Jesus' life and message or in the lives of his first disciples.

Gospels of Sin Management

The overarching metaphor Willard uses to describe the effect his two main critiques have had on modern evangelicalism is encompassed in the term "sin management." Willard uses this term to illustrate those religious ideologies formed as a means to deal with the guilt experienced in relation to the continued lack of effectual change, despite the application of religious effort and belief. Therefore, sin management strategies are a means for the religiously devoted to "manage" the lingering negative effects of a guilt-ridden conscience. The doctrinal beliefs one applies to manage or assuage this guilt are defined by Willard as the left and right "gospels," or constructed religious methods, that create and fund the "sin management" rationale. The ultimate goal of the sin management system is to only diminish the effects of the continuing presence of the sin condition, while remaining impotent to eliminate or transform the source.[20] This section will pursue the nature of the sin management ideology and how Willard sees its effects on contemporary forms of evangelical religion.

There are two main systems of sin management, one representing the conservative "right" and one for the liberal "left" wings of evangelicalism. Both are active in contemporary evangelicalism today and have risen to an acute stage. Additionally, both systems contain views of redemption that pay little to no attention to the everyday human condition and its transformational necessities. Willard writes,

> History has brought us to a point where the Christian message is thought to be essentially concerned only with how to deal with sin; with wrongdoing, and wrong-being and its effects. Life, our actual experiences, is not included in what is now presented

20. Galli, "Downsizing Sin."

> as the heart of the Christian message, or it is included only marginally.[21]

Both sin management strategies have effectively highlighted the means of justification over and above sanctification as the primary objective to evangelical Christianity. On this shift, Willard refers to Karl Barth's comments that early evangelicalism in America developed as "absorption of Christology into soteriology."[22] This absorption brought a gaping loss of "Christological concern" regarding the nature and substance of one's own salvation or the effect Christ's life and influence should have on society at large.[23]

As a result, the conservative (right) evangelical sin management proposal presumes a Christ with no serious work other than to atone for sin. Willard describes this view as a "vampire faith."[24] This is a version of evangelicalism that requires a profession of belief in the necessity of accepting Jesus' blood for penal substitutionary atonement while largely ignoring commitment and devotion to a discipled life of obedience. Such a theology marginalizes anything more from relationship with Jesus other than relief from the intrapsychic terrors of fundamentalist versions of hell in contrast to the glories of heaven. Therefore, the conservative sin management system assuages the greatest of fears through the proclamation of appropriate beliefs in certain theories of the atonement discussed earlier. If one never develops a Christlike character or endeavors to be an obedient disciple, this may be unfortunate but not considered necessary nor exclusionary.

For liberals (left), Willard suggests the sin management aim is displayed differently. Unlike doctrinally focused conservatives, liberals tend to apply a contextualized degree of Pharisaic activism to their sin management endeavors. Such activism centers on displaying self-determined acts of righteousness that often benefit some disenfranchised people group, cause, or charity. Such benevolent activities are deemed to demonstrate a heart worthy of acceptance by God or, at least, a valiant attempt at applying the social mores evident in the actions of Jesus. Faith in the historicity of Jesus, his divine attributes or activities, or the reality of his theo-ontological kingdom are marginalized. Primacy is placed on the accumulation of "good acts" in relation to "bad acts" for achieving a level of confidence in the quality of one's existential virtue. Like conservatives, the liberal sin management system eliminates the greatest fear by creating a means of gauging self-righteousness and assuring a preferred condition.

21. DC, 41.

22. DC, 42, n. 8.

23. Willard quotes, Berger, "Crisis in Continental Theology," 255.

24. Willard, "Why Bother with Discipleship?"

In terms of responding to both the "left" and the "right," Willard quotes A. W. Tozer who suggested there is absolutely nothing in what Jesus himself or his early followers taught that suggests one can decide to manage their sin alone,

> . . . at Jesus' expense and have nothing more to do with him. To this point, Tozer expressed feeling that "a notable heresy has come into being throughout evangelical Christian circles—the widely-accepted concept that we humans can choose to accept Christ only because we need him as Savior and that we have the right to postpone our obedience to him as Lord as long as we want to!" . . . [S]alvation apart from obedience is unknown in the sacred Scriptures.[25]

Willard suggests such a "heresy" creates a situation where modern Christians find it quite acceptable to be "vampire Christians" on the right or "activist" Christians on the left. Put simply, Willard suggest the veracity of one's Christian faith or the presence of a saved condition is best determined through the overwhelming existential reality of a Christlike character emblematic of *agape* love. Instead, the two sin management systems seek to answer this same question through ascertaining proper beliefs (right) or proper behaviors (left).

Specifically considering the sin management of the "right," Willard roundly disagrees with the proposition that the gospel of Jesus almost exclusively advocates for the eternal benefits that come from the "forgiveness of sin." Discussed at length earlier in regards to a particular version of the atonement, the "right" suggests the cross presents the beginning and end motivation of the entire story of God's hope for humanity. Therefore, the Great Commissioning task is to spread the atonement message of trading eternity in hell for life in heaven after death.[26] Willard recognizes the popular bumper sticker that states the theological position, "Christians aren't perfect, just forgiven."[27] Here he senses such an idea gives the impression that Christianity is all or "just" about forgiveness of sin.

In regards to the sin management systems of the "left," Willard proposes the emphasis on righteous acts devoted to liberation or social justice advocates for more than political correctness, but rather "general correctness."[28]

25. GO, 13. The Tozer quote is from Tozer, *I Call It Heresy*, 5.

26. This is a significant issue in Willard's writing, perhaps due in part to the heritage from which his faith ensues in the fundamentalist evangelical tradition of the Southern Baptists. See SD, 33–34

27. Willard, "Why Bother with Discipleship?" Also DC, 35, SD, 23.

28. DC, 51.

He points to liberal theologians, such as James Findlay, who suggest that those involved in the social gospel movement experience significant life-transforming moments and events associated with their activism.[29] Thus, Findlay remarks, many see social activism and its transformative benefits as the primary and best uses of the Christian church and its constituent members. The language and hope of the kind of life that those leading the civil rights movement offered, in Willard's view, was not simply the hope of the outcome of their religion. Rather, such a liberating hope was the entire purpose of the religion altogether. Commitment to the oppressed, or simply to the "community," became the fulfillment of what was essential to liberal views of Christian commitment. The gospel, or good news, on this view was that God himself stood behind liberation, equality and community, and that Jesus died to promote them, or at least endeavored to correct the lack of these virtues. As a result Jesus is seen to either metaphorically or metaphysically "live on in all efforts and tendencies favoring them."[30] This focus on the oppressed and their cause became the overwhelming message of liberal evangelicalism—the activities that determine appropriate Christian behavior—and thus the totalizing view of God's mission on earth. Hence, Jesus becomes diminished to a motivating instrument used for further liberating political and civil causes.[31]

What both gospels of the "left" and "right" have accomplished is to divorce the personal integrity of their adherents to the namesake of their faith. Jesus' current effect on the lives of their adherents and his example for how life can and should be lived is a secondary consideration, if at all. "Both lack any essential bearing upon the individual's life as a whole, especially upon occupations of work time, and upon the fine texture of our personal relationships in the home and neighborhood."[32]

In the end, Willard considers both sin management systems largely irrelevant and ineffectual in their ability to effect human transformation due

29. Findlay, *Church People in the Struggle.*

30. DC, 51.

31. Ibid. Willard sees the myopic focus of the liberationist gospel as presenting a message different from that proffered by the likes of liberal theologians and pastors such as Schleiermacher or Niebuhr. Liberation theologians presented theologies, views of God, as a kind of liberator, which is different from presenting the entire *missio Dei* with a culminating soteriological end of liberation and holistic freedom. Schleiermacher and Niebuhr's social gospel offered a social ethic that valued freedom and could be shared culturally but did not require reliance on God or a living Christ for its fulfillment. As such, the social gospel, different from the liberationist gospel, valued a "total inclusivism of all beliefs and practices except oppressive ones, such as the exclusivism of traditional Christianity itself." See DC, 51.

32. DC, 54.

to their almost singular focus on the removal of sin guilt through either socially constructed and approved behaviors or beliefs. There is no expectation of effectual transformation of individual human lives towards increasing obedience to the example of Christ. "That real life goes on despite them is a natural consequence of this."[33] In effect, both of these ideologies categorize the work of Jesus as a means to their own end. Thus, Willard suggests both systems offer the ability for their constituencies to resist the call of the protoevangelical vision and instead take the anti-evangelical position, "But I don't care to be your student or have your character. In fact, won't you just excuse me while I get on with my life, and I'll see you in heaven."[34]

Such a stance is inconceivable to what Willard suggests is found in protoevangelicalism presented by Jesus in the New Testament gospels and of that lived by the early church. To this, Willard asks how such a faith, if not based on supreme confidence in Jesus, could be relied upon for anything if one is unwilling or unable to trust Christ for anything other than sin guilt or social reform. Willard states, "one can't trust [Jesus]without believing that he was right about everything and that he alone has the key to every aspect of our lives here on earth. But if you believe that, you will naturally want to stay just as close to him as you can, in every aspect of your life."[35]

In an analogy to describe the effect of sin management gospels in practice, Willard uses the example of what he terms "barcode faith."[36] The illustration draws on the popular retail barcoding system displayed on the outside of most packaging materials. When the barcode is laser scanned at the register, a listing of the item and its price are called up and added to the list of items on the receipt. The pricing system automatically assumes what is represented on the barcode accurately reflects the product contained inside the box or package. Whether the barcode is accurate is never questioned. Likewise, Willard argues Christianity has for centuries endeavored to answer the question of how one can gain assurance their outside behaviors (the barcode) accurately reflect the internal condition of the heart (the actual product). The answer to that question has brought different responses theologically and ecclesiologically over the past several millennia.

Willard recognizes how the modernist/fundamentalist controversy that consumed American religion for many decades is still at work and powerfully divisive on this question and has led different wings of Christianity

33. DC, 54.

34. Chapter 2 of GO, 14. First published October, 1996 as "Why Bother with Discipleship?"

35. GO, 14.

36. DC, 36.

coming to develop their own "barcode" identifiers.[37] The Protestant conceptualization of "grace" confounds this problem because it holds that "we can do nothing" in relation to our eternal destiny. Much of orthodox evangelicalism holds that salvation is the result of only God's act of grace and thus a work of unmerited favor of which humans play no part. Thus, salvation is totally independent of human activity, including one's character, whether for the better or worse. By implication there is little to no concern for what type of person one is to become while alive on earth. God alone is responsible for the redemption of the elect.

In such a system, personal character formation is ancillary and subordinate to the greater focus of either the effect of works (social gospel faiths), sacraments, ritual (high church/liturgical faiths), and/or doctrinal correctness (conservative fundamentalists). Each of these brands of Christian expression advocates its own esoteric sin management ideology as "the" orthodox "barcode" representation of "proper" faith. Each unique outward manifestation of these faiths is positioned as containing those qualities of Christian expression that will assure God's acceptance (pass the scanner). Finally, a cosmic exchange is made somewhere in God's economy, and debts are paid for or credit is extended. Some Christian traditions suggest the "account" has to receive regular deposits (gospel of the "Left") while others believe the account has an endless supply once it is opened in your name (gospel of the "Right"). Either way, Willard suggests both ideologies are caught focusing almost exclusively on the problems and effects of sin.

It is not then necessary, in a sin management system, to be or become a morally upright person of character. It is only necessary to be considered by God as having the appropriate "barcode" which designates one "good" or "worthy." Willard sees this as a massive means of "working the system" to the point where "doing good," (gospel of the "Left") or "believing good" (gospel of the "Right") are the means by which people get what they want. Both strategies overlook the integrity of their faith and therefore seldom engage the option of actually "being good." This integrity is found in the process of transformation into the type of person Jesus demands of those who would follow him.

As such, sin management systems appear very pagan and idolatrous in their conception. To search for a means of either placating a god from wrath, proving one's meritorious condition, or enticing divine favors are all indicative of exactly the kind of paganism the Scriptures specifically prohibit. Unfortunately, neither the gospel of the Right or Left places its primary concern on what the product of the faith results in, or what the subject

37. DC, 41.

or person who advocates either of these ideologies becomes internally. The only interest in these "barcode" systems of faith is the outward appearance and end result of passing God's "scanner" and avoiding the potential consequences of condemnation.

Here, Willard asks the question centered on *essentia Dei:* "Would God really do it this way?"[38] Thinking that one can really "get away" with either developing or "working" such a religious system, in Willard's view, reveals both foolishness and a theology that positions God as a fool, as well.

> No one need worry about getting the best of God in some bargain with him, or that we might somehow succeed in using him for our purposes. Anyone who thinks this is a problem has seriously underestimated the intelligence and agility of our father in the heavens. Any arrangement God has established will be right for him and right for us. We can count on it.[39]

Ultimately, Willard recognizes that "barcode Christianity" has not worked. To illustrate this, Willard quotes Mike Yaconelli[40] and Phillip Yancey[41] as examples of evangelicals who have lost their faith in evangelicalism's ability to actually change people.[42] These key figures admit their brand of evangelical faith has failed their best attempts to apply its ethos. Willard suggests evangelicalism is not what fails them, despite their honest efforts. Rather, it is precisely because of the sin management systems inherent to their faith structure that their efforts have remained largely impotent.[43] Thus, like the ECM leaders who began to read his works, Willard suggests that the poor results evangelical faith has demonstrated in the many recent emperical socio-religious studies mentioned previously "is not in spite of what we teach and how we teach, but precisely because of it."[44] Willard quotes the works of Neil Hamilton who marks the degeneration of these opposing sin management systems in general terms.[45] Hamilton describes how each of these parties, being most proud of not being the other, is nonetheless helpless to demonstrate its theological propositions as "transcendent life forces powerful enough to threaten the structures of secular existence.[46]

38. DC, 37
39. Ibid.
40. Yaconelli, "The Terror of Inbetween-ness."
41. Yancey, "Be Ye Perfect, More Or Less."
42. DC, 40.
43. Ibid.
44. Ibid. See pages 48-50.
45. Hamilton, *Recovery of the Protestant Adventure.*
46. SD, 22. cf. 27.

Doctrine of God

It follows then that to assume the life of a disciple of Jesus, and to live life in his kingdom, the first and primary task of a disciple is to put on the "mind of Christ."[47] This presents the key intellectual opportunity Jesus presents to humanity and becomes one of the primary goals of a disciple.[48] It is in discerning the foundational knowledge and personal, interactive experience with God that Jesus both demonstrated and advocated where we find the third of Willard's critiques of modern evangelical theology and practice. As referenced earlier, Willard is often observed asking the question of a certain belief system, theological doctrine, or description of God's activity, "If that were true, what kind of God would that be?"[49] This mode of inquiry was most evident in his class lectures and in personal interviews. In his textual work, Willard presents the question in *Divine Conspiracy* regarding the common understanding of the evangelical doctrine of atonement, "Would God really do things in that way?"[50] In another instance, he discusses the conflicting theological images of God portrayed in various evangelical doctrines. Such conflicts are regularly demonstrated in images of an angry, wrath-filled God, which dominate conservative doctrines of hell, double-predestination, substitutionary atonement, the pre-millennial tribulation theories, and many others.[51] Willard juxtaposes these images to those describing and articulating a loving, grace-filled, kind, patient and benevolent God Jesus is seen describing in chapter three of John's Gospel.[52] Again, Willard asks the question about the efficacy of the images these opposing theological propositions portray of a God who is finally, and always,

47. 1 Cor 2:16. The concept of the "mind of Christ" in Willardian theology represents the concept of coming into the same type of knowledge Jesus possessed about God, the human condition, and the world at large. This does not mean human beings will have an exacting replication of divine omniscience. Rather, disciples of Jesus progressively learn how to realize the essential aspects of God's character and his creation, which makes life in his kingdom both possible, peaceful, and fulfilling. This is an example of Willard's theology being affected by his realist philosophical positions. See SD, 210, DC, 24, ROH, chapter 6.

48. DC, 323.

49. DC, 38.

50. DC, 37.

51. As to the issues related to substitutionary atonement and the assumption of conservative evangelical theology as to the doctrine of God's represented in common views on the crucifixion, see Willard, "The Craftiness of Christ."

52. Moon, "Getting the Elephant Out of the Sanctuary. "

described in the Scriptures as more than loving, but the very fulfillment and perfection of love itself.[53]

Perhaps one of Willard's best and most detailed illustrations in regards to the application of thinking through the *essentia Dei* doctrine is found in his unpublished article concerning the problem of good and evil.[54] Using logic and his *a priori* understanding of *essentia Dei*, Willard argues a proof against one of the more historically difficult problems related to Christian theodicy. Willard proposes that, by necessity, the nature of freedom requires the presence of choice. This includes the choice for humanity to maintain the free ability to choose good or evil. Additionally, such a choice is also required to build human character. A person without a choice cannot build a character from which good choices are made and discernment is built. Consequently, without the freedom incumbent for choice, one could not develop the values that proceed from the outcomes of morally weighted decisions.

Willard argues God's loving character works to provide freedom and, therefore, hope for humanity to develop such a moral character. Love funds his desire for persons to make moral decisions well. Hence, the ability to choose poorly must remain a viable option. There is no logical alternative. Thus, God's love and character make possible the situation in which freedom is allowed and character is developed in the humanity he values so deeply. However, it is also the case that God's love makes it impossible to restrict the alternative of a poor choice. Further, any assertion God did not provide or demonstrate an omnipotent ability to create a situation that disallows poor choices and the consequential evil that often proceeds is an illogical argument. Such an option does not exist, since it is impossible. Something that does not exist is nothing. Nothing, by definition, is not something that can be considered in any form or substance. Therefore, God cannot be accountable for not accomplishing something that does not exist. It follows then that God's nature of love, and his love of humanity, demands the possibility of evil as a consequence to human freedom.

In this argument, like all of Willard's theological pursuits, God is presented as acting consistently within his characteristic *agape* nature. Since

53. Willard makes the point that 1 John 4 says explicitly that God is the personification of *agape*. This is much more than stating that God acts lovingly. Rather, God's essence is the totality of all agape can claim to be. See ROH, chapter 10. Further, Willard pursues these questions with secular representations of God, as well. For instance, in commenting on books and movies such as *The Da Vinci Code* and *The Last Temptation of Christ,* Willard wonders if a person could imagine the saints and martyrs believing in, thinking about, or laying their lives down for the type of person characterized or portrayed of either Christ or God in these works.

54. Willard, "Good and the Problem of Evil."

agape is the primary component that informs the *essentia Dei,* it is the position from which all biblical theological inquiry should proceed and the point from which discipleship commences. Any doctrine or dogma that does not conform to the *agape* nature cannot be assigned or attributed to the actions, will, or providence of God. Put simply, Willard has stated often that one should never believe anything bad about God.[55]

When considering all the characterization and actions attributed to God that flow from past and present versions of evangelical doctrine and biblical interpretation, such common sense theological wisdom can be difficult to apply. One can quickly find a significant number of Christian pastors, leaders and theologians placing seemingly heinous proclivities and/or motives at God's feet. Even in learned evangelical circles there are often attitudes and actions attributed to God that are far afield from anything even remotely demonstrative of a loving, or even a considerate—much less moral—act, even by human standards of ethics. A prime example is found in televangelist and one time presidental candidate Pat Robertson's declaration that Haiti's earthquake, which killed ten's of thousands of Haitians, was a direct result of a divine "curse."[56] Another popular evangelical pastor and writer, John Piper, made headlines when he interpreted the divine purposes of a significant tornado that ripped through Minneapolis. Piper suggested the tornado's damaging of a particular Lutheran church that was considering a vote on ordination of homosexual clergy was a "gentle but firm warning" of God's disapproval.[57]

55. This statement was regularly offered during his class sessions at Fuller Theological Seminary's DMIN cohort. So much so that at Willard's funeral service, Dr. Keith Matthews, a co-instructor with Willard for over a decade, mentioned this during his eulogy as one of Willard's most memorable pieces of wisdom.

56. Robertson claimed the earthquake was a punishment for an ancestral "pact" Haitian slaves were rumored to have made with Satan in the late eighteenth century to barter their freedom. Representatives for Robertson were quick to declare he did not directly say the earthquake was a specific act of God's wrath. However, the felt need to clarify (spin) Robertson's statement is itself evidence that wrath was exactly what anyone listening to Robertson believed him to communicate. It would be the exception that anyone would assume him to communicate anything but that very idea. See Zajac, "Pat Robertson Links Haiti Quake to Pact with Devil."

57. There were many other properties not connected to the church that were damaged as well. Piper, who is from Minneapolis, wrote an interpretation of the tornado strike. He surmises, "*Conclusion*: The tornado in Minneapolis was a gentle but firm warning to the ELCA (Evangelical Lutheran Church of America) and all of us: Turn from the approval of sin. Turn from the promotion of behaviors that lead to destruction. Reaffirm the great Lutheran heritage of allegiance to the truth and authority of Scripture. Turn back from distorting the grace of God into sensuality. Rejoice in the pardon of the cross of Christ and its power to transform left and right wing sinners." See Piper, "The Tornado, the Lutherans, and Homosexuality."

These examples are used here to illustrate what kind of God, what character, nature or essence such a God must maintain, in order to be rightly assigned responsibility for such capricious acts. To consider these possibilities is to begin to grasp the dichotomy Willard recognizes within evangelical theology. Such stark contrast in depictions of God's person represents some insight into what many "post," "ex," or "anti" evangelicals vehemently protest within modern evangelicalism's dispensational pre-millennial theology and penal substitutionary atonement theories. Such characteristics assumed in the evangelical doctrine of God require something of a theological schizophrenia, or a divine multiple personality disorder, to explain a theological system that simultaneously describes a deity who "loves me and has a wonderful plan for my life" yet is also willing and able to randomly kill tens of thousands of Haitians or send tornadoes to destroy neighborhoods surrounding "liberal" churches.[58] This conundrum and dichotomy illustrates how deeply Willard's *essentia Dei* departs from and critiques the more standard conservative evangelical doctrines of God.

From the discussion above some may wonder if Willard is "soft" on God, ascribing only "warm and fuzzy" attributes to God's character. Therefore, it is important to note Willard is not a Universalist. He fully recognizes the presence and importance of evil in both the physical and spiritual realms. He recognizes there will be a time and place, "the day of the Lord," wherein "justice roll down like waters, and righteousness like an ever-flowing stream."[59] Unfortunantly, for those set against justice and righteousness, their wills will be overcome by such a flood to the point every knee will bow whether it wants to or not. Willard fully acknowledges that for the heart turned away from God, drowning—even in goodness—will be a most unpleasant reality.

Furthermore, there is no suggestion in the span of Willard's corpus for an acceptance or assumption of the doctrine of annihilation. In fact, Willard's anthropology specifically states that human beings are eternal in nature and essence with a destiny in God's universe.[60] However, Willard is reticent to suggest exactly what that destiny consists of. However, he does believe in a hell, while humbly resisting to define it in exacting terms. In an e-mail conversation on the topic with this author Willard suggests,

> Basically, I think hell is God's best for some people. I don't know what the furniture is like, but God has arranged for people who

58. The phrase "God loves you and has a wonderful plan for your life" is from Bill Bright's Four Spiritual Laws. See Bright, *Four Spiritual Laws.*

59. Amos 5:24.

60. GO, 20.

> don't love him and can't worship him to be "somewhere else," where they will have to endure the person they have become forever. Here are some lines from Bunyan:
> *Sin is the living worm, the lasting fire;*
> *Hell soon would lose its flames could sin expire.*
> *Better sinless in Hell, than to be where*
> *Heaven is, and to be found a sinner there.*
> *One sinless with infernals might do well,*
> *But sin would make of heaven a very hell.*
> *Look to thyself then, keep it out of door,*
> *Lest it get in and never leave thee more.*
> What is fundamental is that God is good, and all his deeds merciful, that he will not break down the will that sets itself against him, and that at some point character is irreversible to the one who has it. "Better to reign in Hell than to serve in heaven!" Who said that? Unfortunately, these words which Milton put in Satan's mouth are on the lips of many persons, and they may never get them off.[61]

In the end, the reliance on mere belief versus biblical faith, the proliferation of sin management systems, and the increasing focus on a wrathful and angry doctrine of God within contemporary forms of evangelicalism have become more obvious to the world, in general, and increasingly so to postevangelicals. Yet, more than modern evangelical theology caused the postevangelical protest and its progression toward Willardian theology. Postmodern epistemology was also a key factor. Willard's philosophical training in epistemology and phenomenology places him in a unique position to speak to these complicated but essential questions. It is to these final key philosophical issues we now turn.

61. Willard, Personal E-mail to author Re: Hell, July 12, 2008. For Bunyan quote see Bunyan, *The Complete Works of John Bunyan*, 1000.

Chapter Five

Realism, Postmodernism, and Willardian Theology

It is a significant irony that many postmodern Christian leaders and writers list Willard as a key influence, specifically in light of the fact Willard was most certainly neither a modern nor a postmodern philosopher or theologian. Willard's commitment to direct realism is a unique departure from modern constructivism and its postmodern spawn. Constructivism is what Willard calls "Midas touch epistemology," and its application has, in his view, wreaked havoc and confusion in contemporary thought, education, and theology.[1] This chapter will consider Willard's specific responses to the modern/postmodern epistemological duel. It will first discuss the nature of direct realism and then pursue the effects postmodernity has made on contemporary evangelical theology and Willard's perspectives on these issues.

Willard admitted that Edmund Husserl's interest in realism and its influence on his work in phenomenology were the primers that carried Willard into the discipline of philosophy. Early in his studies, Willard came to recognize Husserl stood relatively alone in defending realism against the rising influence of constructivist idealism and linguistic nominalism in the Continental schools of philosophy gathering steam during the late nineteenth and early twentieth centuries.[2] Husserl first sought to disprove Giambattisa Vico and later Immanuel Kant's constructivist assertions using mathematics. Kant's famous remark that the greatest problem of philosophy is the question of how anything in the mind can be a representation of anything outside the

1. Willard, "Predication as Originary Violence," 120–36.

2. Willard handles this in "Attaining Objectivity: Phenomenological Reduction and the Private Language Argument," 15–21.

mind remains the integral issue in the debate.[3] Kant's conclusion that things inside the mind cannot be proven to be represented outside the mind has been widely termed the "Copernican revolution" of modern philosophical thought.[4] What Kant's German idealism forged was a lineage of constructivist philosophical inquiry Husserl directly opposed but which philosophers such as Hegel, Heidegger, Wittgenstein, Nietzsche, and later the French philosophers such as Derrida widely assumed and propagated.[5]

Taking Husserl's lead, Willard's doctoral thesis applied Husserl's phenomenological platform as a logically and methodologically sound means of assuring the veracity of the classical logocentric roots of traditional philosophy.[6] Throughout his professional career, Willard consistently worked to produce detailed, logical arguments for the realist position, its claims regarding the attainability of knowledge, and the existence of an objective reality undergirding the pursuits of metaphysics, ethics, epistemology, logic, and theology. Willard saw constructivism as the primary opponent of realism.

Contrary to Kantian constructivism Willard found in Husserlian phenomenology proofs for exactly what constructivists sought to undermine—namely the foundational ontological presence of objects existing outside the mind. Husserl's work established "the possibility of human interaction with objects, as they are, in and of themselves, apart from any individual's knowledge or interpretation of them."[7] Willard argued the effect of Husserlian phenomenology is the maintenance of the logocentric objective, often referred to as the "God's Eye View" of reality.[8] In contrast to Kantian constructivism, which differentiates and separates things "inside" the mind from those "outside" the mind, Willard suggested realism establishes,

> As G. E. Moore saw a century ago, we are already outside the circle of ideas merely by having a thought or sensation. We are outside precisely because thought and sensation do not produce anything by being what they are. We are outside because there is no inside. The inside is produced by the Kantian illusion that the touch of the mind (language, culture, history)

3. Willard, "How Concepts Relate the Mind to Its Objects."
4. Rockmore, *In Kant's Wake*, 37.
5. Ibid., and Rockmore, *Kant and Idealism.*
6. Willard, "Meaning and Universals in Husserl's Logische Untersuchungen"
7. Willard, "Historical and Philosophical Foundations of Phenomenology"
8. This is a term of Hillary Putnam referred to in Willard, "How Concepts Relate the Mind to Its Objects: The God's Eye View Vindicated." Also see Putnam, *Reason, Truth, and History*, 50.

> produces things that form a wall over which we cannot logically or epistemically get.[9]

Willard's theology, in concert with his realist philosophy, holds that an objective "God's eye view" does exist and is both accurate in its perspective on all reality and, therefore, wholly independent of human description or claims to its knowledge.

Direct realism, however, does not intimate any person or community understands, or any one theory perfectly describes, objective reality. Rather, direct realism, similar to critical realism, holds only that thoughts and their concepts do not affect objects, but merely describe—accurately, inaccurately, or partially—their existence or nature. Direct realism holds there is a "way things are" but refrains from pursuing or advocating certainty and absolutism regarding knowledge of reality.

> The vagaries, indeterminacies, differing viewpoints and so on that are unmistakable and irremovable characteristics of our experience of the world do not transfer to the world itself, and do not erect a wall that encloses us from the world as it is without regard to our experience of it.[10]

What Willard found interesting in the constructivist argument is that, at its conclusion, all knowledge becomes unattainable, even for God. For strict constructionists, even the construct of "God" must remain unconscious of objects, since God does not engage in sense perception. Therefore, Kant's conclusion that concepts without precepts (meaning things have to be conceived in the mind before they can begin to be understood) is an impossibility. Hence, God too must remain ignorant of the world and just as void of reason as any other perception-disabled entity remains destined to be.[11] The point of this line of inquiry is to illustrate that the theism of the Christian point of view posits a God who, if he so desired, could and does reach beyond the limitations of human knowledge, consciousness, and language to bring human beings revelations of reality apart from human descriptions. Yet, constructivism creates a platform where nothing, not even a divine figure, can escape its epistemological limitations. For the constructivist, nothing exists outside of constructivism or the constructed state. The idea of autonomy is impossible in the Kantian design due in large measure to his proposal of how concepts (things) come before the mind. In

9. Ibid.

10. Ibid.

11. Here one can reason where Willard moves pointedly against strict openness theism or the more progressive process theology of Whitehead or Hartshorne.

the closed system of "insider-outsider" imagery, everyone and everything is trapped inside the constructivist loop, including the divine. Further, if God could escape into the outside world of objectivity, constructivism necessitates such a God would still be limited in his inability to communicate to humanity through language. Thus Willard recognizes,

> We are left to construct [God] and what he says, along with everything else, from within our circle of ideas of our language. Prospects for revelation of divine truth are pretty gloomy, to say the least. Construction and reconstruction are the only possibilities, and even then can only be constructions if we are to be consistent. Then consistency too is only . . ."[12]

Postmodernism

The implications of the realist perspective appear to decimate the "hard" concepts of pluralism, relativism, constructivism, and deconstructionism that tend to bracket most every tenet of postmodern thought. Yet, the importance of Willard's realism in his philosophy and theology is to offer a reasoned approach to epistemology that is not forced into the "all or nothing" dilemma of a modern vs. postmodern constructivism. Again, Willard is not arguing that direct realism proposes certainty and empirical superiority, only that objectivity exists and the human mind is specifically able to engage reality and experience objects apart from the need to have omniscient knowledge of them. Willard claims that from the inception of Husserlian phenomenology realism sought to

> ...respond to the increasingly subjectivistic and skeptical interpretations of human consciousness which have somewhat paradoxically accompanied the rise and development of modern science and undermined the cognitive status of all, or nearly all, claims or beliefs about the meaning and nature of human existence.[13]

Husserl described the essence of phenomenology as a "general doctrine of essences within which the science of the essence of cognition finds its place."[14] Consequently, Willard proposes the phenomenologist is regularly wary of definitions tending to incorporate unchecked prejudices with re-

12. Willard, *God's Eye View Vindicated*. 6.
13. Willard, "Historical and Philosophical Foundations of Phenomenology."
14. Ibid.

gard to a subject or conceptualization. "He never works from [subjects or conceptualizations] alone or primarily."[15]

In this regard, Willard's direct realism offers a significant critique to the hubris in modern empericism that totalizes scientific method and values only emperical rationalism, naturalism and physicalism. A similar protest becomes a major focal point and theme behind the works of postmodern philosphers Jacques Derrida, Michel Foucault, Jean-Francios Lyotard. Although critical of Derrida, Lyotard and Foucault's epistemological means and philosphical method, Willard appears largely empathetic to some of their motives and concerns. The abuse of power and the over-enthusiastic myopia of humanistic and scientistic metanarratives are a shared concern for Willard. The impetus of materialism, naturalism, empiricism, utilitarianism, and physicalism—arising from the Enligtenment and extending through modernity—have been used for both good and ill effects. However, Willard's major complaint has been with the academy's unwarranted move to establish an authoritarian plane of knowledge using only emperical, rational foundations as a valid epistemological base. These have been topics of concern in Willard's writings for decades.[16]

Willard approaches the pursuit of all intellectual work with the goal of distinguishing things one from another. Therefore, the postmodern goal of critiquing the modern hubris of scientism, individualism, consumerism, and even systematic theology, is an equally valuable and essential task. However, Willard argues that Lyotard's and Foucault's critique of modernism overlooks key *a priori* assumptions—perhaps even abuses—in their own reconstruction of yet another power-filled, language-gaming, postmodern metanarrative. Furthermore, Derrida's deconstruction also fails to deconstruct the "foundational" constructivist theory in his own philosophy.

Therefore, the choice for postmodern epistemology is limited to determining not if, but only what, constructivist method is deemed appropriate to its agenda. A selective deconstructivism or critique, matched with a new metanarrative, are the final results.[17] For example, postmodern metaphysics defers its epistemological base to the local, communal context in order to save their constructivist assumptions. Yet, there is little differentiation to be found between a preference for the universal and the postmodern appeal

15. Ibid.

16. Willard, "Utilitarianism and Phenomenology," "Knowledge and Naturalism," and, "Non-Reductive and Non-Eliminative Physicalism."

17. Willard, "Degradation of Logical Form"

to the particular.[18] Neither position resists constructivism and therefore largely, if not intentionally, eludes the realist perspective altogether.[19]

Perhaps the most significant effect postmodernism has made on contemporary evangelicalism is found in Derrida's program of deconstruction. Derrida's deconstructive ideology builds on previous works by Peirce, Heidegger, and Saussure to form esoteric concepts such as *difference,* signs and signifieds, and the erasure of the transcendental signified.[20] Although interesting and complex, these issues are tangential to the specific interests related to evangelicalism and Willardian theology. It is Derrida's infamous phrase, "there is nothing outside the text" that most directly relates to this work and has created a firestorm of critique. Conservative evangelicals fear the effect Derrida's linguistic constructivism, idealism, and the implications these ideologies have on divine revelation and Scripture. Simply stated, Derrida's claim for indeterminacy in texts is only a clarification or exponent of the constructivist project. Nothing, including texts, can have any transcendent effect, intent, or meaning "outside" the contextual limitations of a reading or reader. No meaning, reality, or authorial intent exists in a text and thus cannot be conveyed and maintained across time, history, and experience. Strict constructivists such as Derrida propose no text, because no object—no "thing"—is independent of reader response and subjective interpretation.

Therefore, Derridian deconstruction proposes all things, including texts, are ultimately subordinated to the inherent subjectivism of individual or communal constructivist hermeneutics. There is no objective or logocentric metaphysical and ontological basis for knowledge.[21] Nothing is outside the eye of the beholder since there is no "thing" behind the text to which the text can refer. The temporal interpretation of the texts, as with all things engaged or encountered in human life, is forever limited by the subjective application of whatever hermeneutic is chosen. There are no objects; only subjects and ideals, with subjective interpretations and ideological constructions of objects, can come before the mind.

18. For an excellent discussion on this, see Best and Kellner, *Postmodern Theory: Critical Interrogations*, 172.

19. A prime example of this tension is seen in one of the early dealings with postmodern theory by evangelicals in Tomlinson, *The Post Evangelical*, 82–83. An excellent description of the post-evangelical tension, Tomlinson stresses the need to break the hold of metanarratives but struggles to recognize, describe, or reconstruct a more valid epistemology or metaphysics.

20. Derrida, *Of Grammatology*, 326. And, Llewelyn, *Derrida on the Threshold of Sense*, xi.

21. This is discussed in greater detail in the chapter on Willard's theology and philosophical realism.

This concept is what D. A. Carson has termed "hard postmodernism."[22] In analyzing the implications of Derrida's postmodern constructivist epistemology, Carson argues no Christian can reasonably assume a "hard" postmodern worldview. However, it is not just Christianity that stands opposed to "hard" constructivism. Any knowledge claim, religious or not, that points to even a semblance of potential for objectivity or realism in areas of logic, epistemology, metaphysics, or ethics is anathema to a "hard" constructivist position.[23]

Willard's most detailed critique of postmodernism is saved for Derrida.[24] Willard suggests Derrida's misinterpretation and misapplication of Husserl has done nothing less than "unhinge the American mind" and cause a crisis in the university system of education.[25] In summary, Willard suggests Derrida's theories of texts and deconstructionism announced the elimination of "transcendental signifieds," the non-existence of "original data" or new concepts, and the inability to access "real stuff" apart from that which is shaped and formed by language.[26] If rigidly applied, the results of Derridian deconstruction will not form coherent methods of thought but instead only a set of claims about thought and a discourse on the meaning of thought. Hence, Willard argues that the sum total of the Derridian corpus presents very little in terms of a result. Instead, Derrida makes many claims, sets definitions, plays on words, and presents stories while providing precious few discernible arguments for his conclusions.

Willard recognizes Derrida's popularity is unmistakable. Nevertheless, style appears to have largely been mistaken for substance. However

22. Carson, *Becoming Conversant with the Emerging Church*, 104. Scot McKnight makes a similar claim. See McKnight, "What is Emerging Church."

23. It is mentioned here to recognize the continuing struggle to define postmodernism due to the ambiguous and perhaps misunderstood nature of the endeavor. Secondly, what needs be highlighted is not so much the real or imagined threat Derrida makes to Christianity. Instead, it is essential to note constructivism is in no way a postmodern invention. Constructivism has a long history dating back to Giambattista Vico, a great admirer of Cartesian philosophy who first defined the constructivist paradigm. Therefore, there appears to be a significant misnomer in most claims regarding the "post" nature of postmodernism. Since constructivism is tightly connected to Cartesian and Kantian thought, which is then modified and expounded on by Wittgenstein, Heidegger, Nietzsche, and finally Derrida, the concepts of deconstruction do not arise after the modern enterprise but right in the middle of it. See Gruender, "Constructivism and Learning," 21–29; Delanty, *Social Science*, 39–47; Dusek, *Philosophy of Technology*, 199.

24. Willard has several articles on this subject. See McKenna, "Is Derrida's View of Ideal Being Rationally Defensible?" 23–41, and "Prediction a Originary Violence: A Phenomenological Critique of Derrida's View of Intentionality," 120–36.

25. Willard, "Unhinging of the American Mind—Derrida as Pre-Text," 3–20.

26. Ibid.

unsubstantiated Derrida's philosophical constructs may be, Willard recognizes Derrida's brilliance and the fascination his theories have developed in popular culture. What concerns Willard most is the tragic impact Derridian thought has made on higher education. Willard writes,

> The undermining of the normative power of the disciplines [and their texts] seems at the popular level to open the way to saying that any reading of a text by anybody has a certain legitimacy to it—and this can be rationalized in various ways—or by saying that the reading of the text that is socially sustainable at present is the right one, as long as it is socially sustainable. . . And the intellectual atmosphere at the teacher student nexus is thick with such views, coming from both sides. This goes along with the view, commonly defended or assumed that all texts are as good or can be as good as any other since there is no objective ordering of text as to their value, no "canon" other than what is politically enforced.[27]

What is reconstructed in Derrida's deconstruction, if anything, remains a mystery. Willard argues the effect of deconstruction is to engage in endless pursuits of reduction to the point of eliminating any possible foundation (logos) upon which any authoritative position could rest even if such a premise were desirable. Therefore, it would seem Derridian thought pursues the epistemological virtue of "singularity," where no single idea or thought is foundational enough to be built upon. Yet, Derridian singularity itself proves this a practical impossibility since the deconstructive effort employs an immense and intricate theory, representing no less an accumulation of ideological constructs than those of any metanarrative or text it seeks to undermine.

Postmodern Theological Praxis

Willard recognizes how *en vogue* postmodern language and thought have become in theology over recent years. Although not agreeing with all of the many descriptions and applications of postmodernism to Christian thinking and life, Willard is sympathetic to much of the impetus for change and the critique of modern hubris postmodernism carries. However, several postmodern/postevangelical Christians tend to assume there is a connection between the Willardian critiques of evangelical or Christian thought to a version or type of postmodern deconstruction. This is an unfortunate error that reveals a lack of understanding of the philosophical underpinnings

27. Ibid.

of Derridian thought in specific and postmodern epistemology or intellectual process in general. Willard employs nothing of the Derridian concept of deconstruction in his reconsidering of evangelical theology and praxis. Yet, the misunderstanding is both interesting and instructive.

When deconstruction moves from the ideological/philosophical framework of postmodern*ism* into the popular, cultural articulation of postmodern*ity*, the philosophical assumptions of Derrida's deconstructive process are widely eschewed and replaced with a form of wholesale critique and analysis. The result is a form of intellectual investigation that is not nearly as ambiguous or constructivist and, consequently, one with little to no nihilistic bite. Within the postevangelical/ECM contexts mentioned earlier, the overwhelming majority of intellectual reconsiderations done under the banner of "deconstruction" actually resembles only a scant reflection of the enterprise Derrida actually proposed.[28]

In other words, in philosophical postmodern*ism*, deconstruction functions as a noun. In the cultural representation of postmodern*ity*, where most postevangelical/ECM activity eventuates, the concept of deconstruction works like a verb or an adjective to describe the attempt to apply what is very similar to the phenomenological exercise of "bracketing." This is why Willard's application of the Husserlian concept of the *epoche* is crucial. It also gives insight into why Willard's theological method is so attractive to postevangelical leaders reconsidering their evangelical theology and praxis. Husserl's phenomenological process describes in detail the essential requirement of separating ideas about a thing from the thing itself.[29] Therefore, one "brackets" or sets aside thoughts and ideas about a thing, including all preconceived notions and assumptions, and focuses only on the experience of the object itself. This is Husserl's method for clearing out any clouded and confusing delimiters that prevent the engagement of an object as it is "in and of itself."

In similar but not identical fashion, Willard's theological methodology and philosophy prioritizes the "bracket." He often sets aside preexisting

28. In general terms, whenever there is a claim that "truth" or "reality" or "facts" are completely and totally inaccessible, one is often presented with a Derridian form of deconstruction. However, in interviews with most EC leaders, very few actually take this "hard" epistemological position. Although there remains disagreement on the vague notion regarding the degree to which certainty and truth are conjoined in conversations about knowledge, see McKnight's, "What is Emerging Church?" However, many ECM leaders make very strong and visceral truth claims, not the least of which is Rob Bell and Dan Kimball: Kimball's *The Emerging Church*; Bell, *Sex God: Exploring the Endless Connections between Sexuality and Spirituality*; Bell, *Velvet Elvis*; Bell, *Love Wins*; Bell, *Drops Like Stars: What We Talk About When We Talk About God*; and Bell and Golden, *Jesus Wants to Save Christians.*

29. Kockelmans and Husserl, *Edmund Husserl's Phenomenology*, 124.

statements, claims, or doctrinal beliefs about the world, philosophical assumptions, theological doctrines, self-evident propositions, and dogmas of Christian faith. When used appropriately, the bracket allows Willard and his readers to prioritize and then pursue a more "unvarnished" description of the experience of life and its objects as they appear in the world and the lives of individuals. In this process, direct realism combines with phenomenological methodology as a means to search for a more direct vision and experience of the world. This is crucial to understanding the foundational framework that undergirds the Willardian concepts of life in the kingdom of God and the experience of the theo-ontological reality.

The result of this approach presents an epistemological position unique to Enlightenment empiricism, modern constructivism, or postmodern deconstruction. Theologically, from this epistemological platform, Willard argues the teachings of Jesus, and much of the body of knowledge passed down through the intellectual Christian tradition, while perhaps imperfect in regards to specifics, has rather competently articulated the metaphysical, ethical, logical, and epistemological reality of human life and existence. While these efforts are not finished, by any means, pursuing and probing the realities of the kingdom of God is a life-long and eternal task that is both possible and experientially verifiable. Hence, accurate conclusions, although perhaps partial or incomplete, can be discovered and articulated.

Consequentially, there is a sense in which Willard's phenomenological methodology "deconstructs" or "distinguishes" assumption, preconception, supposition, conjecture, and theory from the actual experience Jesus described and offered in the kingdom of God. What appears to be often confusing to postmoderns reading Willard's work is his frequent highlighting of the contradictory distinctions between Jesus' description of "life in the kingdom" to that of the traditional categories and doctrines of evangelical theology. Willard's "bracketing" of contemporary lenses and their assumptions can often be interpreted and misunderstood as a Willardian application of Derridian deconstruction. In fact, the opposite is true. Willard's bracketing is instead the simple, free, and fearless intellectual pursuit to discover and experience the essential nature of Christian thought and life. Such an inquiry requires a willingness to consider every claim and doctrine based upon its own merit and devoid of the implicative baggage attached to it.

Such intellectual work is significant and intrinsically valuable, especially for postevangelicals, many of whom were reared in anti-intellectual and legalistic backgrounds where intellectual inquiry is often considered oppositional to faith. Willard's work tends to elicit a poignant and liberating experience that sets an example and standard of intellectual excellence for both evangelicals and postevangelicals to pursue. However, Willard's methodology is in no way affiliated with the Derridian deconstructive exercise. To assume so is to miss the critical epistemological difference between the role logocentrism plays in both realism and constructivism. Willard is seeking, and describing the discovery of, exactly what Derrida claims does not exist and cannot be known. Willard claims to have found, is continuing to find, and is providing knowledge to others about the very point, realm, and reality of the biblical text which Derrida contends has no external referent and lives only in the minds of the reader.

Moderating the Divide

Important in this brief backdrop are the specific effects philosophical postmodernism have made on mainstream evangelical theology. First, conservative evangelicals sense "hard" postmodernism violates the modern assumption that humanity, or the critical self, is capable and competent to consciously discern the world through the employment of empirical and rational means. Instead, the skeptical nature of postmodernism argues the modern "Enlightened" self, which has come to comprehend selfhood through its stories, texts, (especially the Bible), vocations, and its intellectual history is severely affected by a myopic epistemological hubris and cultural blindness of the certainty, absolutism, and the delusion of humanistic mastery. ECM leaders tend to apply this same critique to the doctrinal certainty present in systematic evangelical theology and praxis. Postevangelicals perceived the political power of the Religious Right, the CGM ecclesiology, and neo-evangelical dogmas of premillennial eschatology and biblical literalism as contemporary manifestations of Foucault, Lyotard, and Derrida's warnings against modernity's manipulation of language games, abuses of power, and dominating metanarratives to subvert any and all competing claims for epistemological authority.

There are other conflicts that have arisen between modern evangelicals and postmodern ECM advocates. Yet, none is perhaps greater than the struggle between postmodern hermeneutics and its direct threat to evangelical biblicism. ECM leaders suggest that evangelicalism's *a priori* assumptions regarding Scriptural inerrancy, infallibility, and divine revelation must reconnect with the advent of postmodern deconstruction and the anthropomorphic temptation to abuse such grand claims to knowledge. Further, Derrida's employment of textual criticism calls for an investigation beyond traditional evangelical presentational and representational ways of describing texts, revelation, and modern forms of discerning metaphysics.[30]

30. Derrida, *Dissemination*, 43–46. Also, John Caputo's work on the metaphysics of presence is a substantial problem for many evangelicals. See Caputo, *Radical*

As a result, the attempt of modern evangelical theologians to undergird their biblicist priority through the application of modern hermeneutical methodology, systematic theological rationalization, or historical context comes under increased scrutiny. Postmodern hermeneutics places suspicion on each of the evangelical attempts to validate and authorize a totalizing structure of the biblical metanarrative.[31]

These epistemological differences leave modern evangelicals at somewhat of a logical impasse with postmodern philosophy in general and postmodern evangelicals in specific. As a result, the ECM began to distance themselves, not so much from the underlying theological objectives of historical evangelicalism, much of which many ECM leaders have retained. Rather, postevangelicals seek to create separation from the modern methodological and epistemological devotions within evangelical theology. Postmodern evangelicals argue the neo-evangelical devotions to modern foundationalism, universalization, rationalism, totalitarianism, and exclusivism threaten the veracity of the very gospel they profess. ECM leaders argue such fidelity seems more a product of modern fundamentalist arrogance than divine inspiration.

Conversely, for conservatives, postmodernism represents nothing short of a reconstruction of theological liberalism, which threatened to eviscerate not just evangelicalism but historic Christian orthodoxy. ECM advocates often contend mainstream evangelicalism remains encumbered by the undercurrent of fundamentalism and its hopelessly logical, consistent, and rationalistic form of Christian faith. To the ECM, such a rigid Christianity is left devoid of mystery, miracle, transcendence, and awe, all characteristics unworthy of a limitless God evangelicals claim to worship. Postmodernism contends for a paradoxical epistemology modern evangelical rationalism cannot endure. The uncertainty, nuance, and mystery despised in modernism is equally valued and celebrated in postmodernism. Modern Christian apologetics melded a paradox into their systematic theology by interpreting the super-natural acts of God in very natural, rational and methodologically consistent ways. Mysterious, miraculous wonders became rational events completely within the comprehension and explanation of the modern systematic theology. Other metaphysical biblical concepts such as the Incarnation and the atonement of sin followed suit.

Modern evangelicals continually triumphed the virtues of method and consistency. A daily devotional "quiet time" of daily prayer and Bible

Hermeneutics: Repetition, Deconstruction, and the Hermeneutic Project and *The Prayers and Tears of Jacques Derrida: Religion without Religion.*

31. Fekete, *The Structural Allegory*, Intro.; and Attridge, *Post-structuralism and the Question of History*, 6–11.

reading, weekly church attendance, and Bible memorization programs were touted as the proven methods for reliably achieving a "Christian life." Yet, the evidence of personal transformation into Christ-likeness resulting from the applications of these methods was far from obvious or consistent. Worse, to postmodern evangelicals such reductionistic methods effectively eliminated the awe-inspiring power, transcendence, and ambiguity inherent to the supernatural. What conservative evangelicals feared a century earlier from liberal theology has come to pass. Ironically, the nominalism and diminishment of the divine within their own ranks did not come from the result of theological liberalism but through the heavy-handed legalism, rationalism, and reductionism of their own theological platform.

Eventually, various ECM leaders began to try their hand at forming alternative, postmodern theological platforms. Theologians and philosophers such as Stanley Grenz, Ray Anderson, Robert Webber, Carl Raschke, John Milbank, James K. A. Smith, and others have each attempted to create a meaningful epistemological framework that remains true to key Christian distinctives but arrives at theological conclusions through "softer" postmodern proclivities. Others have attempted to use the works of theologian Jürgen Moltmann,[32] philosopher/theologians Mark C. Taylor,[33] Thomas Altizer,[34] John Caputo, and Jeffery Robbins,[35] to develop "hard" postmodern theologies that employ more constructivist, relativist, and pluralist epistemologies. These theologies often highlight ambiguity, communal discernment, contextual dependence, and dialectical engagement of idiosyncratic semantic definitions of theological concepts. As such, their conclusions routinely present proposals tied to few if any evangelical priorities. Even popular ECM writer and speaker Brian McLaren's most recent attempt at forming a postmodern/postevangelical theological praxis in *A New Kind of Christianity* has struggled to gain traction.[36] Although an interesting and insightful writer, McLaren's latest publications do not appear to have garnered the same effect of his earlier works.[37]

The inability to make any truth claim capable of withstanding the nullifying subjectification within Derridian deconstruction eviscerates much

32. Moltmann, *Experiences in Theology*, 258.

33. Taylor, *Erring: A Postmodern a/Theology*, and Taylor, *After God*.

34. Altizer, *Living the Death of God*.

35. Robbins, *Between Faith and Thought*, and, Robbins *In Search of a Non-Dogmatic Theology*.

36. McLaren, *A New Kind of Christianity*.

37. See McKnight's and Brink's review of McLaren's *A New Kind of Christianity*, Brink, "A Review of a New Kind of Christianity," and McKnight, "Review: A New Kind of Christianity," 59–66.

of the postmodern's theological objectives. The lack of an undergirding theological framework has caused some leaders in the ECM to split ranks, suggesting "hard" postmodernism threatens an irretrievable loss of any coherent, substantive argument for a consistent and defensible concept of knowledge or truth in general.

It is in these dilemmas—whether in an ambiguous state of postmodern constructivism or a closed state of modern, totalitarian, and absolutist dogmatism—where many contemporary postevangelicals lament their faith. It is also where the protoevangelical theology offered by Willard has provided increasing numbers of postevangelical hopefuls a reasonable, encouraging, biblically-grounded alternative. The protoevangelicalism Willard articulates should not be confused with a pursuit of the "first" version of American evangelicalism. Rather, Willard's protoevangelicalism seeks something of a moratorium, or an escape from the trappings and limitations of the modern/postmodern, sacred/secular, revelational/communal, fundamentalist/liberal "insider" theological debates, alterations, and standards of evangelical orthodoxy. Instead, Willard seeks to recapture the transcendent quintessential goodness and opportunity Jesus first taught, demonstrated, and manifested in the New Testament.

There are other aspects of the postmodern move Willard appreciates and supports. One such facet is the positive attention postmodernism has brought to abuse of power, manipulation, and increased proclivity to defend the marginalized voice of the "other." Here, Willard and other evangelical theologians seek to bolster the postmodern aim. Historically, several political and military régimes have used authority, propaganda, and manipulation to articulate a metanarrative and a theology for abusive ends. Some postevangelical theologians such as Grenz,[38] Walsh, and Middleton,[39] as well as more popular writers such as McLaren,[40] Jones,[41] and Pagitt,[42] pick up on Foucault's argument.[43] They also suggest the effect of modern metanarratives and language manipulation, within contemporary culture in general,

38. Grenz, *A Primer on Postmodernism*, 45.

39. Middleton and Walsh, *Truth Is Stranger Than It Used to Be*, 70–75.

40. McLaren, *A New Kind of Christianity*, 265.

41. Jones, *The New Christians*, 139–41, 229. Jones does speak to metanarratives in this work, but his interpretation of the effect of metanarratives and subsequent preference of "communal discernment" and a "hermeneutics of humility" are the terms he uses.

42. Pagitt, "The Emerging Church and Embodied Theology," 127; Pagitt, *Preaching Re-Imagined*. Like Jones, Pagitt responds to the metanarrative hegemony by choosing instead to enlist a local, communal hermeneutic.

43. Foucault, *Power/Knowledge*, and Foucault and Khalfa, *History of Madness*, 333.

and evangelical theology in specific, has been to oppress the minority view and create a moral crisis of elitism and separatism.[44]

However, the greatest degree of commonality between postmodernism and Willardian thought is found in the critique of the modern construction of the self and rejection of the optimism and myopia of anthropocentrism within secular humanism.[45] Willard agrees the modern hubris of the Enlightenment narrative has largely lost its influence on Western humanity. He discusses at length the fracturing of the human soul, the loss of selfhood, and the consequential devolving condition of both society at large and the local church in specific. Additionally, Willard would agree with Middleton and Walsh's ironic suggestion that "*homo autonomous* is reconstituted as *Homo linguisticus*," not as a truth statement as much as a recognition of the pragmatic reality inherent to postmodernity.[46] Willard would also agree with Kenneth Gergen's conclusion that in such a linguistic-centric paradigm, where words do not reflect reality itself but only representations of reality that may or may not be accurate, the idea of constructing a knowable and reliable concept of the self is also "effectively dismantled," since the autonomous self is a particular construct of the Enlightenment ethos.

The fact that postmodernism tends to reflect almost exclusively on the negative aspects of individualism, consumerism, and humanism results in the emergence of an identity gap within much of Western society. Willard describes this gap in both *The Divine Conspiracy* and *Renovation of the Heart* as the ruined soul that has struggled to land on a worthy cause or substance for its existence largely to no avail. A significant part of Willard's theological corpus is devoted to the concepts surrounding the topic of spiritual formation.[47] These works keenly describe how and why the human soul is frequently fractured and the results of the dis-integration of the individual aspects of a person that form a single personality.[48] Without a focus, purpose, or central motivating vision for life, Willard suggests "the greatest obstacles to effective spiritual formation in Christ today is the simple failure to understand and acknowledge the reality of the human situation as it affects Christians and non-Christians alike. We must start from where we really are."[49] And unfortunately, Willard recognizes people in a postmod-

44. Middleton and Walsh, *Truth is Stranger Than it Used to Be*, 71.

45. An excellent discussion on this and the effects of postmodernism at large on the evangelical theology is found in Knowles, *Beyond Evangelicalism*, 22–26.

46. Middleton and Walsh, *Truth Is Stranger Than It Used to Be*, 51.

47. Lifton, *The Protean Self*.

48. See Willard's description of the self in ROH, chapter 2.

49. ROH, chapter 3.

ern consumeristic society find themselves in a state of what he calls "helter skelter."[50]

Attempting to further explain this concept, Robert Lifton describes what he terms the "protean self," named after the Greek god of the sea who was able to take on multiple forms as circumstances require. Likewise, Lifton concludes the postmodern construct of the self propagates destabilization and thus demands a new search for fulfillment.

> We are left in a permanent flux of relativity. In many cases . . . postmodern anthropology seems now to go to the other extreme. Instead of certainty and purpose, there is now play; for determinacy there is indeterminacy; fixed ideas are replaced by process; the heterogeneous properties of the postmodern self come to the fore. The notion of a de-centered self results in a self that is not anchored to anything. It is a self that floats upon the waters of postmodernity like a fragment of driftwood, on tides of momentary desires and needs, and tossed about by the latest whims, fads, and fascinations. Who you are depends on where you are, who you are with, what you are doing, and the time that you are doing it. This fragmentation of the self produces a chameleon-like self, and a very insecure chameleon at that.[51]

To this chameleon-like existence, Willard recognizes American evangelicalism has drawn itself to consumerism like a moth to a flame.[52] Willard also speaks to the consumerism in the church as a natural consequence of the unhinging of the self from the traditional understanding of the self conveyed in Scripture. The consumer-focused identity is a form of materialism that indicates a pronounced dearth of appreciation for the spiritual nature of Christian life and reality.[53] The "have it your way" priority of consumer satisfaction has created an expectation that religiously minded consumers are equally able, and have the self-evident authority, to mix and match the elements of their faith as easily as they can specify their preferences for a

50. Helter Skelter is a term from a early rock and roll song that was popularized for its use in the Charlie Manson murders in northern California in the late 1970's. Commenting on Manson's use of the song to characterize and instill the state of confusion among his followers and himself, Willard suggests, "in a state of helter skelter, nothing makes sense. And everything makes as much sense as anything else. So for example when you cut someone's throat or stab them repeatedly and they die, you didn't really kill them and they didn't really die. That was Manson's [constructivist] teaching." See ROH, 43–44.

51. Knowles, *Beyond Evangelicalism*, 26.

52. GO, 52.

53. SD, 56–95.

hamburger. Willard is critical of modern evangelicalism in the way it panders to the lowest common denominator of consumerism in terms of filling seats and membership lists to the detriment of forming the human spirit in discipling relationships to Christ.[54]

Several key concepts of postmodernism—namely the demise of metanarrative and its power plays, the impact of deconstruction, and their combined effects on the fracturing of the postmodern self—are emblematic of the similar if not the same primary issues concerning postevangelicals. As a philosopher and theologian, Willard is uniquely positioned to explicitly engage these critical issues. Although Willard has not specifically dealt with each of these concepts in his theological writing, his philosophical works engage, critique, and challenge the foundational assumptions of nominalism and constructivism, which he contends undergirds the entire postmodern enterprise and the theology that proceeds from the same.

Summary

To summarize this section, Willard departs from many of his evangelical peers in their sometimes hyper-reactive response to all things postmodern. Willard is sympathetic to the universal claims of scientism and recognizes the harmful effects modern hubris has wrought. Additionally, Willard is a proponent for "deconstruction," albeit not at all the Derridian form previously described. Instead, Willard advocates for a continual, diligent search for increasing levels of knowledge and discernment within all texts, methodologies, and knowledge claims alike. This he understands as the primary motive of intellectual work: to distinguish and delineate things, one from another. Thus, "deconstructing" hermeneutical tools and their products is a beneficial and necessary endeavor. However, unlike Derrida, Willard contends that there is something behind, underneath, and/or above the texts that the texts aim to describe. Context matters, of course. Yet, an essential distinction for Willard would be his assertion that context is only a shaper, not a determiner, of reality. Taking an Aristotelian and Husserlian position, Willard holds reality can be engaged, albeit humbly, fleetingly and incompletely, but essentially, through the intentional processes of honest intellectual pursuit.

An example of this distinction is seen in Willard's treatment of the Bible as a specific text. He holds the Bible as open to interpretation and as such allows for pluralism and subjectivism to a degree. Application of hermeneutical

54. Willard, "Rethinking Evangelism," and "The Failure of Evangelical Political Involvement in the Area of Moral Transformation," 74–91.

lenses is unavoidable since humans are subjects and apply filters through which experience is shaped. This would include culture, environment, tradition, etc. However, that humans are subjects does not logically demand that Scripture, directed by the *Logos*, cannot transcend the limits of subjectivity and convey objectivity to human subjects if desired. Hence, Willard reasserts direct realism and logocentrism into his conceptualization of Scripture. From that position, Willard asserts the claims of the Bible can be tested to determine their veracity. No constructivism is required.

Willard would agree with Derrida that an appropriate means to discern objectivity is found in community. However, Willard is quick to note communal discernment is neither the only nor the exclusive means of accurate discernment, due to the "mobs'" ability to both mislead and be misled. Instead, Willard holds that knowledge of the world is possible, desirable and essential for life and flourishing both individually and corporately. Additionally, he holds that knowledge, along with grace and love, is a primary benefit of the life Jesus describes in the kingdom of God. Willard does not share the modern assumptions of certainty, either individually or corporately, as offered in the Enlightenment's optimistic notion of objective truth. Nor is he confident in the application of methodological rigor and strict empiricism present in many modern systematic theologies. However, Willard does hold firmly to the existence of truth, not as an idealist but as a realist. Communal consensus can assist in the process of discernment between good or better interpretations, since there is a point of measurement from which members can gauge progress. Therefore, faith communities establish credibility and determine meaning from a preexisting point of reality, and interpretations are guarded and guided by the Holy Spirit into all "truth."

This pneumatological aspect is certainly not without its vulnerabilities and abuses of power. Authority for determining veracity of an interpretation and its advocation from the Holy Spirit remains a point of contention. Yet, Willard would argue that abuse is not to be eliminated in the Christian life. Abuse is an ever-present necessity for the relationship of free beings.[55] Thus, the character or underlying intent and desire (want) rises to primacy in Willard's theology. If one wants to abuse a text, twist a metanarrative, manipulate relationships, or even delude the self, self-determinacy allows and funds such an agenda. Like Foucault, Willard recognizes the potential abuse of power is incumbent in all human activity. But Foucault was not a complete skeptic, nor was he fatalistic about human power relations. "It is precisely the positive mechanism [of power] that needs to be investigated, and here one must free oneself from all the previous characterizations of the

55. Willard, "Good and the Problem of Evil."

nature of power."[56] Foucault encouraged reconsideration of human/power relations, so too, Willard's focus on the development of a transformed character, which can assume the responsibility to engage real states of affairs on their own terms and the power that position conveys without requiring some self-preserving or protecting epistemological maneuver or the marginalization of the "other."

This is the ultimate goal of Willard's theo-ontology. Willard's view of the gospel describes the pursuit and attainment of a quality of personal integration and security of will that effectively eliminates the impetuses that have caused the abuses of power, dominating delusions of grandeur or self-centeredness, and the egomaniacal pursuits postmodernism so vitally protests. Thus, Willard's vision of the Christian life appeals to those sympathizing with the postmodern rejection of modernism and asserts the kingdom of God described by Jesus has as much a claim of legitimacy as any other worldview and should, therefore, be judged by its results on an equal playing field in the marketplace of ideas.

For Willard, the ability and essentiality of distinguishing things one from another is a basic tenet of all intellectual endeavors. However, for evangelicalism, such a pursuit may represent either a lost art or, unfortunately, a moot point. Yet, it is in this dogged pursuit of distinguishing, clarifying, and discriminating where a majority of postevangelicals are increasingly drawn to Willardian thought and theological process. If ideological analysis and separation does not occur among one's feelings, thoughts, opinions, or traditions about an object or subject, making a thing independent and distinct in itself, then definitions, meanings, purposes, concepts, and structures progressively lose all power and authority over life. A migration occurs toward a self-defining reality. This is Willard's argument for bracketing.

In like manner, evangelicals have largely not learned to separate feelings, needs, and experiences about theological issues or ideas from the theological ideas themselves. Therefore, staunch anti-constructivist evangelicals have unwittingly begun to employ the disastrously ironic facilities of constructivism in practice, which they diametrically oppose in theory. Willard highlights these ironies continuously. His works regularly seek to separate and distinguish, for instance, the popular evangelical ideas of the "church" from the biblical concept of kingdom of God. Likewise, Willard spends a great deal of time distinguishing the concepts surrounding "salvation" as articulated in Scripture from the sermonized reductionism in popular evangelical theology that often limits salvation to attaining the destination of heaven in the afterlife.

56. Foucault, *Power and Knowledge*, 120–22.

There are several examples where Willard separates what contemporary evangelicalism has coalesced. Many of these have already been reviewed in previous chapters. The point to make here is that postevangelicals appreciate and respond to Willard's overt resistance to evangelical convolution and interchanging of key theological ideas, their negative implications, and the confusion which results. Most troubling, Willard contends this theological negligence, by default, creates a constructivist playground where an alternative, anthropomorphic religious enterprise is humanly constructed under the banner of a historically sound and biblically Christian theological framework. Willard argues it is exactly this misappropriated endeavor Jesus staunchly opposed and attempted to correct in first century Judaism.[57]

Therefore, Willard proposes ongoing vigilance in all theological and epistemological endeavors inside Christian circles. The constructivist "enemy" is inside the camp, as it were, and not simply an outside threat. "Judgment starts with the house of God" Willard writes.[58] This clarification appears to be the underlying motive for Willard—to both seek and achieve a more radical, authentic, and metaphysically real protoevangelical theology and practice. It is also this drive and motive that draws postevangelicals to his works.

57. Willard makes a continuing point of this in his deep discussion of chapter 3 of John's Gospel where Jesus talks to an apparently confused and unenlightened religious leader, Nicodemus. DC, 68. ISOG, chapter 7 and KC, 195.

58. GO, 225.

Chapter Six

Conclusion

To Willard's thinking, the current reality in American evangelicalism represents the dire condition of the construction and application of alternative gospels highlighted in the previous chapters. In differing degrees and with differing effects, the preponderance of American evangelicalism and its organizations are mired in one version or another of these non-orthodox visions of Christian faith. The ability to pick and choose among different manifestations of these gospels, in somewhat of a "buffet style" selection process, represents a distinctly Americanized version of evangelicalism that pays homage to consumer culture.[1]

This is not the evangelicalism that proceeded from the late eighteenth and early nineteenth century. In his article for the *Oxford Handbook of Evangelical Theology*, Willard recognizes that the brand of evangelicalism marked by Edwards, Wesley, Whitefield, and Finney would have little continuity with contemporary versions of evangelicalism in America.[2] He sees the evangelical "revivals" of the first half of the eighteenth century and moving into the first half of the nineteenth century as a very different kind of endeavor from the revivalism of the Billy Graham era that swept the country after WWII. The evangelistic "revivals" of Wesley and others intended to "revive" that which was once "alive" but had become listless. These revivals were efforts targeted at retrieving a *protoeuangelion* that targeted Christians and strived to redirect and spur them on toward Christlikeness and righteous living. According to Willard, these earlier evangelicals believed righteous living (*dikaiosune*), not evangelical forms of proselytizing, was the primary means of establishing and bearing witness to the veracity of their faith to non-believers.

1. DC, 303.
2. Willard, "Discipleship," 239.

The Divine Conspiracy intones exactly how Willard views the contemporary systems of sin management and the ignominious affect a "barcode" type of faith have made on the broader culture of western civilization. He states his hope for *The Divine Conspiracy* was to give the gospel of Jesus a new and fresh hearing, "especially among those who believe they already understand him. In this case . . . quite frankly, presumed familiarity has led to unfamiliarity, unfamiliarity has led to contempt, and contempt has led to profound ignorance."[3] Thus, ignorance of and/or apathy for the original message of Jesus and it effects have allowed other intentions and motives to overpower and control evangelical Christianity, essentially separating the religion from its namesake and thus threatening elimination of the original impetus altogether.

In conforming the gospel of Jesus to fit contemporary motives, Willard proposes the message has ceased to make sense and seeks to elicit compliance only from moralizing the negative. Instead, Willard believes the message Jesus presented must remain "free of the deadening legalisms, political sloganeering, and dogmatic traditionalism long proven by history to be soul-crushing dead-ends. Obviously, [the gospel Jesus himself believed and taught] does not come to us now, and this is a fact widely recognized."[4]

The implications of Willard's statements here are stunning to consider. They also illuminate the heart of what may be the single differentiating insight into Willardian theology. Simply stated, Willard seems to be communicating that the vision of the kingdom of God, or the primary point of the enterprise of Christianity itself, has been altered over time in such a way that the corpus of the entire vision or mission of God has been either lost or replaced by another message. Willard is unqualifying in his statement that

> . . . serious difficulties currently bar people of good intent from an effectual understanding of Jesus' gospel for life and discipleship in the kingdom. . . . If we cannot remove [these difficulties] no gospel we bring can have the natural tendency to lead onward into a life of discipleship to Jesus and to personal fulfillment in the kingdom of the heavens.[5]

It is not an exaggeration to suggest that Willard's critique of contemporary evangelicalism places him as one who generally views the enterprise as focused on objectives often contradictory to those presented as the *missio Dei* throughout the whole of Scripture. Secondly, Willard also senses the institutions and organizations of evangelicalism have largely ignored or turned away

3. DC, xv.
4. DC, 59.
5. Ibid.

from the application of Jesus' specific teachings and their values. Throughout his works, Willard continually illuminates his views on the results of the re-institutionalization and advocation of a different, and one could say un-Christlike, gospel. That these alternative gospels are widely professed from America pulpits and embodied in a multitude of Christian organizations is the single reason, Willard proposes, for the impotency of the Christian religion to manifest an overwhelmingly beneficial movement for good in contemporary society.

Further, Willard's alternative vision of the kingdom is not to be confused as a critique of a slightly misguided recontextualization of Christianity. Willard is not suggesting that the evangelical gospels currently articulated are biblically orthodox but have only been overly contextualized to a twenty-first-century culture. Rather, he suggests the evangelical message itself has become substantially and essentially altered to focus on ends different from those valued and presented by Jesus. However, with ample weight given to Willard's claims of unorthodoxy mentioned above, perhaps his greatest critique is levied at the exclusivity modern evangelicalism currently places on the "conversion" experience as opposed to the decision for discipleship to Jesus. Willard states that current expressions of evangelicalism within more conservative and fundamentalist churches since WWII have presented "very little . . . about discipleship except what is anecdotal—and there is not a lot of that."[6]

All of these previous critiques and the alternative gospels that have been articulated earlier result in the increasing distance between stated beliefs in appropriate Christian doctrines and the application of said beliefs in the lives of evangelical proponents. In street language, Willard suggests the evangelical "talk" does not have a "walk." In Willard's view, a doctrine of belief that does not entail commensurate action is ineffectual. Further, Willard contends such an understanding of belief itself is both psychologically impossible and biblically false.[7]

Nevertheless, this impotence of belief has grown within recent forms of evangelicalism. Willard argues the spread of conservative forms of evangelicalism, which developed a resistance to acknowledging Jesus as a master teacher, is a key factor. To consider or advocate for Jesus as a teacher became a "code" word that hinted at a liberal theology that dismissed Jesus' divinity and valued only his wise teachings. This conservative generalization resulted in the gradual elimination of the view of Jesus as a master teacher of life, one who actually is giving direction on how to live. Instead, conservative

6. Ibid.

7. Ibid.

theology elevated Jesus' sacrificial value, highlighting the "lamb of God" characteristic to coincide with their particular atonement theory.

On the left, considering Jesus as a good teacher and not also "divine" equally diminishes Christ's influence. Such a view relegates Jesus to only one of many good teachers with something valuable to add to the cacophony of wisdom offered down through the ages. As such, excluding Jesus as equally manifesting his person as the Son of God reduces confidence in his claims and the veracity of his miraculous deeds. Consequently, Christians on both the "left" and "right" marginalize their faith in, and knowledge of, Jesus altogether. The evidence for this claim, in Willard's perspective, is found in the broadening disappearance of moral knowledge and the elimination of the Christian worldview as a field of knowledge altogether.

This, Willard sees as a failure of the church to take the God-given and critically essential place within broader society to both articulate, demonstrate, and make manifest the wisdom of Christ. This is not simply the wisdom that argues for social activism or the wisdom that articulates a means of attaining bliss in the afterlife. Nor is it a wisdom that advocates for membership in a local church. Rather, Willard sees the church catholic as given the unique task to be a beacon of light to the world, illuminating the knowledge of Christ as the wisdom of God.[8] Such knowledge must be proven in displays of the knowledge of Christ and his ways, and a character formed around the essence of *agape* love. This, in Willard's view, was the divine plan for evangelism all along.[9]

It is the strength and vitality of Willard's positions on these key blights within modern evangelical Christianity that initially struck a deep chord in the hearts and minds of many young ECM and postevangelical leaders. Combined with their negative encounters of conservative, neo-evangelicalism's wrath-filled premillenial dispensationalism, the polarization of the Religious Right, and the individualistic consumerism of the CGM, Willard's protoevangelicalism forged an ideological bridge with increasing numbers of disaffected Christians. This connection would eventually lead to new attempts at reimagining evangelical theology and to the consideration of different praxis by which to express the gospel of Jesus in a twenty-first-century context. *The Divine Conspiracy* positioned Willard as a popular theologian in the manner of C. S. Lewis, offering a rather radical revision to and/or protest against much of what had become modern evangelical orthodoxy.

8. 2 Cor 4:6.

9. DC, 311.

As a result, *The Divine Conspiracy* became the work many postevangelicals still recognize and point to as a monumental catalyst for their intellectual and spiritual transformation as both Christians and leaders. Rob Bell, arguably the most renowned postmodern pastor, author, and speaker to emerging generations of Christians notes, "[Divine Conspiracy] has been the single most influential book in my life. I've read that same copy over and over again. Richard Foster said it's the book he waited all of his life for. I can say the same thing."[10] A similar refrain comes from Dieter Zander. Zander took nearly two years studying *The Divine Conspiracy* after he left the mega-church model of Willow Creek. His well-worn copy of the book provided a guide in the reconfiguring and deconstruction of his theological and ecclesiological understandings. Notably, early postevangelical leaders Mark Scandrette, Todd Hunter, Linda Bergquist, and Rod Washington accompanied Zander in this deconstruction of evangelicalism all using Willard's *Divine Conspiracy* to chart their way through unfamiliar waters.[11]

Willard encouraged this change and met with several young leaders at critical points during their deconstruction of modern evangelical ethos. His initial support was indicative of his belief that, as a whole, mainstream Christian leaders were not demonstrating or teaching about the availability and potency of the kingdom of God. The obvious demonstrative failure of this leadership responsibility, in Willard's view, represented the cause and effect of an increasingly inconsequential evangelical church. Willard uses a common saying among business management experts: "Their system is perfectly designed to yield the results they are getting."[12]

Postevangelicals appear to appreciate Willardian theology on two levels.[13] First, Willard seeks to correct contemporary evangelical systematic theology that has too often abused New Testament hermeneutics to satisfy a modern obsession with sectarian divisions, atonement theories, and doctrinal correctness. Willard's suggestion of modern eisegesis in the conservative evangelical theology appears to dovetail with the postmodern deconstructive exercise of bracketing (*epoche*). Willard argues modern

10. Bell, "E-mail Correspondence with Author."

11. Willard and Zander, "The Apprentices," 20–25.

12. DC, 58.

13. Willard is mentioned widely by many ECM leaders and specifically postevangelical writers. This fact will be widely discussed throughout this work. Here, two key texts are mentioned. Gibbs and Bolger, *Emerging Churches*, 49. And Tomlinson, *The Post Evangelical*, 11–15. Willard's most popular work *The Divine Conspiracy* received book of the year awards from conservative evangelical periodical *Christianity Today*. Scheller, "A Divine Conspirator," See also Bill Hull's discussion of this in "A Reluctant Prophet" 283–95.

evangelicalism has in places proceeded far afield from historically orthodox Christian theology and has effectively lost the "forest for the trees" in relation to the purpose and intent of the Christian gospel. However, unlike many postmodern/Emergent theologians who tend to exacerbate relativism and pluralism, which produces an unending list of equivocations, Willardian theology rests on a direct, epistemologically realist platform. Hence, Willardian theology offers a positive corrective that reestablishes the New Testament gospels as the entre' into the ontological and existential reality Jesus reveals and manifests as life in the kingdom of God.

In the process, Willard also reinvigorates past streams of pietistic Christianity that have been more recently overshadowed or forgotten amidst the modernist/fundamentalist dichotomies, culture wars, and politicized agendas that plagued the later half of twentieth-century evangelicalism. Simultaneously, Willard has consistently advocated a distinctively apolitical, ecumenically inclusive, culturally engaging, intellectually robust and personally transforming gospel message. Hence, in a time when evangelical theology may be approaching an epistemological crossroads where authority and authenticity are becoming increasingly reconsidered, Willardian theology presents a forceful critique and correction to many aspects of mainstream evangelicalism's religious doctrines and institutional accommodation to American culture.

The second level of appreciation for Willardian theology lies in what can be called its "crossover" appeal. While Willard's works have been widely referenced as inspiring the pursuit of early ECM leaders to recapture a more robust, integrated, and authentic Christian expression, he has also maintained broad welcome and acclaim within mainstream evangelicals circles. To postevangelicals, Willard's pursuit of the reality and effect of the "original" gospel represents a poignant reprisal to the modern Enlightenment hubris pervasive inside conservative evangelical theology. Yet, to conservatives, Willard provides insight and exposition on the inherent shortcomings of an increasingly secular, postmodern, relativist, and constructivist epistemology and psychology.

However, Willardian theology does not stop at critique. Instead, Willard articulates a positive alternative to the shortcomings of conservative, liberal, and postmodern manifestations of contemporary evangelical religion. Unlike many theologians and leaders in the ECM who have thus far offered only helpful insights, assessments, or sweeping deconstructive critiques, Willardian theology erects a complete vision of a viable Christian faith that does not leave adherents in a state of either paralyzing doubt, pluralistic relativism, or eternal equivocations. Yet, neither does Willard take the hyper-critical, legalist path of evangelical fundamentalism, often anathematized by many postmodern Christians.

The unique ability to blend both stinging critiques with enlivening encouragements for both postevangelicals and evangelicals alike places Willardian theology in a rare position to bridge what has often been perceived as an ever widening divide. Willardian theology redefines, reestablishes, and distinguishes a protoevangelical position on a few core biblical foundations based on a philosophically rooted, direct realism and promotes a gospel centered on the *agape* character of God. Together, his Scripturally dependent, agape centric, pneumatological, and theo-ontological realism appear to effectively bridge the progressive postmodern and conservative modern evangelical constituencies. At its end, the protoevangelical perspective marries a de-institutionalized, un-acculturated, un-politicized, non-legalistic, and relational postevangelical sentiment with a biblically centered, discipleship funded, historically orthodox, experiential, and theologically evangelical core.

Finally, Willardian theology—while proceeding from an evangelical perspective—is in its essence a distinct and concerted effort to transcend the limits and myopia of American evangelical religion. It seems Willard's long engagement with evangelicalism is not by choice or intent. Rather, Willard, as a product of his culture, has become chronologically and contextually well positioned to correct, admonish, and encourage contemporary Christians—many of whom have chosen to be evangelical. In essence, protoevangelicalism has a plasticity that reacts and responds to all the evangelical brands of faith it encounters. There is a palpable sense in which protoevangelical faith assumes a foundation that rises above or goes beyond all the current evangelical distinctives, interests, and proclivities. Thus, on several subjects and interests, Willard's theology is antithetical to American evangelicalism in specific, and perhaps, even large portions of Western Christianity in general.

This point is significant to bear in mind due to the fact that protoevangelicalism is best understood when compared against evangelical Christianity in America. It is important to remember they are not the same but are at times strikingly oppositional and often seek to produce an altogether different end. Protoevangelical theology seeks to surpass the limitations of contemporary evangelical expressions and return to a primal gospel that escapes the social adaptations, political trappings, and cultural contextualization that have historically devolved into faint resemblances or distant echoes of the original message of Jesus. In so doing, protoevangelicalism carries both a substantive reproach and reminder. It corrects the lingering effects and influence of fundamentalism, individualism, philosophical constructivism, materialism, and consumerism that have gained increasing dominion both inside and outside all forms of American Christianity. Yet, this corrective is neither the re-creation of a new evangelicalism nor a new Christianity. Rather, the protoevangelical objective is to recapture the first key priorities of the *euangelon* represented in earlier Christian priorities and values of holiness, pietism, character formation, discipleship, and a holistic vision of individual and communal life within the realm of God's kingdom centered on agape love. Willard suggests this is the central message Jesus both advocated and demonstrated in the biblical gospels. The rearticulation of this vision appears to be providing increasing numbers of twenty-first-century Christians the ability to recapture key distinctives of a faith presented by earlier generations of Christians while simultaneously remaining committed to the courage and integrity required in an increasingly secular, postmodern, and post-Christian world.

A Restorer, Reformer, or Transformer?

Willardian thought and theology has certainly gained the attention of many who consider the current manifestation of Christian expression in some way lacking. Whether this lack is in the area of spirituality, spiritual formation, soteriology, or discipleship, the success of Willard's work has evidentially hit a felt need within some constituencies inside the evangelical church. Some consider Willard something of a restorationist—a voice calling evangelicals back to their original roots—where Christians are encouraged to restore their confidence in the contemporary applicability of Jesus' brilliance brought to bear in everyday situations. The restorationist perspective suggests the modern focus on doctrines and propositional faith statements brought to the forefront through growing application and instruction in systematic theologies have produced a deadening impotency in contemporary Christian life. To these individuals, Willard appears to validate their views that dead doctrine is as damaging to evangelical Christianity as was the first-century Judaism as expressed in the heavy legalistic burdens of Pharisaism. Restorationists appreciate Willard's argument against the primacy placed on doctrinally focused theologies and the forms of externalism that act as a form of law that "kills." This is in contrast to the theological method of inquiry demonstrated by Jesus that "brings life."[14]

Others, perhaps more radical evangelicals, see Willard's views as presenting an entirely different gospel that demands a wholesale reformation of evangelicalism. Those carrying this perspective sense that it is not the method of theological inquiry that requires change, but rather a

14. ROH, 22.

new vision of American Christianity in total must be reconstructed. The misapplication of such critical concepts as grace, spirituality, salvation, discipleship, eternal life, and the role of the church and its authority carry deeply imbedded conceptualizations within the evangelical ethos. Therefore, to change or alter these concepts and their meanings, in some opinions, is to radically reform the entire enterprise of Christian faith. For perhaps a majority of modern evangelicals, the potential of such a drastic change brings increasing levels of fear and uncertainty to the point where many will resist the ideas themselves simply in order to ignore the consequences such ideas could facilitate.

Nonetheless, there is ample evidence in the effect of Willard's work to justify both a restorationist and reformer opinion. However, at its end, Willard's protoevangelical vision attempts to move beyond the fettered adaptations centuries of American evangelical heredity has wrought. And in this pursuit, Willard was pointedly direct in his reprisals of evangelical hubris and its ill effects. Willardian theology strives to aid not only evangelicals, but all Christians, to escape and evade the enduring oxymoronic dilemma that all Christian faith proclaiming a gospel attributed to Jesus should at its heart epitomize an attainable reality that is very, very good. Nothing less is worthy of a Christ-centered message.

Willard's view of the protoevangelical message of Jesus presents a vision of life and living that would re-center both post- and traditional evangelical theology around the nature, availability, and pursuit of a good God reigning over a transformative kingdom. Such a pursuit seeks a contemporary articulation of the original gospel represented by Jesus in the New Testament regarding the reality of God's kingdom being available to all who would desire it with their whole heart. Evangelization of this hopeful message, the cornerstone of evangelicalism, in Willard's view, should point toward the present and future theo-ontological and soteriological reality Jesus made available to all persons. Any reductionistic perspective of a gospel focused solely or primarily on eternal life in heaven after death, but has little if any redeeming qualities for contemporary life and existence, is not only less than what Christ offers, but counterproductive. Willard makes the very stark point that confidence in Jesus' provision for sin is a very different matter from a wholesale commitment to an eternally relevant Christocentric worldview.

Therefore, in a definitive way, Willard suggests that both acceptance of and entrance into the theo-ontological reality of the kingdom of God represent simultaneously the salvific message and the sum total of salvation itself. Such a protoevangelical view seeks to correct most of the essential postevangelical concerns regarding mainstream evangelical theology previously stated. The kingdom of God can triumph over all opposing "kingdoms," including those religious kingdoms established under similar sounding—but often antithetical—ends. Therefore, Willardian theology represents a clear and poignant warning to modern evangelicalism's tendency toward self-idolatry under the guise of personal piety or populist forms of religiosity.

Ironically, Willard is attractive to postevangelicals due to his theological application of his direct realism. Surprisingly and unexpectedly, postevangelicals appreciate Willard's protoevangelicalism largely because he allowed them to retain much if not all their past evangelical or theological categories. The key to the attractiveness of protoevangelicalism is not that it offers a replacement to a modern epistemology, theology, or ontology. Rather, Willard provides a more appropriate lens (a realist perspective) through which postevangelicals can reconceptualize the very same objects and subjects that have been the cause of their angst. This comes from Willard's skillful application of phenomenological bracketing. The result is a feeling of redemption or a salvaging of beliefs and ideas that are equally as precious as they have been painful. Postevangelicals appear relieved to discover their evangelical heritage has not been completely dysfunctional or totally ill conceived. Much of this anxiety is eliminated after realizing that the gospel of Jesus was not failing them, only modern evangelicalism, and they are not the same. Metaphorically, Willardian theology provides the potential of removing the corrective, contextual lenses of modernity or postmodernity to gain a new, more realistic perspective on some very old evangelical concepts. His protoevangelical perspective provides a new vision that has increasing numbers of postevangelicals moving toward a brighter and more hopeful future.

In conclusion, simply articulating or spreading knowledge of Willard's protoevangelical theology will likely not generate a new future for American evangelicalism. Huge numbers of evangelicals and postevangelicals alike have already read his works and give mental assent to his theology. Unfortunately however, familiarity and agreement with Willard is too often the beginning and end of their engagement with his work. The process of *metanoia* too often stops at agreement. Yet, agreement is not the most crucial aspect involved in change. To adapt Mark Noll's concept of the "missing" evangelical mind, the new scandal in evangelicalism may be found in the well-worn path of giving intellectual assent to a revolutionary or attractive theological platform, while never intending to apply or practice any of its truths.

Still, Willard reminds that true change cannot be forced. It has to be chosen. There is nothing inherent to Willard's works that can upend a will set on maintaining the status quo. This is true even if the status quo is to value the ethic and pursuit of change while never intentionally engaging the activities necessary to actuate change. Key to change is the human heart.

Willard's words and insights, as powerful, insightful, and instructive as they may be, cannot change evangelicalism or evangelicals, no matter how widespread agreement or advocation of his views may become. Ironically, that is the final focus of all his works. The lone qualifier of an orthodox faith is evidenced in the manifest reality of a heart and life full of *agape* love. In Willardian protoevangelical faith, that alone is the demonstrable proof of the presence and power of the eternal life Jesus provides.

Bibliography

Adam, Andrew Keith. *What is Postmodern Biblical Criticism?* Minneapolis: Fortress, 1995.

Ahlstrom, Sydney E., and David D. Hall. *A Religious History of the American People.* 2nd ed. New Haven, CT: Yale University Press, 2004.

Bob, Allen. "*Southern Baptist Seminary Professors Attack New Book By Brian McLaren.*" (2010) http://www.abpnews.com/content/view/4983/53/ (accessed 10/16/2012).

Althaus, Horst. *Hegel: An Intellectual Biography.* Oxford: Polity-Blackwell, 2000.

Altizer, Thomas J. J. *Living the Death of God: A Theological Memoir.* Albany, NY: State University of New York Press, 2006.

Ameriks, Karl. The *Cambridge Companion to German Idealism.* Cambridge: Cambridge University Press, 2000.

Ammerman, Nancy T. *Baptist Battles: Social Change and Religious Conflict in the Southern Baptist Convention.* New Brunswick, RI: Rutgers University Press, 1990.

———. "Culture and Identity in the Congregation." In *Studying Congregations: A New Handbook*, edited by Nancy Ammerman et al., 91–92. Nashville: Abingdon, 1998

———. *Pillars of Faith: American Congregations and Their Partners.* Berkeley, CA: University of California Press, 2005.

Anderson, Leith. *A Church for the 21st Century.* Minneapolis: Bethany House, 1992.

———. *Dying for Change: An Arresting Look at the New Realities Confronting Churches and Para-Church Ministries.* Minneapolis: Bethany House, 1990.

Anderson, Ray S. *An Emergent Theology for Emerging Churches.* Downers Grove, IL: Intervarsity, 2006.

Anderson, Robert Mapes. *Vision of the Disinherited: The Making of American Pentecostalism.* Peabody, MA: Hendrickson, 1992.

Andrews, Alan. *The Kingdom Life: A Practical Theology of Discipleship and Spiritual Formation.* Colorado Springs, CO: NavPress, 2010.

Anheier, Helmut K., and David C. Hammack. *American Foundations: Roles and Contributions.* Washington, D.C.: Brookings Institution Press, 2010.

Anscombe, Elizabeth. "Modern Moral Philosophy." *Philosophy* 33.124 (1958) 1–19.

Archer, Ken. "A Review of D. A. Carson's *Becoming Conversant with the Emerging Church.*" (2006): http://kenarcher.typepad.com/CarsonEmergingChurchBookReview.pdf (accessed 12/14/2012).

Armstrong, Chris. "How John Wesley Changed America." *Christian History and Biography* (2008) http://www.christianitytoday.com/ch/news/2003/jun20.html (accessed 4/14/2010).

Armstrong, John H. *Reforming Pastoral Ministry: Challenges for Ministry in Postmodern Times.* Wheaton, IL: Crossway, 2001.

Astin, Alexander, Helen Astin, and Jennifer Lindholm. *The Spiritual Life of College Students: A National Study of College Student's Search for Meaning and Purpose.* Los Angeles: University of California, Los Angeles, Higher Education Research Institute, 2003.

Auslander, Philip. *Presence and Resistance: Postmodernism and Cultural Politics in Contemporary American Performance.* Ann Arbor, MI: University of Michigan Press, 1992.

Bachyrycz, David J. "The Epistemological Foundation of Transcendental Phenomenology: Husserl and the Problem of Knowledge." *Ph.D Dissertation.* Georgetown University, 2009.

Bader-Saye, Scott. "The Emergent Matrix." *Christian Century*, Nov 30, 2004, 20.

Bader, Christopher, Kevin Dougherty, and Paul Froese. *American Piety in the 21st Century: New Insights to the Depth and Complexity of Religion in the U.S.* Waco, TX: Baylor Institute for Religious Studies, 2006.

Bader, Christopher, F. C. Mencken, and P. Froese. "American Piety 2005: Content and Methods of the Baylor Religion Survey." *Journal for the Scientific Study of Religion* 46.4 (2007) 447–63.

Bader, Jesse M. *Evangelism in a Changing America.* St. Louis, MO: Bethany, 1957.

Bakker, Jay. *Fall to Grace: A Revolution of God, & Society.* New York, NY: FaithWords, 2011.

Balmer, Randall Herbert. *Encyclopedia of Evangelicalism.* Waco, TX: Baylor University Press, 2004.

———. *The Making of Evangelicalism: From Revivalism to Politics, and Beyond.* Waco, TX.: Baylor University Press, 2010

———. *Mine Eyes Have Seen the Glory: A Journey Into the Evangelical Subculture in America.* 4th ed. New York: Oxford University Press, 2006.

Balz, Horst Robert and Gerhard Schneider, *Exegetical Dictionary of the New Testament* vol. 2, Grand Rapids: Eerdmans, 1990.

Baringer, Sandra. *The Metanarrative of Suspicion in Late Twentieth Century America.* New York: Routledge, 2004.

Barna, George. *Baby Busters: The Disillusioned Generation.* Chicago: Northfield, 1994.

———. *Casting the Net: The Unchurched Population in the Mid-Nineties.* Glendale, CA: Barna Research Group, 1995.

———. *Evangelism That Works: How to Reach Changing Generations with the Unchanging Gospel.* Ventura, CA: Regal, 1995.

———. *Generation Next: A Probing Examination of America's Teenagers.* Glendale, CA: Barna Research Group, 1995.

———. *Growing True Disciples.* Ventura, CA.: Issachar Resources, 2000.

———. *The Habits of Highly Effective Churches: Being Strategic in Your God-Given Ministry.* Ventura, CA.: Regal, 1999.

———. *The Invisible Generation: Baby Busters.* Glendale, CA.: Barna Research Group, 1992.

———. *Marketing the Church.* Colorado Springs, CO.: NavPress, 1988.

———. "Number of Unchurched Adults Has Nearly Doubled Since 1991." (2004) http://www.barna.org/barna-update/article/5-barna-update/140-number-of-unchurched-adults-has-nearly-doubled-since-199 (accessed 10/14/2010).

———. *The Power of Team Leadership: Achieving Success through Shared Responsibility.* Colorado Springs, CO: WaterBrook, 2001.
———. *Re-Churching the Unchurched.* Ventura, CA.: Issachar Resources, 2000.
———. *Revolution.* Wheaton, IL: Tyndale House, 2005.
———. *The Second Coming of the Church.* Nashville, TN: Word, 1998.
———. *Third Millennium Teens: Research on the Minds, Hearts and Souls of America's Teenagers.* Ventura, CA: Barna Research Group, 1999.
———. *Today's Pastors: A Revealing Look At What Pastors Are Saying about Themselves, Their Peers, and the Pressures They Face.* Ventura, CA: Regal, 1993.
Barna, George, and Mark Hatch. *Boiling Point: It Only Takes One Degree: Monitoring Cultural Shifts in the 21st Century.* Ventura, CA: Regal, 2001.
Barna, George, and William Paul McKay. *Vital Signs: Emerging Social Trends and the Future of American Christianity.* Westchester, IL: Crossway, 1984.
Barth, K. *Church Dogmatics,* Vol I, Pt.2 the Doctrine of the Word of God. New York: T. & T. Clark, 1956.
Bartholomew, Craig G., Colin Greene, and Karl Möller, editors. *Renewing Biblical Interpretation.* Carlisle, UK: Paternoster, 2000.
Bartlett, Anthony W. *Cross Purposes: The Violent Grammar of Christian Atonement.* Harrisburg, PA: Trinity, 2001.
Barton, J. *The Cambridge Companion to Biblical Interpretation.* Cambridge: Cambridge University Press, 1998.
Basden, Paul, and David S. Dockery. *Southern Baptists & Evangelicals: The Conversation Continues.* Nashville: Broadman & Holman, 1993.
Bass, Diana Butler. *Christianity for the Rest of Us: How the Neighborhood Church is Transforming the Faith.* San Francisco: HarperSanFrancisco, 2006.
———. *A People's History of Christianity: The Other Side of the Story.* New York: HarperOne, 2009.
———. *Strength for the Journey: A Pilgrimage of Faith in Community.* San Francisco: Jossey-Bass, 2002.
Bauckham, Richard. See Richard J. Bauckham, 2 *Peter, Jude.* Word Biblical Commentary vol. 50, Dallas, TX: Word Incorporated, 2002.
———. *The Theology of Jürgen Moltmann.* London: T. & T. Clark, 1995.
Bauman, Zygmunt. *Intimations of Postmodernity.* London, UK: Routledge, 1992.
———. *Modernity and Ambivalence.* Ithaca, NY: Cornell University Press, 1991.
———. *Postmodern Ethics.* Oxford: Wiley-Blackwell, 1993.
Baumgartner, Frederic J. *Longing for the End: a History of Millennialism in Western Civilization.* New York, NY: Palgrave, 2001.
Beal, T. *Religion in America: A Very Short Introduction.* Oxford: Oxford University Press, 2008.
Bebbington, D. W. *The Dominance of Evangelicalism: The Age of Spurgeon and Moody.* Downers Grove, IL: InterVarsity, 2005.
———. *Evangelicalism in Modern Britain: A History From the 1730s to the 1980s.* Boston: Unwin Hyman, 1989.
———. *Patterns in History: A Christian Perspective on Historical Thought.* Grand Rapids: Baker, 1990.
Beisner, E. Calvin. *Where Garden Meets Wilderness: Evangelical Entry into the Environmental Debate.* Grand Rapids: Eerdmans, 1997.

Bennetch, Rebekah. J. "The Gospel according to Glamour: A Rhetorical Analysis of Revolve: The Complete New Testament." Masters diss., University of Saskatchewan, 2009.

Benson, April Lane. *I Shop, Therefore I Am: Compulsive Buying and the Search for Self.* Northvale, NJ: Aronson, 2000.

Benson, Bruce Ellis, and Peter Heltzel. *Evangelicals and Empire: Christian Alternatives to the Political Status Quo.* Grand Rapids: Brazos, 2008.

Berger, Peter L. "Crisis in Continental Theology." In *European Intellectual History since Darwin and Marx*, edited by W. W. Wager, 255. New York: Torchbooks, 1966.

Bergquist, Linda, and Allan Karr. *Church Turned Inside Out: a Guide for Designers, Refiners, and Re-aligners.* San Francisco, CA: Jossey-Bass, 2010.

Berlet, Chip, and Matthew Nemiroff Lyons. *Right-Wing Populism in America: Too Close for Comfort.* New York: Guilford, 2000.

Berry, P., and A. Wernick. *Shadow of Spirit: Postmodernism and Religion.* New York: Taylor & Francis, 1992.

Bertens, Hans. "The Postmodern Weltanschauung and Its Relation to Modernism: An Introductory Survey." In *A Postmodern Reader*, edited by Joseph P. Natoli and Linda Hutcheon, 25–71. Albany. NY: State University of New York Press, 1993.

Bertens, Johannes Willem. *The Idea of the Postmodern: A History.* London: Routledge, 1995.

Bertens, Johannes Willem, and Douwe Wessel Fokkema. *International Postmodernism: Theory and Literary Practice.* Philadelphia: Benjamins, 1997.

Best, Steven, and Douglas Kellner. *Postmodern Theory: Critical Interrogations.* New York: Guilford, 1991.

Best, Steven, and Douglas Kellner. *The Postmodern Turn.* New York: Guilford, 1997.

Bielo, James. "The 'Emerging Church' in America: Notes on the Interaction of Christianities." *Religion* 39 (2009) 219–32.

Bishop, Bill, and R. G. Cushing. *The Big Sort: Why the Clustering of Like-Minded America is Tearing Us Apart.* New York: Mariner, 2009.

Black Jr., Gary. "Returning to Protoevangelical Faith: The Theology and Praxis of Dallas Willard." Ph.D. diss., University of Exeter, 2012.

Blackaby, Henry T. *Experiencing the Cross.* Sisters, OR: Multnomah, 2005.

Blake, Nigel, Richard Smith, and Paul Smeyers, editors. *Education in an Age of Nihilism.* New York: Routledge-Falmer, 2000.

Blanchard, K. H., Bill Hybels, and Phil Hodges. *Leadership by the Book: Tools to Transform Your Workplace.* Multnomah, OR: Waterbrook, 1999.

Blomberg, Craig, and Sung Wook Chung. *A Case for Historic Premillennialism: An Alternative to "Left Behind" Eschatology.* Grand Rapids: Baker Academic, 2009.

Blumenfeld, Laura. "The Nominee's Soul Mate." *Washington Post*, September 10, 1991.

Blumhofer, Edith Waldvogel. *The Assemblies of God: A Popular History.* Springfield, MO: Radiant, 1985.

Blumhofer, Edith Waldvogel, and Joel A. Carpenter. *Twentieth-Century Evangelicalism: A Guide to the Sources.* New York: Garland, 1990.

Boas, Maxwell, and Steve Chain. *Big Mac: The Unauthorized Story of McDonald's.* New York: Dutton, 1976.

Bohannon, John S. "Preaching and the Emerging Church: An Examination of Four Founding Leaders." Ph.D. diss., Southeastern Baptist Theological Seminary, 2010

Boice, James Montgomery, and Philip Graham Ryken. *The Doctrines of Grace: Rediscovering the Evangelical Gospel*. Wheaton, IL: Crossway Books, 2002.

Bolt, John. "Sola Scriptura as an Evangelical Theological Method." In *Reforming Or Conforming? Post-Conservative Evangelicals and the Emerging Church*, edited by Gary Johnson and Ronald Gleason, 90. Wheaton, IL: Crossway, 2008.

Booker, M. Keith. *Postmodern Hollywood: What's New in Film and Why It Makes Us Feel So Strange*. Westport, CN: Praeger, 2007.

Borg, Marcus J., and N. T. Wright. *The Meaning of Jesus: Two Visions*. San Francisco: HarperSanFrancisco, 1999.

Bosch, Henk van den. "Emergence: How Christianity is Changing and Why—By Phyllis Tickle." *Religious Studies Review* 35 (2009) 253.

Bousa, Jess. *Confessions of a Wanna-be Megachurch Pastor: I Was Wrong about the Seeker-Sensitive Movement*. Havre de Grace, MD: Bousa, 2009.

Bowler, Peter J. *Monkey Trials and Gorilla Sermons: Evolution and Christianity from Darwin to Intelligent Design*. Cambridge: Harvard University Press, 2007.

Boyd, Gregory A. *The Myth of a Christian Nation: How the Quest for Political Power is Destroying the Church*. Grand Rapids: Zondervan, 2005.

Brabazon, Tara. *From Revolution to Revelation: Generation X, Popular Memory, and Cultural Studies*. Aldershot, UK: Ashgate, 2005.

Bradley, Ian C. *God is Green: Ecology for Christians*. New York: Image, 1992.

Bright, Bill. *Four Spiritual Laws*. Peechtree City, CA: Bill Bright Media Foundation, 2007.

Brint, Steven G., and Jean Reith Schroedel. *Evangelicals and Democracy in America*. New York: Russell Sage Foundation, 2009.

Bromley, David G., and Anson D. Shupe. *New Christian Politics*. Macon, GA: Mercer, 1984.

Brown, Colin, editor. *The New International Dictionary of New Testament Theology. Vol. 3*. Exeter, UK: Paternoster, 1986.

Brown, Dale W. *The Christian Revolutionary*. Grand Rapids: Eerdmans, 1971.

Brown, Robert McAfee. *The Spirit of Protestantism*. New York: Oxford University Press, 1961.

Brown, William. "Theology in a Postmodern Culture: Implications of a Video-Dependent Society." In *The Challenge of Postmodernism: An Evangelical Engagement*, edited by David Dockery, 318. Grand Rapids: Baker, 1995.

Brumfitt, J. H. *The French Enlightenment*. London: Macmillan, 1972.

Bryant, Barry. "Original Sin." In *The Oxford Handbook of Methodist Studies*, edited by William J. Abraham and James E. Kirby, 536–38. New York: Oxford University Press, 2009.

Bucke, Emory Stevens. *The History of American Methodism*. New York: Abingdon, 1964.

Burke, Spencer, and Barry Taylor. *A Heretic's Guide to Eternity*. San Francisco: Jossey-Bass, 2006.

Burke, Spencer. *Out of the Ooze: Unlikely Love Letters to the Church from Beyond the Pew*. Colorado Springs, CO: NavPress, 2007.

Burke, Spencer, and Colleen Pepper. *Making Sense of Church: Eavesdropping on Emerging Conversations about God, Community, and Culture*. Grand Rapids: Zondervan, 2003.

Burnaby, John, PA. *Augustine: Later Works*. Philadelphia: Westminster, 1955.

Bushman, Richard L. *The Great Awakening; Documents on the Revival of Religion, 1740–1745*. New York: Atheneum, 1970.

Butler Jr., Farley P. "Billy Graham and the End of Evangelical Unity." Ph.D. diss., University of Florida, 1976.

Butler, Jennifer, Grant Wacker, and R. H. Balmer. *Religion in American Life: A Short History*. New York: Oxford University Press, 2007.

Butler, Jennifer S. *Born Again: The Christian Right Globalized*. Macon, GA: Pluto, 2006.

Butler, Jon. *Awash in a Sea of Faith: Christianizing the American People*. Cambridge: Harvard University Press, 1990.

———. "Jack-in-the-Box Faith: The Religion Problem in Modern American History." *Journal of American History* 90.4 (2004) 1357–78.

Buzzard, A. F. *The Coming Kingdom of the Messiah*. Wyoming, MI: Ministry School, 1988.

Byrne, James. *Religion and the Enlightenment: From Descartes to Kant*. Louisville, KY: Westminster, 1997.

Calvin, John. *Golden Booklet of the True Christian Life*. Grand Rapids: Baker, 1955.

Cameron, Euan. *The European Reformation*. Oxford: Clarendon, 1991.

Campolo, Anthony. *Speaking My Mind. Nashville*, TN: Word, 2004

———. *Red Letter Christians: a Citizen's Guide to Faith & Politics*. Ventura, CA: Regal, 2008.

Caputo, J. D. "The Economy of Signs in Husserl and Derrida: From Uselessness to Full Employment." *Deconstruction and Philosophy: The Texts of Jacques Derrida.7* (1987) 99–133.

"Husserl, Heidegger and the Question of a 'Hermeneutic' Phenomenology." *Husserl Studies 1.1* (1984) 157–78.

———. *Heidegger and Aquinas: An Essay on Overcoming Metaphysics*. Bronx, NY: Fordham University Press, 1982

———. "Mysticism and Transgression: Derrida and Meister Eckhart." *Derrida and Deconstruction 3* (1989) 24–39.

———. *Radical Hermeneutics: Repetition, Deconstruction, and the Hermeneutic Project*. Bloomington, ID: Indiana University Press, 1987.

———. *What Would Jesus Deconstruct? The Good News of Postmodernism for the Church*. Grand Rapids: Baker Academic, 2007.

Caputo, J. D., and Michael J. Scanlon. *God, the Gift, and Postmodernism*. Bloomington, IN: Indiana University Press, 1999.

Caputo, J. D., Gianni Vattimo, and Jeffrey W. Robbins. *After the Death of God*. New York: Columbia University Press, 2007.

Carpenter, Joel A. *Revive Us Again: The Reawakening of American Fundamentalism*. New York: Oxford University Press, 1997.

Carpenter, Joel A., Harold Lindsell, and Carl F. H. Henry. "Two Reformers of Fundamentalism: Harold John Ockenga and Carl F. H. Henry." *Fundamentalism in American religion, 1880–1950, Vol. 45*, New York, NY: Garland, 1988.

Carroll, Jackson, and Wade Clark Roof. *Beyond Establishment: Protestant Identity in a Post-Protestant Age*. Louisville, KY: Westminster John Knox, 1993.

Carson, D. A. *Becoming Conversant with the Emerging Church: Understanding a Movement and Its Implications*. Grand Rapids: Zondervan, 2005.

———. *The Gagging of God: Christianity Confronts Pluralism*. Grand Rapids: Zondervan, 1996.

Catherwood, Christopher. *The Evangelicals: What They Believe, Where They Are, and Their Politics.* Wheaton, IL: Crossway, 2010.

Celek, Tim, and Dieter Zander. *Inside the Soul of a New Generation: Insights and Strategies for Reaching Busters.* Grand Rapids: Zondervan, 1996.

Chandler, Michael. "Stumping for Progress in a Postmodern World." In *Change and Development: Issues of Theory, Method, and Application,* edited by Eric Amsel and K. Ann. Renninger, 1–54. Mahwah, NJ: Erlbaum, 1997.

Charles, Larry, director. *Religulous.* Los Angeles: Lions Gate Entertainment, 2008.

Cherry, Conrad. *The Theology of Jonathan Edwards: A Reappraisal.* Bloomington, IN: Indiana University Press, 1990.

Chia, Loyd. "Emerging Faith Boundaries: Bridge-Building, Inclusion and the Emerging Church Movement in America." Ph.D. diss., University of Missouri-Columbia, 2010.

Chomsky, Noam. *Knowledge of Language: Its Nature, Origin, and Use.* Westport, CT: Praeger, 1986.

Claiborne, Shane. *The Irresistible Revolution: Living as an Ordinary Radical.* Grand Rapids: Zondervan, 2006.

Claiborne, Shane, and Chris Haw. *Jesus for President: Politics for Ordinary Radicals.* Grand Rapids: Zondervan, 2008.

Claiborne, Shane, and Jonathan Wilson-Hartgrove. *Becoming the Answer to Our Prayers: Prayer for Ordinary Radicals.* Downers Grove, IL: InterVarsity, 2008.

Clark, Adam. "Definition of God." In Cyclopedia of Biblical, Theological and Ecclesiastical Literature, McLintock and Strong, editors, 903–904. New York, NY: Harper, 1894.

Clark, David K., and John S. Feinberg. *To Know and Love God: Method for Theology.* Wheaton, IL: Crossway Books, 2003.

Clarke, Peter B. *New Religions in Global Perspective: A Study of Religious Change in the Modern World.* London: Routledge, 2006.

Clayton, Philip, and Tripp Fuller. *Transforming Christian Theology: For Church and Society.* Minneapolis: Fortress, 2010.

Clearwater, Richard. *The Bible: The Unchanging Evangelical Volume.* Shawnee, KS: Central Baptist Theological Seminary Press, 1956.

Clendenen, E. Ray., and Brad J. Waggoner. *Calvinism: A Southern Baptist Dialogue.* Nashville: B & H Academic, 2008.

Cobb, John B., and David Ray Griffin. *Process Theology: An Introductory Exposition.* Philadelphia: Westminster, 1976.

Coffman, Elisha. "Open Debate in the Openness Debate." *Christianity Today,* February (2001): 34–37.

Colson, Charles. "The Postmodern Crackup: From Soccer Moms to College Campuses; Signs of the End." *Christianity Today,* Dec 2003, 72.

Colson, Charles, M. S. Horton, J. I. Packer, R. C. Sproul, and A. E. McGrath. *Power Religion: The Selling Out of the Evangelical Church?* Chicago: Moody, 1992.

Conder, Tim. *The Church in Transition: The Journey of Existing Churches into the Emerging Culture.* Grand Rapids: Zondervan, 2005.

Conkin, Paul. *When All the Gods Trembled: Darwinism, Scopes, and American Intellectuals.* Lanham, MD: Rowman & Littlefield, 2001.

Corbett, Michael, and Julia Corbett Hemeyer. *Politics and Religion in the United States.* New York: Garland, 1999.

Cordeiro, Wayne. *Attitudes That Attract Success*. Ventura, CA: Regal, 2001.

———. *Doing Church as a Team*. Ventura, CA: Regal, 2001.

Corduan, Winfried. *Mysticism: An Evangelical Option*. Grand Rapids: Zondervan, 1991.

———. "Transcendentalism: Hegel." In *Biblical Inerrancy: An Analysis of Its Philosophical Roots*, Norman Geisler, editor, 81–101. Grand Rapids: Zondervan, 1981.

Cori, Patricia. *Beyond the Matrix: Daring Conversations with the Brilliant Minds of Our Times*. Berkeley, CA: North Atlantic, 2010.

Cornwell, John, and Michael. McGhee. *Philosophers and God: At the Frontiers of Faith and Reason*. New York: Continuum, 2009.

Couch, Mal. *Dictionary of Premillennial Theology*. Grand Rapids: Kregel, 1996.

———. *The Fundamentals for the Twenty-First Century: Examining the Crucial Issues of the Christian Faith*. Grand Rapids: Kregel, 2000.

Craig, Edward. *Routledge Encyclopedia of Philosophy*. London: Routledge, 1998.

Croft, Steven J. L. *Mission-Shaped Questions: Defining Issues for Today's Church*. London: Church House, 2008.

Cronk, George. *The Message of the Bible: An Orthodox Christian Perspective*. Crestwood, NY: St. Vladimir's Seminary Press, 1982.

Crouch, Andy. "The Emergent Mystique." *Christianity Today* 48.11 (2004) 37–38.

Cupp, S. E. *Losing Our Religion: The Liberal Media's Attack on Christianity*. New York: Threshold, 2010.

Cupp, S. E., and Brett Joshpe. *Why You're Wrong about the Right: Behind the Myths: The Surprising Truth about Conservatives*. New York: Threshold, 2008.

Dale, Tony, Felicity Dale, and George Barna. *The Rabbit & the Elephant: Why Small is the New Big for Today's Church*. Carol Stream, IL.: Tyndale House, 2009.

Dalhouse, Mark Taylor. *An Island in the Lake of Fire: Bob Jones University, Fundamentalism, and the Separatist Movement*. Athens, GA: University of Georgia Press, 1996.

Daniels, C. Wess. "Four Models of Emerging Churches." http://gatheringinlight.com/2008/01/13/the-four-models-of-emerging-churches/ (accessed 22/5/2010).

Darby, John Nelson. *Notes on the Book of the Revelation*. London: Forgotten, 2007.

Davies, Howard. *The Financial Crisis*. London: Blackwell, 2010.

Davis, Marshall. *More Than a Purpose: An Evangelical Response to Rick Warren and the Megachurch Movement*. Enumclaw, WA: Pleasant Word, 2006.

Davis, Stephen T., Daniel Kendall, and Gerald O'Collins. *The Resurrection: An Interdisciplinary Symposium on the Resurrection of Jesus*. New York: Oxford University Press, 1997.

Davis, Walter. *Inwardness and Existence: Subjectivity in/and Hegel, Heidegger, Marx, and Freud*. Madison, WI: University of Wisconsin Press, 1989.

Dayton, Donald. "Are Charismatic-inclined Pietists the True Evangelicals?" *Modern Reformation* 10.2, (2001) 40–49.

———."The Limits of Evangelicalism: the Pentecostal Tradition." In *The Variety of American Evangelicalism*, Donald W. Dayton, and Robert K. Johnston, editors, 49–51. Downers Grove, IL: InterVarsity Press, 1991.

de Chardin, Teilhard Pierre. *The Phenomenon of Man*. New York: Harper, 1959.

de La Mettrie, Julien Offray. *Machine Man and Other Writings*. Edited by Ann Thomson. Cambridge: Cambridge University Press, 1996.

Delanty, Gerard. *Social Science: Beyond Constructivism and Realism.* Minneapolis, MN: University of Minnesota Press, 1997.

Derrida, Jacques, *Dissemination.* Chicago: University of Chicago Press, 1981.

———. *Edmund Husserl's Origin of Geometry: An Introduction.* Lincoln, NE: University of Nebraska Press, 1989.

———. *Of Grammatology.* Translated by Guyatri C. Spivak. Baltimore, MD: Johns Hopkins University Press, 1976.

———. *The Problem of Genesis in Husserl's Philosophy.* Chicago: University of Chicago Press, 2003.

———. *Writing and Difference.* Translated by Alan. Bass. London: Routledge, 1978.

Dever, Mark. *Proclaiming a Cross-Centered Theology.* Wheaton, IL: Crossway, 2009.

DeWaay, Bob. *Redefining Christianity: Understanding the Purpose Driven Movement.* Springfield. MO: 21st Century Press, 2011.

DeYoung, Kevin. "Christianity and McLarenism." (2010) http://www.facebook.com/note.php?note_id=370885922784 (accessed 3/5/2010).

Dickerson, John S. "The Decline of Evangelical America." *New York Times Sunday Review,* December 15, 2012.

———. *The Great Evangelical Recession: 6 Factors That Will Crash the American Church—and How to Prepare.* Grand Rapids: Baker, 2013.

Dienstag, Joshua F. *Pessimism: Philosophy, Ethic, Spirit.* Princeton, NJ: Princeton University Press, 2006.

Djupe, Paul A., and Laura R. Olson. *Encyclopedia of American Religion and Politics.* New York: Hermitage Facts On File, 2003.

David Dockery, editor, *The Challenge of Postmodernism: An Evangelical Engagement.* Grand Rapids: Baker Academic, 1995.

———. *Southern Baptists & American Evangelicals: The Conversation Continues.* Nashville: Broadman & Holman, 1993.

———. *Southern Baptist Identity: An Evangelical Denomination Faces the Future.* Wheaton, IL: Crossway, 2009.

Dockery, David S., and Gregory Alan. Thornbury. *Shaping a Christian Worldview: The Foundations of Christian Higher Education.* Nashville: Broadman & Holman, 2002.

Dockery, David S., Ray Neste Van, Jerry N. Tidwell, and R. Albert Mohler. *Southern Baptists, Evangelicals, and the Future of Denominationalism.* Nashville: B. & H. Academic, 2011.

Dodson, Edward O. *The Phenomenon of Man Revisited: A Biological Viewpoint on Teilhard De Chardin.* New York: Columbia University Press, 1984.

Dollar, George W. *A History of Fundamentalism in America.* Bloomfield, IN: Bob Jones University Press, 1973.

Domke, D. S., and K. M. Coe. *The God Strategy: How Religion Became a Political Weapon in America.* New York: Oxford University Press, 2008.

Donahue, Bill. *The Willow Creek Guide to Leading Life-changing Small Groups.* Grand Rapids: Zondervan, 1996.

Donahue, Bill, and Russ Robinson. *Building a Church of Small Groups: a Place Where Nobody Stands Alone.* Grand Rapids: Zondervan, 2001.

Dooley, Mark. *A Passion for the Impossible: John D. Caputo in Focus.* Albany, NY: State University of New York Press, 2004.

Dooley, Thomas P. *Praying Faith: I Live By the Faith of the Son of God*, Shippensburg, PA: Destiny Image, 2004.

Dorrien, Gary. *The Making of American Liberal Theology*. Louisville, KY: Westminster John Knox, 2001.

———. *The Remaking of Evangelical Theology*. Louisville, KY: Westminster John Knox, 1998.

———. *Social Ethics in the Making: Interpreting an American Tradition*. Chichester, UK: Wiley-Blackwell, 2009.

Douglass, Herbert E. *Truth Matters: An Analysis of the Purpose Driven Life Movement*. Nampa, ID: Pacific, 2005.

Downes, Martin. "Entrapment: The Emerging Church Conversation and the Cultural Captivity of the Gospel." In *Reforming Or Conforming? Post-Conservative Evangelicals and the Emerging Church*, edited by Gary Johnson and Ronald Gleason, 225. Wheaton, IL: Crossway, 2008.

Dreyfus, Hubert L., and Paul. Rabinow. *Michel Foucault: Beyond Structuralism and Hermeneutics*. Brighton, NY: Harvester, 1982.

Driscoll, Mark. "Acts 29 Network Doctrine." http://www.acts29network.org/about/doctrine/ (accessed 8/3/2010).

———. *Confessions of a Reformission Rev.: Hard Lessons From an Emerging Missional Church*. Grand Rapids: Zondervan, 2006.

———. "The Emerging Church." *The Convergence Conference* (2007) http://theresurgence.com/2008/02/27/convergent-conference-session-3-the-emerging-church (accessed 2/9/2010).

———. "The Emerging Church Highway." *Christian Research Journal* 31.4 (2008) 12–21.

———. "A Pastoral Perspective on the Emergent Church." *Criswell Theological Review* 3.2 (2006) 87–93.

———. *The Radical Reformission: Reaching Out Without Selling Out*. Grand Rapids: Zondervan, 2004.

———. *Religion Saves: And Nine Other Misconceptions*. Wheaton, IL: Crossway, 2009.

Driscoll, Mark, and Gerry Breshears. *Doctrine: What Christians Should Believe*. Wheaton, IL: Crossway, 2010.

———. *Vintage Church: Timeless Truths and Timely Methods*. Wheaton, IL: Crossway, 2009.

———. *Vintage Jesus: Timeless Answers to Timely Questions*. Wheaton, IL: Crossway, 2007.

Drucker, Peter F. *Managing the Non-Profit Organization: Practices and Principles*. New York: HarperCollins, 1990.

———. "The Non-Profits Quite Revolution." *Wall Street Journal*, Jan 4, 1988.

———. *Post-Capitalist Society*. New York: HarperBusiness, 1993.

Duin, Julia. *Quitting Church: Why the Faithful Are Fleeing and What to Do About It*. Grand Rapids: Baker, 2008.

Duncan, J. Ligon, Dan Kimball, Michael Lawrence, Timothy C. J. Quill, Dan Wilt, Mark Dever, and J. Matthew Pinson. *Perspectives on Christian Worship: 5 Views* Nashville: B. & H. Academic, 2009.

Dusek, Val. *Philosophy of Technology: an Introduction*. Malden, MA: Blackwell Publishers, 2006.

Dyck, Drew. *Generation Ex-Christian: Why Young Adults Are Leaving the Faith—and How to Bring Them Back*. Chicago: Moody, 2010.

Easum, William M. *Dancing with Dinosaurs: Ministry in a Hostile and Hurting World.* Nashville: Abingdon, 1993.

———. *Sacred Cows Make Gourmet Burgers: Ministry Anytime, Anywhere, By Anybody.* Nashville: Abingdon, 1995.

Easum, William M., and Herb Miller. *How to Reach Baby Boomers.* Nashville: Abingdon, 1991.

Editorial. "God Vs. God." *Christianity Today*, February (2000): 12.

Editorial. "Is Evangelical Theology Changing?" *Christian Life Magazine* 17.11 (1956) 16–19.

Edwards, Jonathan. *Sinners in the Hands of an Angry God and Other Puritan Sermons.* New York: Dover, 2005.

Edwards, Jonathan and T. M. Moore, *Pursuing Holiness in the Lord.* Phillipsburg, NJ: P & R Pub., 2005.

Efird, James M. *Left Behind? What the Bible Really Says About the End Times.* Macon, GA: Smyth & Helwys, 2006.

Eidsmoe, John. *Christianity and the Constitution: The Faith of Our Founding Fathers.* Grand Rapids: Baker, 1987.

Einstein, Mara. *Brands of Faith: Marketing Religion in a Commercial Age.* London: Routledge, 2008.

Elisha, Omri. *Moral Ambition: Mobilization and Social Outreach in Evangelical Megachurches.* Berkeley, CA: University of California Press, 2011.

Elliot, Ralph H. "Dangers of the Church Growth Movement." *Christian Century,* August, 1981, 799–801.

Ellis, John M. *Against Deconstruction.* Princeton: Princeton University Press, 1989.

Elnes, Eric. *Asphalt Jesus: Finding a New Christian Faith along the Highways of America.* San Francisco: Jossey-Bass, 2007.

Emerson, Michael O., and Christian Smith. *Divided By Faith: Evangelical Religion and the Problem of Race in America.* Oxford: Oxford University Press, 2000.

Engle, Randall D. "Book Review: The Divine Conspiracy." *Calvin Theological Journal* 36. 1 (2001) 217–19.

Erasmus, Desiderius, and Martin Luther. *Discourse on Free Will.* Translated by Ernst Winter. New York: Continuum, 1961.

Erasmus, Desiderus, and Martin Luther. *Luther and Erasmus: Free Will and Salvation.* Edited by E. Gordan Rupp and Philip Watson. Louisville, KY: Westminster, 1969.

Erdmann, Katrin. So *Help Me God: The Influence of the Religious Right on the Campaigning of George W. Bush.* Hamburg, Germany: Lit, 2006.

Erickson, Millard J. *Christian Theology.* 2nd ed. Grand Rapids: Baker, 1998.

———. *The Evangelical Left: Encountering Postconservative Evangelical Theology.* Grand Rapids: Baker, 1997.

———. *Postmodernizing the Faith: Evangelical Responses to the Challenge of Postmodernism.* Grand Rapids: Baker, 1998.

———. *The Postmodern World: Discerning the Times and the Spirit of Our Age.* Wheaton, IL: Crossway, 2002.

Erickson, Millard J., Paul Kjoss Helseth, and Justin Taylor. *Reclaiming the Center: Confronting Evangelical Accommodation in Postmodern Times.* Wheaton, IL: Crossway, 2004.

Erre, Mike. *Death By Church: Rescuing Jesus From His Followers, Recapturing God's Hope for His People.* Eugene, OR: Harvest House, 2009.

———. *The Jesus of Suburbia: Have We Tamed the Son of God to Fit Our Lifestyle.* Nashville: Thomas Nelson, 2006.

Eskridge, L. "'One Way': Billy Graham, the Jesus Generation, and the Idea of an Evangelical Youth Culture." *Church History: Studies in Christianity and Culture* 67.1 (2009) 83–106.

Etziomo-Halevy, Eva. "The New Theories of Postmodernity and Hypermodernity: Social/Ideological Context and Implications for Inequality." In *Ideology and the Social Sciences,* edited by Graham Charles Kinloch and Raj P. Mohan, 87–106. Westport, CN: Greenwood, 2000.

Fahlbusch, Erwin, and Geoffrey William Bromiley, editors. *The Encyclopedia of Christianity,* Vol. 4. Grand Rapids: Eerdmans, 1999.

Feinberg, Charles Lee. *Millennialism, the Two Major Views: The Premillennial and Amillennial Systems of Biblical Interpretation Analyzed and Compared.* 3rd ed. Chicago: Moody, 1980.

Feinberg, John S., David. Basinger, and Randall Basinger. *Predestination & Free Will: Four Views of Divine Sovereignty & Human Freedom.* Downers Grove, IL: InterVarsity, 1986.

Fekete, John. *Life after Postmodernism: Essays on Value and Culture.* Hampshire, UK: Macmillan Education, 1988.

Findlay, James F. *Church People in the Struggle: the National Council of Churches and the Black Freedom Movement, 1950–1970.* New York: Oxford University Press, 1993.

Finney, Charles. *Sanctification.* Edited by W. E. Allen. Cleveland, OH: Christian Literature Crusade, 1989.

Finney, Charles and Louis Gifford Parkhurst, *Principles of Holiness: Selected Messages on Biblical Holiness* (Minneapolis, MN: Bethany House, 1984.

Fishwick, Marshall William., and Ray B. Browne. *The God Pumpers: Religion in the Electronic Age.* Bowling Green, OH: Bowling Green State University Popular Press, 1987.

Fitts, Robert. *The Church in the House.* Salem, OR: Prepare the Way, 2001.

Flannely, Kevin, Kathleen Galek, Jackson Kytle, and Nava Stilton. "Religion in America, 1972–2006: Religious Affiliation, Attendance and Strength of Faith." *Psychological Reports* 106.3 (2010) 875–90.

Flory, Richard W., and Donald E. Miller. *Finding Faith: The Spiritual Quest of the Post-Boomer Generation.* Rutgers, NJ: Rutgers, 2008

———. *Gen X Religion.* New York: Routledge, 2000.

Ford, David, and Rachel Muers, editors. *The Modern Theologians: An Introduction to Christian Theology Since 1918.* 3rd ed. Malden, MA: Blackwell, 2005.

Foster, Hal. *The Anti-Aesthetic: Essays on Postmodern Culture.* New York: New Press, 2002.

Foster, Richard. *Celebration of Discipline: the Path to Spiritual Growth.* New York, NY: HarperOne, 1988.

Foucault, Michel. *Discipline and Punish: The Birth of the Prison.* London: Allen Lane, 1977.

———. "Kant on Enlightenment and Revolution." *Economy and Society* 15.1 (1986) 88–96.

———. *Power/Knowledge: Selected Interviews and Other Writings, 1972–1977.* Edited by Colin Gordon. New York: Pantheon, 1980.

———. *What is Enlightenment? The Foucault Reader.* New York: Penguin, 1984.

Foucault, Michel, and Jean Khalfa. *History of Madness*. New York: Routledge, 2006.

Fowler, Robert Booth. *Religion and Politics in America: Faith, Culture, and Strategic Choices*. 4th ed. Boulder, CO: Westview, 2010.

Franke, J. R., and P. A. Hatfield. "Barth Redivivus: Karl Barth, Postmodernity, and Evangelical Theology." Paper given at the Annual meeting of the Evangelical Theological Society, Toronto, 2002.

Froese, P., C. Bader, and B. Smith. "Political Tolerance and God's Wrath in the United States." *Sociology of Religion* 69.1 (2008) 29–44.

Frykholm, Amy Johnson. *Rapture Culture: Left Behind in Evangelical America*. Oxford: Oxford University Press, 2004.

Gabardi, Wayne. *Negotiating Postmodernism*. Minneapolis: University of Minnesota Press, 2001.

Gadamer, Hans-Georg. *Truth and Method*. Translated by Joel Weinsheimer and Donald G. Marshall. New York: Continuum, 2004.

Galli, Mark. "Downsizing Sin: Willard Believes Discipleship is Not as Hard as We Make it." *Leadership Journal* 19.3 (1998) 105–6.

Gallion, Matt. "The Death of the Emerging Church." http://matthewgallion.wordpress.com/2010/01/12/the-death-of-the-emerging-church/ (accessed 1/12/2010).

Gangel, Kenneth O. "Education for Renovation: An Executive Summary of Dr. Dallas Willard's Presentation at the 2004 NAPCE Conference." *Christian Education Journal* 2.1 (2005) 154–61.

Garrett, Greg. *We Get to Carry Each Other: The Gospel according to U2*. Louisville, KY: Westminster John Knox, 2009.

Garrison, Becky, *Jesus Died for This? A Satirist's Search for the Risen Christ*. Grand Rapids: Zondervan, 2010.

———. *Red and Blue God, Black and Blue Church: Eyewitness Accounts of How American Churches Are Hijacking Jesus, Bagging the Beatitudes, and Worshiping the Almighty Dollar*. San Francisco: Jossey-Bass, 2006.

———. *Rising From the Ashes: Rethinking Church*. Google Books.Com, 2007.

Gasper, Louis. *The Fundamentalist Movement*. The Hague, Germany: Mouton, 1963.

Gates, David. "Pop Prophets." *Newsweek*, April (2004) 45–50.

Gay, Peter. *Age of Enlightenment*. New York, NY: Time, Inc., 1966.

Genda, J. K. *Republican Conservative Hypocrisy: The Gop Has Successfully Linked Christian Conservatism to Filthy Politics in the Battle for Religious Votes*. Bloomington, IL: Author House, 2010.

George, Carl F. *Prepare Your Church for the Future*. Grand Rapids: Baker, 1991.

George, Timothy. *Pilgrims on the Sawdust Trail: Evangelical Ecumenism and the Quest for Christian Identity*. Grand Rapids: Baker Academic, 2004.

Gerber, Kent. "Behind the Prosperity Gospel." *US News and World Report*, July, 2008.

Gergen, Kenneth J. *The Saturated Self: Dilemmas of Identity in Contemporary Life*. New York: Basic, 1991.

Gibbs, Eddie. *Churchnext: Quantum Changes in How We Do Ministry*. Downers Grove, IL: InterVarsity, 2000.

Gibbs, Eddie, and Ryan K. Bolger. *Emerging Churches: Creating Christian Community in Postmodern Cultures*. Grand Rapids: Baker Academic, 2005.

Gilbert, Greg. "Saved from the Wrath of God: An Examination of Brian McLaren's Approach to the Doctrine of Hell." In *Reforming Or Conforming? Post-Conservative*

Evangelicals and the Emerging Church, edited by Gary Johnson and Ronald Gleason, 278–82. Wheaton, IL: Crossway, 2008.

Gish, Arthur. *The New Left and Christian Radicalism*. Grand Rapids: Eerdmans, 1970.

Goff, James R., and Grant Wacker. *Portraits of a Generation: Early Pentecostal Leaders*. Fayetteville, AR: University of Arkansas Press, 2002.

Goldstein, Laura. "Obama Made Gains among Younger Evangelical Voters, Data Shows." *New York Times*, Nov 6, 2008.

Gortner, David. *Transforming Evangelism*. New York, NY: Church Publishing, 2008.

Graham, Billy. *Just as I Am: The Autobiography of Billy Graham*. San Francisco, CA: HarperOne, 1999.

Grant, J. T. "Measuring Aggregate Religiosity in the United States, 1952–2005." *Sociological Spectrum* 28.5 (2008) 460–76.

Grant, Michael. *Jesus: A Historians Review of the Gospels*. London, UK: Weidenfeld and Nicolson, 1977.

Green, Bradley. *The Gospel and the Mind: Recovering and Shaping the Intellectual Life*. Wheaton, IL: Crossway, 2010.

Green, D. M. "The End of Identity? The Implications of Postmodernity for Political Identification." *Nationalism and Ethnic Politics* 6.3 (2000) 68–90.

Green, Joel B., and Mark D. Baker. *Recovering the Scandal of the Cross: Atonement in New Testament & Contemporary Contexts*. Downers Grove, IL: InterVarsity, 2000.

Green, Joel B., Scot. McKnight, and I. Howard Marshall, editors. *Dictionary of Jesus and the Gospels*. Downers Grove, IL: InterVarsity, 1992.

Green, John Clifford, Mark J. Rozell, and Clyde Wilcox. *The Christian Right in American Politics: Marching to the Millennium*. Washington, DC: Georgetown University Press, 2003.

Greenough, William, Thayer Shedd and Alan W. Gomes. *Dogmatic Theology*, 3rd ed. Phillipsburg, N.J.: P & R Pub., 2003.

Greenwald, Glenn. *Great American Hypocrites: Toppling the Big Myths of Republican Politics*. New York: Crown, 2008.

Gribben, Crawford. *Writing the Rapture: Prophecy Fiction in Evangelical America*. New York: Oxford University Press, 2009.

Griffin, D. R. *Founders of Constructive Postmodern Philosophy: Peirce, James, Bergson, Whitehead, and Hartshorne*. Albany, NY: State University of New York Press, 1993.

———. *God and Religion in the Postmodern World: Essays in Postmodern Theology*. Albany, NY: State University of New York Press, 1989.

Grossman, Cathy Lynn. "Most Religious Groups in USA Have Lost Ground Survey Finds." *USA Today*, March 17, 2009.

Gruber, J., and D. M. Hungerman. "The Church Versus the Mall: What Happens When Religion Faces Increased Secular Competition?" *Quarterly Journal of Economics* 123.2 (2008) 831–62.

Grudem, Wayne A. *Systematic Theology: An Introduction to Biblical Doctrine*. Grand Rapids: Zondervan, 1994.

Gruender, D. C. "Constructivism and Learning." *Educational Technology* 36.3 (1996) 21–29.

Guder, Darrel L. *The Continuing Conversion of the Church*. Grand Rapids: Eerdmans, 2000.

———. *Missional Church: A Vision for the Sending of the Church in North America*. Grand Rapids: Eerdmans, 1998.

Guinness, Os. *The Devil's Gauntlet: The Church and the Challenge of Society.* Downers Grove, IL: InterVarsity, 1989.
———. *Dining with the Devil: The Megachurch Movement Flirts with Modernity.* Grand Rapids: Baker, 1993.
———. *The Dust of Death: The Sixties Counterculture and How it Changed America Forever.* Wheaton, IL: Crossway, 1994.
———. *Fit Bodies, Fat Minds: Why Evangelicals Don't Think and What to Do About It.* Grand Rapids: Hourglass, 1994.
———. *The Last Christian on Earth: Uncover the Enemy's Plot to Undermine the Church.* Ventura, CA: Regal, 2010.
———. "Sounding Out the Ideals of the Church." In *No God But God,* edited by Os Guinness and John Seel, 92–154. Chicago: Moody, 1992.
Habel, Norman C., and Vicky Balabanski. *The Earth Story in the New Testament.* Sheffield, UK: Sheffield Academic Press Pilgrim Press, 2002.
Habermas, Jürgen. "Modernity Versus Postmodernity." *New German Critique* 22 (1981) 3–14.
———. *Theory and Practice.* London, UK: Heinemann, 1974.
———. *Time of Transitions.* Cambridge, UK: Polity, 2006.
Hankins, Barry. *American Evangelicals: A Contemporary History of a Mainstream Religious Movement.* Lanham, MD: Rowman & Littlefield, 2009.
———. *Evangelicalism and Fundamentalism: A Documentary Reader.* New York: New York University Press, 2008.
Hansen, Collin. Young, *Restless, Reformed: A Journalist's Journey with the New Calvinists.* Wheaton, IL: Crossway, 2008.
Harley, Kenneth. *Thirty-Three Academic Reflections on the Emerging Church.* Long Beach, CA: Harley, 2006.
Harnack, Adolf von. *What is Christianity.* New York: Harper, 1957.
Harper, Steve. *The Way to Heaven: The Gospel according to John Wesley.* 2nd ed. Grand Rapids: Zondervan, 2003.
Harris, Brian. "Beyond Bebbington: The Quest for an Evangelical Identity." *Churchman* 12.23 (2008) 201–19.
Harris, Harriet A. *Fundamentalism and Evangelicals.* New York: Clarendon, 1998.
Harris, Robert Laird, and Bruce Waltke. *Theological Workbook of the Old Testament.* Chicago, IL: Moody Press, 2003.
Harrison, Rodney, Tom Cheyney, Don Overstreet, Elmer L. Towns, and Ed Stetzer. *Spin-Off Churches: How One Church Successfully Plants Another.* Nashville: B. & H. Academic, 2008.
Harrold, Philip. "Deconversion in the Emerging Church." *International Journal for the Study of the Christian Church* 6.1 (2006) 79–90.
Hart, D. G. *Defending the Faith: J. Gresham Machen and the Crisis of Conservative Protestantism in Modern America.* Baltimore, MD: Johns Hopkins University Press, 1994.
———. *The Lost Soul of American Protestantism.* Lanham, MD: Rowman & Littlefield, 2002.
———. *That Old-Time Religion in Modern America: Evangelical Protestantism in the Twentieth Century.* Chicago: Dee, 2002.
Harvey, David. *The Condition of Postmodernity: An Enquiry into the Origins of Cultural Change.* Oxford: Blackwell, 1989.

Hassan, Ihab. *The Postmodern Turn: Essays in Postmodern Theory and Culture.* Columbus, OH: Ohio State University Press, 1987.

Hatch, Nathan O. *The Democratization of American Christianity.* New Haven, CT: Yale University Press, 1989.

Hatch, Nathan O, and Mark A. Noll. *The Bible in America: Essays in Cultural History.* New York: Oxford University Press, 1982.

Hauerwas, Stanley. *With the Grain of the Universe: The Church's Witness and Natural Theology: Being the Gifford Lectures Delivered at the University of St. Andrews in 2001.* Grand Rapids: Brazos, 2001.

Hawkins, Greg, Cally Parkinson, and Eric Arnson. *Reveal: Where Are You?* Barrington, IL: Willow Creek Resources, 2007.

Haykin, Michael, et. al. *The Advent of Evangelicalism: Exploring Historical Continuities.* Nashville, TN: B & H Academic, 2008.

Haynes, Jeffrey. *Routledge Handbook of Religion and Politics.* New York, NY: Routledge, 2009.

Heelas, Paul, David Martin, and Paul Morris. *Religion, Modernity, and Postmodernity.* Oxford: Blackwell, 1998.

Heelas, Paul. *Spiritualities of Life: New Age Romanticism and Consumptive Capitalism.* Malden, MA: Blackwell, 2008.

Hegel, Georg Friedrich. *Introduction to the Philosophy of History: With Selections from the Philosophy of Right.* Translated by Leo Rauch. Indianapolis, IN: Hackett, 1988.

———. *Phenomenology of Spirit.* Translated by A.V. Miller. Delhi: Motilal Banarsidass, 1998.

Helm, Paul. "Calvin, A. M. Toplady and the Bebbington Thesis." In *The Advent of Evangelicalism: Exploring Historical Continuities*, edited by Michael A. G. Haykin, Kenneth J. Stewart, and Timothy George, 199–220. Nashville: B. & H. Academic, 2008.

Heidegger, Martin. *Being and Time.* New York, NY: Harper, 1962.

———. Identity and Difference. New York, NY: Harper & Row, 1969.

Henry, C. F. H. *Evangelicals at the Brink of Crisis.* Waco, TX: Word, 1967.

———. *The Uneasy Conscience of Modern Fundamentalism.* Grand Rapids: Eerdmans, 1947.

Herzog, William R. *Parables as Subversive Speech: Jesus as Pedagogue of the Oppressed.* Louisville, KY: Westminster/John Knox, 1994.

Hesselgrave, David J. "The Changing of the Guards: Missiological Legacies of Donald A. McGavran, John R. W. Stott, Carl F. H. Henry and Ralph D. Winter." http://weblog.wordcentered.org/files/Hesselgrave_TheChangingsoftheGuards.pdf (accessed 9/29/2010).

Hilary, G., and K. W. Hui. "Does Religion Matter in Corporate Decision Making in America?" *Journal of Financial Economics* 93.3 (2009) 455–73.

Hirsch, Alan. *The Forgotten Ways: Reactivating the Missional Church.* Grand Rapids: Brazos, 2006.

Hirsch, E. D. *The Aims of Interpretation.* Chicago: University of Chicago Press, 1976.

Hoekendijk, Johannes Christian. *The Church Inside Out.* Philadelphia: Westminster, 1966.

Holmes, David L. *The Faiths of the Founding Fathers.* Oxford: Oxford University Press, 2006.

Hoover, Stuart M. "The Cross at Willow Creek: Seeker Religion and the Contemporary Marketplace." In *Religion and Popular Culture*, edited by Bruce David Forbes and Jeffrey Mahan, 145–60. Berkeley, CA: University of California Press, 2000.

Hounshell, David A., and John K. Smith. *Science and Corporate Strategy: Du Pont R&D, 1902–1980*. Cambridge: Cambridge University Press, 1988.

Hudson, Curtis. *New Evangelicalism: Enemy of Fundamentalism*. Murfreesboro, TN: Sword of the Lord, 1984.

Hudson, Trevor. *Discovering Our Spiritual Identity: Practices for God's Beloved*. Downers Grove, IL: InterVarsity, 2010.

Hughes, R. Kent. and John H. Armstrong. *The Coming Evangelical Crisis: Current Challenges to the Authority of Scripture and the Gospel*. Chicago: Moody, 1996.

Hull, Bill. *Choose the Life: Exploring a Faith That Embraces Discipleship*. Grand Rapids: Baker, 2004.

———."A Reluctant Prophet." Journal of Spiritual Formation and Soul Care 3.2, (2010) 283–95.

Hunsberger, George, and Craig Van Gelder, editors, *The Church between Gospel and Culture: The Emerging Mission in North America*. Grand Rapids: Eerdmans, 1996.

Hunter, James Davison. *American Evangelicalism: Conservative Religion and the Quandary of Modernity*. New Brunswick, NJ: Rutgers University Press, 1983.

———. *Evangelicalism: the Coming Generation*. Chicago: University of Chicago Press, 1993.

———."The New Class and the Young Evangelicals." Review of Religious Research 22.2 (1980) 155–69.

———. *To Change the World: the Irony, Tragedy, and Possibility of Christianity in the Late Modern World*. New York: Oxford University Press, 2010.

Hunter, Todd D. *Christianity beyond Belief: Following Jesus for the Sake of Others*. Downers Grove, IL: InterVarsity, 2010.

Husserl, Edmund. *The Idea of Phenomenology*. Translated by Lee Hardy. Boston: Kluwer Academic, 1999.

———. *Introduction to Logic and Theory of Knowledge: Lectures 1906/07*. Translated by Clair Ortz Hill. Dordrecht, Netherlands: Springer, 2008.

———. *Philosophy of Arithmetic: Psychological and Logical Investigations: With Supplementary Texts from 1887–1901*. Translated by Dallas Willard. Boston: Kluwer Academic, 2003.

Hutcheon, Linda. "Beginning to Theorize Postmodern." In *A Postmodern Reader*, edited by Joseph P. Natoli, and Linda Hutcheon, 261. Albany, NY: State University of New York Press, 1993.

Hutchison, William R. *The Modern Impulse in American Protestantism*. Durham, NC: Duke University Press, 1992.

———. *Religious Pluralism in America: The Contentious History of a Founding Ideal*. New Haven, CT: Yale University Press, 2003.

Hybels, Bill. *Courageous Leadership*. Grand Rapids: Zondervan, 2002.

———. *The Volunteer Revolution: Unleashing the Power of Everybody*. Grand Rapids: Zondervan, 2004.

Hybels, Bill, and Mark Mittelberg. *Becoming a Contagious Church: Increasing Your Church's Evangelistic Temperature*. Grand Rapids: Zondervan, 2007.

Hybels, Lynn, and Bill Hybels. *Rediscovering the Church*. Grand Rapids: Zondervan, 1995.

Isaac, Gordon L. *Left Behind Or Left Befuddled: The Subtle Dangers of Popularizing the End Times.* Collegeville, MN: Liturgical, 2008.

Isaacson, Walter. "Einstein & Faith." *Time,* June 2007.

Israel, Jonathan I. *Radical Enlightenment: Philosophy and the Making of Modernity 1650–1750.* Oxford: Oxford University Press, 2002.

Jackson, Bob. *Hope for the Church: Contemporary Strategies for Growth.* London: Church House, 2002.

Jenkins, Phillip. "The Next Christianity." *The Atlantic Monthly* 290.3 (2002) 53–68.

Jethani, Skye. *Discovering a Faith Beyond Consumer Christianity.* Grand Rapids: Zondervan, 2009.

Johns, Kenneth D. *The Popes of Pentecostal Television.* Longwood, FL: Advantage, 2005.

Johns, Paul A. "Book Review: A Conspiracy Revealed." *Journal of Psychology and Theology* 28.4 (2000) 327–32.

Johnson, Gary L. W., and Ronald Gleason, editors, *Reforming Or Conforming? Post-Conservative Evangelicals and the Emerging Church.* Wheaton, IL: Crossway, 2008

Johnson, Jan. "Guilt Odyssey." (2011): http://www.janjohnson.org/march_2011_wisbits.html (accessed April, 12, 2013).

Johnson, Jan, Keith Matthews, and Dallas Willard. *Dallas Willard's Study Guide to the Divine Conspiracy.* San Francisco: HarperOne, 2001.

Johnson, William Stacy. "Rethinking Theology: A Postmodern, Post-Holocaust, Post-Christendom Endeavor." *Interpretation: A Journal of Bible and Theology* 55.1 (2001) 5–19.

Johnston, Graham. *Preaching to a Postmodern World: A Guide to Reaching Twenty-First-Century Listeners.* Grand Rapids: Baker, 2001.

Jones, Andrew. "Emerging Church Movement 1989–2009?" http://tallskinnykiwi.typepad.com/tallskinnykiwi/2009/12/emerging-church-movement-1989---2009.html (accessed 4/11/2011).

———. "Five Models of Emerging Church From 1999." http://tallskinnykiwi.typepad.com/tallskinnykiwi/2008/01/models-of-emerg.html (accessed 4/20/2010).

Jones, Lindsay, Mircea Eliade, and Charles J. Adams. Encyclopedia of Religion. Vol. 5. 2nd ed. Detroit, MI: Macmillan Reference, 2005.

Jones, Tony. "Andy Crouch Responds." http://theoblogy.blogspot.com/search?q=andy+crouch (accessed 4/13/2010).

———. "The Church Is Flat: The Relational Ecclesiology of the Emerging Church Movement." Ph.D. diss., Princeton Theological Seminary, 2011.

———. "Is Emergent the New Christian Left?" http://www.outofur.com/archives/2006/05/is_emergent_the.html#more (accessed 6/10/2010).

———. "Is Emergent the New Christian Left? Tony Jones Responds to Critics. Part 1 and Part 2." (2006) http://www.outofur.com/archives/2006/05/is_emergent_the.html (accessed 8/11/2010).

———. "Pentecostalism and Emergence." Paper presented at the Society of Pentecostal Studies, March 4–6, 2010 (2010) http://blog.tonyj.net/tag/pentecostalism/ (accessed 1/3/2011).

———. *Postmodern Youth Ministry: Exploring Cultural Shift, Creating Holistic Connections, Cultivating Authentic Community.* Grand Rapids: Youth Specialties, 2001.

———. *Pray.* Colorado Springs, CO: TH1NK, 2003.

———. *The New Christians: Dispatches From the Emergent Frontier*. San Francisco: Jossey-Bass, 2008.

———. *The Sacred Way: Spiritual Practices for Everyday Life*. Grand Rapids: Zondervan, 2004.

———. "Theoblogy: Which Missional Church." (2011) http://www.patheos.com/blogs/tonyjones/2011/01/27/which-missional-church/ (accessed 2/11/2011).

Jones, Tony, Keith Matthews, Scot McKnight, and Diana Butler Bass. "The Emerging Church." Session at American Academy of Religion, November 2007.

Jorstad, Erling. *Evangelicals in the White House: The Cultural Maturation of Born Again Christianity, 1960–1981*. New York: Mellen, 1981.

———. *The Politics of Moralism: The New Christian Right in American Life*. Minneapolis,: Augsburg, 1981.

Joubert, Johannes Jacobus. "A Pentecostal Theological Reflection on the Emerging Church Movement." Ph.D. diss., University of Johannesburg, 2010.

Kant, Immanuel. *Critique of Pure Reason*. Edited by Paul Guyer and Allen Wood. Cambridge: Cambridge University Press, 1999.

———. "What is Enlightenment?" In *The Philosophy of Immanuel Kant: Immanuel Kant's Moral and Political Writings*, edited by Carl J. Friedrich, 132–41. London: Random House, 1949.

Kärkkäinen, Veli-Matti. *The Spirit in the World: Emerging Pentecostal Theologies in Global Contexts*. Grand Rapids: Eerdmans, 2009.

Kasemann, Ernest. *Commentary on Romans*. Translated by Geoffrey W. Bromiley. Grand Rapids. MI: Eerdmans, 1980.

Keck, Eric. *Pneumanaut: Demonstrate, Embody, Announce*. Montpelier, VT: Grease Monk's Garage, 2006.

Keel, Tim. *Intuitive Leadership: Embracing a Paradigm of Narrative, Metaphor, and Chaos*. Grand Rapids: Baker, 2007.

Keffe, Derek. "Tony Jones Out as Emergent Village Head." *Christianity Today*, November 2008, 13.

Keifert, Patrick R. *Testing the Spirits: How Theology Informs the Study of Congregations*. Grand Rapids: Eerdmans., 2009.

Kell, Carl L. *Exiled: Voices of the Southern Baptist Convention Holy War*. Knoxville, TN: University of Tennessee Press, 2006.

Keller, Timothy J. *The Prodigal God: Recovering the Heart of the Christian Faith*. New York: Dutton, 2008.

———. *The Reason for God: Belief in an Age of Skepticism*. New York: Dutton, 2008.

Kemeny, Paul Charles. *Princeton in the Nation's Service: Religious Ideals and Educational Practice, 1868–1928*. New York: Oxford University Press, 1998.

Kidd, Thomas S. *The Great Awakening: The Roots of Evangelical Christianity in Colonial America*. New Haven, CT: Yale University Press, 2007.

Kimball, Dan. *The Emerging Church: Vintage Christianity for New Generations*. Grand Rapids: Zondervan/Youth Specialties, 2003.

———. *They Like Jesus But Not the Church: Insights From Emerging Generations*. Grand Rapids: Zondervan, 2007.

Kimbrough, S. T. *Orthodox and Wesleyan Ecclesiology*. Crestwood, NY: St. Vladimir's Seminary Press, 2007.

Kinnaman, David, and Gabe Lyons. *Unchristian: What a New Generation Really Thinks About Christianity and Why it Matters*. Grand Rapids: Baker Books, 2007.

King, Darren. "Interview with Brian McLaren." *Precipice Magazine* (2007) http://www.precipicemagazine.com/brian-mclaren-interview.htm (accessed 6/30/2010).

Kirn, Walter. "What Would Jesus Do?" *GQ Magazine* September 2002.

Kirsch, Jonathan. *A History of the End of the World: How the Most Controversial Book in the Bible Changed the Course of Western Civilization*. San Francisco: HarperSanFrancisco, 2006.

Klauber, Martin I., and Scott M. Manetsch. *The Great Commission: Evangelicals and the History of World Missions*. Nashville: B. & H., 2007.

Kleiner, Art. *The Age of Heretics: A History of the Radical Thinkers Who Reinvented Corporate Management*. 2nd ed. San Francisco: Jossey-Bass, 2008.

Klodawsky, Helene, director. "Malls R Us." New York: Icarus Films, 2009.

Kockelmans, Joseph J., and Edmund Husserl. *Edmund Husserl's Phenomenology*. West Lafayette, IN: Purdue University Press, 1994.

Kohut, Andrew, and Carrol Doherty. *Trends and Attitudes toward Religion and Society*. Washington, DC: Pew Research Center, 2007.

Kohut, Andrew. *The Diminishing Divide: Religion's Changing Role in American Politics*. Washington DC: Brookings Institution, 2000.

Kosmin, Barry, and Ariela Keysar. *American Religious Identification Survey*. Harford, CT: Trinity College, 2009.

Kosmin, Barry A., and Ariela Keysar. *Religion in a Free Market: Religious and Non-Religious Americans: Who, What, Why, Where?* Ithaca, NY: Paramount Market, 2006.

Köstenberger, Andreas J., R. Albert Mohler, J. P. Moreland, and Kevin J. Vanhoozer. *Whatever Happened to Truth?* Wheaton, IL: Crossway, 2005.

Kostlevy, William. *Holiness Manuscripts: A Guide to Sources Documenting the Wesleyan Holiness Movement in the United States and Canada*. Philadelphia, PA: Scarecrow Press, 1994.

Kraft, Charles H., and Dean S. Gilliland. *Appropriate Christianity*. Pasadena, CA: William Carey Library, 2005.

Krapohl, Robert H., and Charles H. Lippy. *The Evangelicals: A Historical, Thematic, and Biographical Guide*. Westport, CT: Greenwood, 1999.

Kriegel, Robert J., and David. Brandt. *Sacred Cows Make the Best Burgers: Paradigm-Busting Strategies for Developing Change-Ready People and Organizations*. New York: Warner, 1996.

Kristof, Nicholas. "Apocalypse (Almost) Now." *New York Times*, Feb 24, 2004.

Kushiner, James. "Decline of Catholicism in the Northwest 'Stunning' and other Survey Notes." *Touchstone: A Journal of Mere Christianity* (2009): http://touchstonemag.com/merecomments/2009/03/decline-of-catholicism-in-the-northeast-stunning-other-survey-notes/ (accessed 4/11/2012).

Kwon, Lillian. "Interview: Brian Mclaren on Sin, Hell, New Kind of Christianity." The Christian Post (2010) http://www.christianpost.com/news/interview-brian-mclaren-on-sin-hell-new-kind-of-christianity-44159/ (accessed 1/5/2012).

Kyle, Richard G. *Evangelicalism: An Americanized Christianity*. New Brunswick, NJ: Transaction, 2006.

———. *The Last Days Are Here Again: A History of the End Times*. Grand Rapids: Baker, 1998.

Ladd, George Eldon. *The Gospel of the Kingdom: Scriptural Studies in the Kingdom of God*. Grand Rapids: Eerdmans, 1959.

LaHaye, Tim F. *Revelation Unveiled*. Grand Rapids: Zondervan, 1999.

LaHaye, Tim F., and Jerry B. Jenkins. *Left Behind: A Novel of the Earth's Last Days*. Wheaton, IL: Tyndale House, 1995.

Larsen, Timothy. "Defining and Locating Evangelicalism." In *The Cambridge Companion to Evangelical Theology*, edited by Timothy Larsen and Deniel Trier, 125–43. Cambridge: Cambridge University Press, 2007.

Larson, Bruce, and Ralph Osborne. *The Emerging Church*. Waco, TX.: Word, 1970.

Larson, Edward J. *Summer for the Gods: The Scopes Trial and America's Continuing Debate over Science and Religion*. New York: Basic, 1997.

Lawless, Charles E. *The Great Commission Resurgence: Fulfilling God's Mandate in Our Time*. Nashville: B. & H. Academic, 2010.

———. *Membership Matters: Insights from Effective Churches on New Member Classes and Assimilation*. Grand Rapids: Zondervan, 2005.

Lawlor, Leonard. *Derrida and Husserl: The Basic Problem of Phenomenology*. Bloomington, IL: Indiana University Press, 2002.

Lawton, Kim. "The Emerging Church, Part 1 and 2." *Religion and Ethics Newsweekly Episodes* (broadcast on PBS, 2005). http://video.pbs.org/video/2254457300/ and http://video.pbs.org/video/2254533020/.

Lecky, W. E. H. *History of European Morals: From Augustus to Charlemagne*. London, UK: Watts & Co., 1911.

Lee, Shayne, and Phillip Luke Sinitiere. *Holy Mavericks: Evangelical Innovators and the Spiritual Marketplace*. New York: New York University Press, 2009.

Leeman, Jonathan. *The Church and the Surprising Offense of God's Love: Reintroducing the Doctrines of Church Membership and Discipline*. Wheaton, IL: Crossway, 2010.

Leitch, Vincent B. *Deconstructive Criticism: An Advanced Introduction*. New York: Columbia University Press, 1983.

Lewis, C. S. *The Weight of Glory and Other Addresses*. San Francisco, CA: Harper, 2001.

Lewis, Gordon R., and Bruce A. Demarest. *Integrative Theology*. Grand Rapids: Zondervan, 1996.

Lewis, Michael, and Tanja Staehler. *Phenomenology: An Introduction*. New York: Continuum, 2010.

Liebman, Robert C., Robert. Wuthnow, and James L. Guth. *The New Christian Right: Mobilization and Legitimation*. Hawthorne, NY: Aldine, 1983.

Liederbach, Mark, and A. L. Reid. *The Convergent Church: Missional Worshipers in an Emerging Culture*. Grand Rapids: Kregel, 2009.

Lienesch, Michael. *In the Beginning: Fundamentalism, the Scopes Trial, and the Making of the Antievolution Movement*. Chapel Hill, NC: University of North Carolina Press, 2007.

Lifton, Robert Jay. *The Protean Self: Human Resilience in an Age of Fragmentation*. New York: Basic, 1993.

Lindner, E. W. *Yearbook of American & Canadian Churches*. Nashville: Abingdon, 2010.

Lindsay, D. Michael. *Faith in the Halls of Power: How Evangelicals Joined the American Elite*. New York: Oxford University Press, 2007.

Lindsell, Harold. *The Battle for the Bible*. Grand Rapids: Zondervan, 1976.

———. *The Bible in the Balance*. Grand Rapids: Zondervan, 1979.

———. *God's Incomparable Word*. Minneapolis, MN: World Wide, 1977.

Lippy, Charles H. *Being Religious, American Style: A History of Popular Religiosity in the United States*. Westport, CT: Greenwood, 1994.

Livingston, James C., Francis Schüssler Fiorenza, and Sarah Coakley. *Modern Christian Thought: The Twentieth Century.* 2nd ed. Minneapolis, MN: Fortress, 2006.

Llewelyn, John. *Derrida on the Threshold of Sense.* Ann Arbor, MI: University of Michigan, 1986.

Lloyd-Jones, David Martyn. *What is an Evangelical?* London: Banner of Truth, 1992.

Long, Jimmy. *Emerging Hope: A Strategy for Reaching the Postmodern Generations.* Downers Grove, IL: InterVarsity, 2004.

Long, Kathryn. *The Revival of 1857–1858: Interpreting an American Religious Awakening.* New York: Oxford University Press, 1998.

Longenecker, Richard N. *The Christology of Early Jewish Christianity.* Naperville, IL: A. R. Allenson, 1970.

———. *Patterns of Discipleship in the New Testament.* Grand Rapids: Eerdmans, 1996.

Lovelace, Richard F. *Dynamics of Spiritual Life: an Evangelical Theology of Renewal.* Downers Grove, IL: Inter-Varsity Press, 1979.

Loveland, Anne C., and Otis B. Wheeler. *From Meetinghouse to Megachurch: A Material and Cultural History.* Columbia, MO: University of Missouri Press, 2003.

Lucke, Glenn. "Church Growth Movement." In *Religion and American Cultures: An Encyclopedia of Traditions, Diversity, and Popular Expressions*, edited by Gary Laderman and Luis D. León, 319–20. Santa Barbara, CA: ABC-CLIO, 2003.

Lugo, Luis, and Smith Gregory. *Many Americans Mix Multiple Faiths.* Washington, DC: Pew Forum on Religious and Public Life, 2009.

Lutzer, Erwin W. *All One Body: Why Don't We Agree.* Wheaton, IL: Tyndale House, 1989.

Lyons, Gabe. *The Next Christians: the Good News About the End of Christian America.* New York, NY: Doubleday Religion, 2010

Lymann, Geoffrey C, and Laura S. Hussey. "George W. Bush and Evangelicals: Religious Commitment and Partisan Change Amount Evangelical Protestants 1960–2004." In *A Matter of Faith? Religion and the 2004 Election*, edited by David E. Campbell, 180–98. Washington, DC: Brookings Institute, 2004.

Lyon, David. *Jesus in Disneyland: Religion in Postmodern Times.* Oxford: Blackwell, 2000.

Lyotard, Jean-François. *The Postmodern Condition: A Report on Knowledge.* Minneapolis, MN: University of Minnesota Press, 1984.

MacArthur, John. *Ashamed of the Gospel: When the Church Becomes Like the World.* 3rd ed. Wheaton, IL: Crossway, 2010.

———. *Charismatic Chaos.* Grand Rapids: Zondervan, 1992.

———. *Experiencing the Passion of Christ.* Nashville: Nelson Reference & Electronic, 2004.

———. *The Truth War: Fighting for Certainty in an Age of Deception.* Nashville: Thomas Nelson, 2007.

MacArthur, John, Nathan Busenitz, Scott Lang, and Phillip R. Johnson. *Fool's Gold?: Discerning Truth in an Age of Error.* Wheaton, IL: Crossway, 2005.

Machen, J. Gresham. *Christianity and Liberalism.* New York: Macmillan, 1923.

Madsen, Deborah L. *Postmodernism: A Bibliography, 1926–1994.* Netherlands: Rodopi, 1995.

Magliola, Robert R. *Derrida on the Mend.* West Lafayette, IN: Purdue University Press, 1984.

Mahaney, C. J. *Why Small Groups*. Gaithersburg, MD: People of Destiny International, 1996.

Malley, Brian. *How the Bible Works: An Anthropological Study of Evangelical Biblicism*. Walnut Creek, CA: AltaMira, 2004.

Malphurs, Aubrey. *Planting Growing Churches for the 21st Century: A Comprehensive Guide for New Churches and Those Desiring Renewal*. 3rd ed. Grand Rapids: Baker, 2004.

———. *Strategy 2000: Churches Making Disciples for the Next Millennium*. Grand Rapids: Kregel Resources, 1996.

Mannion, Gerard, and Lewis Seymour Mudge. *The Routledge Companion to the Christian Church*. New York: Routledge, 2008.

Mansfield, Stephen. *Rechurch: Healing Your Way Back to the People of God*. Carol Stream, IL: Barna/Tyndale House, 2010.

Marler, P. L., and C. K. Hadaway. "Being Religious Or Being Spiritual in America: A Zero-Sum Proposition?" *Journal for the Scientific Study of Religion* 41.2 (2002) 289–300.

Marsden, George. "Defining Fundamentalism." *Christian Scholar's Review* 1.2 (1980) 141–51.

———. *The Evangelical Mind and the New School Presbyterian Experience: A Case Study of Thought and Theology in Nineteenth-Century America*. New Haven, CT: Yale University Press, 1970.

———. *Evangelicalism and Modern America*. Grand Rapids: Eerdmans, 1984.

———. "The Gospel of Wealth, the Social Gospel, and the Salvation of Souls in Nineteenth-Century America." *Fides et Historia* 5 (1972) 10–21.

———. *Fundamentalism and American Culture: The Shaping of Twentieth Century Evangelicalism, 1870–1925*. New York: Oxford University Press, 1981.

———. *Fundamentalism and American Culture*. New York: Oxford University Press, 2006.

———. "Fundamentalism as an American Phenomenon: A Comparison with English Evangelicalism." *Church History: Studies in Christianity and Culture* 46.2 (2009) 215–32.

———. *Jonathan Edwards: A Life. New Haven:* Yale University Press, 2003.

———. *Reforming Fundamentalism: Fuller Seminary and the New Evangelicalism*. Grand Rapids: Eerdmans, 1995.

———. *The Soul of the American University: From Protestant Establishment to Established Nonbelief*. New York: Oxford University Press, 1996.

———. *Understanding Fundamentalism and Evangelicalism*. Grand Rapids: Eerdmans, 1991.

Marsden, George, and B. J. Longfield. *The Secularization of the Academy*. New York: Oxford University Press, 1992.

Marsden, George, and L. S. William. "Evangelical and Fundamental Christianity." In *The Encyclopedia of Religion*, vol. 5, edited by Mircea Eliade, 190–97. New York: Macmillan, 1987.

Marsh, J. L., J. D. Caputo, and M. Westphal. *Modernity and Its Discontents*. New Jersey, NJ: Fordham University Press, 1992.

Martin, William C. *With God on Our Side: The Rise of the Religious Right in America*. New York: Broadway, 1996.

Marty, M. E. *Accounting for Fundamentalisms: The Dynamic Character of Movements.* Chicago: University of Chicago Press, 2004.

———. “Fundamentalism as a Social Phenomenon.” *Bulletin of the American Academy of Arts and Sciences* 42.2 (1988) 15–29.

———. *Fundamentalism and Evangelicalism.* New York: Saur, 1993.

———. *The Fundamentalism Project: Fundamentalism Observed, Vol. 1.* Chicago: The University of Chicago Press, 1991.

———. *The Glory and the Power: The Fundamentalist Challenge to the Modern World.* Chicago: Beacon Press, 1992.

———. *The New Shape of American Religion.* San Francisco: Harper, 1959.

———. *Modern American Religion.* Chicago: University of Chicago Press, 1986.

———. *Modern American Religion, Volume 1: The Irony of it All, 1893–1919.* Chicago: University Of Chicago Press, 1997.

———. *Modern American Religion, Volume 2: The Noise of Conflict, 1919–1941.* Chicago, IL: University Of Chicago Press, 1997.

———. *Modern American Religion, Volume 3: Under God, Indivisible, 1941–1960.* Chicago: University Of Chicago Press, 1999.

———. *A Nation of Behavors.* Chicago: University of Chicago Press, 1976.

———. *Religion and Republic: The American Circumstance.* Boston: Beacon, 1987.

———. *Righteous Empire: The Protestant Experience in America.* New York: Dial, 1970.

Marty, M. E., and Merle Peek. *Christianity in the New World: From 1500 to 1800.* Minneapolis: Winston, 1984.

Marty, M. E., and R. S. Appleby. *Fundamentalisms Comprehended.* Chicago: University of Chicago Press, 1991.

McClymond, Michael James. *Embodying the Spirit: New Perspectives on North American Revivalism.* Baltimore, MD: Johns Hopkins University Press, 2004.

———. “Revivals.” In *The Blackwell Companion to Religion in America. Revivals*, edited by Philip Goff, 306–20. Sussex, UK: Blackwell, 2010.

McDannell, C. *Material Christianity: Religion and Popular Culture in America.* New Jersey, NJ: Yale University Press, 1998.

McDermott, Gerald R. *The Oxford Handbook of Evangelical Theology.* New York: Oxford University Press, 2007.

McDowell, Josh. *Evidence That Demands a Verdict: Historical Evidences for the Christian Faith.* Nashville: Thomas Nelson, 1993.

———. *More Evidence That Demands a Verdict: Historical Evidences for the Christian Scriptures.* San Bernardino, CA: Here’s Life, 1981.

———. *The New Evidence That Demands a Verdict.* Nashville: Thomas Nelson, 1999.

McElvaine, Robert S. *Grand Theft Jesus: The Hijacking of Religion in America.* New York: Broadway, 2009.

McGavran, Donald A. *Church Growth and Christian Mission.* New York: Harper & Row, 1965.

———. *The Conciliar-Evangelical Debate: The Crucial Documents, 1964–1976: Expanded Edition of Eye of the Storm, the Great Debate in Mission, Including Documents on Bangkok and Nairobi.* South Pasadena, CA: William Carey Library, 1977.

———. *How Churches Grow: The New Frontiers of Mission.* London: World Dominion, 1959.

McGavran, Donald A., and Winfield C. Arn. *Back to Basics in Church Growth.* Wheaton, IL: Tyndale House, 1981.

———. *How to Grow Your Church*. Dallas, TX: Gospel Light, 1988.

McGavran, Donald A., and C. Peter. Wagner. *Understanding Church Growth*. Grand Rapids: Eerdmans, 1990.

McGee, Gary. *Miracles, Missions, and American Pentecostalism*. Maryknoll, NY: Orbis, 2010.

McGiffert, Arthur Cushman. *Christianity as History and Faith*. New York: Scribner's Sons, 1934.

McGrath, A. E. *A Passion for Truth: the Intellectual Coherence of Evangelicalism*. Downers Grove, IL: InterVarsity Press, 1996.

———. *Christianity's Dangerous Idea: the Protestant Revolution-a History From the Sixteenth Century to the Twenty-first*. New York: HarperOne, 2007.

———. *Christian Theology: An Introduction*. Oxford: Wiley-Blackwell, 2006

———. *The Future of Christianity*. Oxford: Blackwell, 2002.

McIntyre, John. *The Shape of Soteriology: Studies in the Doctrine of the Death of Christ*. Edinburgh: T. & T. Clark, 1992.

McIntyre, Patrick. *The Graham Formula: Why Most Decisions for Christ Are Ineffective*. Mammoth Springs, AR: White Harvest, 2006.

McKnight, Scot. "The Five Streams of the Emerging Church." *Christianity Today* 51.2 (2007) 33–38.

———. "The Ironic Faith of the Emergent's: McLaren Shows Us Not Only Where 'Post-Evangelicals' Are Going, But Also How They Get There." *Christianity Today* 52.9 (2008) 63–65.

———. "Review: A New Kind of Christianity." *Christianity Today* 54.3 (2010) 59–66.

———."What is Emerging Church?" Westminster Theological Seminary, Contemporary Issues Conference, Fall 2006.

McKnight, Scot, Kevin Corcoran, Jason Clark, and Pete Rollins. *Church in the Present Tense: A Candid Look at What's Emerging*. Grand Rapids: Baker, 2011.

McLain, Alvin J. "Is Theology Changing in the Conservative Camp." *The Brethren Missionary Herald*, Feb 23, 1957.

McLaren, Brian D. *The Church on the Other Side*. Grand Rapids: Zondervan, 2003.

———. *Everything Must Change: When the World's Biggest Problems and Jesus' Good News Collide*. New York: Thomas Nelson, 2009.

———. *Finding Faith: A Search for What is Real*. Grand Rapids: Zondervan, 2007.

———. *Finding Our Way Again: The Return of the Ancient Practices*. Thomas Nelson, 2008.

———. "Four Points toward Peace in the Middle East." *Sojourners* (4/16/19) http://blog.sojo.net/2009/04/16/four-points-toward-peace-in-the-middle-east/ (accessed 7/10/2012).

———. *A Generous Orthodoxy: Why I Am a Missional, Evangelical, Post/Protestant, Liberal/Conservative, Mystical/Poetic, Biblical, Charismatic/Contemplative, Fundamentalist/Calvinist, Anabaptist/Anglican, Methodist/Catholic, Green/Incarnational, Depressed-Yet-Hopeful, Emergent, Unfinished Christian*. Grand Rapids: Zondervan/Youth Specialties, 2006.

———. *The Last Word and the Word After That: A Tale of Faith, Doubt, and a New Kind of Christianity*. San Francisco: Jossey-Bass, 2005.

———. "The Method, the Message and the Ongoing Story." *In Church in Emerging Culture: Five Perspectives*, edited by Leonard Sweet, 191. Grand Rapids: Zondervan/Youth Specialties, 2003.

———. *More Ready Than You Realize.* Grand Rapids: Zondervan, 2002.

———. *A New Kind of Christian: A Tale of Two Friends on a Spiritual Journey.* San Francisco: Jossey-Bass, 2001.

———. *A New Kind of Christianity: Ten Questions That Are Transforming the Faith.* New York: HarperOne, 2010.

———. *Reinventing Your Church.* Grand Rapids: Zondervan, 1998.

———. *The Story We Find Ourselves in: Further Adventures of a New Kind of Christian.* San Francisco: Jossey-Bass, 2003.

———. *The Secret Message of Jesus: Uncovering the Truth That Could Change Everything.* Nashville: Thomas Nelson, 2006.

———. *The Voice of Luke: Not Even Sandals.* Nashville: Thomas Nelson, 2007.

———."Why I'm Voting for Obama and Why I Hope You Will Too." (2008) http://www.brianmclaren.net/archives/blog/why-im-voting-for-obama-and-why.html (accessed 1/15/2012).

McLaren, Brian D., and Anthony Campolo. *Adventures in Missing the Point: How the Culture-Controlled Church Neutered the Gospel.* El Cajon, CA: EmergentYS, 2003.

McLoughlin, W. G. *The American Evangelicals, 1800–1900; an Anthology.* New York: Harper & Row, 1968.

———. *Modern Revivalism: Charles Grandison Finney to Billy Graham.* New York: Ronald, 1959.

McNeal, Reggie. *Revolution in Leadership.* Nashville: Abingdon, 1998.

———. *A Work of the Heart: How God Shapes Spiritual Leaders.* San Francisco: Jossey-Bass, 2000.

———. *Missional Renaissance: Changing the Scorecard for the Church.* San Francisco: Jossey-Bass, 2009.

McQuade, Pamela. *How Do I Get to Heaven? Knowing the Romans Road.* Uhrichsville, OH: Barbour, 2011.

McVeigh, Rory, and David Sikkink. "God, Politics, and Protest: Religious Beliefs and the Legitimation of Contentious Tactics." *Social Forces* 79 (2000) 1425–58.

Mead, S. E. "Denominationalism: The Shape of Protestantism in America." *Church History* 23.4 (1954) 291–320.

Meacham, Jon. "From the Editors Desk." *Newsweek* 46, (2006): 6.

Megill, Allan. *Prophets of Extremity: Nietzsche, Heidegger, Foucault, Derrida.* Berkeley, CA: University of California Press, 1985.

Meissner, W. W. *Thy Kingdom Come: Psychoanalytic Perspectives on the Messiah and the Millennium.* Kansas City, MO: Sheed & Ward, 1995.

Merchant, Dan, director, Lord Save us From Your Followers, Big Finish Media, 2008.

Mermann-Jozwiak, E. *A New Cultural Politics: Women Writers and Postmodernism.* Madison, WI: University of Wisconsin Press, 1993.

Merritt, Jonathan. *Green Like God: Unlocking the Divine Plan for Our Planet.* New York: FaithWords, 2010.

Meyer, Keith. *Whole Life Transformation: Becoming the Change Your Church Needs.* Downers Grove, IL.: InterVarsity, 2010.

Meyers, Robin R. *Why the Christian Right Is Wrong: A Minister's Manifesto for Taking Back Your Faith, Your Flag, Your Future.* San Francisco: Jossey-Bass, 2006.

Middleton, J. Richard, and Brian J. Walsh. *Truth Is Stranger Than It Used to Be: Biblical Faith in a Postmodern Age.* Downers Grove, IL: InterVarsity, 1995.

Milbank, John. "The End of Dialogue." In *Christian Uniqueness Reconsidered: The Myth of a Pluralistic Theology of Religions*, edited by Gavin D'Costa, 174–91. New York: Orbis, 1990.

———. "Problematising the Secular: The Post-Modern Agenda." In *Shadows of Spirit: Postmodernism and Religion*, edited by Philippa Berry and Andrew Wernick, 31. London: Routledge, 1992.

———. *The Word Made Strange: Theology, Language, Culture*. London: Wiley-Blackwell, 1997.

Milbank, John, Catherine Pickstock, and Graham Ward. *Radical Orthodoxy: A New Theology.* London: Routledge, 1999.

Milbank, John, T. Longman, R. Q. Ford, P. R. Davies, and W. T. Cavanaugh. "Postmodern Critical Augustinianism." *Modern Theology* 7 (1991) 228–41.

Miller, Donald. *Blue Like Jazz: Nonreligious Thoughts on Christian Spirituality*. Nashville: Thomas Nelson, 2003.

Miller, Donald E. *Reinventing American Protestantism: Christianity in the New Millennium*. Berkeley, CA: University of California Press, 1997.

———. "The Reinvented Church: Style and Strategies." *Christian Century* 116 (1999) 1250–52.

———. "Routinizing Charisma: the Vineyard Christian Fellowship in the Post-wimber Era." *Pneuma: The Journal of the Society for Pentecostal Studies* 25.2 (2003) 216–239.

Mitchell, Susan. *Generation X: Americans Aged 18 to 34*. 3rd ed. Ithaca, NY: New Strategist, 2001.

Mohanty, Satya. *Literary Theory and the Claims of History: Postmodernism, Objectivity, Multicultural Politics*. New York: Cornell University Press, 1997.

Mohler, R. Albert. "A Conflict of Visions: The Theological Roots of the Southern Baptist Controversy." *Southern Baptist Theological Journal* 7 (2003) 4–11.

———, editor. Confronting Postmodernism edition. *Southern Baptist Theological Journal* 5.2 (2001).

———. *Culture Shift: Engaging Current Issues with Timeless Truth*. Colorado Springs, CO: Multnomah, 2008.

———. *He is Not Silent: Preaching in a Postmodern World*. Chicago: Moody, 2008.

———. *The Disappearance of God: Dangerous Beliefs in the New Spiritual Openness*. Colorado Springs, CO: Multnomah Books, 2009.

Mohler, R. Albert, Bruce Ware, Jim Hamilton, Gregory Wills, and Stephen Wellum. "Southern Seminary Panel Discussion on Brian McLaren's *A New Kind of Christianity*." (2010) http://www.sbts.edu/resources/chapel/chapel-spring-2010/panel-discussion-a-new-kind-of-christianity-brian-mclaren-recasts-the-gospel/?play=true (accessed 10/13/2012).

Mohler, R. Albert, and D. G. Hart. *Theological Education in the Evangelical Tradition*. Grand Rapids: Baker, 1996.

Moltmann, Jürgen. *The Coming of God: Christian Eschatology.* Translated by Margaret Kohl. London: SCM, 1996.

———. *Experiences in Theology: Ways and Forms of Christian Theology*. Minneapolis: Fortress, 2000.

Moltmann, Jürgen., M. Douglas Meeks, and Theodore Runyon. *Hope for the Church: Moltmann in Dialogue with Practical Theology.* Nashville: Abingdon, 1979.

Moon, Gary W. *Apprenticeship with Jesus: Learning to Live Like the Master*. Grand Rapids: Baker, 2009.

———. "Getting the Elephant Out of the Sanctuary: An Interview with Dallas Willard, Expanded Text." *Conversations Journal* 8.1 (2010) 17–23.

Moon, Gary W., and Gary Porter. Special Theme Issue: Dallas Willard and Spiritual Formation. *Journal of Spiritual Formation and Soul Care* 3.2 (2010).

Moore, R. L. *Selling God: American Religion in the Marketplace of Culture*. Oxford: Oxford University Press, 1995.

Moore, Russell. *The Kingdom of Christ: the New Evangelical Perspective*. Wheaton, IL: Crossway Books, 2004.

Moreland, J. P., and Dallas Willard. *Love Your God With All Your Mind: The Role of Reason in the Life of the Soul*. Grand Rapids: NavPress, 1997.

Moritz, Joshua. "Beyond Strategy, towards the Kingdom of God: The Post-Critical Reconstructionist Mission of the Emerging Church." *Journal of Theology* 47.1 (2008) 27–36.

Moritz, Thorsten, and Craig G. Bartholomew. *Christ and Consumerism: Critical Reflections on the Spirit of Our Age*. Carlisle, UK: Paternoster, 2000.

Moynagh, Michael. *Emerging Church: An Intrroduction*. Oxford: Monarch, 2009.

Mullin, Robert Bruce. *A Short World History of Christianity*. Louisville, KY: Westminster John Knox, 2008.

Murphy, M. "The Next Billy Graham." *Esquire*, October, 1978.

Murphy, Nancy C. "Non-Reductive Physicalism: Philosophical Issues." In *Whatever Happened to the Soul? Scientific and Theological Portraits of Human Nature*, edited by Nancey C. Murphy, H. Newton Malony, and Warren S. Brown, 127–48. Minneapolis: Fortress, 1998.

———."Religion and Science." In *Routledge Encyclopedia of Philosophy: Questions to Sociobiology*, Vol. 8, edited by Edward Craig, 224–29. New York: Routledge, 1998.

Murray, Beth. *When the Church Stops Caring*. Victoria, BC: Trafford, 2005.

Murray, Stuart. *Church After Christendom*. Carlisle, UK: Paternoster, 2004.

Myers, D. G., and M. E. Marty. *The American Paradox: Spiritual Hunger in an Age of Plenty*. Princeton: Yale University Press, 2001.

Newport, Kenneth G. C., and Crawford Gribben. *Expecting the End: Millennialism in Social and Historical Context*. Waco, TX: Baylor University Press, 2006.

Nezar, AlSayyad., and Mejgan. Massoumi. *The Fundamentalist City?: Religiosity and the Remaking of Urban Space*. New York, NY: Routledge, 2011.

Nichols, Stephen J. Jesus *Made in America: A Cultural History from the Puritans to the Passion of the Christ*. Downers Grove, IL: InterVarsity, 2008.

Nichols, Stephen *J. J. Gresham Machen: A Guided Tour of His Life and Thought*. Phillipsburg, NJ: P. & R., 2004.

Niebuhr, H. R. *Christ and Culture*. New York: Harper, 1951.

Noll, M. A. *American Evangelical Christianity: An Introduction*. New York: Blackwell, 2001.

———. *The Civil War as a Theological Crisis*. Chapel Hill, NC: University of North Carolina Press, 2006.

———. "Evangelicalism." In *A Companion to American Thought*, edited by Richard Wightman Fox and James T. Kloppenberg, 222. Malden, MA: Blackwell, 1995.

———. *A History of Christianity in the United States and Canada*. Grand Rapids: Eerdmans, 1992.

———. *The Old Religion in a New World: The History of North American Christianity.* Grand Rapids: Eerdmans, 2001.

———. *Religion and American Politics: From the Colonial Period to the 1980s.* New York: Oxford University Press, 1990.

———. *The Rise of Evangelicalism: The Age of Edwards, Whitefield and the Wesleys.* Downers Grove, IL: InterVarsity, 2004.

———. *The Scandal of the Evangelical Mind.* Grand Rapids: Eerdmans, 1995.

———. *Turning Points: Decisive Moments in the History of Christianity.* Baker, 1998.

———. "Where We Are and How We Got Here." *Christianity Today* (2006)

Noll, M. A., D. W. Bebbington, and G. A. Rawlyk. *Evangelicalism: Comparative Studies of Popular Protestantism in North America, the British Isles, and Beyond, 1700–1990.* Oxford: Oxford University Press, 1994.

Noll, M. A., and Luke E. Harlow. *Religion and American Politics: From the Colonial Period to the Present.* 2nd ed. New York: Oxford University Press, 2007.

Noll, M. A., N. O. Hatch, and G. M. Marsden. *The Search for Christian America.* Colorado Springs, CO: Helmers & Howard, 1989.

Numbers, Ronald L. *Darwinism Comes to America.* Cambridge: Harvard University Press, 1998.

Oakland, Roger. *Faith Undone: The Emerging Church—A New Reformation Or an End-Time Deception?* Silverton, OR: Lighthouse Trails, 2007.

Obrien, Brandon. "Emergent's Divergence." *Christianity Today* Jan 2008, 13–14.

Oden, Thomas C. *After Modernity—What?: Agenda for Theology.* Grand Rapids: Academie, 1990.

Oden, Thomas C., Kenneth Tanner, and Christopher A. Hall. *Ancient & Postmodern Christianity: Paleo-Orthodoxy in the 21st Century: Essays in Honor of Thomas C. Oden.* Downers Grove, IL: InterVarsity, 2002.

Ogden, Greg. *The New Reformation: Returning the Ministry to the People of God.* Grand Rapids: Zondervan, 1991.

Ogden, Steven G. *The Presence of God in the World: A Contribution to Postmodern Christology Based on the Theologies of Paul Tillich and Karl Rahner.* Bern, Switzerland: Lang, 2007.

Oldfield, D.M. *Right and the Righteous.* New York, NY: Rowman & Littlefield, 1996.

Olson, David T. *The American Church in Crisis: Groundbreaking Research Based on a National Database of Over 200,000 Churches.* Grand Rapids: Zondervan, 2008.

Olson, Roger. *A–Z of Evangelical Theology.* London: SCM, 2005.

———. *Arminian Theology: Myths and Realities.* Downers Grove, IL: InterVarsity, 2006.

———. *How to be Evangelical Without Being Conservative.* Grand Rapids: Zondervan, 2008.

———. "Postconservative Evangelicals Greet the Postmodern Age." *The Christian Century* 112.15 (1995) 480–83.

———. *The Story of Christian Theology: Twenty Centuries of Tradition & Reform.* Grand Rapids: InterVarsity, 1999.

———. editor. *The Westminster Handbook to Evangelical Theology.* Louisville, KY: Westminster John Knox, 2004.

Olson, Roger, and Stanley Grenz. *20th Century Theology: God and the World in a Transitional Age.* Downers Grove, IL: InterVarsity, 1992.

Olson, Ted."Ets Leadership Issues Recommendations on Kicking Out Open Theists." *Christianity Today,* October (2003): 27–29.

———."The Evangelical Electorial Map." *Christianity Today,* November, 2008.

Ortberg, John. *The Life You've Always Wanted: Spiritual Disciplines for Ordinary People.* Philadelphia, PA: Running Press, 2004.

"Rethinking the Kingdom of God: The Work of Dallas Willard and Some Applications to Psychotherapeutic Practice." *Journal of Psychology and Christianity* 14.4 (1995) 306–17.

Ortberg, John, and Dallas Willard. "What Makes Spirituality Christian?" *Christianity Today,* March 6, 1995, 16–17.

Ostwalt, Conrad Eugene. *Secular Steeples: Popular Culture and the Religious Imagination.* Harrisburg, PA: Trinity, 2003.

Packer, J. I. *Concise Theology: A Guide to Historic Christian Beliefs.* Wheaton, IL: Tyndale House, 1993.

Packer, J. I., and Thomas C. Oden. *One Faith: The Evangelical Consensus.* Downer's Grove, IL: InterVarsity, 2004.

Pagitt, Doug. *A Christianity Worth Believing: Hope-Filled, Open-Armed, Alive-and-Well Faith for the Left Out, Left Behind, and Let Down in Us All.* San Francisco: Jossey-Bass, 2008.

———. *Church in the Inventive Age.* Minneapolis, MN: Sparkhouse, 2010.

———. "The Emerging Church and Embodied Theology." In *Listening to the Beliefs of Emerging Churches: Five Perspectives,* edited by Robert. Webber, 127. Grand Rapids: Zondervan, 2007.

———. *Preaching Re-Imagined: The Role of the Sermon in Communities of Faith.* Grand Rapids: Zondervan/Youth Specialties, 2005.

———. *Reimagining Spiritual Formation: A Week in the Life of an Experimental Church.* Grand Rapids: Youth Specialties, 2004.

Pagitt, Doug, and Tony Jones. *An Emergent Manifesto of Hope.* Grand Rapids: Baker, 2007.

Patrick, Darin. "Emerging Church Part 1 and Part Deux." http://journeyon.net/blogs/darrin-patrick/emerging-church-pt-1 (accessed 4/23/2012).

Patterson, James T. *Restless Giant: The United States From Watergate to Bush V. Gore.* New York: Oxford University Press, 2005.

Patton, C. Michael. "Would the Real Emerger Please Stand Up?" http://www.reclaimingthemind.org/blog/2008/02/would-the-real-emerger-please-stand-up-complete/ (accessed 6/4/2012).

Paulson, Henry M. *On the Brink: Inside the Race to Stop the Collapse of the Global Financial System.* New York: Business Plus, 2010.

Peck, Andy. "Kingdom Living: Interview With Dallas Willard." *Christianity & Renewal Magazine* (2002). http://www.dwillard.org/articles/artview.asp?artID=92 (accessed 5/2/2012).

Peck, M. Scott. *People of the Lie: The Hope for Healing Human Evil.* New York: Simon and Schuster, 1983.

Pelosi, Alexandra, director. "The Trials of Ted Haggard." Home Box Office Productions, 2008.

Penrod, Diane. "Logocentrism." *In Encyclopedia of Postmodernism,* edited by V. E. Taylor, and C. E. Winquist, 323–25. London: Routledge, 2003.

Percy, Martyn. "Review of *Reinventing American Protestantism: Christianity in the New Millennium*." *Journal of Contemporary Religion* 13.3 (1998) 406–8.

Peshkin, Alan. *God's Choice: The Total World of a Fundamentalist Christian School.* Chicago: University of Chicago Press, 1986.

Pettegrew, Larry D. "Evangelicalism, Paradigms, and the Emerging Church." *The Master's Seminary Journal* 17.2 (2006) 159–75.

Piper, John. *The Future of Justification: A Response to N. T. Wright.* Wheaton, IL: Crossway, 2007.

———. *Jesus: The Only Way to God: Must You Hear the Gospel to be Saved?* Grand Rapids: Baker, 2010.

———. *The Purifying Power of Living By Faith in Future Grace.* Sisters, OR: Multnomah, 1995.

———. "The Tornado, the Lutherans, and Homosexuality." (2009) http://www.desiringgod.org/blog/posts/the-tornado-the-lutherans-and-homosexuality (accessed 5/12/2012).

———. *Tulip: The Pursuit of God's Glory in Salvation.* Wheaton, IL: Crossway, 2009.

Piper, John, D. A. Carson, Mark Driscoll, and Tim Keller. "The Supremacy of Christ and Truth in a Postmodern World." Desiring God Conference 2006.

Piper, John, and Justin Taylor. *The Supremacy of Christ in a Postmodern World.* Wheaton, IL: Crossway, 2007.

Plantinga, Alvin. *Not the Way It's Supposed to Be: A Breviary of Sin.* Grand Rapids: Eerdmans, 1995.

Platt, David. *Radical: Taking Back Your Faith From the American Dream.* Colorado Springs, CO: Multnomah, 2010.

Pollock, J. C. *Billy Graham: The Authorized Biography.* New York: McGraw-Hill, 1966.

Porter, Steven. "The Willardian Corpus." *Journal of Spiritual Formation and Soul Care* 3.2 (2010) 239–66.

Press, Bill, *How the Republicans Stole Christmas: The Republican Party's Declared Monopoly on Religion and What Democrats Can Do to Take it Back.* New York: Doubleday, 2005.

Price, V., and A. Romantan. "Confidence in Institutions Before, During, and After 'Indecision 2000.'" *The Journal of Politics* 66.3 (2008) 939–56.

Pritchard, G. A. *Willow Creek Seeker Services: Evaluating a New Way of Doing Church.* Grand Rapids: Baker, 1996.

Prosser, Peter E. *Dispensationalist Eschatology and Its Influence on American and British Religious Movements.* Lewiston, NY: Mellen, 1999.

Putnam, Hilary. *Reason, Truth, and History.* New York: Cambridge University Press, 1981.

Quebedeaux, Richard. *The Worldly Evangelicals.* San Francisco: Harper & Row, 1978.

———. *The Young Evangelicals: Revolution in Orthodoxy.* New York: Harper & Row, 1974.

Queen, Edward L., Stephen R. Prothero, and Gardiner H. Shattuck. *Encyclopedia of American Religious History.* Vol. 1. New York, NY: Hermitage Facts on File, 2001.

Rainer, Thom S. *Breakout Churches.* Grand Rapids: Zondervan, 2005.

———. *Eating the Elephant: Bite-Sized Steps to Achieve Long-Term Growth in Your Church.* Nashville: Broadman & Holman, 1994.

———. *Effective Evangelistic Churches: Successful Churches Reveal What Works, and What Doesn't.* Nashville: Broadman & Holman, 1996.

———. "Evangelicals Engaging Emergent: A Discussion of the Emergent Church Movement," edited by William Henard and Adam Greenway, 28–33. Grand Rapids: B. & H. Academic, 2009.
Randall, Kelvin. *Evangelicals Etcetera: Conflict and Conviction in the Church of England's Parties.* Aldershot, UK: Ashgate, 2005.
Raschke, Carl. *The Next Reformation: Why Evangelicals Must Embrace Postmodernity.* Grand Rapids: Baker Academic, 2004.
Rauschenbusch, Walter. *A Theology for the Social Gospel.* New York: Macmillan, 1917.
Reichley, James. *Religion in American Public Life.* Washington, DC: Brookings Institution, 1985.
Rice, John R., *We Can Have Revival Now* Murfreesboro, TN: Bob Jones University Press, 1992.
———.*The Charismatic Movement*, Murfreesboro, TN: Sword of the Lord, 1977.
Rich, Mark. "The Cultural Warriors Get Laid Off." *New York Times*, March 3, 2009.
Risen, Richard. "Jesus the Logician: A Very Modest Proposal." *Christian Scholar's Review* 34.3 (2005) 35–39.
Ritzer, George. *The McDonaldization of Society: An Investigation Into the Changing Character of Contemporary Social Life.* Thousand Oaks, CA: Pine Forge, 1996.
———. *Postmodern Social Theory.* New York: McGraw-Hill, 1997.
Robbins, Jeffrey W. *Between Faith and Thought: An Essay on the Ontotheological Condition.* Charlottesville, WV: University of Virginia Press, 2003.
———. *In Search of a Non-Dogmatic Theology.* Aurora, CO: Davies Group, 2003.
———."The Problem of Ontotheology: Complicating the Divide Between Philosophy and Theology." *The Heythrop Journal* 43.2 (2002) 33–38.
Roberts, Wes, and Glenn Marshall. *Reclaiming God's Original Intent for the Church.* Colorado Springs, CO: NavPress, 2004.
Robinson, John P., and Steven Martin. "More Cold Water from the General Social Survey (GSS) and the American Time-Use Survey." *Social Science Computer Review* 28.1 (2010) 45–63.
Rockmore, Tom. *In Kant's Wake: Philosophy in the Twentieth Century.* Oxford: Blackwell, 2006.
———. *Kant and Idealism.* New Haven, CT: Yale University Press, 2007.
Rogers, Jack B, and DK McKim. *The Authority and Interpretation of the Bible: an Historical Approach.* New York, NY: Harpercollins, 1979.
Roof, Wade Clark. *Contemporary American Religion.* New York: Macmillan, 2000.
———. *A Generation of Seekers: The Spiritual Journeys of the Baby Boom Generation.* San Francisco: HarperSanFrancisco, 1993.
———. *Spiritual Marketplace: Baby Boomers and the Remaking of American Religion.* Princeton: Princeton University Press, 1999.
Rosenau, Pauline M. *Post-Modernism and the Social Sciences: Insights, Inroads, and Intrusions.* Princeton, NJ: Princeton University Press, 1992.
Rosin, H. H. *Missio Dei: an Examination of the Origin, Contents and Function of the Term in Protestant Missiological Discussion.* Leiden, Netherlands: Interuniversity Institute for Missiological and Ecumenical Research, 1972.
Rossing, B. R. *The Rapture Exposed: The Message of Hope in the Book of Revelation.* Boulder, CO: Basic, 2004.
Ryrie, Charles C. *So Great Salvation: What it Means to Believe in Jesus Christ.* Wheaton, IL: Victor, 1989.

Sandeen, Ernest Robert. *The Roots of Fundamentalism; British and American Millenarianism, 1800–1930*. Chicago: University of Chicago Press, 1970.

Sanford, Charles. *The Religious Life of Thomas Jefferson*. Norfolk, VA: University of Virginia Press, 1984.

Sanguin, Bruce. *The Emerging Church: A Model for Change & a Map for Renewal*. British Columbia, Canada: CooperHouse, 2008.

Sargeant, Kimon Howland. *Seeker Churches: Promoting Traditional Religion in a Nontraditional Way*. New Brunswick, NJ: Rutgers University Press, 2000.

Scandrette, Mark. *Soul Graffiti: Making a Life in the Way of Jesus*. San Francisco: Jossey-Bass, 2007.

Schaeffer, Francis. *A Christian Manifesto*. Colorado, Springs, CO: Crossway, 2005.

———. *The Complete Works of Francis a. Schaeffer: A Christian Worldview*. Wheaton, IL: Crossway, 1985.

Scheller, Christine A. "A Divine Conspirator." *Christianity Today*, September 2006.

Schnelle, Udo. Theology of the New Testament. Grand Rapids: Baker Academic, 2009.

Scribner, Robert. "The Reformation, Popular Magic, and the Disenchantment of the World." *Journal of Interdisciplinary History* 23.3 (1993) 475–94.

Seller, Ron. *America's Definition: What is an Evangelical Christian?* Phoenix, AZ: Grey Matter Research and Consulting, 2008.

———. *Defining Evangelical in Polling and Research: Are We Speaking the Same Language*. Phoenix, AZ: Grey Matter Research and Consulting, 2008.

Sheilds, Stephen. "Ten Years Out: A Retrospective on the Emerging Church in North America." *NextWave Church and Culture* 121 (2009) 13–18.

Shelley, Bruce L. *Evangelicalism in America*. Grand Rapids: Eerdmans, 1967.

Shelton, W. B. "Resounding the Chicago Call: A Plea to Restore Evangelicalism's Theological and Historic Foundation." *Reformation and Revival Journal* 13.1 (2004) 43–57.

Shepherd, Victor. *Our Evangelical Faith*. Toronto, ON: Clements, 2006.

Shibley, Mark A. *Resurgent Evangelicalism in the United States: Mapping Cultural Change Since 1970*. Columbia, SC: University of South Carolina Press, 1996.

Shields, Jon A. *The Democratic Virtues of the Christian Right*. Princeton: Princeton University Press, 2009.

Shurden, Walter B., and Randy. Shepley. *Going for the Jugular: A Documentary History of the SBC Holy War*. Macon, GA: Mercer, 1996.

Sider, Ronald J. *The Scandal of Evangelical Politics: Why Are Christians Missing the Chance to Really Change the World*. Grand Rapids: Baker, 2008.

Sim, Stuart. *The Routledge Companion to Postmodernism*. 3rd ed. New York: Routledge, 2011.

Sire, James W. *The Universe Next Door: A Basic Worldview Catalog*. 5th ed. Downers Grove, IL: InterVarsity, 2009.

Skinner, Tom, and Edward Gilbreath. *Reconciliation Blues: A Black Evangelical's Inside View of White Christianity*. Downers Grove, IL: InterVarsity, 2006.

Smart, Barry. *Michel Foucault: Critical Assessments*. Vol. 4. London: Routledge, 1995.

———. *Postmodernity*. London: Routledge, 1993.

Smietana, Bob, "High Tech Circuit Riders." *Christianity Today* 9, 2005, 9–11.

———."Southern Baptists Consider New Name to Broaden Appeal." *USA Today*, Sept 11, 2011.

Smith, Anthony D. *Nationalism in the Twentieth Century*. New York: New York University Press, 1979.

Smith Jr., Chuck. *The End of the World—As We Know it: Clear Direction for Bold and Innovative Ministry in a Postmodern World*. Colorado Springs, CO: WaterBrook, 2001.

Smith, Christian, M. L. Denton, R. Faris, and M. Regnerus. "Mapping American Adolescent Religious Participation." *Journal for the Scientific Study of Religion* 41.4 (2002) 597–612.

Smith, Christian, K. Den Dulk, B. Froehle, J. Penning, and S. Monsma. *The Disappearing God Gap? Religion in the 2008 Presidential Election*. New York: Oxford University Press, 2010.

Smith, Christian, and Michael Emerson. *American Evangelicalism: Embattled and Thriving*. Chicago: University of Chicago Press, 1998.

Smith, Christian, R. Faris, M. L. Denton, and M. Regnerus. "Mapping American Adolescent Subjective Religiosity and Attitudes of Alienation Toward Religion: A Research Report." *Sociology of Religion* 41.4 (2002) 597–612.

Smith, James Bryan. *The Good and Beautiful God: Falling in Love With the God Jesus Knows*. Downers Grove, IL: InterVarsity, 2009.

———. *The Good and Beautiful Life: Putting on the Character of Christ*. Downers Grove, IL.: InterVarsity, 2009.

———. *The Good and Beautiful Community: Following the Spirit, Extending Grace, Demonstrating Love*. Downers Grove, IL: InterVarsity, 2010.

———. *The Kingdom and the Cross*. Downers Grove, IL: InterVarsity, 2010.

Smith, James K. A. *After Modernity? Secularity, Globalization, and the Re-Enchantment of the World*. Waco, TX: Baylor University Press, 2008.

———. *The Devil Reads Derrida: And Other Essays on the University, the Church, Politics, and the Arts*. Grand Rapids: Eerdmans, 2009.

———. *Introducing Radical Orthodoxy: Mapping a Post-Secular Theology*. Grand Rapids: Baker Academic, 2004.

———. *Jacques Derrida: Live Theory*. New York: Continuum, 2005.

———. "Limited Inc/Arnation: Revisiting the Derrida/Searle Debate in Christian Context." In *Hermeneutics at the Crossroads*, edited by Kevin J. Vanhoozer, 112. Bloomington, IN: Indiana University Press, 2006.

———. "A Little Story about Metanarratives: Lyotard, Religion and Postmodernism Revisited." In *Christianity and the Postmodern Turn: Six Views*, edited by Myron B. Penner, 123–40. Grand Rapids: Brazos-Baker, 2005.

———. "What God Knows." *Christian Century* 122.14, (2005): 56–61.

———. *Who's Afraid of Postmodernism? Taking Derrida, Lyotard, and Foucault to Church*. Grand Rapids: Baker Academic, 2006.

Smith, James K. A., and James H. Olthuis. *Radical Orthodoxy and the Reformed Tradition: Creation, Covenant, and Participation*. Grand Rapids: Baker Academic, 2005.

Smith, James K. A., Henry Isaac Venema, and James H. Olthuis. *The Hermeneutics of Charity: Interpretation, Selfhood, and Postmodern Faith*. Grand Rapids: Brazos, 2004.

Smith, Nicholas H. *Charles Taylor: Meaning, Morals and Modernity*. Cambridge: Polity, 2002.

Smith, Peter. "Southern Baptist Fret of Decline as Meetings Begin." *USA Today*, 2008.

Smith, R. Scott. *Truth and the New Kind of Christian: The Emerging Effects of Postmodernism in the Church*. Wheaton, IL: Crossway, 2005.

Smith, Tom W. *Intergroup Relations in a Diverse America: Data From the 2000 General Social Survey*. New York: American Jewish Committee, 2001.

———. "The National Spiritual Transformation Study." *Journal for the Scientific Study of Religion* 45.2 (2006) 283–96.

Smith, Timothy L. "The Evangelical Kaleidoscope and the Call to Christian Unity." *Christian Scholar's Review* 15.2 (1986) 125–140.

Smith, Wilbur M., and Charles Edward Fuller. *A Voice for God the Life of Charles E. Fuller, Originator of the Old Fashioned Revival Hour*. Boston: Wilde, 1986.

Snider, Phil, and Emily Bowen. *Towards a Hopeful Future: Why the Emergent Church is Good News for Mainline Congregations*. Cleveland, OH: Pilgrim, 2010.

Snowball, David. *Continuity and Change in the Rhetoric of the Moral Majority*. New York: Praeger, 1991.

Solomon, Robert C. "The Christian Positivism: Hegelian Interpretation." In *Religious Positivity*, edited by S. M. Tripathi, and N. K. Singh, 95. Delhi: Global Vision, 2001.

———. *In the Spirit of Hegel; a Study of Phenomenology of Spirit*. Oxford: Oxford University Press, 1983.

Sosnik, Doug., Matthew J. Dowd, and Ron Fournier. *Applebee's America: How Successful Political, Business, and Religious Leaders Connect With the New American Community*. New York: Simon & Schuster, 2006.

Spencer, Michael. "The Coming Evangelical Collapse." *The Christian Science Monitor*, March 11, 2009. Editorial. http://www.csmonitor.com/Commentary/Opinion/2009/0310/p09s01-coop.html/(page)/2 (accessed 6/1/2012).

Spong, John. *A Call for a New Reformation*. San Francisco: Harper, 1998.

Sproul, R. C., R. Albert Mohler, and Ravi Zacharias. "Christianity and Postmodernism Q and a #2." Paper given at the Contending for the Truth Conference 2007.

Stark, Rodney. *Cities of God: Christianizing the Urban Empire*. San Francisco: Harper, 2006.

Stark, Rodney, and Roger Finke. *The Churching of America, 1776–2005: Winners and Losers in Our Religious Economy*, New Brunswick, NJ: Rutgers University Press, 2005.

Stark, Rodney, and William Sims Bainbridge. *The Future of Religion: Secularization, Revival, and Cult Formation*. Berkeley: University of California Press, 1985.

Stephanson, Anders. "Interview with Cornel West." In *Universal Abandon? The Politics of Postmodernism*, edited by Andrew Ross, 269–86. Minneapolis, MN: University of Minnesota Press, 1988.

Stetzer, Ed. "The Emergent/Emerging Church: A Missiological Perspective." *Journal for Baptist Theology and Ministry* 5.2 (2008) 63–97.

———. "The Evolution of Church Growth, Church Health, and the Missional Church: An Overview of the Church Growth Movement from, and Back to, Its Missional Roots." Paper given at the American Society of Church Growth, Biola University, 2008.

———. "First Person: Understanding the Emerging Church." (2006) http://www.crosswalk.com/1372534/ (accessed 6/20/2010).

———. *Planting New Churches in a Postmodern Age*. Nashville: Broadman & Holman, 2003.

———. *Planting Missional Churches*. Nashville: Broadman & Holman, 2006.

———."A Year is Not a Trend." Blog (2008) http://www.edstetzer.com/2008/04/a_year_is_not_a_trend_decline_1.html (accessed 10/12/2010).

Stetzer, Ed, and Warren Bird. *Viral Churches: Helping Church Planters Become Movement Makers*. San Francisco: Jossey-Bass, 2010.

Stetzer, Ed, Richie Stanley, and Jason Hayes. *Lost and Found: The Younger Unchurched and the Churches That Reach Them*. Nashville: B. & H., 2009.

Stewart, Kenneth. *Continuities in Evangelical History: Interactions with David Bebbington*. Downer's Grove, IL: InterVarsity, 2007.

———."Did Evangelicalism Predate the Eighteenth Century? An Examination of David Bebbington's Thesis." *Evangelical Quarterly* 77.2 (2005) 152–63.

Stott, John R. W. *Evangelical Truth: A Personal Plea for Unity, Integrity, and Faithfulness*. Leicester, UK: InterVarsity, 1999.

Stott, John R. W., and Alister McGrath. *The Cross of Christ*. Downers Grove, IL: InterVarsity, 2006.

Swatos Jr, W. H. "Beyond Denominationalism?: Community and Culture in American Religion." *Journal for the Scientific Study of Religion* 12,7 (1981) 35–41.

Sweeney, Douglas A. *The American Evangelical Story: A History of the Movement*. Grand Rapids: Baker Academic, 2005.

Sweet, Leonard. *The Evangelical Tradition in America*. Macon, GA: Mercer University Press, 1984.

———. *Post-Modern Pilgrims: First Century Passion for the 21st Century World*. Nashville: B. & H., 2000.

Sweet, Leonard, Andy Crouch, Brian D. McLaren, Erwin Raphael McManus, and Michael Horton. *Church in Emerging Culture: Five Perspectives*. Grand Rapids: Zondervan/Youth Specialties, 2003.

Sweet, William Warren. *Revivalism in America: Its Origin, Growth, and Decline*. Gloucester, MA: Smith, 1965.

Sweetnam, Mark. "Defining Dispensationalism; a Cultural Studies Perspective." *Journal of Religious History* 34.2 (2010) 191–212.

Taylor, Charles. *Modern Social Imaginaries*. Durham, NC: Duke University Press, 2004.

———. *A Secular Age*. Cambridge, MA: Belknap, 2007.

———. *Sources of the Self: The Making of the Modern Identity*. Cambridge: Harvard University Press, 1989.

Taylor, Kevin M. *American Evangelicals and Religious Diversity: Subcultural Education, Theological Boundaries, and the Relativization of Tradition*. Greenwich, CT.: Information Age, 2006.

Taylor, Mark C. *After God*. Chicago: University of Chicago Press, 2007.

———. *Erring: A Postmodern A/Theology*. Chicago: University of Chicago Press, 1984.

Taylor, Victor E., and Charles E. Winquist, editors. *Encyclopedia of Postmodernism*. New York: Routledge, 2001.

Tennant, Agnieszka. "The Making of the Christian: An Interview with Richard Foster and Dallas Willard." *Christianity Today*, Oct 12, 2005, 42–44.

Terry, John Mark, "The Great Commission and International Missions: A Historical Look," in *The Challenge of the Great Commission: Essays on God's Mandate for the Local Church*, Chuck Lawless and Thom S. Rainer, editors, Louisville, KY: Pinnacle Publishers, 2005.

Thomas, Cal, and Ed Dobson. *Blinded By Might: Why the Religious Right Can't Save America*. Grand Rapids: Zondervan, 2000.

Thompson, John. "Voting Games and Belief Reorganization." *Simulation and Gaming* 8.1 (1977) 121–31.

Thorne, P. R. *Evangelicalism and Karl Barth: His Reception and Influence in North American Evangelical Theology*. Tuckerton, NJ: Pickwick, 1995.

Thuesen, Peter Johannes. *Predestination: The American Career of a Contentious Doctrine*. New York: Oxford University Press, 2009.

Thumma, Scott, and Warren Bird. "Not Who You Think They Are: The Real Story of People Who Attend America's Megachurchcs." *Harford Institute of Religious Research* (2009): http://hirr.hartsem.edu/megachurch/megachurch_attender_report.htm (accessed 7/13/2012).

Thumma, Scott, and Dave Travis. *Beyond Megachurch Myths: What We Can Learn From America's Largest Churches*. San Francisco: Jossey-Bass, 2007.

Tickle, Phyllis. *The Great Emergence: How Christianity is Changing and Why*. Grand Rapids: Baker, 2008.

Tischler, Nancy M. *Encyclopedia of Contemporary Christian Fiction: From C. S. Lewis to Left Behind*. Santa Barbara, CA.: Greenwood, 2009.

Tomlinson, Dave. *The Post Evangelical*. London: Triangle, 1995.

———. *The Post Evangelical*. Rev. North American ed. El Cajon, CA: Emergent YS/ Zondervan, 2003.

———. *Still Waters and Skyscrapers: The 23rd Psalm for the 21st Century*. Grand Rapids: Baker, 2006.

Torrey, R. A., Charles Lee Feinberg, and Warren W. Wiersbe. *The Fundamentals: The Famous Sourcebook of Foundational Biblical Truths*. Grand Rapids: Kregel, 1990.

Towns, Elmer L., and Gary McIntosh. *Evaluating the Church Growth Movement: 5 Views*. Grand Rapids: Zondervan, 2004.

Towns, Elmer L., and Ed Stetzer. *Perimeters of Light: Biblical Boundaries for the Emerging Church*. Chicago: Moody, 2004.

Towns, Elmer L., John N. Vaughan, and David J. Seifert. *The Complete Book of Church Growth*. Wheaton, IL: Tyndale House, 1981.

Towns, Elmer L., C. Peter Wagner, and Thom S. Rainer. *The Every-Church Guide to Growth: How Any Plateaued Church Can Grow*. Nashville: Broadman & Holman, 1998.

Tozer, A. W. *I Call it Heresy*. Harrisburg, PA: Christian, 1974.

Tracy, Joseph. *The Great Awakening. A History of the Revival of Religion in the Time of Edwards and Whitefield*. New York: Dayton & Newman;, 1842.

Trujillo, Kelli. *The Future of the Church*. Carol Stream, IL: Christianity Today International, 2008.

Tubbs, Brian. "A Review of Dallas Willard's Classic Book on Spiritual Disciplines." (2006) http://www.suite101.com/content/learning-to-live-like-jesus-a8746 (accessed 8/10/2012).

Turner, Brian S. *Max Weber: From History to Modernity*. New York: Routledge, 1993.

Turner, Daniel L. *Standing without Apology: The History of Bob Jones University*. Greenville, SC: Bob Jones University Press, 1997.

Turner, John G. *Bill Bright & Campus Crusade for Christ: The Renewal of Evangelicalism in Postwar America*. Chapel Hill, NC: University of North Carolina Press, 2008.

Utter, Glenn H., and John W. Storey. *The Religious Right: A Reference Handbook*. Santa Barbara, CA: ABC-CLIO, 2001.

Utter, Glenn H., and James L. True. *Conservative Christians and Political Participation: A Reference Handbook*. Santa Barbara, CA: ABC-CLIO, 2004.

Vallicella, William F. "The Moreland-Willard-Lotze Thesis on Being." *Philosophia Christi* 6.1 (2004) 27–58.

Van Biema, David. "Can Megachurches Bridge the Racial Divide?" *Time*, Jan 11, 2010, 45–47.

Van Der Weele, Steven. "Book Review: the Divine Conspiracy." *Christian Century* 7.7 (1999) 36.

Van Gelder, Chris. "Mission in the Emerging Postmodern Condition." In *The Church between Gospel and Culture: The Emerging Mission in North America*, edited by George Hunsberger and Craig Van Gelder, 113–39. Grand Rapids: Eerdmans, 1996.

Vanhoozer, Kevin J., and Martin Warner. *Transcending Boundaries in Philosophy and Theology: Reason, Meaning and Experience*. Burlington, VT: Ashgate, 2007.

Vine, W. E. Vine's *Expository Dictionary of Old & New Testament Words*. Nashville, TN: T. Nelson Publishers, 2001.

Viola, Frank. *Finding Organic Church: A Comprehensive Guide to Starting and Sustaining Authentic Christian Communities*. Colorado Springs, CO: Cook, 2009.

———. *Pagan Christianity?: Exploring the Roots of Our Church Practices*. Gainsville, FL: Present Testimony Ministry, 2003.

———. *Reimagining Church: Pursuing the Dream of Organic Christianity*. Colorado Springs, CO: Cook, 2008.

———. *So You Want to Start a House Church?: First-century Styled Church Planting for Today*. Gainsville, FL: Present Testimony Ministry, 2003.

———. *The Untold Story of the New Testament Church: An Extraordinary Guide to Understanding the New Testament*. Shippensburg, PA: Destiny Image, 2004.

Vu, Michelle. "Rick Warren Aids Summit Aims to Disturb Christians." *Christianity Today*, Nov 30, 2007, 29–31.

Wacker, Grant. "Billy Graham's America." *Church History: Studies in Christianity and Culture* 78.3 (2009) 489–511.

———.*Heaven Below: Early Pentecostals and American Culture*. Cambridge, MA: Harvard University Press, 2001.

———. "Uneasy in Zion: Evangelicals in Postmodern Society." *Evangelicalism and Modern America* (1984): 17–28.

Wald, Kenneth D. *Religion and Politics in the United States*. 4th ed. Lanham, MD: Rowman & Littlefield, 2003.

Waldrep, B. Dwain. "Fundamentalism." In *Encyclopedia of Religion in the South*, edited by S. S. Hill, C. H. Lippy, and C. R. Wilson, 335. Macon, GA: Mercer University Press, 2005.

Wall, Kevin A. *Relation in Hegel: The Doctrine of Relation in Hegel*. Ann Arbor, MI: University Press of America, 1983.

Wallis, Jim. *The Great Awakening: Reviving Faith & Politics in a Post-Religious Right America*. New York: HarperOne, 2008.

Walsh, Brian J., and J. Richard Middleton. *The Transforming Vision: Shaping a Christian World View*. Downers Grove, IL: InterVarsity, 1984.

Walvoord, John F. *The Millennial Kingdom*. Grand Rapids: Zondervan, 1959.

Ward, Graham. *Barth, Derrida and the Language of Theology*. Cambridge: Cambridge University Press, 1999.

———. "Barth and Postmodernism." *New Blackfriars* 74.877 (2007) 550–56.

———, editor. *The Blackwell Companion to Postmodern Theology*. Oxford: Wiley-Blackwell, 2001.

———. *Cities of God*. London: Routledge, 2000.

———. "The Future of Religion." *Journal of the American Academy of Religion* 74.1 (2006) 179–86.

———. *Theology and Contemporary Critical Theory*. London: Palgrave Macmillan, 2000.

———. "A Postmodern Version of Paradise." *Journal for the Study of the Old Testament* 20.65 (1995) 3–12.

———. *The Postmodern God: A Theological Reader*. Oxford: Wiley-Blackwell, 1997.

Warren, Richard. *The Purpose Driven Church: Growth without Compromising Your Message & Mission*. Grand Rapids: Zondervan, 1995.

———. *The Purpose-Driven Life: What on Earth Am I Here For?* Grand Rapids: Zondervan, 2002.

Watson, J. B., and Walter Scalen. "'Dining with the Devil': The Unique Secularization of American Evangelical Churches." *International Social Science Review* 83.3 (2008) 171–80.

Wauzzinski, Robert A. *Between God and Gold: Protestant Evangelicalism and the Industrial Revolution, 1820–1914*. Rutherford, NJ: Associated University Presses, 1993.

Webber, Robert. *Ancient-Future Faith: Rethinking Evangelicalism for a Postmodern World*. Grand Rapids: Baker, 2003.

———.*Who Gets to Narrate the World? Contending for the Christian Story in an Age of Rivals*. Downers Grove, IL: InterVarsity, 2008.

———. *The Younger Evangelicals: Facing the Challenges of the New World*. Grand Rapids: Baker, 2002.

Webber, Robert., and Donald G. Bloesch. *The Orthodox Evangelicals: Who They Are and What They Are Saying?* Nashville: Thomas Nelson, 1978.

Webber, Robert, John Burke, Dan Kimball, Doug Pagitt, Karen M. Ward, and Mark Driscoll. *Listening to the Beliefs of Emerging Churches: Five Perspectives*. Grand Rapids: Zondervan, 2007.

Weber, Timothy. "Fundamentalism Twice Removed." In *New Dimensions in American Religious History*, edited by Jay Dolan, and J. P. Wind, 428–30. Grand Rapids: Eerdmans, 1993.

———. *Living in the Shadow of the Second Coming: American Premillennialism, 1875–1925*. New York: Oxford University Press, 1979.

———. "Premillennialism and the Branches of American Evangelicalism." In *The Variety of American Evangelicalism*, edited by Donald W. Dayton, and Robert K. Johnston, 12. Downers Grove, IL: InterVarsity, 1991.

———. *On the Road to Armageddon: How Evangelicals Became Israel's Best Friend*. Grand Rapids: Baker Academic, 2004.

Webster, John. "Barth, Modernity, and Postmodernity." In *Karl Barth: A Future for Postmodern Theology*, edited by Christian Mostert and Geoff Thomson, 1–28. Wayville, South Africa: ATF, 2001.

Wells, David. *Above All Earthly Powers: Christ in a Postmodern World*. Grand Rapids: Eerdmans, 2005.

———. *No Place for Truth, Or, Whatever Happened to Evangelical Theology*, Grand Rapids: Eerdmans, 1993.

Wesley, John. "What is Man Sermon 109." In *Sermons on Several Occasions*, edited by John Emory, 363–68. New York: Mason, 1835.

Wesley, John and Clare G. Weakley, *The Nature of Holiness*, Minneapolis, MN: Bethany House, 1988.

West, Cornel. *The American Evasion of Philosophy: A Genealogy of Pragmatism*. Madison, WI: University of Wisconsin Press, 1989.

Westphal, Merold. *Overcoming Onto-Theology: Toward a Postmodern Christian Faith*. New York: Fordham University Press, 2001.

White, Ronald C., and Charles Howard Hopkins. *The Social Gospel: Religion and Reform in Changing America*. Philadelphia, PA: Temple University Press, 1976.

White, Thomas, and John M. Yeats. *Franchising McChurch: Feeding Our Obsession with Easy Christianity*. Colorado Springs, CO: Cook, 2009.

Whitehead, A. N. *Science and the Modern World*. New York: Free, 1997.

Whitehead, James D., and Evelyn Eaton. *Whitehead: Method in Ministry: Theological Reflection and Christian Ministry*. Lanham, MD: Rowan and Littlefield, 1995.

Wicker, Christine. *The Fall of the Evangelical Nation: The Surprising Crisis Inside the Church*. New York: HarperOne, 2008.

Wilcox, Clyde, Sharon Linzey, and Ted Jelen. "Reluctant Warriors: Pre-Millennialism and Politics in The Moral Majority." *Journal for the Scientific Study of Religion* 30 (1991) 245–58.

Willard, Dallas. "The Absurdity of Thinking in Language." *The Southwestern Journal of Philosophy* 4 (1973) 125–32.

———. "Against Nominalism." In *History as the Story of Freedom: Philosophy in Intercultural Context*, edited by Clark Butler, 94–97. New York: Rodophi, 1995.

———. "Attaining Objectivity: Phenomenological Reduction and the Private Language Argument." In *Topics in Philosophy and Artificial Intelligence*, edited by Lillian Abertazzi and Alberto Poli, 15–21. Bozen, Italy: Istituto Mitteleuropeo di Cultura, 1991.

———. "Beyond Moral Bewilderment: Where is Moral Knowledge?" *Provocations: A Journal from The Trinity Forum* (2007) 13–18.

———. "Beyond Pornography: Spiritual Formation Studied in a Particular Case." Paper given at the Talbot School of Theology Christian Spirituality and Soul Care conference, 2008.

———. "The Craftiness of Christ in Mel Gibson's 'Passion' and Philosophy." In *Challenges in the Trial, Conviction, and Crucifixion of Christ*, edited by Jorge Gracia, 167–78. Chicago: Open Court, 2004.

———. "Crucial Error in Epistemology." *Mind* LXXVI.304 (1967) 513–23.

———. "Degradation of Logical Form." Lecture in Logic (2005): http://www.dwillard.org/articles/artview.asp?artID=24

———."Discipleship." In *The Oxford Handbook of Evangelical Theology*, edited by Gerald R McDermott, 236–46. New York: Oxford University Press, 2010.

———. "Discipleship: For Super-Christians Only?" *Christianity Today* 24.17 (1980) 24–27.

———. *The Divine Conspiracy: Rediscovering Our Hidden Life in God*. San Francisco: Harper, 1996.

———. "The Failure of Evangelical Political Involvement in the Area of Moral Transformation." In *God and Governing: Reflections on Ethics, Virtue and Statesmanship, edited by* Roger Overton, 74–91. Eugene, OR: Wipf and Stock, 2009.

———. "The Faith of Unbelief." Unpublished article (2004) http://www.dwillard.org/articles/artview.asp?artID=27 (accessed 1/12/2012)

———. "Good and the Problem of Evil." unpublished article (2010) http://www.dwillard.org/articles/artview.asp?artID=30 (accessed 11/15/2012).

______. "The Good Person: A Matter of the Heart." unpublished article (2010): http://www.dwillard.org/articles/artview.asp?artID=59 (accessed 9–11, 2010).

———. *The Great Omission: Reclaiming Jesus' Essential Teachings on Discipleship*. San Francisco: HarperOne, 2006.

———. *Hearing God: Developing a Conversational Relationship with God*. Downers Grove, IL: InterVarsity, 1999.

———. "Historical and Philosophical Foundations of Phenomenology." In *Phenomenology and Counseling*, edited by Paul Bloland, forthcoming.

———. "How Reason Can Survive the Modern University: The Moral Foundations of Rationality." Lecture at American Maritain Association, Notre Dame, 2000.

———. *In Search of Guidance: Developing a Conversational Relationship with God*. Ventura, CA: Regal, 1983.

———. "Is Derrida's View of Ideal Being Rationally Defensible?" In *Derrida and Phenomenology*, edited by William McKenna, 23–41. Boston: Kluwer Academic, 1995.

———. "Jesus the Logician." *Christian Scholar's Review* 27.4 (1999) 605–14.

———. *Knowing Christ Today: Why We Can Trust Spiritual Knowledge*. San Francisco: HarperCollins, 2009.

———. "Knowledge." In *Cambridge Companion to Husserl*, edited by Barry Smith and David Woodruff Smith, 138–67. Cambridge: Cambridge University Press, 1995.

———. "Knowledge and Naturalism." In *Naturalism: A Critical Analysis*, edited by William.L. Craig and J. P. Moreland, 24–48. New York: Routledge, 2000.

———. *Logic and the Objectivity of Knowledge: A Study in Husserl's Early Philosophy*. Athens, OH: Ohio University Press, 1984.

———. "My Journey to and beyond Tenure in a Secular University. C. S. Lewis Foundation Summer Conference." Faculty Forum, University of San Diego, 2003.

______."Non-Reductive and Non-Eliminative Physicalism." Unpublished article (2001): http://www.dwillard.org/articles/artview.asp?artID=48 (accessed 2–23, 2011).

———. "Observations on Current Leadership Issues in Higher Education." Lecture, Christian College and Universities Forum (1995)

———. "Postmodern Holiness." Lecture: Malcolm R. Robertson Lectureship on Holy Living Azusa, CA: Azusa Pacific University (2010).

———. "Prediction a Originary Violence: A Phenomenological Critique of Derrida's View of Intentionality." In *Working through Derrida*, edited by G. B. Madsen, 120–36. Evanston, IL: Northwestern, 1993.

———. *Renovation of the Heart: Putting on the Character of Christ*. Grand Rapids: NavPress, 2002.

———. "Rethinking Evangelism." *Church Planting* 4 (2001) 15–18.

———. *The Spirit of the Disciplines: Understanding How God Changes Lives.* San Francisco: HarperOne, 1991.

———. "Spiritual Disciplines, Spiritual Formation and the Restoration of the Soul." *Journal of Psychology and Christianity* 26.1 (1998) 101–9.

———. "Theory of Wholes and Parts and Husserl's Explication of Possibility of Knowledge in the Logical Investigations." In *Contributions to Phenomenology*, edited by Denis Fisette, 53–68. New York: Kluwer Academic, 2003.

———. "Truth: Can We Do Without it?" *Christian Ethics Today* 21 (1999) 12–19.

———. "Unhinging of the American Mind-Derrida as Pre-Text." In *European Philosophy and the American Academy*, Barry Smith, editor, LaSalle, IL: Hegeler Institute, 1994.

———. "The University's Responsibility for Moral Guidance." *The Real Issue* 1 (2004).

———. "Utilitarianism and Phenomenology." In *Phenomenological Approaches to Moral Philosophy: A Handbook*, edited by John J. Drummond and Lester E. Embree, 69–86. Boston: Kluwer Academic, 2002.

______. "Where is Moral Knowledge." unpublished article (2010): http://www.dwillard.org/articles

———. "Why Bother With Discipleship?" *Renovare Perspective* 5.4 (1995) 8–12.

———. "Who is Your Teacher?" *Promise Magazine* (1996) 34–38.

———. "The World Well Won: Husserl's Epistemic Realism One Hundred Years Later." In *A Hundred Years of Phenomenology*, edited by Robin Small, 69–78. Boston: Kluwer Academic, 2002.

Willard, Dallas, Gayle Beebe, Lynda Graybeal, and Thomas C. Oden. *The With God Bible. New Revised Standard Version.* New York: HarperCollins, 2005.

Willard, Dallas, Daniel Cho, and Sarah Park. *A Place for Truth: Leading Thinkers Explore Life's Hardest Questions.* Downers Grove, IL: InterVarsity, 2010.

Willard, Dallas, and Richard Foster. "Marriage and Divorce." *Quaker Life* (1973) 8–11.

Willard, Dallas, and Randy Frazee. *Renovation of the Heart: Putting on the Character of Christ* (an Interactive Student Edition). Colorado Springs, CO: NavPress, 2005.

Willard, Dallas, Os Guinness, Richard Mouw, Richard George, Jesse Miranda, David Neff, Dick Ohman, and Larry Ross. "Evangelical Manifesto." *National Press Club* (2008): http://www.anevangelicalmanifesto.com/media/manifesto.htm (accessed 5/9/2010).

Willard, Dallas, and Jan Johnson. *Hearing God through the Year.* Downers Grove, IL: InterVarsity, 2004.

———. *Renovation of the Heart in Daily Practice: Experiments in Spiritual Transformation.* Colorado Springs, CO: NavPress, 2006.

Willard, Dallas, and Donald Simpson. *Revolution of Character: Discovering Christ's Pattern for Spiritual Transformation.* Colorado Springs, CO: NavPress, 2005.

Willard, Dallas, and Dieter Zander. "The Apprentices: What is Spiritual Formation and How Does a Church Do it? A Professor and a Pastor Discuss a New Language of Making Disciples." *Leadership Journal* 26.3 (2005) 20–25.

Williams, Daniel K. *God's Own Party: The Making of the Christian Right.* New York: Oxford University Press, 2010.

Winter, Ernest F. *Erasmus-Luther: Discourse on Free Will.* New York: Ungar, 1961.

Witham, Larry. *Marketplace of the Gods: How Economics Explains Religion.* New York: Oxford University Press, 2010.

Witherington, Ben. *The Christology of Jesus.* Minneapolis, MN: Fortress, 1990.

———. *Jesus and Money: A Guide for Times of Financial Crisis*. Grand Rapids: Brazos, 2010.

———. *The Living Word of God: Rethinking the Theology of the Bible*. Waco, TX.: Baylor University Press, 2007.

———. *The Problem with Evangelical Theology: Testing the Exegetical Foundations of Calvinism, Dispensationalism, and Wesleyanism*. Waco, TX.: Baylor University Press, 2005.

Wolfe, Alan. "The Opening of the Evangelical Mind." *The Atlantic Monthly* 286.4 (2000) 74–78.

———. *The Transformation of American Religion: How We Actually Live Our Faith*. New York: Free, 2003.

Wolfe, Alan, and Ira. Katznelson. *Religion and Democracy in the United States: Danger Or Opportunity*. Princeton: Princeton University Press, 2010.

Wood, W. Jay. "More Than Deep Feelings: Dallas Willard Argues We Really Can Know Christ." *Christianity Today* 6 (2009) 55–56.

Woods, Tim. *Beginning Postmodernism*. Manchester: Manchester University Press, 1999.

Woozley, A. D. *Theory of Knowledge; an Introduction*. New York: Barnes & Noble, 1966.

Wrenn, Bruce, Philip Kotler, and Norman Shawchuck. *Building Strong Congregations: Attracting, Serving, and Developing Your Membership*. Hagerstown, MD: Autumn House, 2010.

Wright, B. R. E. "Greg L. Hawkins, Cally Parkinson, Eric Arnson: Reveal: Where Are You?" *Review of Religious Research* 49.3 (2008) 343–44.

Wright, Crispin. *Truth and Objectivity*. Cambridge: Harvard University Press, 1992.

Wright, Christopher J. H. *The Mission of God: Unlocking the Bible's Grand Narrative*. Downers Grove, IL: InterVarsity, 2006.

Wright, N. T. *The Challenge of Jesus: Rediscovering Who Jesus Was and is*. Downers Grove, IL: InterVarsity, 1999.

———. *Evil and the Justice of God*. Downers Grove, IL: InterVarsity, 2006.

———. *Justification: God's Plan & Paul's Vision*. Downers Grove, IL: IVP Academic, 2009.

———. *The Last Word: Beyond the Bible Wars to a New Understanding of the Authority of Scripture*. San Francisco: Harper, 2005.

———. *The New Testament and the People of God*. Minneapolis, MN: Fortress, 1992.

———. *Simply Christian: Why Christianity Makes Sense*. San Francisco: HarperOne, 2010.

———. *Surprised By Hope: Rethinking Heaven, the Resurrection, and the Mission of the Church*. San Francisco: HarperOne, 2008.

Wright, R. K. McGregor. *No Place for Sovereignty: What's Wrong With Freewill Theism*. Downers Grove, IL: InterVarsity, 1996.

Wuthnow, Robert. *After the Baby Boomers: How Twenty- and Thirty-Somethings Are Shaping the Future of American Religion*. Princeton: Princeton University Press, 2007.

———. *After Heaven: Spirituality in America Since the 1950s*. Berkeley, CA: University of California Press, 1998.

———. *Christianity in the Twenty-First Century: Reflections on the Challenges Ahead*. New York: Oxford University Press, 1993.

———. *The Crisis in the Churches: Spiritual Malaise, Fiscal Woe*. New York: Oxford University Press, 1997.

———. *Experimentation in American Religion: The New Mysticisms and Their Implications for the Churches*. Berkeley: University of California Press, 1978.

———. *The Struggle for America's Soul: Evangelicals, Liberals, and Secularism*. Grand Rapids: Eerdmans, 1989.

———. *God and Mammon in America*. New York: Free, 1994.

———. *Saving America? Faith-Based Services and the Future of Civil Society*. Princeton: Princeton University Press, 2004.

Wythe, George. "Pentecostals Celebrate World's Fastest Growing Religion." *Associated Press*, April 24, 2006.

Yaconelli. Mike. *Stories of Emergence: Moving From Absolute to Authentic*. Grand Rapids: Emergent YS Zondervan, 2003.

———."The Terror of Inbetweeness." The Whittenberg Door 4.4 (1992): 22–24.

Yancey, Philip. "Be Ye Perfect, More Or Less: Tolstoy, Dostoevsky and the Impossible Sermon on the Mount." *Christianity Today* July 17, 1995, 38–41.

Yancey, Philip, and Eugene H. Peterson. *Church, Why Bother? My Personal Pilgrimage*. Grand Rapids: Zondervan, 1998.

Yolton, John W. *Thinking Matter; Materialism in 18th-Century Britain*. Minneapolis, MN: University of Minnesota, 1983.

Yong, Amos. *In the Days of Caesar: Pentecostalism and Political Theology*. Grand Rapids, MI: W.B. Eerdmans, 2010.

Young, Julian. *Heidegger's Later Philosophy*. New York: Cambridge University Press, 2002.

Yzerbyt, Vincent, Guy Lories, and Benoit Dardenne. *Metacognition: Cognitive and Social Dimensions*. London: Sage, 1998.

Zahavi, Dan, and Frederik Stjernfelt. *One Hundred Years of Phenomenology: Husserl's Logical Investigations Revisited*. Boston: Kluwer Academic, 2002.

Zajac, Andrew. "Pat Robertson Links Haiti Quake to Pact With Devil." *Los Angeles Times*, Jan 13, 2010.

Zdero, Rad. *The Global House Church Movement*. Pasadena, CA: William Carey Library, 2004.

———. *Jesus and Money: A Guide for Times of Financial Crisis*. Grand Rapids: Brazos, 2010.

———. *The Living Word of God: Rethinking the Theology of the Bible*. Waco, TX.: Baylor University Press, 2007.

———. *The Problem with Evangelical Theology: Testing the Exegetical Foundations of Calvinism, Dispensationalism, and Wesleyanism*. Waco, TX.: Baylor University Press, 2005.

Zodhiates, Spiros and James Strong. *The Complete Word Study New Testament: King James Version*. Chattanooga, TN: AMG Publishers, 1991.

Glossary of Terms

***A priori* assumptions:** a Latin term describing the kind of reasoning that is done independent of sensory experience. One gains knowledge a priori when she reasons about the nature of things independent of sensory experience; or reasons from self-evident propositions to a conclusion about the thing or proposition in question.

Activism: in Christian religious terms, the view that the result of being influenced by the gospel will necessarily cause one to assume priorities and values that form certain and specific actions and behaviors.

Agape: a Greek word describing a divine form of love. Such a love described in the Scriptures is generally assumed to convey moral goodwill and esteem for oneself and others that proceeds from high principle, or duty, rather than attraction or charm. Such a love is undeserving, despite disappointment and rejection and therefore is unconditional in both nature and affect.

Anthropology: the multiple methods and areas of study related to both the individual human being and humanity at large.

Atonement: a doctrine that describes the means through which human beings can be, and are, reconciled to God.

Biblicism: the view that assumes all essential truth, and/or spiritual truth, is contained in the biblical text.

Christology: the study of the work and person of Jesus Christ.

Constructivism: the theory that individuals and/or groups construct mental models to understand, describe, or create knowledge of, and/or engagement with, the world around them.

Consumerism: the socio-economic state that encourages, supports, and proliferates the purchasing of goods and services in increasing amounts and degrees.

Contextualization: in general, placing an idea or belief within a proper, perhaps larger, setting (context) in order to acquire a more complete and accurate understanding.

Conversionism: a view that places value and priority on the religious process human persons engage to alter their previous state of being as a result of experiencing, or coming to understand, the nature of God's will and way for life and living.

Crucicentrism: a system of belief that places a prioritization on the nature and effect of the transcendent and imminent realities demonstrated through Christ's work accomplished as a result of his crucifixion, death, and resurrection.

Dikaiosune: Greek word for "righteousness." Conveys the sense of developing and/or maintaining the ability to both know and do the right thing.

Dispensationalism: a theological set of beliefs that proposes God relates to humanity in distinctive ways under different circumstances, conditions, or eras of time (dispensations).

Ecclesiology: the theological study of the origins, purposes, practices, leadership, destiny, and functions of the Christian church.

Egalitarianism: the belief in human equality, specifically within social, political, and religious affairs.

Eisegesis: the process of inserting an interpretation into a text.

Epistemology: the branch of philosophical inquiry dedicated to pursuing the nature and scope of knowledge, what knowledge is, and how knowledge is acquired on any given subject or entity.

Epoche¢: a Greek term used in philosophy to describe the act of suspending (bracketing) judgments, interpretations, or thoughts about the existence or characteristics of an object or experience in order to examine the object or experience independently as it manifests itself before the consciousness.

Euangelion: the Greek term for the good news or beneficial information. Often translated in the Bible as "gospel."

Eschatology: the theological study of last things, final events, and/or ultimate destinies.

Essentia Dei: Latin term for "essence of God."

Ethos: Greek term for "character" that is used to describe overarching ideals or beliefs that characterize a community or ideology.

Exclusivism: in theology the doctrine or belief that only one particular religion, worldview, or system of belief is accurate. This often results in the marginalizing or disregarding other theologies, opinions, or ideas that vary from one's own.

Exegesis: the process of pulling a critical explanation or interpretation from a text.

Existentialism: a philosophical outlook that emphasizes the uniqueness of the individual experience and the importance of freedom in choice and responsibility.

Foundationalism: in philosophy an epistemological theory that holds some of one's core/basic beliefs are not justified on the basis of other beliefs. These basic beliefs, however, may support or justify other beliefs one holds. Such core or basic (foundational) beliefs are self-justified or immediately justified and can be used to justify other contingent beliefs or claims to knowledge.

Fundamentalism: in theology the belief in strict adherence and application of certain basic, essential theological doctrines assumed to promote and assure continuity and accuracy of traditional orthodox Christian belief. Two core beliefs of Christian fundamentalism tend to surround biblicism (see above) and separatism (see below).

Hermeneutics: the art, principles, and theories of interpretation.

Heterogeneous: that consisting of dissimilar or diverse ingredients or constituents.

Idealism: a philosophical position that asserts reality, or reality as it is engaged by human beings, is fundamentally a mental construct and therefore primarily immaterial. Therefore, idealism maintains a skepticism that anything can be known outside the realms of reason and consciousness. Hence, only what is perceived is real.

Ideology: a systematic body of concepts, typically concerned with human life or culture, which constitutes the manner, or characteristic thinking, of an individual, group, or culture.

Individualism: the moral, political, philosophical, and ideological outlook that prioritizes the aspects, interests, freedoms, and necessities of persons as individuals.

Institutionalism: Adherence to, belief in, or proliferation and support of, the established, traditional forms of social organizations and their structures.

Intellectual historiography: the study of the methods, processes, history, development, circumstances, and consequences of ideas and concepts.

Justification: in Christian theology the theory of the means by which God forgives, pardons, removes, or resolves the problem of human sinfulness.

Liberalism: in theology the attempt to open theological inquiry and incorporate the discoveries of many intellectual pursuits and methods, especially those applied in the sciences, into the Christian faith. Theological liberalism tends to emphasize reason, ethics, and experience over doctrine, tradition, or Scriptural authority and therefore is resistant to the parts of Scripture that describe the supernatural activities of God.

Logocentrism: a philosophical position that holds an external point of reference exists on which all forms of thought are either based, refer to, or are pursuing.

***Metanoia*:** Greek word often translated "repentance" in Scripture. Refers to the state of reconsidering one's previous thoughts and beliefs.

Metaphysics: the branch of philosophy that studies the nature and problems related to ultimate reality, which may lie behind or beyond the reach of the physical sciences. Metaphysics often includes the subject of ontology.

Methodology: a body of rules and postulates employed by a discipline. A particular procedure or set of procedures used to analyze or direct an inquiry within a particular field.

Millennialism: a doctrine held by many Christian denominations referenced in Revelation chapter 20 regarding the reign of Christ for a thousand years (millennium).

***Missio Dei*:** Latin term for Mission of God.

Naturalism: in terms of epistemology the position that phenomenon can only be explained and understood in terms of natural causes and laws, in opposition to supernatural or spiritual causes and explanations.

Penal substitutionary atonement theory: refers to a set of beliefs surrounding Christ's death on the cross as a substitute for human sinners. In this theory, God imputed the guilt of all human sin onto to Christ, and he, as a substitute victim, bore the full punishment (crucifixion and death) of human sinfulness. Often this punishment is said to have satisfied both the wrath and the righteousness of God, in order that God could justifiably forgive sinners without compromising a perfect standard of justice.

Phenomenology: the philosophical study of the structures of consciousness and subjective experiences, as they come before the mind, in the first person perspective.

Physicalism: the philosophical position that only the physical world, and its laws, is real. Therefore everything is ultimately dependent upon or necessitated by the physical world and its laws, are real. There is no intervention from "outside" of this world. Also termed metaphysical naturalism.

Pluralism: in philosophy, a theory that there is more than one ultimate reality; and/or a theory that holds there can be more than one accurate "truth" or "reality" even if these "truths" are logically incompatible.

Proselytize: the act of inducing someone to convert to one's faith

Pneumatology: the area in Christian theology dedicated to the study of spirit, spirituality, and the Holy Spirit.

Postevangelicalism: a system of Christian beliefs that protests, corrects, and/or adapts modern evangelical positions and practices connected to individualism, theological politicization, consumerism, denominationalism, and Enlightenment epistemology within theological pursuits.

Postmodernism: Postmodernism represents a reaction to modernism that generates skepticism of the presumed certainty inherent to empirical epistemology and its assumption of objectivity in the task of describing reality. It is "post" due to a denial of modernity's claims to ultimate principles, and a lack of optimism regarding any scientific, philosophical, or religious truth (metanarrative) that accounts for all things. As such, postmodernism is often used as a generally contested and wide-ranging term applied to many subjects such as art, philosophy, architecture, religion, and literary criticism, etc.

Praxis: the process through which a theory is developed into an applied practice or action. Otherwise stated as "understanding in action."

Protoevangelicalism: a system of Christian beliefs based on the premise that one can recapture an understanding and experience the essence of the original gospel message Jesus presented in the first century.

Ontology: a branch of study within philosophy and metaphysics that seeks to understand the nature of being, existence, reality, and their relations.

Orthodoxy: Right or accurate belief and/or doctrine.

Orthopraxis: properly informed action.

Pluralism: in philosophy, a theory that there is more than one of ultimate reality and/or a theory that reality is composed of a plurality of entities.

Rationalism: the epistemological position that reason, and not sensory perception, is the chief and/or exclusive means of acquiring knowledge.

Realism: in specific reference to Willardian thought, the philosophical position that objects exist independently of the mind and present themselves and their properties through sense data and therefore can be engaged and encountered as they are. The sense data itself, compared to the knowledge of that data, may be different and incomplete. Yet, objects remain unaffected by data claims or interpretations.

Reductionism: the explanation of complex life-science processes and phenomena only in terms of the laws of physics and/or chemistry. Also a theory or doctrine that assumes a procedure or theory can reduce complex data and phenomenon to simple terms and/or conclusions.

Relativism: a theory that knowledge is relative to the limited nature of the mind, and that a condition of knowing ethical truths depend on the individuals and groups holding them.

Revivalism: the spirit or activities characteristic of religious revivals.

Sanctification: In Christian theology, sanctification is usually understood as an act or process subsequent to that which renders the believer holy. Sanctification is often juxtaposed to justification, which is God's declaration of pardon.

Secularism: indifference, rejection, or exclusion of religious engagement in theory, philosophy, or action.

Separatism: the belief in, and advocacy of, separation of groups due to specific cultural, ethnic, religious, racial, or political differences.

Soteriology: the study of the religious doctrines of salvation.

Subjectivism: a theory that limits knowledge to subjective experience and stresses the subjective elements in experience, such as feelings or apprehensions, as the ultimate criterion for moral determination.

Taxonomy: the practice and investigation of the process and principles used to classify things and/or concepts.

Teleology: a study or inquiry into the evidences of purposes or design in a phenomenon or nature.

Theo-ontology: the philosophical proposition that all "being," both human and non-human, is contingent upon and engaged with God, God's character, and will.

Totalitarianism: a term used to convey the belief that certain states or beliefs hold uniform authority and control over all things.

Universalization: the idea individuals often unknowingly belong to a larger normalizing group or groups engaging similar or identical events. Thus, these individualized experiences and/or events are argued to be "universal" in nature.

Utilitarianism: a doctrine that usefulness is the highest and best good in determining value. This is often manifested in a theory that the aim of human action and thought should seek the largest possible balance of pleasure over pain, or the greatest happiness of the greatest number.